Navajo Land Use
An Ethnoarchaeological Study

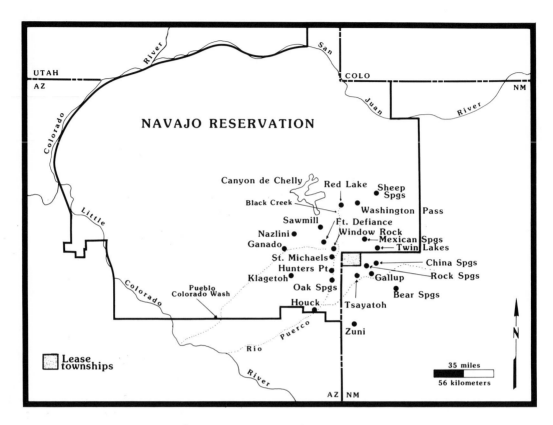

Northwest New Mexico and Northeast Arizona

NAVAJO LAND USE

An Ethnoarchaeological Study

Klara B. Kelley

Navajo Nation
Cultural Resource Management Program
Window Rock, Arizona

1986

ACADEMIC PRESS, INC.
Harcourt Brace Jovanovich, Publishers

Orlando San Diego New York Austin
London Montreal Sydney Tokyo Toronto

ACADEMIC PRESS, INC.
Orlando, Florida 32887

United Kingdom Edition published by
ACADEMIC PRESS INC. (LONDON) LTD.
24–28 Oval Road, London NW1 7DX

LIBRARY OF CONGRESS CATALOGING-IN-PUBLICATION DATA

Kelley, Klara B.
    Navajo land use.

    "January 1985."
    Bibliography: p.
    Includes index.
    1. Navajo Indians—Economic conditions.   2. Navajo
Indians—Land tenure.   3. Indians of North America—
Southwest, New—Economic conditions.   4. Indians of
North America—Southwest, New—Land tenure.   5. Land
settlement patterns—Southwest, New.   I. Title.
E99N3K335   1986   333.73'13'08997   85-13361
ISBN 0-12-404010-1 (alk. paper)
ISBN 0-12-404011-X (paperback)

PRINTED IN THE UNITED STATES OF AMERICA

86 87 88 89   9 8 7 6 5 4 3 2 1

Contents

Figures   ix
Tables   xi
Preface   xv

1. Introduction   *1*

Navajo Family Land Use   *2*
Field Methods   *3*
Analytic Methodology   *4*

2. Navajo Family Land Use and the Political Economy of the United States   *6*

Large-Scale Changes in the National Political Economy   *6*
Capitalist Development and Navajo Family Land Use   *10*

3. The Land and Early Navajo Use   *16*

1700–1800   *16*
1800–1864   *17*
1864–1881   *22*

4. The Railroad Era, 1881–1930   *24*

Historical Background   *24*
Trends in Family Land Use   *30*

5. Family Economy and the Local Environment during the Railroad Era   *33*

Family Sources of Livelihood   *33*
Consumption Patterns   *35*
The Environment   *41*
Conclusion   *43*

6. Family Demography and Land Tenure during the Railroad Era   *44*

    Family Demography   *44*
    Land Tenure   *45*
    Land Tenure in the Tse Bonita Wash–Upper Defiance Draw   *50*
    Land Tenure in the Middle Defiance Draw   *53*
    Land Tenure in the Eastern Flat–Lower Defiance Draw   *55*
    Conclusion   *57*

7. Spatial Aspects of Land Use during the Railroad Era   *59*

    Customary Use Areas   *60*
    Gray-Eyed Woman's Year-Round Customary Use Area   *64*
    Blackgoat's Winter Customary Use Area   *67*
    Grazing Tracts   *68*
    Fields   *72*
    Homesites   *74*
    Conclusion   *77*

8. Technology of the Railroad Era   *79*

    Domestic Technology   *79*
    Stock-Raising Technology   *88*
    Farming Technology   *95*
    Conclusion   *97*

9. The Great Depression and Grazing Regulation, 1930–1950   *98*

    Historical Background   *98*
    Trends in Family Land Use   *102*

10. Family Economy and the Local Environment during the Era of Grazing Regulation   *104*

    Family Sources of Livelihood   *104*
    Consumption Patterns   *108*
    The Environment   *113*
    Conclusion   *114*

11. Family Demography and Land Tenure during the Era of Grazing Regulation *115*

Family Demography   *115*
Land Tenure   *116*
Land Tenure in the Tse Bonita Wash–Upper Defiance Draw   *118*
Land Tenure in the Middle Defiance Draw   *120*
Land Tenure in the Eastern Flat–Lower Defiance Draw   *122*
Conclusion   *122*

12. Spatial Aspects of Land Use during the Era of Grazing Regulation *124*

Customary Use Areas   *124*
The Customary Use Area of Curly Tallman and His Mother   *127*
The Customary Use Area of the Tinhouse Family   *131*
Grazing Tracts   *135*
Fields   *136*
Homesites   *137*
Conclusion   *140*

13. Technology of the Era of Grazing Regulation *141*

Domestic Technology   *141*
Stock-Raising Technology   *144*
Farming Technology   *148*
Conclusion   *150*

14. The Industrial Era, 1950–Present *151*

Historical Background   *151*
Trends in Family Land Use   *154*

15. Family Economy and the Local Environment during the Industrial Era *157*

Family Sources of Livelihood   *157*
Consumption Patterns   *159*
The Environment   *162*
Conclusion   *165*

16.   Family Demography and Land Tenure during the Industrial Era   *166*

Family Demography   *166*
Land Tenure   *168*
Land Tenure in the Tse Bonita Wash–Upper Defiance Draw   *171*
Land Tenure in the Middle Defiance Draw   *174*
Land Tenure in the Eastern Flat–Lower Defiance Draw   *175*
Conclusion   *176*

17.   Spatial Aspects of Land Use during the Industrial Era   *178*

Customary Use Areas   *178*
The Customary Use Area of Gray-Eyed Woman's Grandchildren   *181*
The Customary Use Area of the Tinhouse Family's Successors   *181*
Grazing Tracts   *186*
Fields   *186*
Homesites   *187*
Conclusion   *190*

18.   Technology of the Industrial Era   *191*

Domestic Technology   *191*
Stock-Raising Technology   *195*
Farming Technology   *198*
Conclusion   *199*

19.   The Future   *200*

The Near Future   *200*
The Distant Future   *201*

20.   Navajo Land Use: An Ethnoarchaeological Perspective   *203*

Appendix A. Methodology   *206*
Appendix B. Genealogy   *213*
References   *217*

Index   *227*

Figures

Frontispiece. Northwest New Mexico and Northeast Arizona: places cited in the text.

Figure 3.1   The lease townships and their drainages.   *18*

3.2   The landscape of the lease townships in the 1850s.   *22*

4.1   Navajo family portrait taken in the west-central reservation in 1892–1893.   *25*

4.2   Original claims in the lease townships, ca. 1880–1900.   *29*

4.3   Land ownership in the lease townships by 1912.   *30*

6.1   Land tenure in the Tse Bonita Wash–upper Defiance Draw.   *51*

6.2   Land tenure in the Tse Bonita Wash–upper Defiance Draw, ca. 1920.   *52*

6.3   Land tenure in the upper Defiance Draw, 1910–1930.   *54*

6.4   Land tenure in the middle Defiance Draw, 1910–1930.   *55*

6.5   Land tenure in the Eastern Flat–lower Defiance Draw, 1910–1920.   *56*

7.1   Customary use areas in the lease townships, 1910–1915.   *61*

7.2   Gray-Eyed Woman's use area, ca. 1910–1916.   *64*

7.3   Gray-Eyed Woman's homestead, ca. 1910–1916.   *65*

7.4   Gray-Eyed Woman's winter sheep camp, ca. 1910–1916.   *66*

7.5   Blackgoat's homestead, 1918–1924.   *68*

7.6   Blackgoat's customary use area, 1918–1924.   *69*

7.7   Blackgoat's sheep camp, ca. 1918–1924.   *70*

7.8   Railroad-era fields in the lease townships.   *73*

7.9   All sites with forked-stick hogans inside the South McKinley Mine Lease.   *76*

7.10   Homesites in the lease townships in 1915.   *77*

8.1   A forked-stick hogan of 1892–1893, with a silversmith and his forge outside.   *80*

8.2   A forked-stick hogan as it appears archaeologically.   *81*

8.3   A cribbed-log hogan as it appears archaeologically.   *82*

8.4   Mr. Towering House Clansman's sheep camp, ca. 1910.   *90*

8.5   A lamb pen.   *91*

8.6   A brush corral.   *92*

11.1   Land tenure in the Tse Bonita Wash–upper Defiance Draw, ca. 1937–1945.   *119*

Figure 11.2   Land tenure in the middle Defiance Draw during the 1930s.   *121*

11.3   Land tenure in the Eastern Flat–lower Defiance Draw, ca. 1944.   *123*

12.1   Customary use areas in the lease townships, ca. 1940.   *125*

12.2   Customary use area of Curly Tallman and his mother, 1931–1948.   *128*

12.3   Margaret Thompson's homestead, showing masking by features of later occupations.   *129*

12.4   Curly Tallman's homestead, 1931–1960s, showing earlier and later features.   *130*

12.5   Customary use area of the Tinhouse family, 1930–1941.   *132*

12.6   Homestead of the Tinhouse family.   *133*

12.7   Summer homestead of the Tinhouse family, ca. 1935–1941.   *134*

12.8   Alternate winter homestead of the Tinhouse family, ca. 1935–1941.   *135*

12.9   Fields of the grazing-regulation era in the lease townships.   *138*

12.10   Homesites in the lease townships, 1940.   *139*

13.1   A stock reservoir in the lease townships.   *149*

16.1   Land tenure in the Tse Bonita Wash–upper Defiance Draw, 1950s.   *172*

17.1   Customary use areas in the lease townships, 1978.   *179*

17.2   Customary use area of Gray-Eyed Woman's descendants, 1960s.   *182*

17.3   Winter use area of Smiley's descendants, 1950s.   *183*

17.4   Summer use area of Smiley's descendants, 1950s.   *184*

17.5   Use area of Smiley's descendants, 1970s.   *185*

17.6   Industrial-era fields in the lease townships.   *188*

17.7   Homesites in the lease townships, 1978.   *189*

18.1   A modern homesite in the lease townships.   *192*

18.2   A modern corral.   *196*

18.3   A winter corral with lamb pens and twin corral used 1962–1969.   *198*

Tables

Table 4.1   Comparison of Navajo Wool and U.S. Flour Prices, 1890–1974   *31*

5.1   Number of Livestock Owned by Lease-Township Households, 1915   *34*

5.2   Distribution of Sheep and Goats among Lease-Township Households, 1915   *34*

5.3   Artifacts on Railroad-Era Dwelling Sites on the South McKinley Mine Lease   *36*

5.4   Functional Types of Artifacts on Railroad-Era Sites on the South McKinley Mine Lease   *37*

5.5   Functional Types of Artifacts by Site Type on the South McKinley Mine Lease, 1880–1979   *39*

5.6   Artifact Inventories on a Homestead and a Probable Sheep Camp of the Railroad Era   *40*

5.7   Faunal Remains from Excavated Railroad-Era Sites on the South McKinley Mine Lease   *41*

5.8   Actual 1915 Stocking and Estimated 1941 Carrying Capacities of Subdivisions of the Lease Townships   *42*

6.1   Demographic Characteristics of Lease-Township Households and Residence Groups, 1910–1915   *45*

6.2   Land Tenure in the Lease Townships, 1915   *47*

7.1   Homes of Lease-Township Residents outside the Lease Townships, 1910–1915   *61*

7.2   Inventories of Sites in Customary Use Areas in the Lease Townships, 1915   *62*

7.3   Types of Sites Identified by Local Navajos and Used in 1915   *63*

7.4   Distances from Homesites to Satellite Sites in the Same Customary Use Area, 1915 and 1940   *63*

7.5   Number of Small Stock, Size, and Physiographic Characteristics of Customary Use Areas in the Lease Townships, 1915   *71*

7.6   Distribution of Railroad-Era Fields by Slope Zone   *73*

7.7   Areas of Excavated Homesites on the Lease and Annual Occupation Span, All Historical Periods   *75*

7.8   Situations of Sites on Landforms, Early Railroad Era and 1915   *76*

8.1   Sizes of Railroad-Era Dwellings and Selected Variables on the South McKinley Mine Lease   *83*

Table 8.2   Heating Devices and Ash-Dump Characteristics on
             South McKinley Mine Homesites, 1880–1979   *86*

      8.3   Percentages of Railroad-Era Homesites in the Lease Townships
             with Selected Types of Features   *87*

      8.4   Possible Twin Corrals on Railroad-Era Sites on the South McKinley Mine Lease   *93*

      8.5   Corrals on Railroad-Era Sites on the South McKinley Mine Lease   *94*

      8.6   Corrals Used by Individual Families during the Railroad Era   *96*

      10.1 Number of Small Stock Owned by Lease-Township Residents, 1936–1946   *105*

      10.2 Number of Livestock Owned by Lease-Township Households, 1939   *106*

      10.3 Distribution of Sheep and Goats among Lease-Township Households, 1939   *106*

      10.4 Employment in the Lease Townships, 1940   *108*

      10.5 Household Livestock Holdings and Income by Source in the Lease Townships, 1940   *109*

      10.6 Money Income by Source for Lease-Township Households, 1940   *109*

      10.7 Household Trade and Debt in the Lease Townships, 1940   *110*

      10.8 Consumption of Livestock in the Lease Townships, 1940   *111*

      10.9 Faunal Remains from Excavated Sites of the Era of Grazing Regulation
             on the South McKinley Mine Lease   *111*

      10.10 Functional Types of Artifacts on Sites on the South McKinley Mine Lease,
             1930–1950   *112*

      10.11 Artifacts on Grazing-Regulation–Era Homesites on the South McKinley Mine Lease   *113*

      10.12 Actual 1940 Stocking and Estimated 1941 Carrying Capacities of Subdivisions
             of the Lease Townships   *114*

      11.1 Demographic Characteristics of Lease-Township Households and
             Residence Groups, 1940   *115*

      11.2 Land Tenure in the Lease Townships, 1940   *117*

      11.3 Residence Rights of Households to Main Homesites in the Lease Townships, 1940   *117*

      12.1 Homes of Lease-Township Residents outside the Lease Townships, 1940   *125*

      12.2 Inventories of Sites in Customary Use Areas in the Lease Townships, 1940   *126*

      12.3 Types of Sites Identified by Local Navajos and Used in 1940   *127*

      12.4 Number of Small Stock, Size, and Physiographic Characteristics
             of Customary Use Areas in the Lease Townships, 1940   *136*

      12.5 Distribution of Fields by Slope Zone in the Era of Grazing Regulation   *139*

      12.6 Situations of Homesites on Landforms, 1940   *139*

      13.1 Size of Dwellings on Grazing-Regulation–Era Homesteads and Selected Variables
             on the South McKinley Mine Lease   *143*

      13.2 Percentage of Grazing-Regulation–Era Homesites in the Lease Townships
             with Selected Types of Features   *144*

      13.3 Comparison of Functional Types of Artifacts on the Tinhouses' Winter and
             Summer Sites, 1935–1940   *145*

      13.4 Corrals on Grazing-Regulation–Era Sites on the South McKinley Mine Lease   *148*

      13.5 Corrals Used by Individual Families during the Grazing-Regulation Era   *149*

      15.1 Number of Livestock Owned by Lease-Township Households, 1978   *158*

      15.2 Distribution of Sheep and Goats among Lease-Township Households, 1978   *158*

      15.3 Employment in the Lease Townships, 1978   *159*

      15.4 Household Income by Source, Land Management District 16, 1973   *160*

Table 15.5   Estimated Aggregate Personal Income by Source,
South McKinley Mine Lease Residents, 1978–1979   *160*

15.6   Household Consumption Expenditures, Land Management District 16, 1973   *161*

15.7   Functional Types of Artifacts on Sites on the South McKinley Mine Lease,
1950–1979   *161*

15.8   Artifacts on Industrial-Era Dwelling Sites in the South McKinley Mine Lease   *163*

15.9   Minimal Inventory of Artifacts Observed on a Currently Occupied Homestead
in the Lease Townships   *163*

15.10   Actual 1978 Stocking and Estimated 1941 Carrying Capacities of Subdivisions
of the Lease Townships   *164*

16.1   Demographic Characteristics of Lease-Township Households and Residence Groups,
1978–1979   *167*

16.2   Land Tenure in the Lease Townships, 1978   *170*

16.3   Residence Rights of Households to Main Homesites in the Lease Townships, 1978   *171*

17.1   Homes of Lease-Township Residents outside the Townships, 1978   *179*

17.2   Inventories of Sites in Customary Use Areas in the Lease Township, 1978   *180*

17.3   Types of Sites Used by Local Navajos in 1978   *181*

17.4   Number of Small Stock, Size, and Physiographic Characteristics of
Customary Use Areas in the Lease Townships, 1978   *187*

17.5   Distribution of Fields by Slope Zone in the Industrial Era   *188*

17.6   Situations of Homesites on Landforms, 1978   *190*

18.1   Sizes of Industrial-Era Dwellings and Selected Variables
on the South McKinley Mine Lease   *193*

18.2   Percentage of Industrial-Era Homesites in the Lease Townships
with Selected Types of Features   *194*

18.3   Corrals on Industrial-Era Sites on the South McKinley Mine Lease   *197*

A.1   Site Components by Type in the Positively Identified Sample
in the Lease Townships   *208*

A.2   Site Components by Type in the Limited Site Sample in the Lease Townships   *209*

A.3   Navajo Ethnographic Samples and Estimated Number of Archaeological Sites,
Lease Townships   *210*

A.4   Navajo Sites on the South McKinley Mine Lease in Positively Identified Ethnographic
Sample Compared to Archaeological Survey Inventory by Date   *210*

A.5   Navajo Sites on the South McKinley Mine Lease in Positively Identified Ethnographic
Sample Compared to Archaeological Survey Inventory by Function   *211*

A.6   Navajo Sites on the South McKinley Mine Lease in Positively Identified Ethnographic
Sample Compared to Archaeological Survey Inventory by Location   *212*

Preface

This book develops insights into land use that I have gained during 8 years of life among Navajo Indian families and work on contract archaeology projects around the Navajo country. Because land is central to Native American history, and because the research is interdisciplinary, this book should be relevant not only to ethnologists and archaeologists, but also to historians, researchers in Native American studies, and experts involved in the many facets of Native American economic development.

The book began as a technical report for a contract archaeology project in a working coal strip mine and has been transformed several times since. When I started the fieldwork for the contract project, I had already spent 5 years on various Navajo economic-development research projects and had lived for a year with a Navajo family. Having been the "visiting anthropologist" who, as the saying goes, is part of the typical Navajo family, I knew that hardly an aspect of Navajo life had escaped scholarly scrutiny. As the contract project got underway, however, I learned that surprisingly little was actually known about Navajo family land use. Only one study (Landgraf 1954) treats as parts of a system the ways that families use land for production and domestic maintenance; none analyzes variations among families through time or connects these variations to the evolution of the national political economy, as I have done in this book.

Yet Navajo family land use has been a paramount concern of federal and tribal government policymakers, since it is at the root of both severe overgrazing and local opposition to certain economic-development projects—two problems that have confounded policymakers for most of this century. Since many anthropologists have worked with the federal and tribal governments, the anthropologists' relative inattention to land use cannot be blamed on lack of interest. Instead, I believe that lack of opportunity is to blame. Land-use patterns vary greatly among families, are often geographically extensive, and shift constantly in response to short-term changes in both the physical and political-economic environments. One must therefore observe many families over a long period if one is to see any patterning in their land-use behavior. Most anthropologists have not been able to make such extensive or long-term observations.

But archaeological information about abandoned sites can substitute for long-term direct observation, especially if one can learn, from local people and documents, the land-use behavior associated with each site. If the archaeological information also systematically covers a large geographic area, the data base should be big enough to reveal general patterns. With federal environmental laws of the late 1960s and early 1970s requiring archaeological and historical work on Native American lands that development will disturb, opportunities have now arrived (though the land itself might be destroyed).

This book, then, is the result of an early effort to take advantage of the new "opportunities." With so much to learn about land use and its links to other aspects of Navajo life, I have defined land use very broadly. Land use is here seen as a behavioral system involving not only the family's use of space, but also

xv

family sources of livelihood, the demography of the family (the labor force that works the land), the physiographic environment, land tenure, and technology. I have also connected land use, thus broadly defined, to large-scale historical processes, namely capitalist development in the United States as mediated by federal Indian policy.

During several years and almost as many rewrites, this book has received help from many people. First thanks are due to the people whom I interviewed, especially those willing to tour backcountry tracks and roadless areas in a two-wheel-drive truck that ran less than perfectly. The interpreters Walter Tulley, Pauline Begay, and Timmie Mitchell handled with great aplomb the stupid questions that an ethnologist inevitably asks. Any errors in this work must be blamed on my misunderstanding, not on the failure of local people or interpreters to inform me. Tribal Councilor Willis Peterson and Chuck McKinney, Fritz Gottren, and Howard Draper of the McKinley Mine offered guidance at the start of the contract project. The Franciscan Friars of St. Michaels, Arizona, could not have been more generous in opening their vast store of historical materials to me; I thank especially Father John Lanzrath and Mike Andrews of the St. Michaels Historical Museum. Maurice Kelley of Princeton University was a most tactful editor. Martha Graham and June-el Piper completed the word processing in record time with record accuracy. Emily Garber meticulously drafted all the figures. Finally, I thank Lewis R. Binford of the University of New Mexico, without whose urging this book would never have been published.

Chapter 1

Introduction

Navajos, like many other country people, often assert their unity with the land. This feeling stems from more than just the ideology of tribal sovereignty. It arises from the objective bonds between the land and the people who get their food from it. The flow of family labor into a piece of land produces livestock and crops that in turn sustain the family. The people, in a sense, grow themselves from the land.

This bond between families and the land has endured through Navajo history, although today most families draw little or no sustenance from their land and perhaps are somewhat alienated from it as their forebears were not. Inherited lands nevertheless still offer most families havens from which even poverty and unemployment cannot dislodge them. Many Navajos today consequently fear that if they leave their lands they will lose the last shreds of security. This fear grows in proportion to the number of families displaced by intertribal land disputes and by strip-mining. The bonds between Navajo families and their lands constitute a central, but often neglected, aspect of Navajo society, both past and present.

In this study I describe and explain historical changes in the land-use patterns of families around the south McKinley Mine, a coal strip mine in New Mexico a few miles southeast of Window Rock, Arizona. Only by scrutinizing such small areas can one see in fine detail family land-use patterns and the range of variation among families. In seeking explanations for local changes in family land use, however, I widen the geographical focus to two ultimate causes: first, conquest, colonization, and national oppression of the Navajo nation spearheaded by U.S. mercantile and industrial capitalism; and second, the atomistic decision making about production by individual families that has characterized Navajo society from before the conquest to the present. The results of this work will illuminate family land use elsewhere, not only in Navajoland but also in other places with similar histories of colonialism, national oppression, and mixed pastoral–agricultural production by families.

In addition to providing a more sharply focused view of family land use, this study offers an advance in methodology. This advance lies in the reconstruction of past land-use patterns with an inventory of archaeological sites as a framework, within which oral histories and documents weave a web of links. First, I formulate the relationships between changes in land use and the two proposed causes. Then I describe various aspects of family land use in a series of historical periods, discuss changes in these aspects, and explain the changes in terms of the formulation. Finally, I discuss the ways in which archaeological data reflect changes in land use and their causes. Before plunging into this material, however, I must provide some background information: definitions of the aspects of land use to be described and what I mean by "family"; the field methods used to collect the data; and the analytic methods used to describe and compare each aspect of land use at different times.

Navajo Family Land Use

The first Navajos apparently subsisted mainly by hunting and gathering. By the time they settled around the south McKinley Mine, however, they used land mainly for raising sheep and goats, for farming, and for residence. I have therefore concentrated on these types of land use. I define *land use* itself very broadly here to embrace several interrelated aspects. These include family sources of livelihood, especially how much the items produced on the land contribute to the family's subsistence; the particular environmental characteristics of land needed for production; the demographic composition of the family, which is both the land-using unit and the labor force that works the land; land tenure, that is, the source of the family's right to use particular tracts of land; the use of space, that is, the number, size, and distribution of sites and parcels of land, or tracts, used for production and for residence; and, finally, technology, that is, the division of labor, facilities, tools, and techniques that the family applies to the land to maintain its home and produce its subsistence.

Since this study concerns family land use, I must also define the ambiguous term *family*. Among Navajos, the inhabitants of the individual homesite constitute one kind of family. They usually consist of a couple with their juvenile children, their grown children and grandchildren, or both. These people not only share a homesite, but also cooperate in daily production. These coresident families, often called *camps* in the ethnographic literature but here called *residence groups*, are the most obvious units for the study of family land use.

Nevertheless, I have often chosen the household rather than the residence group for this purpose. As used here, the term *household* ordinarily refers to the occupants of one dwelling. The ethnographic literature on Navajos shows that the people who share a dwelling usually depend on each other economically. Exceptions to this definition are economically semi-productive people with dwellings of their own—teenagers or elderly adults—who I assume are part of the household in the same residence group to which they are most closely related. Although most households are nuclear families, the term is more spatial than demographic or genealogical. It is therefore the most useful term for combining ethnohistorical and archaeological data. The residence group is also a spatial unit but is more ambiguous than the household. Especially in the past, a group of households that would share a homesite and a herd in one season often would disperse to separate homesites in other seasons, sometimes even splitting the herd to do so. The composition of the residence group therefore would vary more and also more systematically throughout the year than would the composition of the household.

A second reason for making the household the analytic unit is the fact that its members depend economically on each other more than do the members of the residence group. Especially today, an older-generation household typically owns most or all the livestock and monopolizes the land, while younger-generation households depend upon wage work. The forces that hold these households together, as is discussed in the following chapters, are often the need of the elderly for able-bodied help in domestic chores (hauling water, hauling and chopping wood) and, today, the need of the younger people for cheap housing.

A third reason for making the household the analytic unit is the fact that the censuses used in this study record data on households but do not show which households shared homesites. Although I use the household as the main unit of analysis, I do not mean to underplay the importance of the residence group in Navajo land use. Throughout this study, I have defined the *residence group* as a fundamental land-using unit and have viewed *households* as its building blocks. I have therefore reconstructed past residence groups whenever possible.

Land-using units composed of two or more residence groups are also known in Navajoland and have been termed variously "outfits" (Kluckhohn and Leighton 1962:109–110; Witherspoon 1975:101), "land-use communities" (Kimball and Provinse 1942), "cooperating groups" (Collier 1951:55–57), and "co-residential kin groups" or "CKGs" (Aberle 1981a, b). That such land-using units also seem to have existed around the south McKinley Mine is one of the interesting results of this study. At the outset of my research, however, I could not assume their composition or even their existence; therefore, they could not serve as basic units for the collection and analysis of information.

Another important kinship grouping among Navajos is the *clan*. These named groups consist of people who usually consider themselves the descendants of a common mythological ancestress but cannot demonstrate actual genealogical links among all members. A person belongs to the clan of his or her mother, and must marry outside that clan. A person is said to be "born for" the clan of his or her father and is also enjoined from marrying into that clan. Marriages between members of the same clan remain rare today even though some young people do not know their own clans. In earlier times, such marriages were almost unheard of. Marriages into fathers' clans were also rare, at least in the last century (although marriages dating to more than 100 years ago in the genealogies of the families studied here seem to favor fathers' clans). Marriages into the clans of the maternal and paternal grandfathers also may be enjoined today but are not uncommon (Aberle 1980; Franciscan Fathers 1910:424–427; Morgan and Lathrop 1979; Reichard 1928; Zelditch 1959).

Most clans have members in many localities throughout the Navajo nation, although a particular clan may have many members in one locality and few in another. This pattern probably developed after a small group of pioneers, representing a small number of clans, settled in an area, monopolized it, and transmitted the land to descendants who tended either to intermarry or to marry outsiders but to transmit land-use rights matrilineally (Aberle 1961, 1963; Kelley 1980; Reichard 1928). All clan members in a given locality are therefore likely to be related genealogically, although as time passes, clan members may not be able to trace the genealogical links. This process of land settlement and inheritance gives rise to *outfits*, each of which has a core of members of a particular clan (Aberle 1981b; Reynolds, Lamphere, and Cook 1967).

Therefore, clans, or at least their localized segments, may seem to be landholding units. They are not, however, and therefore could not serve as basic units of data collection and analysis for this study.

Field Methods

Most of the information for this study was collected during a contract archaeological project that the Office of Contract Archeology (OCA), University of New Mexico, conducted in 1978 and 1979 on the south McKinley Mine lease with funding from the Pittsburg and Midway Coal Mining Company. The lease covers about 22 mi.^{2} south and east of the reservation proper as of this writing; an area of about the same size within the reservation, the north McKinley Mine lease, is still being studied. Parts of about 6 mi.^{2} sections of the south mine lease were strip-mined after 1960. The rest of the lease is to be strip-mined in the next few years. Archaeological surveys by the Museum of New Mexico in 1975 and the Navajo Nation Cultural Resource Management Program in 1977 (Hartman 1977; Koczan 1977) had already covered the whole lease; two additional small tracts were surveyed in 1981 (Eck 1981). The purpose of the OCA project was to gather more information on a sample of sites through the intensive techniques of excavation and ethnohistorical research.

I collected most of the historical and ethnographic data during a year of fieldwork on the south McKinley Mine lease while living with a local Navajo family. I spent the field period reading primary documents, interviewing a total of 87 people both at archaeological sites and at their homes, and doing "participant observation." Archaeological data for the OCA project were collected mainly by OCA field crews during the summer of 1979 and supplemented by observations made during the fall of 1978 and summer of 1979, when I visited most sites on the lease with an archaeologist. The final reports on the project convey this information in technical detail (Allen and Nelson 1982; Kelley 1982a). I have also used material collected for a study of the history of the Black Creek Valley (Kelley 1982b), observations made during the subsequent 6 years of residence in the area, and information from my work on the neighboring north McKinley Mine lease in 1984 and 1985 (Kelley n.d.a).

The area covered by the OCA archaeological project, the south McKinley Mine lease, is an arbitrary unit that does not neatly circumscribe the entire land-use areas of all households and residence groups that have used the lease. This lack of correspondence raises the question of whether the study of sites on the lease can accurately reveal overall family land-use patterns. To overcome this problem, I studied entire family land-use areas, even when they extended outside the lease. Most of these areas lie within the townships that encompass the lease, which are hereafter called the *lease townships*, and make up the basic geographic unit studied here (see Frontispiece). My study therefore is based on entire "natural" land-use areas here called *customary use areas*. This is not, however, a community study. Navajo communities as land-using units may have existed in the nineteenth century (Hill 1940b), but apparently they have not existed since. Probably the most widely recognized geographic community today is the local political unit called *the chapter*, which has jurisdiction over business-site leases and land withdrawals for public use but is not itself a land-using unit. The lease townships are part of one such area, the Tsayatoh chapter. I have also sought to minimize bias in this study by making the size of the sample of families and their customary use areas big enough to exhibit the full range of variation in land-use patterns found in the lease townships and similar localities.

Analytic Methodology

In this work I have sought to explicate Navajo family land use in both scientific and humanistic terms. The scientific explication is based on aggregate statistical data on the families that occupied the lease townships at various times. I have isolated each aspect of family land use for statistical description and explanation. The statistics come from various sources—documents, oral histories, and the archaeological record—but all represent basically the same families.

The high degree of overlap in the families represented by these sources was possible only through the use of the complete archaeological inventory survey as a control. Through visits to archaeological sites on

and off the lease with local Navajos, I constructed a list of former users of the lease. I made the list as representative as possible by trying to match the frequencies of sites of particular types, dates, and locations identified by interviewees with the corresponding frequencies in the archaeological survey inventory. I maximized the completeness of this list by trying to identify the largest possible number of sites. Then, when I consulted the documents, I was able to identify users of the lease townships, not only by the particular localities in which they were reported, but also by name in other localities outside the lease townships.

Some aspects of land use, however, such as land tenure and the spatial aspects, involve large-scale, long-term processes that do not show clearly in statistical data on a small geographical area. Only the humanistic method of historical reconstruction can reveal these processes. For each of three main divisions of the lease townships, I first used documents, oral histories, and archaeological data to chronicle the subdivision of the land and the functioning of each family subdivision at particular times. These chronicles are too long and tedious to be included, but I have summarized blocks of this material to supplement the statistical analyses of land tenure and the spatial aspects of land use.

I have organized this study by dividing lease-township history into several periods, each of which begins with an event that ultimately transformed the local production system and, therefore, family land use. These same events have transformed the general Navajo production system and land use. During the first few periods (1700–1880), Navajos were recorded, mainly by military observers, in only the general vicinity of the lease townships; sources on these periods also suggest where the actual ancestors of the first settlers of the lease townships were living. This information is given straightforwardly as a chronicle and does not require further discussion here.

The documents, statements of local Navajos, and archaeological data specific to the lease townships cover the interval from 1880 to the present, which I have divided into three periods: 1880–1930, 1930–1950, and 1950–present. Within each period, various types of censuses and other documents are available for a short span, or baseline interval. I have integrated all the information sources on each period by using the document data for each baseline interval as a framework on which to anchor contemporary data from the other sources. The resulting reconstruction of land use in each baseline interval does not, however, necessarily represent the whole period. I have therefore added any available information on the rest of the period for comparison with the reconstructed baseline.

The different sources of information illuminate different aspects of land use. The document sources and my own field census of 1978 provide the most reliable picture of family sources of livelihood, the environment, and demography, although oral histories constitute an essential supplement. These sources, however, offer little information on land tenure, the spatial aspects of land use, and technology—the topics on which interviewees and the archaeological record shed the most light. Because different sources must be used for different aspects of land use, the fact that all sources represent basically the same families is especially important.

The various sources of information and their comparability are discussed in Appendix A. This appendix shows a great overlap in the groups of families identified by the various sources. This overlap means that the sources include most families in the lease townships, and that this study offers a representative picture of their land-use patterns.

Chapter 2

Navajo Family Land Use and the Political Economy of the United States

My aim in this book is to show through both ethnohistorical and archaeological evidence how processes within a conquering, colonizing, capitalist society and within a conquered, colonized, tribal society have interacted to change family land-use patterns. The process within the capitalist society is the shift from dominance by merchant capital to dominance by industrial capital. The process in the tribal society is the atomistic decision making by the families that are its basic production units. In this chapter I lay out my argument. First I discuss the large-scale changes in U.S. capitalism and how these changes affected Navajo families through the medium of federal Indian policy. Then I show how these larger changes acted on atomistic family decision making to change family land-use patterns. The chapters that follow this one document and add detail to this formulation.

Large-Scale Changes in the National Political Economy

U.S. capitalism has transformed the Navajo political economy from a self-sufficient one, based on the family's production for its own consumption, to one with families thoroughly integrated into the complex national division of labor and class system. This process of change also reflects the concurrent evolution of U.S. capitalism: the gradual replacement of merchant capitalism as a dominant economic and political force by industrial monopoly capitalism (Kelley 1977; Lamphere 1976; Ruffing 1979; Weiss 1984; White 1983).

Merchant capital comes from the profits that merchants derive from buying goods cheaply and selling them dearly. Often the trade involves small-scale family producers, like the Navajos, who trade their products at low prices for other goods at high prices. Industrial capital comes from profits on the mass production of goods by large machine industry. Capitalism first developed in Europe after the Middle Ages as merchant capital slowly gave rise to industrial capital. Merchants invested their profits in specialized manufacturing concerns. These became increasingly mechanized, and the division of labor within them increasingly specialized, as manufacturers tried to produce goods more cheaply than their competitors and thereby enhance their profits. The large landowners who supplied these manufacturers with raw materials (especially for textiles) in turn saw a chance to profit by reorganizing their land-based production to minimize the labor involved. They evicted tenants in droves, who formed a pool of cheap, landless labor that fueled the ongoing growth of manufacturing. The colonization of the New World was part of this process. It generated a large share of the raw materials and merchants' profits that went into manufacturing in Europe and also absorbed many of the dispossessed European farmers and tenants (Marx 1967:713–774).

In the United States the process continued during the eighteenth and nineteenth centuries, but change did not proceed evenly in all parts of the country. It was most advanced in the Northeast and most retarded in the West. Industrialization was driving small farmers off the land in the Northeast, and many moved westward, along with the continuing stream of European immigrants, to take up their own farms or to become tenants of large landholders. The merchants accompanied these settlers, of course, even drew them by speculating in large tracts of land to subdivide and sell to them (Carstensen 1963; Chandler 1945).

Thus, even though industrial monopoly capital was becoming, by the late nineteenth century, the dominant force in the national economy, the merchants and land speculators were able to dominate the West for a while longer. They therefore were able to influence strongly federal Indian policy, which applied mainly to the West, until industrial monopoly capital consolidated its economic dominance throughout the country during the 1920s (Debo 1970; Means 1964).

The westward extension of merchant capital and its eventual capitulation to industrial capital show in the shifts of federal Indian policy that have affected Navajo families. Elsewhere (Kelley 1979) I have formulated the relationship between federal Indian policy and capitalist development in the United States. That formulation I summarize here, emphasizing the most profound effects on the Navajo political economy.

Between 1850 and 1875, federal Indian policy tended to reflect the interests of land speculators and merchants (often one and the same). The federal government served these interests by confining certain tribes to reservations and offering the rest of their land either at public sale in large tracts or as railroad grants. This policy enhanced the speculators' profits by allowing a few investors to monopolize the lands opened for sale to small farmers and ranchers. Once the farmers and ranchers came in, the merchants, of course, profited. The Indians were to be contained on reservations,

rather than simply "removed" to uncolonized territory, because, by this time, settlers were overrunning the entire West, and various states and territories were refusing to accept Indians who had been removed from neighboring regions (Priest 1942:6–19).

The Navajo tribe was among those that the United States conquered during this period. The Navajo homeland was part of the land that Mexico gave up to the United States in 1848, after the Mexican War. For the next 15 years, partly because the Navajos impeded travel to and from the California gold fields, the U.S. Army steadily intensified its hostilities with the Navajos. Finally, in 1864, about half the tribe surrendered. Their conquerors forced them to walk several hundred miles from their homes in the New Mexico and Arizona territories to a small reservation at Fort Sumner, New Mexico. There they starved for 4 years, until the government agreed to establish a reservation in their homeland and allowed them to return. The return may have ultimately been prompted by the filling of the West, for there was no place else for the Navajos to go. Speculators, moreover, held no immediate interest in the land after its supposed mineral riches were not found.

Between 1875 and 1890, merchants kept their grip on federal Indian policy, but speculators lost some of their influence to the impoverished small farmers who were settling the West. These farmers pressed the federal government to offer land in small tracts either free or on easy terms. Even in the several decades before 1875, Congress had responded to these farmers by gradually reducing the minimum acreage required for public land purchases, and especially by passing the Homestead Act of 1862 (Gates 1936). Some see in these statutes a "safety valve" that kept an impoverished, landless proletariat from growing in the Northeast faster than urban industry could absorb it (see Shannon, 1936, for a summary of and argument with this view). The influence of small farmers on federal Indian policy was greatest between 1875 and 1920, because that is when many were losing land in the East (and especially in the South after the Civil War) and were also pressed by waves of immigrants from Europe.

The influence of these farmers and the merchants who profited from them culminated in the General Allotment Act of 1887, the sponsor of which had backing from an association of Boston merchant-philanthropists (Otis 1973; Priest 1942:78–79). The act allowed the federal government to allot to the head of each Indian household a 160-acre piece of reservation land, and then to add the land left over to the public domain. Partly to keep the Indian allottees from losing their land to unscrupulous buyers and becoming destitute burdens on the body politic, the act also enjoined allottees from selling their allotments for 25 years. The federal government mostly used this statute to break up reservations and offer their unallotted portions under the Homestead Act in territories like Oklahoma, where droves of settlers were moving. The influence of the speculators nevertheless persisted, as is evident in the 25-year trust provision of the General Allotment Act; in the failure of Congress to flood the land market by breaking up many reservations, including the Navajo; and in the disposal of a large proportion of "surplus" Indian lands at public sale rather than through the provisions of the Homestead Act (Gates 1936).

The allotment policy as applied to the Navajo country thus owes much to the influence of distant speculators. Merchants also exerted a strong influence. In 1866, Congress had given the Atlantic and Pacific Railroad Company a land grant in the homeland of the newly conquered Navajos to finance the construction of a transcontinental railroad. The railroad finally materialized in 1881 and swept in a flurry of traders eager to capture the Navajo wool trade. The merchants soon transformed the Navajos from self-sufficient producers of their own subsistence into small-scale, semi-commercialized sheep ranchers. The merchants achieved this transformation by extending credit to Navajo families who were only slowly rebuilding herds ravaged during conquest and temporary removal, and who could no longer get help from rich headmen, who before the conquest had held groups of families together in economically interdependent communities but who had lost their political authority (and often much of their livestock) during the conquest. The merchants further undercut the headmen and other economic ties among families, destroying the self-sustaining indigenous political economy, preserving the family as the production unit, and replacing help from other families with trading-post credit as the main source of economic security. Growing indebtedness then forced families to allocate more and more of their production to the traders. Families became isolated from each other and forced into par-

tial dependence on the national capitalist economy, generating profits for the traders.

Distant land speculators and especially local merchants, then, influenced federal policy toward the Navajos much more than did the clamor of land-hungry farmers and ranchers, but the land-hungry were not entirely absent. By the early twentieth century, settlers were moving into the area east of the Navajo Reservation, where since 1866 most land had belonged to the railroad or the public domain, but both before and after the conquest had been occupied by Navajos. In an atypical application of the allotment policy, the federal government began in 1906 to secure Navajo tenure on this land by allotting the public domain to them. The next year, the government extended the reservation eastward. The small-scale settlers, allied with the more powerful large-scale merchant ranchers who were also moving into the country, then pressured Congress to return the land to the public domain at the same time that they also forced the federal government to slow the allotting. That the merchants had made the Navajos themselves small-scale, semi-commercial ranchers probably protected Navajo land from more encroachment and prevented the allotting from ending altogether.

Although the merchants, speculators, and farmers exerted the greatest influence on federal Indian policy during the 1875–1890 period, industrial capitalists also began to make themselves felt. Their interests were (and still are) best served by the transfer of large tracts of Indian land to the public domain, from which it is leased only long enough for the industrialists to strip it of its marketable resources. It is also in the industrial capitalist's best interest to lease from the government rather than from private landholders or Indian tribes. The private owners try to extract profits that the government would not try to extract, while federal public-land leasing laws tend to be more liberal than the laws that apply to Indian lands (Sutton 1975:17), hedged about as those lands often are by legally binding treaties.

If the government transferred all reservation lands to the public domain, however, a crisis of public finance to support the destitute, expropriated Indians would follow. This course therefore has never been politically feasible. If Indians are to retain some lands, these lands usually serve industrialists best if they are preserved in large tracts as reservations, especially if the tribes themselves do not compete with the industrialists for resources. Splitting these lands into allotments is undesirable, for then the industrialists must arrange a plethora of leases with individual small landholders. The emerging influence of industrial capitalism during the 1890–1920 period is perhaps the reason that the government did not allot many reservations and restored the land's timber and mineral resources to the public domain by executive order (Sutton 1975:71). Parallel developments in public-land policy include such statutes as Congress's authorization of the National Forests in 1891 and the Mineral Leasing Act of 1920. These statutes gave industrialists liberal access to public lands (Clawson and Held 1957:25).

Since 1920, industrial capital has superseded merchant capital in dominating federal Indian policy. In a parallel development, the federal government has increased its public landholdings and their use by industrial capital (Clawson 1967:1; Clawson and Held 1957:24, 27–36). In the Navajo country, industrial capital made its emerging dominance felt first through the creation, in 1922, of the Navajo Tribal Council, a representative body of Navajos that was to sign leases arranged between the Bureau of Indian Affairs (BIA) and private oil companies. The next, and more transforming, manifestation of industrial capital's rise was the grazing-regulation program of the 1930s. The industrial growth of southern California required that Navajos reduce their livestock to stem overgrazing and the resulting soil erosion, which threatened to silt up Boulder Dam, the source of electricity that was to power California's growth. By cutting Navajo livestock holdings in half, this program destroyed family livestock production as the foundation of the Navajo economy and, in the process, undermined the merchants.

Since 1945, the federal government has made tribal governments more responsible for developing infrastructure and social services to tribal members and has funded much of this development (Tyler 1973:151–279). The Navajo–Hopi Long-Range Rehabilitation Act of 1950 funded such development in the Navajo country. The federal government has thereby authorized tribal governments to groom tribal lands for private industry and to maintain their

members as "industrial reserve armies"—workers available for any upsurge in industrialization, however temporary. The troops of the industrial reserve army are the workers last hired and first fired, and their employment is most strongly affected by business cycles—cycles of boom and bust, overproduction, and the compensatory curbing of production. This extreme lack of job security makes the industrial reserve army the most readily exploited segment of the labor force, the most oppressed, and the most dependent on welfare for survival. The industrial reserve army is the segment of the labor force that has absorbed most employable Navajos.

The financial responsibility of maintaining both the Navajo industrial reserve army and infrastructure to attract the enterprises that will employ it has set tribal governments, including that of the Navajos, on a collision course with those very enterprises. Continually pressed for money, tribal governments have started their own enterprises, pushed for larger lease and royalty payments from private enterprises on tribal lands, and imposed taxes on these enterprises. These adverse relations between the tribes and private industry have become especially acute during economic downturns, and not by accident, federal proposals for termination have become most frequent at these times. Industrial capital has tended to exploit rural labor mainly during boom periods, then to recede into the cities during busts (Mandel 1976). As rural industry withdraws from the reservations, Indian people who have remained on their reservations are thrown out of work, while many who had moved to the cities to work return unemployed. As these people raise the demand for social services and tribal-government jobs, the tribal governments must try to squeeze money out of the industries that are left—mainly those with long-term leases on natural resources—through taxes, demands for more lease and royalty payments, and so forth.

The response of industry shows in the termination resolution that the U.S. House of Representatives passed in 1953 and the clamor for termination between the late 1970s and this writing (Gallup *Independent*, February 8, 1983, p. 2; *Navajo Times*, March 9, 1983, p. 2; Johansen 1978; Rogal 1976). *Termination* means that the federal government unilaterally withdraws its recognition of all tribes, thus no longer protecting the sovereignty of tribes over lands that they reserved for themselves in treaties with the United States. That the government has actually terminated few tribes, however, is probably owing to a lack of enthusiasm among the state governments, which would be responsible for supporting the Indian industrial reserve army (Debo 1970:306–317). As I show in the following chapters, the relationship among lease-township residents, the Navajo tribal government, and the McKinley Mine exemplifies the results of federal policy since 1945.

Capitalist Development and Navajo Family Land Use

The foregoing account shows that slow shifts in the capitalist sectors that dominated federal Indian policy did not affect the Navajos strongly until those shifts were well advanced. Thus, although speculators and merchants had dominated federal Indian policy since the eighteenth century, they had not seen the Navajos conquered until 1864 and did not fully transform the Navajo economic base from self-sufficient to market-oriented production until after the railroad arrived in 1881. Likewise, industrial capital, although dominant after 1920, required the two decades between 1930 and 1950 to destroy family production for the market as the Navajo economic base. Only since 1950 has industrial capital replaced this base with wage work and welfare.

However tardily, capitalist development, mediated by federal Indian policy, has produced a two-stage class transformation among the Navajos. During the railroad era (1881–1930), autonomous and interdependent family production units became isolated and market oriented, driven by the profit motive of the merchants. Then, through the influence of industrial capital during the era of grazing regulation (1930–1950) and the industrial era (1950–present), the market-oriented family production units have given way to families of wage workers or welfare recipients and their dependents. Family land use has undergone a corresponding two-stage transformation in these three historical periods.

Larger forces outside Navajo society have changed family land-use patterns by interacting with the atomistic decision making of Navajo families. This type of decision making is a major source of contradictions within the Navajo family production system and has kept the system from maintaining itself at a constant state. Perhaps the central contradiction is that between the small scale on which these decisions are made and their capacity to ramify throughout entire regions. As individual families make production decisions, particularly regarding the use of land, the resulting shifts in land use could impinge on neighboring families, whose responses in turn could impinge on their neighbors, and so on. Such ramified changes are especially likely when a particular type of stress falls on many families. Sources of stress might include population increase, changes in the physical environment, and shifts in relations with outsiders (here, the colonial and national powers). For the Navajos, the stress of outsiders has been the most important, especially since 1864; in fact, as later chapters show, Navajo relations with merchant capitalists seem to have encouraged overexploitation of the land and environmental degradation, even perhaps population growth.

During the railroad era of 1881 to 1930, merchant capital acted on, or even enhanced, the atomism of family decision making to change various aspects of family land use in several ways. Merchant capitalism lessened the family's direct dependence on land-based production by forcing the family to depend more and more on weaving blankets and making silver jewelry for the market. It also caused families to specialize in one form of land-based production, the raising of sheep and goats, and thereby to substitute a growing variety of mass-produced goods for home-produced food crops and other items. Impoverished from warfare, conquest, and captivity, families became indebted to traders. To pay their debt, they stepped up their weaving, their silversmithing, and their extracting of products from herds (wool, lambs, hides, and even butchered meat). Many became more deeply enmeshed in producing handicrafts for the market as successive generations subdivided the land, and the herds of individual families shrank proportionally. Families also lost land to the wealthy, whom the merchants encouraged to expand their own livestock production and allocate their surplus to the market rather than to their poorer relations. On top of the long-term trend of expanding handicraft production for the market, cyclical decreases in raw wool prices encouraged increases in craft production (weaving), which added value to the raw wool.

At the same time, the trading posts reduced family dependence on farming. People could then move into lands, like the lease townships, that were too dry for crops to grow dependably. Rich stockowners, whom the merchants encouraged to enlarge their herds and landholdings, also forced smaller owners into such marginal lands. The lack of reliable natural water in summer at first restricted all but a few families to living in the newly settled lands only in winter, and to returning to the better watered lands of their forebears in summer. As population grew and land subdivision progressed in the summer range, however, more and more families were forced to stay in the new lands year-round, and they began to improve springs and build dams to catch runoff moisture. The range filled and fragmented while alternatives to land-based production remained limited, because the merchants invested their profits wherever they could realize the highest return—mainly outside the region. The natural environment therefore changed. Many families would not reduce their herds below the minimum they needed to support themselves, especially knowing that their neighbors would then assert traditionally inherited residual rights and overrun the land. The result was overgrazing and soil erosion that bled the range dry.

Market production also created residence groups with a size and demographic composition that could supply enough able-bodied workers for the variety of tasks that market production and domestic maintenance demanded. Mercantile trade steadily demanded more labor from families as they sank into debt. It forced them both to diversify and to increase, if possible, their production. By the time a couple was middle aged, they were losing helpers as their children grew up, formed households of their own, and moved away where they could keep the herd they needed to support themselves. Perhaps at least partly to keep up the family labor force, women bore many children, beginning when they were very young and continuing until menopause. An unintended result of the individual family preference for many children was the growing speed with which families filled and subdivided the land. Impoverishment and range degradation followed close behind.

The communal land tenure of the time before the conquest could barely survive the mercantile onslaught. The old communities fell apart and families became isolated both economically and politically. The rights of individual families to monopolize land became stronger, and individuals began to receive range-use rights from their parents. The inheritance of land-use rights was matrilineal, because that principle was compatible with earlier forms of inheritance. Because mercantile trade encouraged land fragmentation and range degradation, however (and also perhaps because the semiarid environment has always been unpredictable), people also asserted residual rights to the lands of matrilateral relatives. Thus, a vestige of communal tenure survived in the residential kin group or outfit, that is, the set of several residence groups that share a land base.

Merchant capitalism affected the numbers and sizes of grazing tracts, fields, and homesites most directly by encouraging families to fill the range and then subdivide it. Subdivision increased the number of grazing tracts, so that the size of each one shrank. Families at first did not need to farm as much as their forbears had, and most of their fields remained in the wetter ancestral lands where they spent the summer. As land subdivison proceeded in the ancestral range, howver, more families began to live all year in the new range and thus to farm there. The number of fields in the new land then increased. These fields could not produce crops as dependably as those along the permanent streams and would have been inadequate for families before the arrival of the trading posts. Augmented by trading-post credit, however, they were enough for the families of the late railroad era.

The natural population growth in the new lands would have increased the number of homesites there between the early and late railroad era. Homesites also grew in size as range subdivision shrank the grazing tracts. Families were able to exploit more of each smaller tract from a given homesite and therefore did not need to move so often. Because families stayed longer on each homesite, they used fewer homesites during the year. It might have been this settling down that kept the number of homesites from growing as fast as population. If families had reduced their homesites on the ancestral lands only to spend most or all of the year on the new lands, however, the number of homesites on the new land might have increased as fast as population.

The natural-resource needs of families, especially water, forage, wood, and shelter, affected the distribution of both grazing tracts and homesites across the landscape. Because the distribution of water changed seasonally, families shifted seasonally among homesites. Their grazing tracts encompassed forage areas that included, or were at least near, water sources viable in different seasons. They situated their fields in the parts of their range with slope and soil types best suited to farming. If acceptable farmland was widespread, as in the lease townships, fields were often situated near homesites. In the lease townships, however, grazing needs exerted a stronger influence over homesite locations than did farming needs, especially because many families did not farm at all.

The longer stays of families on homesites that land subdivision encouraged influenced not only the spatial aspects of land use, but also productive and domestic technology. So did trading-post credit, by bringing families mass-produced tools and equipment, such as plows, wagons, stoves, and kerosene lanterns. Merchant capitalism affected family technology most strongly, however, through the unrelenting pressure that indebtedness imposed on the family labor pool to diversify and, if possible, increase production. Everybody in the family therefore worked. Only adults were adept enough or strong enough for most handicrafts and for such domestic chores as hauling water and getting wood. The less specialized, physically less taxing work of daily herding therefore fell to the children.

As they stayed longer on homesites and produced more handicrafts, families enlarged the sizes and forms of their dwellings for more indoor storage and work space. Even if household sizes did not change, families enlarged the floor areas of their dwellings and replaced the pre-conquest conical form, the "forked-stick hogan," first with the domelike form ("round hogan") and later with the rectangular form (cabin). Because longer seasonal stays also imposed on families a wider variety of outdoor tasks, they built more facilities on their homesites and also left more nonstructural evidence of activities (such as hearths) on their homesites. They enlarged the work area in front of each dwelling by dumping refuse farther away from it. They bought at the trading posts whatever domestic tools and equipment they could afford. These were labor-saving devices and items that they lacked the time or expertise to make for themselves and that native craft specialists no longer made because they,

too, were producing for the national market. Larger dwellings induced families to buy stoves, if they could afford them, which in turn necessitated lamps and kerosene to compensate for the firelight that people lost when they abandoned the open heating hearth.

The longer annual stays and growing family labor burden also affected herding technology by influencing the construction of corrals and pens. People built more and bigger corrals for their herds on homesites where they spent the longest periods of the year, because muck, which makes the sheep wet, cold, and sick in winter, would not accumulate so fast in the bigger corrals. Corrals also saved labor by allowing people to leave the herd unattended so that they could do other chores. Specialized corrals and pens for lambs orphaned or rejected by their mothers saved the family work by segregating those animals that needed special feeding to survive. Tools and equipment for both herding and farming, although minimal, also reflect the family's need to save labor in production. For example, one can shear a given amount of wool in less time with mass-produced clippers than with the tin cans or knives that Navajos used in the early days. The plows and iron hoes that farmers bought at the trading posts saved work in planting and cultivating.

The second stage of the Navajo class transformation, and the corresponding changes in family land use, began with the grazing-regulation era of 1930 to 1950 and have been more or less completed during the present industrial era, 1950–present. Industrial monopoly capital overrode mercantile interests in influencing federal Indian policy. The federal government then abruptly imposed grazing regulation to stop the market-induced range degradation that had been widespread for at least a generation. Regulation on its own, however, could not curb trends in family land use that mercantile trade had set in motion. By reducing family herds, grazing regulation forced families to subsist on less produce from the land but did not automatically provide other sources of livelihood. Therefore, it failed to eliminate the family as the basic production unit and to lessen the family's dependence on land-based production and trading-post credit. It only deepened their poverty. Grazing regulation also failed to lighten the labor burden on the family or to stop the subdivision of the range—two immediate causes of many changes of family land use under merchant capitalism. Only when wage work and welfare became widespread would most trends in family land use stop or change direction. Wage work and welfare did not become available to most Navajos until after World War II, and cyclical economic downturns since then have made growth uneven.

After 1950, as industry began to move into the Navajo country, and with welfare programs in place, wage work and welfare replaced family land-based production as the foundation of the Navajo economy. Mercantile capitalism thereby lost its sway over the family. People now relied on money income eked out with short-term credit from city stores.

Still, industrialization has not lessened the shortage of family labor for land-based production, nor has it stopped the shrinking of the family land base. Indeed, it has worsened these problems, but not in the same ways as merchant capitalism did. Merchant capitalism increased the work of the family in production (land-based and handicraft) and increased the number of families competing for land. It forced families to intensify production, that is, to get more product from a given expenditure of labor and raw materials. Technology (especially water development), diversified land-based production (through farming), and overgrazing were the means to this end.

In contrast, industrialization has transferred the most able-bodied family members from land-based and other family production (and domestic maintenance) to wage jobs and has taken land from families for such industrial uses as strip mining. These withdrawals indirectly provide the money income that has replaced land-based and other family production in supporting the family. These other means of support have relieved the pressure on families to intensify production and have also helped them to buy more labor-saving items. People cannot quit family production, however, nor can they stop exploiting natural resources for domestic maintenance, because industrialization has not yielded enough money income to free them entirely. Wages and welfare do not provide enough income without supplemental herding and farming. Nor has industrialization brought most people public utilities, like electricity, running water, or heat, which would save domestic labor.

The various aspects of family land use reflect these changes that industrialization has wrought. I have already mentioned the change in one aspect of family land use: the family's dwindling dependence on its own production, both land-based and handicraft. A corollary development is that mass-produced goods have almost entirely replaced home-produced goods.

Industrialization has altered little the natural resources that families need for land-based production or domestic maintenance, because it has not eliminated family land-based production nor offered families the full range of public utilities. Industrialization has, however, reduced land-based production and provided some families with some utilities. It has thereby reduced the pressure on most resources. In the lease townships, industrialization has more or less replaced overgrazing with another form of environmental degradation, strip-mining, which is supposed to be only temporary but may nevertheless prevent individual families from using the fragile, reclaimed land. If grazing is possible on the land after mining, families may only be able to renew their use of it by pooling their livestock and managing it cooperatively.

So far, industrialization has not broken down the residence groups that the labor demands of mercantile capitalism required. The households of old and young still must band together to accomplish all the unchanged work of domestic maintenance, with the elderly still involved in stock raising and farming and the young often working for wages. In fact, by eliminating stock raising as the economic mainstay of all families, industrialization has removed the factor that limited the size of residence groups. In the railroad and grazing-regulation eras, younger couples left the parental homesite as their herds grew and the range accessible from the homesites became insufficient for the sheep of all the households. Today, younger couples do not accumulate sheep. Moreover, because many households want to live near a paved road or maintain dwellings in homesites where they cannot live when they are working, industrialization has actually made some residence groups bigger than in earlier times. Nevertheless, residence groups are also beginning to break down at homesites where elderly people are the only permanent residents, and the younger households only visit the dwellings they maintain there.

Land withdrawals for industry and government have already displaced many families, while others have moved to be near the paved roads that link them to schools, stores, social services, and jobs. Still others, especially younger families, shift their homes as often as they change jobs or ride out stints of unemployment. These families have exercised their residual rights to land expediently and thereby have kept the larger land-using group, the outfit, alive. The principle of matrilineal inheritance and the control of the outfit's land by matrikin are, however, in jeopardy. Older couples have always tended to live virilocally, that is, with the husband's family, almost as often as uxorilocally, that is, with the wife's family. In the past, however, only the children of the uxorilocal couples would ordinarily stay on their parents' land, thus living with their mothers' families. Now, the grown children of many virilocal couples are also staying on their parents' land, thus living with their fathers' families even after the parents die, because land withdrawals and overcrowding prevent them from moving in with their mothers' families. Within an outfit, members whose use rights came from their mothers in the traditional matrilineal way may contest the rights of members whose use rights came through their fathers. The resulting disputes might, in the long run, destroy the outfit.

Industrialization has also forced more families either to safeguard more of their traditional claims through a growing variety of legal means or to lose the traditional claims to outsiders. Families have also started to invoke these legal rights in land disputes among themselves. The legal principle of inheritance is bilateral and has been applied to most allotted land by probate court. Many people with legal rights therefore lack traditional, matrilineal rights. When these people invoke their legal rights in land disputes, they are essentially using legal tenure to undermine traditional tenure. At the same time, industrialization and the federal Indian policy that so often serves it have made these legal safeguards less than ironclad. Lease-township families discovered that the federal government had negotiated leases with the Pittsburg and Midway Coal Mining Company behind their backs. Their control of the very allotments that safeguarded their land rights proved to be incomplete.

Industrialization has also transformed the use of space. As families no longer depend on land-based production, the number of grazing tracts and fields has hardly changed, even as population has grown. By eliminating some tracts altogether, strip-mining has also kept the number of grazing tracts in the lease townships from increasing. Strip mines and other land withdrawals have reduced the size of grazing tracts as well. As the lessened importance of farming prompts more families to limit themselves to kitchen gardens, fields seem to have shrunk. Diminished stock raising has restricted virtually all families to living year-round in the lease townships, so that the number of homesites per family has dwindled with the loss of the summer range. The number of homesites in the lease townships, however, has almost kept pace with population. Because many homesites contain more households, one would expect industrial-era homesites to be bigger than those of earlier times. The bigger houses that money income allows families to build and heat may also enlarge industrial-era homesites. But other facilities, such as corrals, barns, corn-drying places, and the like, disappear from homesites as family production dwindles, so that the homesites may shrink instead.

Industrialization has not changed the distribution of homesites, grazing tracts, or fields across the landscape in relation to natural resources, because the natural resources that families need have not changed. Besides taking much acreage from family use, industrialization has affected the spatial distribution of homesites and grazing tracts by bringing paved roads. Now that the national economy has thoroughly enmeshed families, their ready access to this link with the outside world is essential. Families have therefore moved their homesites as near the road as possible and have reoriented their grazing tracts accordingly.

Industrialization has, however, altered domestic, herding, and farming technology. I have already mentioned the new family division of labor in which most herding and farming chores, as well as much of the domestic work, fall on old people if the younger, working people live away from the homesite. The quest for labor-saving devices is therefore intense. Families now have the money to buy more mass-produced devices than ever before, the pickup truck being paramount. Some also have the money to hire help in herding, farming, hauling and cutting wood, and to take trips to the outside world. Wage relations thus have penetrated even the domain of traditional, unpaid family labor.

The vast growth of money income also shows in the bigger dwellings that people build during the industrial era to house their growing inventory of possessions, and which they can now afford to heat with stoves of adequate size. Money also shows in the mass-produced building materials that today make up most dwellings, and many corrals and barns. Many families no longer have other home-made facilities, such as ovens and sweathouses, that families once built for their various productive and domestic tasks. Some of these facilities have given way to mass-produced equipment such as kitchen ranges, often kept in the house. Others, like corrals, are no longer needed since many families have abandoned the production that these facilities served.

These are the changes in family land use and their causes that have passed through the lease townships, as later chapters show. Before beginning that detailed demonstration, however, I recount in the following chapter the history of the lease townships and their settlers before these changes began.

Chapter 3

The Land and Early Navajo Use

1700–1800

During the seventeenth century, the Navajos were living in Dinetah. That wooded mesa-and-canyon country lies along the San Juan River and its southern tributaries, Largo and Gobernador drainages, in what is now northwestern New Mexico (see Frontispiece). Archaeological and ethnohistorical works on the period show that Navajos lived in dispersed small groups that probably consisted of extended families. They subsisted by growing corn and other crops, hunting, and gathering (see Vivian, 1960, for a review of sources). They also sustained raids, mainly from the Spanish colonists to the east along the Rio Grande, who took Navajo slaves. The Navajos reciprocated in kind, either by retaliating or by taking livestock (McNitt 1972:3–26). At first they seem to have eaten the livestock, just as they would have done with wild game. By about 1700, however, Navajo families were augmenting their farming, hunting, and gathering by raising small herds of sheep and goats (Hill 1940b; Reeve 1958:217). They may also have started to move westward, as they continued to do throughout the eighteenth century, and some settled in the general vicinity of the lease townships.

The move westward may have been the outcome of three sets of conflicts, all responses to Spanish (and some possibly to French) colonial expansion. The first set consists of the Pueblo Revolt of 1680, when the Pueblo Indians drove the Spanish out of the New Mexico Territory, and the Spanish Reconquest of 1692 to 1696, during and after which many Puebloans fled into Dinetah (Reeve 1958). That the first Navajo occupa-

tion of Canyon de Chelly (in what is now Arizona) may date to this time (Brugge 1972:95) suggests that Navajos were moving westward, perhaps because the Puebloan refugees were crowding them out of Dinetah, or because they were fleeing the Spanish.

The second set of conflicts consists of Ute and Comanche raids on the Navajos between about 1710 and the 1760s, with arms possibly furnished by the French (Reeve 1958; Sjoberg 1953:77). These raids forced the Navajos to abandon Dinetah. Many moved southward into the Cebolleta Mountains or westward to the Chuska Range and Canyon de Chelly (Ellis 1974:302–306, 489–490; Hill 1940b:396; Reeve 1959:20, 24). During this time, the Navajos and Spanish were at peace (Reeve 1959), possibly because the Spanish wanted the Navajos as a bulwark against Ute and Comanche attacks and therefore restrained themselves from taking Navajo slaves.

The third set of conflicts came about at least partly because the Spanish settlers spread into Navajo territory around Mount Taylor during the 1760s (Reeve 1959:29–39). The Spanish also renewed the slave trade after the Ute–Comanche alliance fell apart during the 1760s, a change that Brugge (1972:97) sees as the main cause of the renewed slaving.

During this period, Navajos settled in the general vicinity of the lease townships. Mid–eighteenth-century Navajo homesites are located a few miles from the townships, to the south at Manuelito on the Rio Puerco of the West and to the southeast at Rock Springs. During the eighteenth century, Navajos also built antelope-hunting corrals a few miles west of the lease townships in the Black Creek Valley. These corrals suggest that settlement was sparse, for otherwise the sheep would have outcompeted the antelope (Navajo Tribe, Correll Collection [CC] 1962: S-ULC-UP-P, Q, R, AA, OO). Other sites several dozen miles west of the lease townships (near Nazlini and Klagetoh) date to the mid-eighteenth century. The masonry fortifications that make up these sites show that westward migration did not insure the Navajos against attack (Bannister, Hannah, and Robinson 1966:7–8; Brugge 1972:97). Navajos, however, evidently did not settle in the lease townships themselves during this period. The archaeological studies of the lease (Eck 1981; Eck, Boyer, and Kelley 1982; Hartman 1977; Koczan 1977) offer no clear evidence of Navajo residence until the late nineteenth century.

The townships nevertheless would have offered most of the resources that Navajos needed to survive. Farming was important to Navajo livelihood at the time. People would have sought farming sites in places where they could also graze small herds of sheep and goats, find water and firewood, and hide during raids. The lease townships cover a tract between 6500 and 7200 feet in elevation that is rugged and rocky except for the east side. Mixed sagebrush-grassland carpets the broad, low-lying valley bottoms and is interspersed with piñon and juniper woodland in the uplands. Moisture today averages 12.6 inches a year, between a third and a half of which falls as snow (Dames and Moore 1974:37) and is therefore adequate for dry farming. So is the growing season, which usually exceeds the 120–130 frost-free days that corn requires (Knight 1982:52–53). Wide expanses of clay loam with adequate slope for drainage offer cultivable land between the bigger arroyos and outcropping mesas (Nelson and Cordell 1982:872–873).

Sage-grass forage for stock also abounds in the three major drainages of the townships: Tse Bonita Wash, a southwest-flowing tributary of Black Creek that heads north of the lease; Defiance Draw, separated from the Tse Bonita Wash to the west by a yellow sandstone spine and draining southeast into the Puerco; and the Eastern Flat, an eastern tributary of the lower Defiance Draw. The lease also nips off a small side canyon of Black Creek for a bit of a fourth drainage (see Figure 3.1). The townships, then, offered cultivable land, forage, hiding places, wood, and water.

In summer, however, surface water in the townships is scant. No springs or streams are permanent, although layers of water-bearing sandstone and shale underlie the townships. Seepage is mainly confined to the winter, as snow melts and the low temperatures prevent the quick evaporation that occurs in summer. The yellow and brown sandstone crops out in the uplands as caprock with shale underneath or as steep-sided ridges, and the gray shale crops out as badlands. Shales also underlie the lowland sage-grass plains. Overall, the townships dip to the southeast (Dames and Moore 1974:42, 45, 47). Water seeps from the exposed sandstone-shale contacts along the sides of the ridges at various elevations and collects in playas on the flats. The general southeastward dip probably affords seep-fed tributary drainages in the southern and eastern parts of the townships' larger catchment basins than those to the north and west. It also gives the lower Defiance Draw and Eastern Flat more surface water than the Tse Bonita Wash and upper Defiance Draw. The Tse Bonita Wash, however, is longer than the other two drainages. It heads in the foothills of the Chuskas and seems to have more subsurface flow than do the other two, so that one can tap more water by digging shallow wells in its bed.

On the other hand, nearby Black Creek would have run continuously during the eighteenth century before irrigation projects, dams, and wells absorbed some of its flow. From its source about 35 miles northwest of the lease townships, it traversed broad grasslands between the pine-topped red sandstone "haystacks" on the east and the timbered Defiance Plateau on the west, crossed the meadows of Oak Springs, and descended through a canyon to the Rio Puerco of the West, also a permanent stream. People could have farmed near hiding places along the edges of the Black Creek and Puerco valleys and probably would not have needed more range. The lease townships, therefore, may have attracted Navajos of the time only for hunting and gathering. Distance from concentrations of people would have encouraged deer in the area, and perhaps even antelope in the sage-grass flats where two undated antelope corrals still stand.

1800–1864

Hostilities between the Navajos and successive colonial regimes escalated after 1800 (Reeve 1960:235) and especially after 1818 (Brugge 1972:99). The

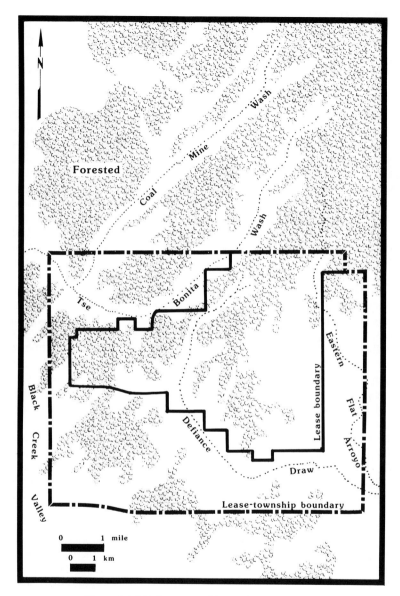

Figure 3.1 The lease townships and their drainages.

Spanish and Mexican colonial governors sanctioned slave raids, and the practice continued after the United States took over the New Mexico Territory in 1848 (Young and Morgan 1952:3). Colonial governors also dispatched military expeditions into the Navajo country. On the Navajo side, small groups of malcontents mounted some raids for livestock and, sometimes, slaves, but large groups evidently also raided the colonials (Reeve 1971:226).

Colonial slaving and military adventures were not the only spurs to Navajo raiding. By the early nineteenth century, great differences in wealth divided

Navajo families and forced the poor to raid. Since early times, Navajos seem to have been organized economically and politically into self-sufficient local groups, each made up of perhaps a few dozen families. Every group had a "headman," who probably settled disputes within the group and acted as its spokesperson to outsiders such as colonial authorities, missionaries, and the like. These headmen were probably chosen by group consensus and exerted "moral suasion" rather than power over their followers (Hill 1940a, b; Reeve 1958). Evidence that these headmen were also wealthy was lacking until the late eighteenth century, when Antonio El Pinto, a headman from the Mount Taylor vicinity, was recognized as such (Correll 1979, Vol. 1:80; Reeve 1960:222). That Navajos around Mount Taylor traded rather extensively with both the Spanish and the Pueblo Indians (Reeve 1960:213) and thus had an incentive to amass wealth suggests that wealth stratification was starting, perhaps encouraged by trade.

After 1800, the Louisiana Purchase and the opening of the Santa Fe Trail inundated the New Mexico Territory with trade goods, much of which flowed into the Indian trade (McNitt 1962:14–17). Unlike earlier documents, those of the nineteenth century portray many headmen as owners of large herds of livestock (Correll 1979; McNitt 1972; Reeve 1957, 1958, 1960, 1971). These *ricos* may have controlled the best range at the expense of their poorer neighbors, *pobres* or *pelados*, who could either become semidependent retainers of the *ricos* or colonize new land and enlarge their herds through raiding.

Narbona of Sheep Springs, on the east side of the Chuskas, perhaps epitomized the *rico*. He had three wives and presided over a sprawling menage in which his first wife's mother cared for almost a dozen children. The family owned 2000 sheep, 200 goats, 50 head of cattle, and 200 horses. The sheep and goats were divided into several flocks, each in the care of two or three herders, while the other herders looked after the horses and cattle. Narbona owned a few slaves (non-Navajo captives taken on raids), but most of the herders were indigent genealogical or clan relatives who worked in exchange for safety and board for themselves and their families. Of the various dependents, the older women wove and the older men made moccasins, saddles, and silver jewelry. Narbona's own homesite consisted of a hogan for each

of his wives, one for his mother-in-law, one for a married daughter, and one for his aunt, as well as a corral built against a sheltering cliff and two sweathouses (small bathing chambers that people heated with rocks and then entered to bathe by sweating), one for women and one for men, dug into the bank of an arroyo nearby. Other corrals dotted the range, as the sheep numbered too many for herders to bring them home every night. Dependents evidently maintained their own homesites some distance from that of Narbona (Newcomb 1964:8–9).

The growing herds of *ricos* like Narbona perhaps forced not only *pobres*, but also the ambitious children of *ricos*, to colonize new land, most of which was to the west.

Perhaps as a result, and also because military campaigns had become "at least an annual event" for the New Mexico colonial government by about 1834 (Wilson 1967:23), the Black Creek Valley seems to have received another wave of settlers during the 1840s. Spanish and Mexican colonial documents indicate little earlier military interest in the area, although it lay between Zuni and the Chuskas, two frequent military targets (Correll 1976; Wilson 1967). Between 1848 and 1868, however, soldiers saw Navajo cornfields in the Black Creek Canyon spilling into the valley of the Rio Puerco and even farther west in the Pueblo Colorado Wash (Reeve 1974:241).

The people who moved into the Black Creek Valley during the 1840s were the headmen Zarcillos Largos and Manuelito and their followers. This group may have included the ancestors of people who later settled the lease townships. Manuelito had moved to Sheep Springs in 1835 when he married Narbona's daughter, and he apparently had raided with the future headman Ganado Mucho. He had moved south along the foot of the Chuskas toward Tohatchi sometime before Narbona was killed in 1849 during a supposedly peaceful encounter with the U.S. Army (Correll 1979, Vol 1:241–242; Hoffman 1974:83–85). Manuelito had possibly also begun to range from Tohatchi across the Chuskas into the Black Creek Valley. Meanwhile, in 1843, Zarcillos Largos and several other headmen notified Mexican colonial officials that they wanted to settle in the Zuni Mountains, at Bear Spring, and in the Chuskas to separate themselves from the "thieves of the tribe" (Correll 1976:151). That these thieves probably emanated from the eastern Navajo country near the Spanish settlements suggests that Zarcillos Largos, too, then lived in the eastern Navajo country.

When the U.S. Army moved into the Black Creek Valley in 1851, however, these men and their followers seem to have already ensconced themselves there. Partly to protect travelers to California from the Navajos, Colonel Edwin Vose Sumner established the first military post inside the Navajo country, Fort Defiance, where Bonito Canyon enters Black Creek about 10 miles northwest of the lease townships (Correll 1976:262–263). Some of the soldiers called the place Hell's Gate (Frink 1968:19), but, according to another contemporary observer, "The location is one of the most eligible ones that can be found in all that region, being at the mouth of *Canoncito bonito* (pretty little canyon), a favorite spot with the Navajos, and near fertile valleys and good water" (Davis 1962:229). Relations between the army, on the one hand, and Manuelito and Zarcillos Largos, on the other, seem to have been uneasy at first and deteriorated thereafter.

In 1853, Territorial Governor David Meriwether designated Zarcillos Largos "head chief" of the Navajos (Correll 1976:322). In the fall of 1854 the civilian Navajo Agent Henry L. Dodge, or Red Shirt, as the Navajos called him, made Fort Defiance his headquarters. For the next year he circulated among that post, Red Lake in the upper Black Creek Valley, and Washington Pass on the trail over the Chuskas to Sheep Springs (McNitt 1972:256, 267). He had reportedly married a niece of Zarcillos Largos (Brugge 1970:12) and was apparently moving within the area that his wife's family used. In July of 1855, Governor Meriwether went to Red Lake, a "pretty little sheet of water among the mountains," where he met with many Navajo headmen to negotiate a boundary for the Navajo territory (Davis 1962:231). At this council, Zarcillos Largos renounced his office as spokesman for the Navajos, and the honor passed to Manuelito. The description of the treaty council by Meriwether's secretary, W. W. H. Davis, reveals the uneasy tone of relations between the Navajos and their would-be colonizers.

> When we returned to our camp we found it surrounded by hundreds of Indians, and some dozen or more greasy fellows were occupying our tent, and smoking in a manner ridiculously cool and independent, but they soon made

> tracks after our arrival. . . . In the evening there was a rumor in camp that the bad men of the tribe intended to attack us during the night, but we viewed it as an idle tale. (Davis 1962:233)

After the chiefs had agreed to the treaty, Meriwether presented them with a wagon-load of gifts. These they distributed among the 2000 buckskin-clad warriors present by throwing them "into the crowd pell-mell. . . . Brass kettles, knives, tobacco, muslin, looking glasses, and various other articles changed owners with magic quickness" (Davis 1962:235).

Notwithstanding this treaty (never ratified by Congress), conflicts between the garrison at Fort Defiance and the local Navajos soon flared. The resulting military observations offer glimpses of the seasonal moves of Manuelito, Zarcillos Largos, and their followers in and out of the Black Creek Valley. Like Narbona, these headmen seem to have dominated large tracts of range; their followers must have herded in the same general areas.

In 1856, for example, Zarcillos Largos was said to have kept a winter home in Oak Springs and a summer home and farm upstream at Red Lake. He also controlled the lush high pastures in the mountains northwest of Fort Defiance, which his brother leased to the army in exchange for gifts and bonuses. In the same year, agent Dodge was confronted by Manuelito, in whose cattle range around Red Lake the soldiers were cutting hay for army livestock (Correll 1979, Vol. 2:44, 100; McNitt 1972:284, 304). Like Zarcillos Largos, Manuelito probably used this range in summer, for he was known to spend the winter far to the southwest in the low-lying open grasslands of the Pueblo Colorado Wash, a range that he apparently shared with Ganado Mucho (Correll 1979, Vol 2:177, 182, 187; Hoffman 1974:91).

In May of 1858, soldiers from Fort Defiance killed 48 of Manuelito's cattle north of Fort Defiance. Apparently in retaliation, a Navajo killed the black slave of the officer in command of Fort Defiance, and the foes plunged into a full-scale war with many engagements in the Black Creek Valley near the lease townships (Correll 1979, Vol. 2:122–131, 133–134, 153–154). An army company skirmished with Navajos at Oak Springs, capturing at least 20 people, including Torrivio, a Hispanic slave of the Navajo headman Herrero, after whom Torrivio Ridge (or Mexican Fall Down Hill, according to local people) in the lease townships may have been named (Correll 1979, Vol. 2:188–189). In the fall of 1858, a contingent from Fort Defiance went to the Pueblo Colorado Wash, where Zuni auxiliaries burned "Manuelito's village" of "wigwams or half cabins" (Correll 1979, Vol. 2:182). Another contingent, dispatched to attack Zarcillos Largos and destroy his "rancheria," failed to find him near either Oak Springs or Red Lake. They finally caught him and his followers at the wheatfields about 10 miles north of Red Lake, where they wounded the headman and took more than 50 horses, many buffalo robes, blankets, saddles, a silver belt, and an opulent coral necklace (Correll 1979, Vol. 2:169–170). Zarcillos Largos survived but was killed 2 years later far to the southwest near Klagetoh, supposedly by New Mexican and Zuni raiders (Correll 1979, Vol. 3:86).

In July of 1858, an army detachment sent to reconnoiter the Navajo country reported a few people in the Black Creek Valley but no livestock. They observed "extensive" cornfields totaling about a 100 acres in the lower valley and about 15 or 20 miles north of there, possibly between the present St. Michaels and Fort Defiance. They saw evidence of "wintering large herds of horses and flocks of sheep" in the lower Black Creek Valley, which they said was too dry for grazing before mid-July. They also noted cornfields, but no stock or people, in Manuelito's winter range on the Pueblo Colorado Wash. On the other hand, they found Red Lake "swarming" with horses and sheep, which they thought people had driven there "by their fear of the Utahs" (Walker and Shepherd 1964:63–64).

Between 1859 and 1861, army scouting parties often led by Ute and New Mexican trackers harassed Navajos in the valley of the Rio Puerco of the West and the Chuskas (Bailey 1964:135; Correll 1979, Vol. 3:98, 100; Jenkins 1980:89–91). Navajos attacked soldiers at a grazing camp in the Cienega Amarilla (now St. Michaels) a few miles south of Fort Defiance in January of 1860 (McNitt 1972:380–381). In April, a force variously reported as 100 to 1000 Navajos under Manuelito and the Canyon de Chelly headman Barboncito attacked Fort Defiance (Correll 1979, Vol. 2:386–393). The attack failed, and later in the year the army established another post, Fort Fauntleroy, near the Puerco about 40 miles southeast of Fort Defiance. Stretched thin after the outbreak of the Civil War, however, the army abandoned Fort Defiance early in 1861. Manuelito immediately moved in with his cattle (Hoffman 1974:91). Later in the year the army also abandoned Fort Fauntleroy (renamed Fort Lyon after its original namesake joined the Confederate Army) after a horse race ended with troops massacring Navajos who had gathered there to receive food rations (Correll 1979, Vol. 3:183–184).

The swirl of events in the Black Creek Valley seems, however, to have bypassed the lease townships completely, as archaeological evidence of Navajo occupation remains absent (Eck, Boyer, and Kelley 1982). If people used the lease townships at all, they probably still confined themselves to hunting and gathering, although Torrivio and his companions may have hidden near the ridge perhaps named after him.

Navajos may also have avoided the lease townships for another reason. In 1853 the army built the wagon road from Fort Defiance through Wingate Valley to Albuquerque (see Figure 3.2), and during the rest of the decade a constant traffic of military expeditions, supply trains, and the like crossed the townships (Frazer 1963:22; Jenkins 1980:44–45; U.S. Department of the Interior [USDI] General Land Office 1882, 1893).

When military activity escalated into warfare after 1858, the military road would have made the lease townships especially unattractive. The abandonment of Fort Defiance would have offered little rest to Navajos nearby, for between 1860 and 1868 many "citizens' expeditions," with the tacit consent of the U.S. government, raided the Navajo country for slaves (Brugge 1972:103). Military observers nevertheless reported Navajos along the wagon road near Rock Springs only a few miles east of the townships in 1858 and 1861 (Littell 1967:229, 232).

The final blow came in the summer of 1863, after General George S. Carleton's troops had secured New Mexico for the Union. Carleton dispatched his troops to Fort Defiance under Kit Carson, who unleashed them and his Ute mercenaries on the Navajos. Carleton apparently believed that the Navajo country concealed rich deposits of gold and silver, in which he hoped to speculate after he had removed the Navajos to make the land safe for mining (Young 1978:33). First Carson had the Utes destroy all fields within a 40-mile radius of Fort Defiance, or an estimated 2 million pounds of grain (Bailey 1964:156; Kelly 1970:38–44). Navajos battled with the army at China Springs, about 10 miles southeast of the lease townships (Van Valkenburgh 1941:63). Throughout the fall and winter of 1863 to 1864, Carson's men continued

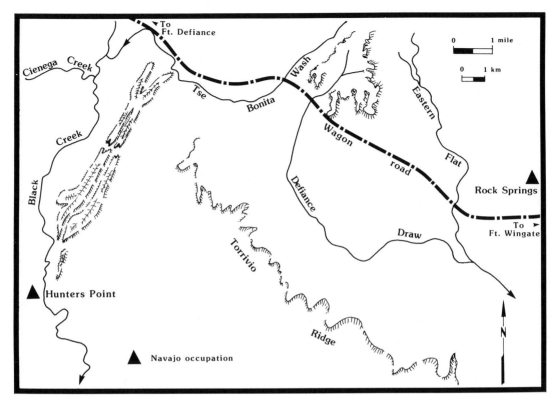

Figure 3.2 The landscape of the lease townships in the 1850s.

to destroy fields and any livestock that they encountered. Carson also asked Carleton to let his Ute mercenaries take Navajos as slaves (Kelly 1970:30–31). These depredations forced Navajos to surrender to Carson at Fort Defiance. During the spring of 1864, groups of 1000 to 2500 people with their remaining livestock began the Long Walk to Fort Sumner in eastern New Mexico, presumably along the military road that crossed the lease townships (Correll 1979, Vol. 4).

1864–1881

While many Navajos languished at Fort Sumner, those who stayed behind fled to the edges of the Navajo country and beyond. The neighborhood of the Black Creek Valley and the lease townships probably was deserted most, but not all, of the time. "Roam-

ing bands who had eluded the troops and scouts of Carson burned the cane and timbered sections of [Fort Defiance], leaving only the thick sod and rubble walls" (Van Valkenburgh 1941:57). In the spring of 1864, Manuelito was reported around Oak Springs and Fort Defiance, together with several other headmen and 1200 followers. Manuelito refused to surrender, reportedly because he expected a massacre at Fort Sumner like the one at Fort Fauntleroy 3 years earlier (Correll 1979, Vol. 4:167–168). The next winter, Manuelito again told emissaries that he would not surrender but would plant crops in the Canyon Bonito. He did, however, reveal the locations of other Navajos, including 40 of them at Oak Springs (Reeve 1974:334).

In the summer of 1865, however, Manuelito with his band of 100, including 25 warriors, had fled 60 miles south of Zuni (Ellis 1974:456). By the summer of 1866, Manuelito was hiding in the Sierra del

Escudilla near present-day Springerville, Arizona. The following September, Manuelito and his followers finally surrendered. They were the last band to turn themselves in (Correll 1979, Vol. 5:368).

Manuelito and his followers remained at Fort Sumner until July of 1868. By that time, the U.S. government had found that the Navajos could not support themselves by farming at Fort Sumner as they could by herding and farming in their homeland. The government therefore established a reservation in the middle of the Navajo country by a treaty that Manuelito and other headmen signed (USDI, Commissioner of Indian Affairs 1868:161–164; Correll and Dehiya 1978:2–7). The treaty reservation extended about 30 mi. on either side of the boundary between the Arizona and New Mexico territories, and from the Colorado–Utah line south as far as the line running east and west from Fort Defiance. An executive order annexation moved the southern boundary south to Cienega Amarilla (St. Michaels) in 1880 (Correll and Dehiya 1978:10–11). The lease townships and lower Black Creek Valley, however, remained outside the reservation.

All Navajos were supposed to stay within the boundaries of the treaty reservation, but many Navajos, when they returned from Fort Sumner in 1868, settled outside. The BIA had supposedly refurbished Fort Defiance to serve as the Navajo agency (although 13 years later it was called "a collection of old dilapidated mud, pig sties and sheep pens"), where government agents distributed rations of grain and beef to help the many destitute families (Bloom 1936:81). That farming was also an economic mainstay is clear from the rations that agents issued for many years to compensate for crop failures. The herds regenerated, however, by the middle 1870s, and Navajo dependence on rations apparently diminished (Bloom 1936:82; USDI, Commissioner of Indian Affairs 1868–1881).

The agents also distributed annuity goods, which the 1868 treaty had promised for 10 years. Periodic distributions continued as late as 1891, however, and included 25,000–44,000 sheep and goats in addition to cloth, coats, shirts, boots, hats, pots and pans, kettles, harness, various small tools, sheep shears, plows, hoes, axes, scrapers, wheelbarrows, cookstoves, and even wagons (Brugge 1980:51–72, 118–121; Correll 1979, Vol. 3:224–225; USDI, Census Office 1890:155; USDI, Commissioner of Indian Affairs 1868–1891;

Young 1961:146). These distributions induced many more Navajos than had previously lived in the Black Creek Valley to settle there. Probably most of the estimated 1500 Navajos who were subsisting on rations in 1871 (Brugge 1980:58) were living in the general vicinity of Fort Defiance. In comparison, the group of followers of a headman during the mid-nineteenth century may have numbered 10–40 families (Hill 1940a:23). The combined followers of Manuelito and Zarcillos Largos probably would have numbered no more than a few hundred.

Among the people who settled in the Black Creek Valley after Fort Sumner were people who were soon to settle in the lease townships, or the forebears of those settlers. Many may have been followers of Manuelito and Zarcillos Largos before Fort Sumner. Circumstantial evidence is that the clans associated with Manuelito, Zarcillos Largos, and their followers were also common among the lease-township residents of 1910 and their forebears (Kelley 1982a:138). Unfortunately, the available sources are too fragmentary to show whether any direct genealogical ties existed between lease-township residents and the two headmen, although some residents are linked indirectly to Manuelito. One of the first settlers of the lease townships after Fort Sumner, moreover, was born around 1850 near Washington Pass, where Zarcillos Largos's band ranged at the time (Navajo Tribe, CC n.d.b).

The forebears of people who moved into the lease townships, then, may have belonged to the bands of Manuelito and Zarcillos Largos before Fort Sumner and perhaps were resettling their former lands after 1868. Manuelito himself, however, was not among them. After 1868 he moved back to his "old home near Tohatchi, south of Sheep Springs" (Hoffman 1974:100). In 1870, the Fort Defiance agent appointed Manuelito head chief, that is, nominal spokesman, of Navajos in the eastern part of the country, and Ganado Mucho chief of those in the west (Van Valkenburgh 1941:90). Manuelito headed the short-lived "Navajo cavalry" (police) and met with two U.S. presidents. He "received many favors from various agents," including "the earliest windmills and wagons, given in the form of annuities [which] were issued to Manuelito and other favored headmen." He fell from favor in 1884 for drunkenness, however, and died 9 years later (Van Valkenburgh 1941:91).

Chapter 4

The Railroad Era, 1881–1930

Historical Background

In 1866, while the Navajos were still at Fort Sumner, Congress granted the Atlantic and Pacific Railroad land in the New Mexico and Arizona territories. This grant ultimately included both surface and mineral rights to all the odd-numbered sections in a swath 50 mi. wide on either side of the right-of-way (Greever 1954:20). It created a checkered pattern of land ownership south and east of the Navajo Reservation that has persisted to this day, although with many modifications. Within this so-called checkerboard area, the right-of-way followed the Rio Puerco 10 mi. south of the lease townships. The Atlantic and Pacific Railroad, later called the Atchison, Topeka and Santa Fe (AT&SF), was built in 1881. Its two most important consequences for land use in the lease townships were the commercialization of Navajo family production and the settlement of the lease townships.

The railroad drew a flood of traders, who saw in the Navajo wool an opportunity to profit from the high wool prices of the early 1880s in U.S. markets that the railroad brought within a few days' travel (U.S. Department of the Treasury [USDT], Bureau of Statistics 1901:447). The Navajos, on their part, were ready to trade their wool, for they were still rebuilding their herds from the Fort Sumner fiasco and needed every source of livelihood they could get. If one considers the primitive shearing tools of the time, tin cans and knives, agents' wool-sales figures suggest that Navajos were shearing most of their sheep by 1880 (USDI, Commissioner of Indian Affairs 1880:131). The traders also sold flour and other mass-produced foods that allowed Navajos to lessen their dependence on farming. The Navajos therefore could settle lands not very well suited to agriculture, such as the lease townships.

Before the railroad, the only trading posts near the lease townships were those in Fort Defiance proper (Kelley 1977:251), where Navajos were exchanging wool for consumer goods by 1876 (USDI, Commissioner of Indian Affairs 1876:109), and one nearby just south of the treaty reservation line near Black Rock, operated by Anson Damon and a man named Neale on Damon's homestead. Damon had been a butcher at Fort Defiance who married a Navajo woman and returned to the Navajo country with her (McNitt 1962:249). His sons were soon to play a role in the settlement of the lease townships.

The railroad gave traders access not only to the wool market, but also to markets for the blankets and silver jewelry that Navajos had previously produced mainly for themselves. By 1890, Navajos were substituting clothing of machine-made calico and woolen blankets

Figure 4.1 Navajo family portrait taken in the west–central reservation in 1892–1893 shows that clothing of machine-made cloth (worn by woman at left and man at right) was replacing home-made clothing (worn by woman second from left and seated woman). Note also the earth-covered, conical dwelling (forked-stick hogan) and sheep bedded without a corral in the background. (Photograph from Smithsonian Institution, National Anthropological Archives, Bureau of American Ethnology Collection).

for their own leatherwork and weaving and were trading a large share of their woven goods (see Figure 4.1). In that year, the Fort Defiance agent reported to the Commissioner of Indian Affairs,

> The proximity of trading posts has radically changed their native costumes and modified many of the earlier barbaric traits, and also affords them good markets for their wool, peltry, woven fabrics, and other products. Bright calicoes and Mexican straw hats are their ordinary summer attire, and they take kindly to our comfortable heavy garments in cold weather. . . . Silver ornaments of their

own manufacture are worn instead of copper or brass. (USDI, Commissioner of Indian Affairs 1890:164)

Falling wool prices spurred this transition, as both weavers and traders could make more money per pound of wool in the form of blankets than in the raw (Amsden 1934:235; Mindeleff 1898:503). By 1914, the Fred Harvey Company, which ran the dining car concession on the AT&SF Railroad and tourist hotels along the way, was to build up "the largest business in Indian blankets, baskets, pottery, and curios in the world" (James 1914:203). The company also launched the commercial production of silver jewelry in 1899, when its representative, Herman Switzer, asked traders to have local smiths make souvenir baubles for railroad tourists (Adair 1944:25–56; Bedinger 1973:118).

On the other hand, sales of sheep, especially of the lamb crop, seem to have been low until the 1920s (Coolidge and Coolidge 1930:69; Harbison 1932:9190; Kelly 1968:113). Agents' reports before 1907, when detailed reports by reservation ceased, mention lamb sales in 1890 only (USDI, Commission of Indian Affairs 1890:162). The reason for the low sales probably was not the lack of a market, for lambs from elsewhere in New Mexico were going to feedlots in the Midwest by the 1890s (Carlson 1969:34; Grubbs 1961:284–285; Kelly 1972:192; Parish 1961:121), and off-reservation feeders were buying Navajo lambs from the traders by late in the railroad era. The government, however, required these buyers to arrange purchases from reservation traders by way of the government agents, who opposed such sales as long as there were Navajos whose lack of stock forced them onto government rations (USDI, Commissioner of Indian Affairs 1905:268; U.S. Senate 1932:9520–9817). Most Navajo families, moreover, were themselves unwilling to sell stock, because they were still trying to build up their herds, and because they ate the surplus animals (male lambs and old, unproductive sheep). They would especially have avoided selling when prices were low around the turn of the century and after World War I (Kelly 1968:113; New Mexico Department of Agriculture [NMDA] 1962:44–45), for the use values of sheep consumed would exceed the exchange values.

As Navajo households began to produce wool and handicrafts for the market, their burden of labor seems to have grown. Even before Fort Sumner, Navajos had marketed some handicrafts; Navajo blankets were traded as far as Saltillo, San Miguel, and Oaxaca, Mexico. Nevertheless, the volume of all craft production except weaving was probably low, and even weaving was mainly for home use (Amsden 1934:133; Matthews 1883; Mera 1947:2). After the railroad opened new markets for handicrafts, however, Navajo families greatly increased their weaving and silverwork. The added labor would have been only partly offset by the possible decline in farming and the labor-

saving methods, such as the substitution of cotton string for homespun warp, which weavers used during the 1890s until the traders found that the cheapened product was not as marketable (Amsden 1934:193).

The volume of weaving in the Navajo country surged during the 1890s, when almost the entire output went to the traders. The estimated value of all Navajo blankets and rugs sold, $24,000 in 1890, more than doubled by 1899 and reached $719,000 by 1911, after which it leveled off (Amsden 1934:182; James 1914:57; USDI, Commission of Indian Affairs 1890:162, 1899:157). Commercial silversmithing evidently did not flourish quite so early, but reached "tremendous proportions" by the 1920s in Gallup and the Navajo communities near the railroad (Adair 1944:9, 28). Because this rapid growth in handicraft production probably was not offset by any great reduction in other demands on family labor, the family's labor burden probably grew. From the very beginning, this trade affected the lease townships. During the 1880s, new stores appeared at Manuelito, Rock Springs, and Cienega Amarilla, (St. Michaels), all within a few miles of the lease townships (Amsden 1934:178; McNitt 1962:49; Van Valkenburgh 1941:90).

The railroad also attracted homesteaders to the public domain that alternated with the railroad sections in the Black Creek Valley outside the reservation, even though Navajos were already living there. That white settlers eschewed the lease townships is probably owing to the lack of reliable water. They did, however, settle nearby at Cienega Amarilla, where two reliable streams come together. Sam E. Day, who had worked on a survey of the northern part of the railroad grant in 1885 and had hauled supplies for the agency at Fort Defiance, staked the first claim in the Cienega Amarilla, where he raised a cabin in 1887. The Navajo named Shorthair, who was already pasturing his stock in the meadow, tried to drive Day out, but Day coopted Shorthair by paying him and nine other men $1.50 a day to help fence the meadow (Wilkin 1955:24). The next year, Joe Wilkin and J. M. Wyant jointly settled two quarter-sections in the Cienega Amarilla and started to trade there. These and other homesteaders soon sold out to the Sisters of the Blessed Sacrament of Philadelphia and the Franciscan Fathers of Cincinnati, who established the St. Michaels Mission in 1898 and gave the Cienega Amarilla the new name of St. Michaels (Wilkin 1955:22–85). All of these settlers played a role in the first settlement of the lease townships.

Meanwhile, other settlers were moving into the Puerco Valley. In 1881, coal mines to supply the railroad drew the first settlers to Gallup, a railroad stop 15 mi. southeast of the lease townships. By 1890, the number of mines had so proliferated that the settlement became a railroad division point and major regional freight depot (Van Valkenburgh 1941:63). By the turn of the century, it had also become a major wholesaling center for the trading posts (McNitt 1962:222–223).

Between 1881 and 1890, the trader–homesteaders in the Black Creek Valley and the settlers of Gallup may have pushed some Navajos into different parts of the lease townships. The first person to move into the Tse Bonita Wash was reportedly Tall Salt Clansman of St. Michaels, a brother of Shorthair. He was a large-scale stock owner whose claim seems to date to the 1880s. The first settlers of the middle Defiance Draw were Smiley and his wife, both of Hunters Point, who moved in a few years after they were married around 1875 (Franciscan Friars n.d.b). The first identifiable users of the Eastern Flat were a group of related women of the Towering House clan and their husbands. After returning from Fort Sumner, this family evidently settled along the Puerco around the future site of Gallup. Some may have lived around Catalpa Canyon in the hills south of Gallup (York 1981); others settled westward around Tsayatoh north of the Puerco; still others moved northward, probably up the Defiance Draw, possibly to Rock Springs and into the lease townships. When this movement began is unclear, but surely the development of Gallup propelled it, especially the opening of coal mines around Defiance and Mentmore near the mouth of Defiance Draw in 1881 (USDI, General Land Office 1881) and in Catalpa Canyon in 1887 (Moore 1981:24).

All these original settlers of the lease townships had herds somewhat larger than average and claimed the biggest sage flats in the bottoms of the three major drainages. They used this land mainly in winter. Figure 4.2 shows the approximate locations of the original claims. These settlers returned to Black Creek and the Puerco in the summer.

Another consequence of the railroad and trade also affected the settlement of the lease townships. During the early years of the railroad era, a class of wealthy Navajos who raised livestock for profit began to form in the Black Creek Valley. Evidence from the vicinity of Chaco Canyon (U.S. Senate 1937:18004) suggests that the men who ran this type of operation were often in debt to the traders who equipped them. This class may have included headmen with family prestige and herds accumulated before Fort Sumner, but also men who had amassed herds through entrepreneurship. Some were mixed-bloods whose knowledge of English gave them an advantage.

Tall Salt Clansman's brother-in-law, Silversmith, though not a mixed-blood, was such a rich man. He moved between his own lands around Crystal in the upper Black Creek Valley and those of his wives in St. Michaels. Together with the homesteaders, he may have forced Tall Salt Clansman from St. Michaels into the lease townships. The epitome of the new *ricos*, however, was Chee Dodge. The son of a Navajo woman and the Hispanic captive–army interpreter Juan Anaya (Borgman 1948:83), or a white army officer, or agent Henry L. Dodge himself (McNitt 1972:295), Chee Dodge learned to speak English at Fort Sumner and returned to Fort Defiance with his mother's sister and her husband, a white supply clerk at the post. Agent Arny hired Chee Dodge as the agency interpreter in 1874 or 1875, and in 1884 Dodge replaced Manuelito as "head chief." (Ganado Mucho apparently had earlier fallen by the wayside.) In the same year, Dodge bought an interest in a northern reservation trading post (USDI, Census Office 1890:156; Van Valkenburgh 1941:90, 127). By the late 1880s, Dodge had reportedly saved thousands of dollars (Hoffman 1974:187–198).

Dodge evidently started running livestock in 1886 (Borgmann 1948). He had several large ranches, including one in the upper Black Creek Valley near Sonsela Buttes, where the range is among the best in the Navajo country (Hoffman 1974:187–198; USDI, BIA, Eastern Navajo Agency n.d.b; USDI, BIA, Fort Defiance Agency n.d.). In 1895 he hired a German architect from Flagstaff to build a big stone house near Sonsela Buttes, in one wing of which he opened a store to provision the herders whom he hired. He also married a woman from Sawmill and therefore may have run stock there as well (Hoffman 1974:187–198). According to the 1915 census of the Fort Defiance Agency, or Southern Navajo Agency jurisdiction

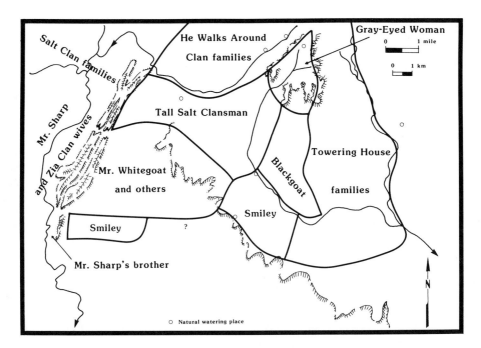

Figure 4.2 Original claims in the lease townships, ca. 1880–1900.

(Paquette 1915), he was running 5000 sheep and over 1000 cattle—figures that may reflect only his holdings on the reservation. He is undoubtedly the unnamed Navajo who, according to the same source, maintained a bank deposit larger than any in McKinley County, New Mexico, except for those of the Gallup coal companies. When the federal government was to organize the first Navajo Tribal Council in 1923, Chee Dodge would be its chairman.

Other wealthy stock owners who had also worked for the agency and were probably running stock in the lush pastures around Sawmill were Anson Damon and his sons. The 1915 census enumerated the sons at Sawmill, where two of them had combined holdings of 3600 sheep and goats; they had probably been using the land earlier along with their father's homestead south of Fort Defiance.

Between 1890 and 1900, the expanding herds of Chee Dodge and the Damons seem to have pushed a second wave of Navajo settlers into the lease townships. Unlike the first wave, these settlers came from the vicinity of Fort Defiance and, according to local Navajos, claimed the rocky upland portions of

the upper Tse Bonita Wash and upper and middle Defiance Draw. All were neighbors and relatives or in-laws of Chee Dodge and the Damon brothers (Franciscan Friars n.d.b). Thus, Louis Reeder, Old Man Curly and other He Walks Around clan people, and a man who may have been Lefthanded Slim settled along the upper Tse Bonita Wash. Louis Reeder and Old Man Curly had married women related to Chee Dodge; Old Man Curly's older wife was also a half-sister of Lefthanded Slim. Old Man Curly and Left-handed Slim came from Natural Bridge near Fort Defiance, the home of the Damons; descendants of a He Walks Around clan settler say that the people moved because the land had become too crowded. Blackgoat, another refugee from Fort Defiance, married a daughter of Smiley in 1895 and herded from his father-in-law's claim northward across the Defiance Draw. Blackgoat's father was a neighbor and possible relative of the Damons; Blackgoat also had a wealthy younger brother, who may have crowded him off the family's land at Red Lake.

Meanwhile, beyond the Black Creek Valley and its neighboring lands, homesteaders and cattlemen were settling throughout the checkerboard area at the same time that Navajos were intensifying their use of those lands. Clashes between the Navajo and non-Navajo stockmen reached peak ferocity during periods of high livestock and wool prices (Brugge 1980:191–243; NMDA 1962:44–45, 56). In 1906, therefore, after 4 years of pressure from the Indian Rights Association, from Father Anselm Weber of the Franciscan Friars in St. Michaels and from others, the BIA took advantage of a slump in the cattle market to authorize the allotment of Navajos on the public domain, including land that alternated with railroad sections. Tracts around water were the first ones allotted (Brugge 1980:204; Tyler 1973:97; USDI, Commissioner of Indian Affairs 1888:191; Weber 1937:17571; Wilkin 1955:199–206). Federal policy there was to grant allotments not only to male heads of households, but also to their wives and all minor children then living (U.S. Senate 1944:3093).

To ease the allotment process, President Theodore Roosevelt in 1907 withdrew from the public domain a large portion of the nonrailroad lands that Navajos occupied in New Mexico and Arizona until all Navajos living on these lands could receive allotments (Brugge 1980:204; Correll and Dehiya 1978:24–29). This area included the lease townships. After allotting some land in the middle Black Creek Valley (including allotments to a few lease-township residents), the government took the railroad land there in exchange for public domain outside the Navajo country and annexed the middle Black Creek Valley to the reservation (Correll and Dehiya 1978:24–29; Greever 1954:86). In New Mexico, however, the railroad kept its lands. Moreover, the large-scale commercial non-Navajo sheep owners, who also used the checkerboard area, were still enjoying high prices and competing intensely for range, and their protests forced the federal government to restore the withdrawn land to the public domain between 1908 and 1911 (Brugge 1980:191–243; Correll and Dehiya 1978:24–20; NMDA 1962:44–45).

Almost all of the public domain in the lease townships was allotted in 1910 (see Figure 4.3), but the allotments were not trust-patented until 1921, possibly because the agent who had taken the applications between Thoreau, New Mexico, and the Arizona line had neglected to file them at the local land office (Kelly 1968:34–35). The federal government retained the rights to coal under these allotments, and thus at any time could sell the coal out from under the allottees and their descendants, displacing them without their consent.[1] For this reason, lease-townships residents can be said to have lived "in the shadow of the dragline" since the time of the allotments.

Having concerned itself with Navajo land rights in the checkerboard area, in 1909 the BIA also established a special agency for that area. This was the last of six agency jurisdictions into which the government had begun to divide the Navajo country around the turn of the century, when successive additions to the reservation had consolidated an area too big for the Fort Defiance agent to administer alone (Young 1978:49–51). The lease townships, although located in the checkerboard area, were nearer to Fort Defiance and therefore included in that jurisdiction (Paquette 1915). They did not come under the jurisdiction of Crownpoint until about 1940. After 1911, lease-township residents were thus moving seasonally between lands on and off the reservation but remaining within one agency jurisdiction.

The agency superintendents, as the agents were now called, often remained aloof from their wards. This aloofness exacerbated another consequence of the railroad and trade, the political weakening of the headmen. The councils of local headmen that the Fort Defiance agents had convened periodically after 1868 had become rare by the 1890s (USDI, Commissioner of Indian Affairs 1870–1897). Wealthy headmen still existed, but trading-post credit probably had undermined the economic source of their local authority, largess to their neighbors, especially after the agents refused to continue distributing annuities through the headmen in the 1870s. The first lease-township settlers probably had heard from the agents through headmen in the settlers' original homes outside the lease townships. These headmen had included Silversmith and perhaps one lease-township resident, Charley Boyd, who had served as a scout in the Apache Wars of 1886 (Navajo Tribe, CC n.d.b). By the early twentieth century, however, the new agency superintendents tended to communicate with local people through schools, traders, missionaries, and a few government

---

[1]Allotment holders have recently sued the U.S. government for the rights to this coal on the ground that the government had no legal basis to reserve the coal in the first place (Snyder and Fyfe 1983).

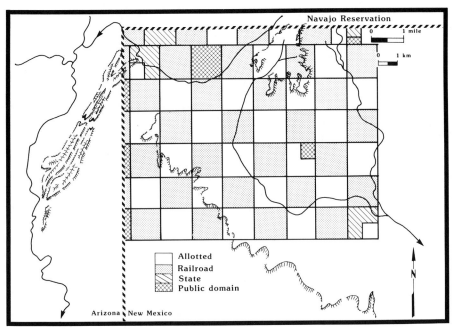

Figure 4.3 Land ownership in the lease townships by 1912.

extension workers, the so-called agency farmers and field matrons, who themselves had ties to traders and missionaries. Lease-township residents probably had more contact with the government through sending their children to the Fort Defiance boarding school, as a very few families did, than through the other channels.

In contrast, lease-township Navajos probably came in contact with traders regularly and increasingly during the early twentieth century as new trading posts began to encircle the lease townships (McNitt 1962:246n, 352; Van Valkenburgh 1941:89–90). The price of western wool in Boston, depressed between the late 1880s and the turn of the century (U.S. Department of Agriculture [USDA] 1910, 1930), had discouraged would-be traders but was now rising again. The growth of wholesaling in Gallup may also have drawn some traders to the countryside nearby. The high wool prices of World War I hastened commercial development even more. By the end of this second influx of traders, the residents of the lease townships were inextricably involved in producing for national markets.

Trends in Family Land Use

During the railroad era, then, the opening of the Navajo country to national markets drew non-Navajo traders and homesteaders and created a class of rich Navajo stock owners, all of whom crowded small stock owners from the Black Creek and Puerco valleys into the lease townships. The federal government and merchant capital also stamped out the vestiges of the old Navajo self-sufficient economy. The process had begun with Kit Carson's destruction of the herds. It continued as agents and traders undermined the political authority and economic responsibility of the rich headmen that had previously bound Navajo families into interdependent, self-supporting communities. The virtual autonomy of Navajo families as units of production, which had weakened community cohesiveness even before Fort Sumner, also kept such communities from reviving. The many livestock-poor households therefore turned for help in hard times to trading-post credit rather than to their wealthier neighbors, and their consequent indebtedness forced them to produce partly for the market. The rich

Table 4.1

Comparison of Navajo Wool and U.S. Flour Prices, 1890–1974[a]

Year	U.S. flour price (cents/lb)	Navajo wool price (cents/lb)	Ratio of wool price to flour price
1890	2.8	9	3.2
1900	2.4	10	4.2
1910	3.5	13	3.7
1920	8.1	28	3.5
1930	4.6	13	2.8
1940	4.5	22	4.9
1946	7.1	30	4.2
1951	10.4	39	3.8
1956	10.8	31	2.8
1974	20.5	30	1.5

[a]From USDC, Bureau of Foreign and Domestic Commerce 1913:502; 1916:556; 1926:324; 1936:308; USDC Bureau of the Census 1961:339; 1975:349; McNitt 1962:81, 196; James 1914:57; U.S. Senate 1932:8962, 8967, 9198, 9560, 9686; Young 1958:376–377; Kelley 1977:249.

also turned to market production so that they could get all sorts of mass-produced goods and even make profits.

Like all merchants, traders maximized their own profits by buying commodities from their customers at low prices and selling mass-produced goods to the same customers at high prices. As a result, the terms of trade for Navajo households deteriorated in the long run (see Table 4.1), although short-term fluctuations in national markets interrupted the general trend. The individual Navajo household was therefore under almost constant pressure both to increase and to diversify its production, particularly during the early railroad era, after wool prices fell.

The effects of this pressure on each aspect of land use, as I show in the next few chapters, were as follows. The pressure to pay their trading post debts (and the possibility of getting more goods and even profits, in some instances) induced families to raise more stock. If that was not enough, they also produced rugs and jewelry for trade. The more time families spent producing for the market, the more mass-produced foods and other items they substituted for the crops they no longer had time to grow or the handicrafts they no longer had time to make for themselves or for exchange with other families. Those who had been crowded into range without summer water, like the lease townships, were further discouraged from farming.

The pressure on families to increase market production also allowed them to survive on marginal range and to colonize more of it, because they no longer needed to farm. Grazing, however, altered the natural environment. As both human and animal populations grew, people colonized more and more land until finally the range was filled. But population growth did not stop, and families continued to depend on livestock production or even expand it, because neither the merchants nor the government offered a nonland-based alternative (wage work), and the demand for handicrafts was too low to support most families. The land consequently became overgrazed and erosion set in.

The pressure on households to produce for the market may have even quickened population growth. Couples may have wanted many children to help them with the diverse productive and domestic tasks that scattered household members from the home to the stock range, the cornfield, the fuelwood grove, and the watering place. Households headed by very young or old people often lacked enough able-bodied members to do all this work. The households of the young and old therefore tended to pair up, sharing a homesite, herd, and labor.

The market orientation of individual households, together with its corollary, the decay of the self-sufficient community, also almost eliminated communal land tenure, the pre–Fort Sumner form. The dominant form of land tenure instead became that of households, singly or in small groups, through original claim or inheritance. A vestige of communal tenure survived, however, in the outfit, as land competition, drought, and range erosion forced many households to seek new land, at least temporarily, at the same time that federal law made both reservation and allotted land unavailable for them to lease or buy.

The pressure on households to produce more for the market also altered the spatial aspects of land use: the number, size, and distribution across the landscape of grazing tracts, fields, and homesites. As market production encouraged families to produce more livestock, they not only filled, but subdivided, the range, both inside and outside the lease townships. Inside the lease townships, the growing number of families partitioned the range into more tracts, which were necessarily smaller on the average and encompassed fewer types of natural resources, especially water. As the same families partitioned their summer range outside the lease townships, some households lost access to the summer range and began to stay in the lease townships all year. As a result, even though most households farmed less than their predecessors had before Fort Sumner, a growing number of households planted fields in the lease townships, and

there the number of fields increased. The number of homesites overall may have grown with population, but the number that each family used probably dwindled. As families filled and subdivided the range, they did not need so many homesites to exploit fully the shrinking tracts. As they consequently settled down longer on each homesite, people engaged in a wider range of activities there, especially weaving, and stored more things. To encompass all this they needed bigger dwellings and more facilities, and their homesites thus grew in size and complexity. Homesites also proliferated in the most marginal range after the better, neighboring range filled up.

Finally, the pressure on households to increase market production shows in domestic, herding, and farming technology. Families responded directly to this pressure by changing the forms and sizes of their dwellings to accommodate more handicraft production, and by adopting as many new labor-saving tools, techniques, facilities, and equipment as they could afford. Families also altered technology (or at least its appearance in the archaeological record), because they settled down longer on each homesite; they built bigger houses and a wider variety of facilities and discarded more varied things on each site.

Chapter 5

Family Economy and the Local Environment during the Railroad Era

Family Sources of Livelihood

The trading posts did not divert Navajo families from the livestock, crops, and handicrafts they had raised and produced before Fort Sumner. By forcing people to allocate more and more for the market to pay their debts, however, the trading posts probably did enhance the importance of handicrafts and diminish that of crops. They also altered the range of items that families consumed by replacing home-produced food (especially meal) and other items with mass-produced goods.

The trading posts, moreover, offered relatively large-scale stock owners, such as those who settled the lease townships, a chance to buy more personal goods. The large owners were often heavily indebted to the traders for subsistence and herders' supplies and consequently were forced to maximize their money return on livestock products by cutting production costs, including the number of dependent herders. The large stock owners of the railroad era were perhaps also unwilling to support as many poor families as did their pre–Fort Sumner predecessors, and they consequently forced the poor into handicraft production and even possibly into wage work to make ends meet.

Although quantitative data from earlier eras for comparison are lacking, the 1915 census of the Southern Navajo Agency jurisdiction and other sources suggest that the impoverishment of many households, the diminution of farming, the expansion of weaving, the beginnings of wage work, and the growth in the use of mass-produced foods and other items were well advanced in the lease townships by the middle of the railroad era.

The 1915 census shows the number of livestock that belonged to households in the lease townships (see Table 5.1). I assume that these figures, which were taken in summer, include lambs and kids, because most Navajos sold little livestock until after the railroad era (as indicated in Chapter 4). The average Navajo family (probably a family of five) reportedly could survive on a minimum of about 100 sheep and goats if it traded the wool (U.S. Senate 1937:20995, 21093; I assume this figure includes young). The

Table 5.1

Number of Livestock Owned by Lease-Township Households, 1915[a]

	Sheep and goats	Cattle
Total no.	4057	67
No. per household	162	2.7
No. per residence group	270	4.5

[a]From Paquette (1915); figures are assumed to include lambs and kids.

average lease-township household, however, kept well over that minimum, with 162 sheep and goats.

Among these households, livestock was nevertheless most unevenly distributed: Most households lacked even the minimum herd of 100 (see Table 5.2); fully one-quarter of the households owned no small stock at all; another half owned 100 or less; and only 16% (four households) owned 500–1000. By World War I, two owners, Blackgoat and Mr. Small (aided by his nephew, Mr. Towering House Clansman), had consolidated even larger herds. Such an uneven distribution forced the impoverished households to depend on the livestock of others (most likely those in the same residence group), on cattle, on crops, on employment as dependent herders for the wealthy minority, on wage work, or on the production of jewelry and rugs.

Sharing among households in a residence group, however, evened out the distribution of sheep only slightly. Of the six lease-township households without sheep, two constituted residence groups, two more combined to make a third residence group, and one was paired in a (reconstructed) residence group with a household of 20 sheep. Only the sixth household was part of a residence group with another household whose herd (180) was big enough to support both. The number of cattle in the lease townships was too low to serve as an alternative to sheep and goats (see Table 5.1).

Whether crops offered a significant alternative in income is hard to say. The relatively large-scale stock owners used most of the agricultural acreage, just as they raised most of the livestock,[1] and a total of 15 households (60%) lacked fields entirely. The large

Table 5.2

Distribution of Sheep and Goats among Lease-Township Households, 1915[a]

No. of sheep and goats	No. of households	% of all households
0	6	24
1–25	2	8
26–50	5	20
51–75	3	12
76–100	0	—
101–200	4	16
201–300	0	—
301–400	1	4
401–500	0	—
501–600	3	12
600–900	1	4
	25	100

[a]From Paquette (1915); figures are assumed to include lambs and kids.

stock owners may have farmed more acreage than did small owners, however, because they were feeding their hired herders, some of whom may have been of poor families.

Local Navajos are not able to say whether any of the households without stock worked for other stock owners, but I believe that at least three of the six herdless households of 1915 did so, and the number may be as high as five. Only the herdless household that formed a residence group with another household owning 180 small stock definitely did not herd for others. Evidence of herdless households herding for others is mentioned in the land-tenure case histories (Chapter 6). Nearly all households in the lease townships, even those without stock of their own, therefore probably lived by herding. Other sources of subsistence, including wage work and craft production, would have been secondary.

Probably few lease-township residents worked for wages. Even Fort Defiance was too far from the lease

---

[1]Households with 400 or more small stock constituted only 20% of all households, and they owned 74% of all small stock and farmed 65% of all crop acreage, whereas owners of 100 small stock or less constituted 64% of all households and yet held as little as 11% of all small stock and 24% of all crop acreage.

townships for most residents to commute over the rudimentary roads of the time. The only jobs available locally would therefore have been at the St. Michaels Mission and at three coal mines in or near the lease townships. The Fort Defiance mine north of the lease supplied coal to the agency and boarding school, probably beginning when the school opened in 1881. At first, "Mexicans" both mined and hauled the coal, probably on contract with the BIA. Navajos worked there after the BIA assumed direct control of the mine late in the period, but all Navajo miners seem to have come from near the mine (Maldonado 1981; Tsosie Blackgoat, personal communication, 1979). The other two mines began operating around 1902 on railroad sections inside the lease townships to supply coal to the St. Michaels and Ganado Presbyterian missions, but neither employed more than a couple of miners. (Demographic evidence that some men emigrated to work is discussed in Chapter 6.) By the late 1920s, a few lease-township men were also working in the Mentmore coal mines.

Unlike wage work, handicraft production undoubtedly engaged many lease-township residents, especially weavers. The railroad brought tourists avid for blankets to Gallup and the trading posts along its route. Around 1900, moreover, when wool prices were low and weaving was consequently up, the Hyde Exploring Expedition of Chaco Canyon operated the Manuelito Trading Post, which was a few miles south of the lease townships, as part of a chain that was intended "to control Navaho weaving at its very source." The Hydes shipped blankets by rail to their retail outlets in Boston, Philadelphia, New York, and the Adirondacks (Amsden 1934:194). Several wholesalers in Gallup also sold rugs through nationwide channels (James 1914:203–204). These firms gave weavers in the lease townships rather direct access to the national market. The nearby railroad also offered a market for silverwork. In discussing the histories of particular archaeological sites, however, local Navajos mention only weaving, not silversmithing, as prevalent during the railroad era.

Consumption Patterns

Around the middle of the railroad era, the Franciscans described Navajo diet thusly:

Withal, the abundance of mutton and beef have practically excluded all other kinds of meat, while the facility with which flour and bread and a large assortment of canned goods may be purchased, has at present limited the various native dishes to a comparative few. (Franciscan Fathers 1910:214)

They also noted that people grew corn, squash, pumpkins, melons, beans, and potatoes wherever possible. At the trading posts, herdless families probably sometimes bought meat the traders had bought from other local families.

Inventories of artifacts and faunal remains on archaeological sites on the lease suggest that lease-township families used such a mixture of home-produced and store-bought goods (botanical specimens are inconclusive). This evidence also suggests that the store-bought goods increased as time wore on.

Table 5.3 lists all dwelling-site components (distinct episodes of occupation) at which artifacts (or their absence) were recorded and which local Navajos have identified with the railroad era. Ceramics (Navajo and historical Puebloan—mainly Zuni—pottery) almost disappeared after 1905 to 1910, while mass-produced small housewares (dishes, pots and pans, and the like) first became common around the same time. Cans, evidence that people ate mass-produced foods, did not appear until after 1905. Glass is common even on early sites, but the few identifiable sherds are from liquor or patent-medicine bottles rather than food containers and may simply mean that local traders did not scorn bootlegging. Other mass-produced items, namely building materials and especially auto parts, are rare on railroad-era sites. These changes seem to track not only the initial penetration of mercantile trade after the railroad, but also the upsurge in that trade after about 1905 to 1910.

Another possible reason for the changes shown on Table 5.3, however, emerges from a consideration of Tables 5.4 and 5.5: the settling down of lease-township families from 1880 to 1979. Table 5.4 provides a more detailed list of types of artifacts on both dwelling and nondwelling site components from 1880 to 1910 and 1910 to 1930. Although the table seems to show the same growing consumption of mass-produced items as seen in Table 5.3, the increase in artifacts may also reflect the fact that three times as many site components with artifacts date to the later interval (1910–1930) than to the earlier interval (1880–1910). Rare artifact types are therefore more likely to appear in the later group of sites than in the earlier, simply

Table 5.3
Artifacts on Railroad-Era Dwelling Sites on the South McKinley Mine Lease[a]

Site no.	Dates[b]	Native historic ceramics	Household items[c]	Mass-produced			Building materials[d]	
				Food		Auto parts	Lumber	Other
				Glass	Cans			
12	1868–1920	x		x				
26	1868–1920							
30	1868–1920							
12814	1880–1910	x		x				
225	1880–1912	x	x	x				
12808	1883–1910							
12809	1886–1910				x			x
80	1895–1910	x		x				
118–121	1900–1935		x	x				
124–125– 131	1905–1920	x	x					
243	1906–1920		x	x	x		x	
12803	1910–1916	x	x	x	x		x	
215.1	pre-1910							
28	1910–1925		x					
12812	1911–1918			x	x			
215.2	ca. 1912		x	x	x		x	
271	1913–1915		x	x	x			
12805	1916–1918	x	x	x	x			
13	1917–1936		x	x		x[e]	x	
272	ca. 1918		x		x			
74	ca. 1918				x			
46	1918–1924		x	x				
48–49	1918–1930		x	x	x	x		x
72	ca. 1920			x	x			
91	1921–1924		x	x	x			
57	1921–1928	x	x	x	x			
183	ca. 1923	x	x	x	x			
179	1925–1935		x	x	x	x	x	
135	ca. 1926		x	x				
73	1927–1937					x		

[a]All sites listed are dwelling components on the lease that were positively identified by interviewees and on which the presence or absence of artifacts was systematically recorded.
[b]Based on both interviewees' statements and archaeological data.
[c]Small housewares, mostly culinary.
[d]Excludes nails.
[e]1930s model car.

because the later group includes more sites. Both interviewees and architectural evidence (see Chapter 8) also suggest, however, that people tended to stay at the earlier dwelling components for shorter stints during the year than they did at the later dwelling components. People consequently discarded fewer types of artifacts on the earlier components than they did on the later ones, so that the later artifact inventories

Table 5.4
Functional Types of Artifacts
on Railroad-Era Sites on the South McKinley Mine Lease

	1880–1910		1910–1930	
	N	%	N	%
Total no. of components[a]	12	100	34	100
No. of components without artifacts	4	33	7	21
Artifacts of production				
lamb nipples	—	—	—	—
sheep rattles	—	—	—	—
salt trough	—	—	1	3
arms/ammunition	—	—	2	6
agricultural implements	—	—	—	—
silversmith equipment	—	—	—	—
weaving equipment	—	—	—	—
Food				
baking powder can	2	17	8	24
vegetable/fruit can/jar	1	8	4	12
milk can/bottle	—	—	2	6
lard can	—	—	4	12
meat can	—	—	1	3
jelly can/jar	—	—	2	6
syrup can/jar	1	8	2	6
Indulgences				
coffee/tea	—	—	5	15
pop	1	8	3	9
liquor	1	8	6	18
tobacco	—	—	3	9
Domestic small technology				
dishes	3	25	11	32
pot/pans	5	42	8	24
utensils	2	17	3	9
mano and metate	—	—	2	6
wash tubs/basins	2	17	3	9
pails	1	8	5	15
Household equipment and furniture				
kerosene lantern	—	—	1	3
other light	—	—	—	—
stove and parts	—	—	2	6
water barrel	—	—	4	12
furniture	—	—	1	3
House construction and maintenance				
locks/chains/hinges	—	—	2	6
ax/shovel/large tools	1	8	5	15
boards	3	25	8	24
tarpaper	—	—	—	—
Personal effects				
patent medicine/cosmetics	2	17	5	15
clothing/buttons/buckles	—	—	3	9
shoes	1	8	7	21

(*continued*)

Table 5.4 (*continued*)

Functional Types of Artifacts
on Railroad-Era Sites on the South McKinley Mine Lease

	1880–1910		1910–1930	
	N	%	*N*	%
Entertainment				
toys	—	—	2	6
musical instruments	—	—	1	3
Transportation				
wagon parts/supplies	—	—	1	3
auto parts/supplies	—	—	2	6
horse gear	—	—	3	9

[a]Includes all sites identified by interviewees on which systematic observations of artifacts were made.

reflect settling down as well as the increasing number of site components.

Interviewees identified a total of 45 railroad-era dwelling-site components (with and without artifacts), 14 of which were occupied for more than 6 months of the year, 15 for less than 6 months, and 16 for unknown durations. For convenience, the sites occupied for 6 months or more of the year are hereafter called *homesteads*, and those occupied for less than 6 months, *sheep camps*. All of the homesteads seem to postdate 1910, but sheep camps and sites of unknown occupation-span are more evenly divided between the two periods. Architectural evidence reviewed in Chapter 8 suggests that most, if not all, sites of unknown occupation-span were also sheep camps. Although people used these camps for different lengths of time within a year, they occupied both homesteads and sheep camps for the same average number of years (9 years for the 11 homesteads with known beginning and ending dates; 8 years for the 5 sheep camps). Differences between the two types of sites mentioned below in this and later chapters cannot therefore be explained by different total lengths of occupation.

Table 5.5 corroborates the notion that a greater variety of items discarded on a site component indicates a longer annual stay. The table shows that homesteads of all periods have more varied artifact assemblages than do sheep camps. The differences between homestead and sheep-camp artifact assemblages suggest that people did not use different items on the two types of sites. Instead, they did not stay long enough on the sheep camps to discard as great a variety

of used items as they did on the homesteads. Table 5.6 supports this notion by comparing what I assume are rather complete artifact inventories from a homestead and from a probable sheep camp. I assume that the artifact inventories are almost complete, because on each site the head of the household died. The still-functional condition of many of the items suggests that the survivors followed the common practice of discarding all possessions of the deceased on the site and then abandoning it. The two sites housed roughly the same number of people for roughly the same total number of months. The two artifact inventories differ very little.

Most differences in artifact inventories between lease-township sites occupied between 1880 and 1910 and those occupied between 1910 and 1930, then, probably reflect the higher ratio of homesteads to sheep camps in the later interval. This change, in turn, indicates that families were staying on fewer sites for longer periods within the year and signals the filling of the range late in the railroad era (see Chapters 6 and 7). The higher ratio of homesteads to sheep camps cannot explain, however, the absence of cans before about 1905 or the substitution of mass-produced small household items for native ceramics. The artifact assemblages, therefore, do also show that people were using more mass-produced items.

Lease-township families also ate home-produced foods during the railroad era, probably more in the beginning than at the end. Botanical remains recovered by flotation from the fill of hearths in three railroad-era sites, however, unfortunately tell little about the local diet. All three sites antedate 1920 and probably

Table 5.5
Functional Types of Artifacts by Site Type on the South McKinley Mine Lease, 1880–1979[a]

	All homesites[b]		Homesteads		Sheep camps		Campsites	
	N	$\%^c$	N	$\%^c$	N	$\%^c$	N	$\%^c$
Total no. components	48	74	17	26	15	23	17	26
No. components without artifacts	4	40	1	10	—	—	6	60
Artifacts of production								
lamb nipples	1	100	1	100	—	—	—	—
sheep rattles	2	100	2	100	—	—	—	—
salt troughs	1	50	—	—	—	—	1	50
arms/ammunition	4	100	3	75	1	25	—	—
agricultural implements	1	100	1	100	—	—	—	—
silversmithing anvil	1	100	—	—	1	100	—	—
Food								
baking powder can	14	93	7	47	4	27	1	7
vegetable/fruit can/jar	11	100	5	45	3	27	—	—
milk can/bottle	5	83	1	17	3	50	1	17
lard can	8	89	6	67	2	22	1	11
meat can	4	100	2	50	1	25	—	—
jelly can/jar	2	100	—	—	1	50	—	—
syrup can/jar	3	100	1	33	1	33	—	—
Indulgences								
coffee/tea	5	83	3	50	2	33	1	17
pop	9	90	7	70	2	20	1	10
liquor	12	92	6	46	5	38	1	8
tobacco	3	75	1	25	2	50	1	25
Domestic small technology								
dishes	24	92	12	46	6	23	2	8
pots/pans	19	95	8	40	4	20	1	5
utensils	6	100	1	17	2	33	—	—
mano and metate	6	100	5	83	—	—	—	—
washtubs/basins	8	89	5	55	1	11	1	11
pails	10	77	5	38	3	23	3	23
Household equipment								
kerosene lamp	3	100	3	100	—	—	—	—
other light	2	67	2	67	—	—	1	33
stove and parts	7	100	6	86	1	14	—	—
water barrel	5	71	3	43	1	14	2	28
furniture	4	100	4	100	—	—	—	—
House construction and maintenance								
locks/chains/hinges	5	100	3	60	2	40	—	—
ax/shovel/large tools	7	88	5	63	1	12	1	12
Personal effects								
patent medicine/cosmetics	20	100	12	60	5	25	—	—
clothing/buttons/buckles	4	67	4	67	—	—	2	33
shoes	11	100	8	73	1	9	—	—
Entertainment								
toys	9	100	7	78	2	22	—	—
musical instruments	1	100	—	—	1	100	—	—

(*continued*)

Table 5.5 (*continued*)

Functional Types of Artifacts by Site Type on the South McKinley Mine Lease, 1880–1979[a]

	All homesites[b]		Homesteads		Sheep camps		Campsites	
	N	%[c]	N	%[c]	N	%[c]	N	%[c]
Transportation								
wagon parts/supplies	4	80	4	80	—	—	1	20
auto parts/supplies	15	88	11	65	4	24	2	12
horse gear	6	100	5	83	1	17	—	—

[a]Includes all homesites and campsites indentified by interviewees on which artifacts were systematically recorded.
[b]Includes homesteads, sheep camps, and homesites of undetermined function.
[c]Percentage of all homesites plus campsites with each type of artifact.

Table 5.6

Artifact Inventories on a Homestead
and a Probable Sheep Camp of the Railroad Era

	Year-round homestead, 1916–1918	Probable sheep camp ca. 1912–1918
Miscellaneous tin cans	x	x
Baking powder cans	x	x
Other identifiable cans	lard	lard
Coffee/tea cans	x	—
Pop bottles	x	x
Liquor bottles/jugs	x	x
Dishes	x	x
Coffee pot	x	x
Other pots/pans	—	x
Basins	x	x
Pails	x	x
Kerosene lamp	x	—
Locks/chains/hinges	chains	hinges
Ax/shovel/other tools	saw	ax/shovel
Patent medicine bottles/jars	x	x
Clothing (buttons)	x	—
Shoes	x	x
Harness	x	x
Wagon parts/supplies	axle grease	x

even 1910, and all were probably sheep camps. The samples contained no remains of cultivated crops and no conclusive evidence that people ate wild plants, although samples from homesteads might have contained such remains (Toll and Donaldson 1982:781–785).

Unlike the plant remains, animal remains do suggest a dietary trend. They suggest that lease-township residents ate less game, and thus a dwindling variety of meat, as the railroad era wore on. Animal remains recovered from excavated railroad-era sites on the lease are listed in Table 5.7. The table shows both the number of elements (bones) identified to each taxon and the minimum number of individual animals those elements represent. Because of decay, the depredations of dogs, and other factors, one cannot assume that

Table 5.7
Faunal Remains from
Excavated Railroad-Era Sites
on the South McKinley Mine Lease

Taxon	No. of elements	MNI
Bird	1	1
Wood rat	1	1
Squirrel	1	1
Rabbit	6	4
Canid	2	2
Sheep and goat[a]	106	22
Horse	19	5
Cow	1	1

[a]Includes unidentified Artiodactyla.

either figure accurately represents the number of each taxon consumed on the site; the numbers delineate solely the minimum and maximum numbers of individuals of which the surviving elements were part. Moreover, one cannot tell which animals people consumed in greater or lesser quantities. Rates of preservation vary among species, and even among different anatomical parts of the same species, according to differences in bone density, in processing and cooking techniques, and so forth (Binford and Bertram 1977). The table does show, however, that inhabitants of the lease townships ate both domestic and wild species, mainly small ones. In addition, the fact that all the wild forms occur on pre-1920 sites suggests that people were hunting less by late in the railroad era. A possible reason for this change is that families were eating more mass-produced foods, which they could have stored for longer periods and therefore would not have needed to supplement by hunting.

The Environment

The valleys are broad, open, flat-floored washes, in many places trenched by narrow arroyos cut in material which covers the rock floor. . . . Gullies rather than hills impede progress. . . . A variety of rank weeds have obtained possession of the sand and adobe flats to the exclusion of forage plants. . . . Grass, though limited in quantity and much overgrazed, is fairly satisfactory in normal seasons, but water is very scarce. (Gregory 1916:26)

The geologist Herbert Gregory's observation of the Manuelito Plateau, the physiographic province that encompasses the lease townships, was soon to apply to the townships themselves. The biggest change in the environment of the lease townships that the railroad and trading posts created was its settlement and eventual overstocking.

A prerequisite for these changes was a change in what Navajo families needed from the environment. The biggest drawback of the lease townships before Fort Sumner was their lack of summer water, especially for cornfields. I have already mentioned that families no longer found the inferior farming potential of the townships a great drawback when they were able to get mass-produced foods at the trading posts. People dealt with the lack of summer domestic and stock water first by confining their stays in the townships mainly to winter, when snow usually covered the ground. Later, toward the end of the railroad era, they built reservoirs.

As early as the beginning of the railroad era, observers were mentioning evidence of overgrazing in some parts of the Navajo country (USDI, Commissioner of Indian Affairs 1883:122, 1892:580). By 1928, the problem was considered widespread (Fonaroff 1963:200). Overstocking seems not to have been a problem in the lease townships, however, as late as 1915. In that year, the actual numbers of sheep and goats in the three major divisions of the townships claimed by the original settlers seem to have reflected, but not exceeded, the different carrying capacities of those divisions.

The best range in the lease townships is in the sage-grass flats of the major drainages, and the widest expanses of sage and grass there are below 6800 ft. in elevation. Of the three major divisions, the Tse Bonita Wash–upper Defiance Draw probably has the lowest carrying capacity, because nearly all of the land lies above 6800 feet. It therefore has more piñon–juniper woodland and smaller clearings of the sage and grass than do the middle Defiance Draw and Eastern Flat–lower Defiance Draw, which probably have similar carrying capacities.

I have counted the stock of each household enumerated in 1915 in the division where members of that household had received allotments in 1910 and where today's local Navajos said the members had lived (see Table 5.8). I have also counted the stock of households not enumerated but mentioned by local

Table 5.8
Actual 1915 Stocking and Estimated 1941 Carrying Capacities of Subdivisions of the Lease Townships

	Small stock per mi.^{2}		
	Tse Bonita Wash–upper Defiance Draw	Middle Defiance Draw	Eastern Flat–lower Defiance Draw
Actual number, 1915[a]	81	159	120
Estimated carrying capacity, 1941[b]	33	46	46
Adjusted 1941 carrying capacity[c]	108	150	150

[a]Includes young; includes stock of households enumerated by the 1915 census (Paquette 1915) and of two other households identified by interviewees.

[b]Mature sheep units year long (SUYL); 1 SUYL = 1 sheep, 1 goat, 0.25 cow, or 0.20 horse. Estimates are based on carrying capacities of three sections in middle Defiance Draw.

[c]Figures multiplied by 1.64 to include young, according to the historical average of young as a percentage of mature animals (Young 1961:167–171), and then doubled to reflect 6-month use.

Navajos. These estimates suggest that the better range in the Eastern Flat and middle Defiance Draw supported higher densities of small stock than did the poorer range of the Tse Bonita Wash and upper Defiance Draw.

Without carrying-capacity estimates from the railroad era, it is impossible to say with certainty whether these numbers of livestock were already excessive. A comparison of these numbers with 1941 carrying capacities, however, suggests that the lease townships were not overstocked in 1910 to 1915 (see Table 5.8). If the same processes of range deterioration had occurred in the lease townships as elsewhere in the Navajo country, the carrying capacity would have declined between the railroad era and 1941. Carrying-capacity estimates are available for three sections in the middle Defiance Draw in 1941 (USDI, Grazing Service 1940–1946). The average carrying capacity of all three sections is expressed in terms of mature sheep units yearlong; a sheep unit is one sheep, one goat, or the equivalent in cattle or horses. Since the topography and vegetation of the middle Defiance Draw and those of the Eastern Flat are similar, I assume that both divisions have the same carrying capacity. One of the three sections resembles the Tse Bonita Wash–upper Defiance Draw; I have thus applied its carrying capacity to that division.

To compare livestock estimates in 1915 with the 1941 carrying capacities, the carrying-capacity figures must be adjusted, because the 1915 estimates include lambs and kids, and because the stock was in the lease townships only for 6 months.[2] The resulting adjusted carrying capacities, shown in Table 5.8, equal or even exceed the actual numbers of stock in 1915. If carrying capacities had been higher in 1915 than in 1941, actual stocking would have stood below carrying capacity in all three divisions.

While the lease townships may not have been overstocked in 1915, however, the number of sheep units yearlong probably climbed above the carrying capacity between World War I and 1930. The reason for the steady increase in livestock seems to be partly that descendants of the original settlers were multiplying both inside the lease townships and outside on the summer range; some descendants then forced others to abandon the summer range in favor of year-round residence on the lease townships (see Chapters 6 and 7). In addition, the low prices for sheep after World War I may have discouraged families from selling their surplus sheep, although all but the largest owners probably would have eaten most of the surplus. Finally, several large stock owners monopolized the best

[2]The 1941 figures must first be inflated by 64% to include lambs and kids, because, reservation-wide, lambs and kids in the early and middle twentieth century numbered, on the average, 64% of all mature animals (Young 1961:167–171). The resulting figures should then be doubled, because theoretically one can graze twice as many animals in an area for 6 months as one can all year.

range in the lease townships. At least two of them seem to have enlarged their herds around World War I, either to take advantage of high wool prices during the war, or because they could not sell all their surplus later. These owners packed their poorer neighbors into every marginal upland cranny, and the poor may not always have been able or willing to reduce their herds to fit these shrunken land bases. As shown in the first part of this chapter, however, many families were herdless and managed to survive, probably by depending mainly on other stock owners and on weaving.

Conclusion

Both documents and the archaeological record show that, during the railroad era among the lease-township families, the main economic trends were the impoverishment of many households, the diminution of farming (overall, not necessarily inside the lease townships), the expansion of weaving, the beginnings of wage work, and the growing use of mass-produced foods and other items. While weaving and wage work may have increased, however, most families still depended mostly on stock raising for trade and home use. Inventories of artifacts on archaeological sites also show that families moved around less as time passed and spent more time on individual sites, probably because population was growing and subdividing the range both inside and outside the lease townships.

As population grew and more people stayed in the lease townships all year, and as stock raising remained their main support, the range became overstocked and degraded. Another spur to overstocking may have been World War I and its aftermath, when large owners, in particular, first enlarged their herds to profit from high wartime prices but then failed to sell off their surplus stock when prices plunged during the postwar depression.

Chapter 6

Family Demography and Land Tenure during the Railroad Era

Family Demography

Market production imposed both much more work and a wider range of tasks upon lease-township households and thereby required many workers. Stock raising, however, forced households to disperse over the range so that each could have as much room as possible for its herd. Individual households therefore chose to live alone or to share a homesite with other households, depending on how many able-bodied workers they could muster. The need for able-bodied workers also may have induced couples to have many children, thus perhaps spurring a population explosion.

In both 1910 and 1915, the average lease-township household consisted of two to three adults (people over age 18 years) and two to three juvenile children (see Table 6.1). More than half of all lease-township residence groups consisted of single households. Most multiple-household residence groups consisted of two households with heads from different generations, usually related as parents and children. Only one plural-household residence group lacked two generations, including instead the households of two men who were probably brothers.

That differences in herd sizes did not alone hold households together is clear from the many herdless households that lived with other herdless households (see Chapter 5). Instead, the main cementing factor seems to have been the shortage of able-bodied workers in one or more of the coresident households. The households most likely to need help were those of old people, whose children had grown up and formed households of their own, and those of young people, whose children were too young to help them. These are exactly the people who teamed up in plural-household residence groups in the lease townships.[1]

Men leaving in the summer to work may have worsened the labor shortage in the family. Evidence that some lease-township men did just that may be seen in the big difference in sex ratios between 1910 and 1915 (shown on Table 6.1). According to the genealogical records used to reconstruct the 1910

[1]The average age of heads of the senior households in this group was 53 in 1910 and 56 in 1915, whereas the heads of the junior households averaged 27 in 1910 and 32 in 1915. Middle-aged people, who had teenage children to help them, did not live with other households; the average age of heads of all single-household residence groups was 42 years in 1910 and 40 in 1915.

Table 6.1
Demographic Characteristics
of Lease-Township Households and Residence Groups, 1910–1915

	1910[a]	1915[b]
Total population	142	131
No. of households	29	25
No. of residence groups	18	15
No. of single-household residence groups	10	8
Population per household	4.9	5.2
Population per residence group	7.9	8.7
Households per residence group	1.6	1.9
Mean age per resident	20.9	22.8
% of population under age 18	55	53
Ratio of males to females	109:100	79:100

[a]Includes 25 allotted households and 4 unallotted households; household composition is reconstructed from genealogical records (Franciscan Friars n.d.b) and allotment records (USDI, BIA, Eastern Navajo Agency n.d.a, n.d.b).
[b]From Paquette (1915).

households, the population of the lease townships included more men than women. The absence of many of these same men from the 1915 census roll therefore suggests that they were away temporarily that summer. They may have joined the several hundred Navajos who worked on the AT&SF Railroad beginning in 1899, or those who picked beets in Colorado after 1901 (USDI, Commissioner of Indian Affairs 1899:157, 1901:180).

Railroad-era couples tended to have many more children than the two they needed merely for biological replacement. Among the 1915 residents of the lease townships, I have identified 12 women who were over age 40 years and for whom I believe I have complete lists of children who survived past early infancy. These women had an average of eight children apiece. Such a phenomenon may simply exemplify the *demographic transition* common in "developing" societies, that is, the temporary historical failure of families to match declining death rates with lower birth rates. I suggest that such population growth may also reflect the desire of couples to mitigate the growing amount of work that market production imposed on them by producing many children to help with the chores.

If either this response to the growing demands for labor or the demographic transition began during the railroad era, one would expect women of earlier times to have had fewer children survive early infancy than did their railroad-era descendants. In the genealogies

of the lease-township residents, I was able to find eight women who were over age 40 years in 1880. These women had an average of only 4.6 children apiece, a figure significantly lower than the average for their 1915 descendants.[2] This test, however, is not very reliable, because the samples are not necessarily random, and because the children of older women are more likely to be undercounted than those of younger women.

Land Tenure

Conquest and merchant capitalism seem to have transformed Navajo land tenure in the same way they transformed the family economy—by breaking up the communities of interdependent families and isolating them economically. Market production thereby all but destroyed communal tenure and replaced it with tenure by individuals and small family groups.

As the history of the southern Navajo country before Fort Sumner suggests, entire Navajo "communities" may have used range land in common. These communities were supposedly groups of 10 to 40 families that monopolized a particular locality and were led by a headman, usually a *rico* (Hill 1940a).

[2]Standard deviations are 3.5 for the 1915 group ($n = 12$) and 2.3 for the 1880 group ($n = 8$); $t = 2.53$ and $p < .025$.

The headmen Manuelito and Zarcillos Largos and their followers, for example, seem to have moved seasonally as a group. At any one time, however, each family had its own customary use area within the communal range. The family agreed to respect the use areas of others, if for no other reason than to avoid the mixing of herds. The boundaries of these areas probably were negotiable, and anyone was probably able to appropriate unused range—a custom recorded immediately after Fort Sumner (Dyk 1938). The rich headmen settled disputes, presumably including those over grazing areas (Hill 1940a), but probably used the lion's share of the range themselves.

Communal tenure, however, was scarcely evident in the lease townships during the railroad era. The headmen had lost so much of their political and economic power to the government agents and the traders that ordinary Navajos no longer depended on the headmen to negotiate peace, organize defense, or give them food during hard times. They therefore did not need to follow the headmen or take their advice in the settlement of land disputes and were able to act more autonomously in managing their own customary use areas.

In the lease townships, each customary use area was a tract of land that a residence group (or small number of residence groups) used for grazing, farming, and residence. The inhabitants of a use area might formalize its boundaries by refusing to share it with other families. The stock owners' need to maximize the amount of goods or profits they received in the market exchange of wool and sheep encouraged many families, especially those of large owners, to assert such monopolies, and these attempts likewise encouraged other neighbors, usually collateral relatives, to do the same. As a result, particular tracts of land tended to pass from parents to children, while transfers among collateral relatives were less common, and transfers among nonrelatives were almost unknown.

The sources of most traditional land-use rights in the lease townships during the railroad era were either original claim or kinship (mainly descent). A separate system of land tenure was the legal system imposed by the federal government. The superimposed legal tenure, which was by virtue of allotment, did not at this stage, however, conflict with the indigenous forms of tenure. The allottees and other lease-township residents whom local Navajos have identified were also the original claimants, their descendents, and, in a few instances, their collateral relatives. The relationships of allottees to people who claimed the land before its allotment show that the residents of the lease townships did not derive their use rights solely from the allotments. The allotments simply formalized preexisting claims.

Moreover, although railroad land alternated with the allotted sections, the railroad did not interfere with Navajo land use. The railroad did not force Navajos to lease railroad lands in the lease townships, as it did elsewhere, perhaps because no cattlemen were interested in taking that scrubby range away from them. Similarly, in 1898, Congress granted Sections 6 and 36 of every township to the Territory of New Mexico for leasing to generate public school revenues, but no one was interested in the lease townships (Mosk 1963:412–413). When Congress also granted Sections 2 and 32 for the same purpose in 1912, the year in which New Mexico became a state, these sections in the lease townships had already been allotted by the federal government.

Table 6.2 shows the source of people's traditional use rights to the principal types of archaeological sites in the lease townships. (In the case of a site claimed by more than one household, I have counted only the rights of the senior- generation household.) I assume that the right to use a site is the same as the right to use the entire surrounding quarter section, unless interviewees have supplied such evidence to the contrary as use-area boundaries that cut across the quarter section. Use rights therefore passed from previous users of the quarter section to subsequent users. The large number of sites in the lease townships identified through interviews allowed me to construct a sequence of users for almost every quarter section in the lease townships. I have analyzed the transfer of land-use rights by focusing on sites rather than tracts of land, because I believe that people identify the users and dates of sites more accurately than those of larger land units, the boundaries of which are often difficult for both interviewer and interviewee to specify accurately.

In 1915, original claims were almost as numerous as rights through descent. The latter included rights received from living parents and grandparents, as well as those inherited from deceased parents and grandparents. The few sites claimed through some other channel were on land that the user shared with col-

Table 6.2
Land Tenure in the Lease Townships, 1915[a]

Source of use rights	Number of sites			
	Homesite	Campsite or isolated corral	Water source	Field
Original claim	4	2	6	3
Descent	12	4	2	2
Other	3	1	—	—

[a]If a site was used by more than one household at the same time, only the rights of the senior-generation household are counted.

lateral relatives who had made the original claim. The rights through descent were about evenly divided between those from the family of the husband and those from the family of the wife. Although sites, not households, are the units counted here, this pattern seems to suggest that rights were transmitted through bilateral, rather than matrilineal, descent. Nevertheless, this pattern could also be consistent with the matrilineal inheritance that is supposed to characterize Navajo society, if, as Aberle (1981a:29) has noted, both husbands and wives gained their use rights from the families of their respective mothers. Because most lease-township adults in 1915 received their rights from original claimants, however, and I consider original claims the joint possession of husband and wife, I cannot attribute most inherited rights to one parent or the other. Only in later periods is it possible to see if a pattern of matrilineal inheritance emerges.

Where couples chose to live after they married (postmarital residence choices) can also shed light on whether land-use rights were commonly transmitted, and ultimately inherited, matrilineally. As Aberle (1981a:29), Bailey and Bailey (1980:1467), and I (Kelley 1982a:92,293) have noted, however, terminology common in the literature on Navajo residence choices is not adequate for this task; conclusions about matrilineality based on this terminology therefore may be misleading. In the literature, residence with the wife's family is often called *matrilocality*, and residence with the husband's family, *patrilocality*, although the proper terms are *uxorilocality* and *virilocality*, respectively. Uxorilocality, or matrilocality, is often considered the first step toward matrilineal inheritance: When the wife's parents die, the uxorilocal couple normally stays on the land, if

not the homesite, of the deceased parents (Shepardson and Hammond 1970:50). In many studies of Navajo social organization (see several examples in Henderson and Levy 1975:138–139), single-household residence groups are labeled *neolocal*, so that the sources of their residence rights remain unknown. Plural-household residence groups are classified according to the residence choice of the junior households. Thus, residence groups that consist of a senior couple and married daughters are called *matrilocal*, while those of a senior couple and married sons are called *patrilocal*, and those with some other composition are called *other*.

When the 15 residence groups of 1915 that local Navajos have identified in the lease townships are classified in this way, a bias toward matrilocality (uxorilocality) is evident.[3] A very different pattern emerges, however, when the 23 individual households with identifiable residence rights are classified according to their relationships to their predecessors on the quarter section where each had its main homesite in 1915. The households are evenly divided among those living on the wife's family land (uxorilocal households), those living on the husband's family land (virilocal households), and those with other use rights.[4] The two methods of classification produce different results, because most junior households in the group were uxorilocal, whereas the senior or

[3]Eight residence groups are neolocal, five are matrilocal (uxorilocal), none are patrilocal (virilocal) or mixed, and two are other types.

[4]The figures are eight uxorilocal households, eight virilocal households, and seven others.

solitary households tended equally toward virilocality and other sources of use rights.[5] Again, one cannot say whether the junior couples exhibited true matrilocal residence, as the literature on Navajo kinship would lead one to expect, because of the large number among their parents who held the land jointly by original claim.

In 1915, at least six lease-township households kept homesites on lands of the families of both husband and wife. In only one of these cases were the lands of both families inside the lease townships; in the other cases, the lands of either the husband's or wife's family were outside. Each of the six households had its main homesite on the lands of one family and one or more sheep camps on the lands of the other. The six households were evenly divided between those living in the lease townships on lands of the husband's family and those on lands of the wife's family.[6] Only one of the six households was among the richest in the townships, but heads of all but one of the remaining households had parents among the richest households. Couples who used lands of both sets of parents seem to have owned herds that reached moderately large sizes after the land filled up. They therefore could no longer claim much new land for their growing herds.

The need for extra land that resulted in these double land claims may help to explain virilocal residence (residence on the husband's family land) among Navajos in general as well as among lease-township residents. Many households classified as virilocal in a particular locality may also have used land elsewhere that belonged to the wife's family. Only three of the eight households that lived virilocally in the lease townships are known to have used such double claims, but another three virilocal households might have done so. The need for land for big herds, which seems to explain dual residence, would then, at least in part, also account for virilocal residence. Heads of most virilocal households in the lease townships included some of the richest stock owners and their children;

this wealthy group included at least four of the six that might have used double claims.

Although virilocality was thus commonplace, people reportedly invoked the principle of matrilineal inheritance of land during the railroad era. One would therefore expect land-use rights not to pass from the virilocal couples of 1915 to their children. (Later chapters show whether this was actually the case.) A 90-year-old local man reported that "in the old days," people inherited land through their mothers. Recognition of the matrilineal principle is also evident in the list of allottees. Very often, the government granted blocks of allotments in the lease townships to a woman and her children, but not to the husband, even when the husband or his relatives had originally claimed the land. Perhaps these men thought that they would jeopardize the chances of their children to inherit the land if they put it in their own names and thus triggered claims from their sister's children.

Although lease-township residents of the railroad era showed a clear tendency to pass specific tracts of land from parents to children, a vestige of communal tenure still survived in the form of larger land-holding groups called (in Chapter 1) outfits or coresidential kin groups (CKGs). Information presented in this chapter and in Chapters 11 and 16 suggests the following formulation of the outfit.

The force that held the outfit together was not the sharing of an entire original claim at any given time so much as residual rights to that claim. People probably cherished these rights, and therefore perpetuated them, as mercantile trade fomented land competition among families and caused them to settle drought-prone lands. With these residual rights, both the fortunate people whose herds had outgrown their original range and the unlucky ones whom the expanding herds of others had crowded out had somewhere else to settle. These rights were especially important, because most land around the lease townships was inalienable reservation and allotted land that even the wealthy stock owners could not buy. These rights also gave families whose water sources had dried up a place to stay while they weathered the drought.

These long-term residual rights seem to have accrued mainly to the matrilineal descendants of the original claimants and to the descendants of their siblings who shared the original claim. If previous range tenure had

---

[5]The figures are as follows: 17 junior households (3 virilocal, 4 uxorilocal) and 16 senior or solitary households (6 virilocal, 4 uxorilocal, and 6 others).

[6]The household with lands in the townships from both sets of parents was classified as uxorilocal, because its main homesite was on land of the wife's family.

been communal, this matrilineal inheritance of range rights would not have been strictly traditional. I have suggested elsewhere (Kelley 1980), however, that farmland, and therefore nearby homesites, may have been inherited matrilineally even before Fort Sumner. Matrilineal inheritance of range-use rights may therefore have been an extension of this earlier principle. In addition to the outfit's core matrikin and their spouses, other users, such as their patrilateral relatives, affines, and the grown children of male core users, might be found on the land at any one time. These people, however, tended not to stay on the land for long or to have their grown children inherit from them; they were "peripheral" users who seem to have owed their tenure to permission from particular members of the core group to whom they had the closest kin or affinal ties.

Land within an original claim, then, might be transferred between collateral relatives from one generation to the next as the herds and land needs of the families waxed or waned. At any one time, however, residence groups, either alone or in cooperation with a few others, monopolized particular parts of the larger claims, that is, customary use areas. Over time, the boundaries of customary use areas within each original claim changed often, and many such areas even overlapped. The boundaries between neighboring original claims, on the other hand, were more stable over time and therefore may have resulted from formal agreements between two neighboring outfits.

At least two interrelated processes, however, undermined the permanence of these boundaries. First, members of neighboring outfits often intermarried and occupied customary use areas in neighboring parts of two original claims. In the early days, these areas often lay in the underused uplands that formed buffer zones between the sage flats where the original claimants had first settled. These interstitial customary use areas blurred the boundaries between the original claims and thereby also the boundaries between neighboring outfits.

When the two intermarried families included a large stock owner, he might have overrun the land bases of both outfits and thereby have consolidated them into one larger outfit. Such outfits, however, were probably unstable. The children of the marriage could not

perpetuate the bond by marrying into the clan of either parent, although collateral relatives might do so. If later generations did not perpetuate the bond, the outfit would probably disintegrate.

Often, however, the boundaries of these interstitial areas would instead become formalized and the areas thus isolated from the lands of both outfits. Sometimes the intermarried couple, or their children, formalized the boundaries of their customary use area to preserve it intact, and sometimes the other members of the two outfits formalized their boundaries with the interstitial area to keep it from becoming a conduit for members of one outfit into the lands of the other.

The second process that undermined the stability of the original-claim boundaries was the tendency of large stock owners to formalize the boundaries of their customary use areas (even noninterstitial ones) to keep their relatives out. They withdrew their customary use areas from the land bases of the rest of their outfits. Often such large owners were also intermarried couples from neighboring outfits.

This notion of the outfit follows closely Aberle's (1981b) model of the CKG. The existence of these large groups has been questioned (Lamphere 1970, 1977), because they are so difficult for one to discern: Their members use the land in severalty, are rarely if ever observed acting in concert, and have land-base boundaries that change over time. The small number of such groups in any one locality, the slowness with which such groups grow or dissolve, and the absence of historical records showing which families used the land all hinder one in showing that such groups exist. I myself at first did not see clearly the groups here called outfits, but rather the rough outlines of the original claims (Kelley 1982a:176). Only later, after I had analyzed the 1940s grazing-permit records and the 1936 livestock records, applied that analysis to seemingly anomalous transfers of use rights among collateral relatives mentioned by interviewees, and read Aberle's (1981b) formulation of the CKG, did I see that the heirs of the original claimants were not simply associated as neighboring, but independent, land users. Instead, they were linked organically by existing (although dormant) residual rights to entire claims.

Through the historical reconstructions of who was where and when, I here try to build a case for the existence of outfits. The histories in the next three sections of this chapter and in the chapters on later periods represent the best approximations I have been able to make with information from a variety of sources. In addition to the recollections of local Navajos, my sources include almost all of the documents on the post–Fort Sumner period listed in the bibliography, aerial photographs (USDA, Soil Conservation Service 1934; USDI, Geological Survey 1952, 1962, 1973; Pittsburg and Midway Coal Mining Company 1976), archaeological reports (Allen and Nelson 1982; Bannister, Hannah, and Robinson 1966; Eck 1981; Hartman 1977; Koczan 1977; Maldonado 1981; Navajo Tribe, CC 1962), and miscellaneous sources (Navajo Tribe, CC n.d.a, n.d.b). In the accounts that follow in this and later chapters, I use pseudonyms for both living and recently deceased people; genealogies are provided in Appendix B.

Land Tenure in the Tse Bonita Wash–Upper Defiance Draw

When Tall Salt Clansman first moved into the lease townships during the 1880s, he reportedly claimed the land along the lower Tse Bonita Wash from the state line several miles eastward across the upper Defiance Draw to Burned Through The Rock Wash (see Figure 6.1). His claim covered the sage flats south of the Tse Bonita Wash and in the upper Defiance Draw near the present south McKinley Mine headquarters. Allotments of Tall Salt Clansman's wife and daughters also bracket this claim (see Figure 6.1). Allotments were placed in Defiance Draw as near as possible to two dug wells in a railroad section, Coyote Drinking Water (W74) and Bubbling Spring (W82), and at the state line near a present-day well, Mud Spring, that may have flowed naturally in earlier times. The allotments therefore seem to have been placed as near to water as possible, as the allotting agents were wont to do. Tall Salt Clansman used this area in winter and apparently summered in the mountains west of St. Michaels.

In 1907, Tall Salt Clansman's family began to intermarry with their neighbors to the north, the family of Bald Head. After returning from Fort Sumner to be near the rations at Fort Defiance, Bald Head had settled in the Black Creek Valley north of the mouth of Tse Bonita Wash. His matrilateral and He Walks Around clan relatives made their homes near St. Michaels Lake and Natural Bridge but soon were crowded out, perhaps by the growing Damon herds. The family then began wintering in the lease townships along the north side of Tse Bonita Wash as far east as Bubbling Spring and Coyote Drinking Water. One of Bald Head's matrilateral relatives, Chopped Hair, married one of Tall Salt Clansman's daughters, while Chopped Hair's mother's brother, Little Warrior, married his daughters to Tall Salt Clansman's sons.

Little Warrior's wives and daughters received allotments in Tall Salt Clansman's claim near another spring south of the Tse Bonita Wash (see Figure 6.1). Bald Head's matrilateral relatives, especially Little Warrior's daughters, therefore seem to have married for land. A possible reason is that in 1907 a son of Anson Damon reportedly asserted a claim to land that impinged even more upon, if it did not overlap, Little Warrior's winter range in the Black Creek Valley (Gallup *Independent*, January 18, 1983, p.1; *Navajo Times*, January 26, 1983, p.1). The resulting expansion of Little Warrior's family into the lease townships thus could be another example of land settlement induced by big Black Creek Valley stock owners.

Meanwhile, sometime after 1900, Cornmerchant started wintering on the ridge that formed the southern edge of Tall Salt Clansman's claim. Cornmerchant may have been a son of Tall Salt Clansman's sister, and he married a former wife of Bald Head. Soon after Cornmerchant moved in, his daughter married Whitegoat Curly, whose mother's brother, Mr. Whitegoat, was evidently the first to use the land bordering Cornmerchant's on the south. Whitegoat Curly secured for various members of his family allotments around a dug well in the Defiance Draw, where Tall Salt Clansman may have previously maintained sheep camps (see Figure 6.2). These allotments were not only for his wives and children, but also for two children of his sister, who never used the land until after Whitegoat Curly died. Cornmerchant and his son-in-law, then, were able to consolidate a customary use area in a little-used band of uplands between earlier claims north and south and to absorb parts of these claims (see Figure 6.2).

Although Cornmerchant had absorbed the far eastern reaches of Tall Salt Clansman's claim, Tall Salt Clansman's children kept the sage flats along the Tse

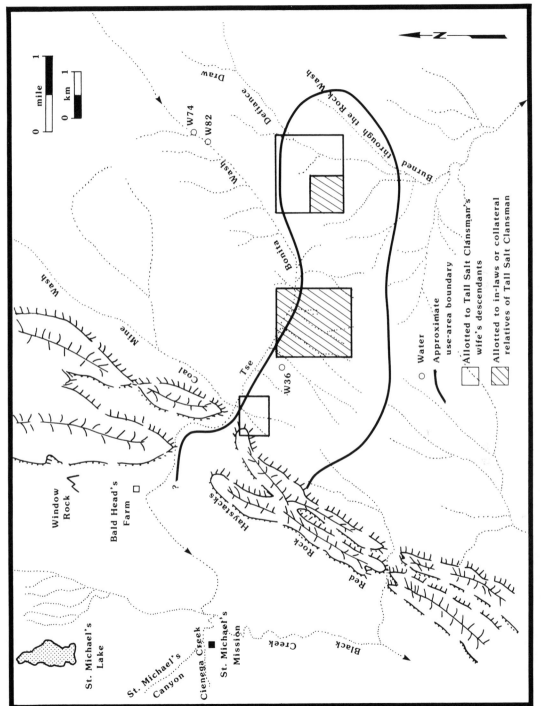

Figure 6.1 Land tenure in the Tse Bonita Wash–upper Defiance Draw: Tall Salt Clansman's claim and 1910 allotments.

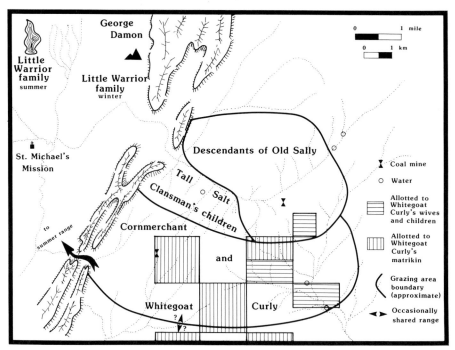

Figure 6.2 Land tenure in the Tse Bonita Wash–upper Defiance Draw, ca. 1920.

Bonita Wash (see Figure 6.2). These children and their in-laws, the family of Little Warrior, lived in summer with Little Warrior's relatives near St. Michaels Lake. They may have farmed there only and herded in the mountains west of St. Michaels, where one of Tall Salt Clansman's sons had an allotment.

Tall Salt Clansman apparently died sometime around 1915, and his daughter's husband, Chopped Hair, left her for a daughter of Tall Salt Clansman's sister. A couple of years later, Chopped Hair's father, Charley Boyd, forced Tall Salt Clansman's daughter off her winter home and allotment in the Defiance Draw. In order to expand his range, he may have been taking advantage of Tall Salt Clansman's death and his daughter's failure to inherit a lot of stock. Although the daughter later remarried into the same family, she never regained her allotment. Charley Boyd's son-in-law, Chee Jim, herded his own sheep and those of his in-laws on the allotment for the next 25 years.

Thus, Tall Salt Clansman, his sister's son (Cornmerchant), and his in-laws (the family of Little Warrior)

seem to have shared the winter range south of the Tse Bonita Wash and in upper Defiance Draw. Whether they also shared farmland and the summer range in Black Creek Valley or the mountains to the west is unclear. These families seem to have constituted an outfit, at least in winter. In summer, Tall Salt Clansman and Cornmerchant may have shared land in the Black Creek Valley with their sister and her children, while Little Warrior may have shared land with his own relatives. If so, the families that formed one small outfit in winter may have separated and joined two larger outfits in summer. Tall Salt Clansman dominated the range of the winter outfit, at least, until late in his life. By the early 1900s, however, the outfit seems to have begun to fall apart. By his death, Tall Salt Clansman's claim had been split between Whitegoat Curly and Cornmerchant on the one hand and Tall Salt Clansman's children and their in-laws on the other.

Of the two resulting outfits, Cornmerchant's included his own household and that of Fat Salt (probably his brother), with one set of homesites and herd (of

1000) for himself and another set of homesites and herd for the household of his daughter and son-in-law, Whitegoat Curly. Although "just an in-law," Little Warrior evidently dominated the other outfit, which included his own household, those of at least two married daughters, and the two households of Tall Salt Clansman's widow and daughter. These people probably maintained no less than two herds and two separate systems of homesites, at least until Charley Boyd evicted Tall Salt Clansman's daughter from the eastern end of the range. Like Tall Salt Clansman's outfit, these two outfits perhaps functioned only in winter, their members joining in summer the other, larger outfits from which they had budded.

Another family, meanwhile, had annexed a separate claim for themselves in the upper Defiance Draw northeast of Tall Salt Clansman's original claim. The claimants were Gray-Eyed Woman and her husband. The husband may have been Left-Handed Slim, an in-law of the He Walks Around clan people whose land north of Tse Bonita Wash bordered Gray-Eyed Woman on the west. Gray-Eyed Woman's immediate family came from Rock Springs and had intermarried with the settlers of the Eastern Flat. Husband and wife, therefore, seem to have belonged to neighboring outfits, and they staked a claim in the interstitial land.

Gray-Eyed Woman and her husband shared their modest herd and a homesite with their daughter and her husband. In 1910, Gray-Eyed Woman's husband and son-in-law applied for allotments in the upper Defiance Draw in their own names, those of their wives, and those of the younger couple's children (see Figure 6.3). The tract included at least one natural spring, Dripping Spring (W03), and adjoined the railroad sections in which Coyote Drinking Water and Bubbling Spring emerged. Gray-Eyed Woman's husband later fenced the entire $2\frac{1}{4}$-mi.^{2} tract with logs and brushwood, possibly to keep out a son of Old Man Curly to the west, who had married into the Eastern Flat family to the east and thereby surrounded Gray-Eyed Woman's claim. Perhaps it also signaled that the family did not want to share the land with their relatives or in-laws on either side, from whose outfits they were evidently breaking away.

The couple nevertheless did share the southern part of the tract, the only part left unfenced, with the household of Gray-Eyed Woman's sister, Margaret Thompson, and with the father of both women before

he died around World War I. The father and sister shared a small herd but lived in two separate residence groups. A fourth residence group of one household, probably distant relatives, lived near the Thompsons for a couple of years.

Between 1911 and 1918, Gray-Eyed Woman, her daughter, and her son-in-law all died; Gray-Eyed Woman's husband died 5 years later. Margaret Thompson adopted her deceased sister's grandchildren. Together with her oldest son and his wife, she used the entire tract year-round until the end of the railroad era. The nascent outfit that consisted of the households of Gray-Eyed Woman, her sister, her daughter, and others then collapsed into a single residence group of two households.

Land Tenure in the Middle Defiance Draw

The founders of what was to become the middle Defiance Draw outfit were Smiley and his wife, who evidently came from Hunters Point during the 1880s. They herded in the broad sage flats south of the draw in winter and returned to Hunters Point in summer. Around 1895 one of their daughters married Blackgoat, who, according to local Navajos, was the first to claim the piñon- and juniper-covered uplands north of his father-in-law's range and the draw (see Figure 6.4).

Local Navajos attributed separate claims to Smiley and Blackgoat, and the two men seem to have confined themselves most of the time to separate areas. Nevertheless, they seem to have managed their range cooperatively. In addition to Blackgoat's wife, Smiley's wife and two of his other daughters had allotments north of the draw in Blackgoat's claim, while three of Blackgoat's children had allotments south of the draw in Smiley's claim. (This block of allotments is another in which the husband, Blackgoat, did not apply for an allotment for himself, but only for his wife and children.) Blackgoat also sent one of his sons to stay with his grandparents south of the draw for at least a couple of years.

The allotments seem to bracket not only the range of the two men but also important water sources (see Figure 6.4). One allotted section south of the draw surrounded a big dam (W20) that Smiley had built,

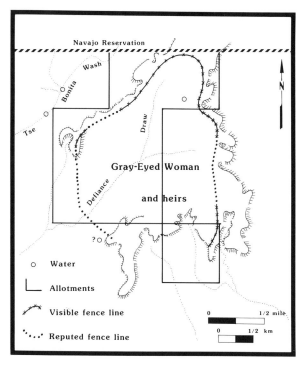

Figure 6.3 Land tenure in the upper Defiance Draw, 1910–1930.

perhaps with Blackgoat's help, and bordered a reliable spring, Smiley's Spring (W38). The allotted section farthest north of the draw adjoined a railroad section where another spring reportedly flowed from the rock just north of the Gallup road. The southeast corner of the combined tract was unprotected, but another of Smiley's sons-in-law, Mr. Towering House Clansman, monopolized the neighboring range to the east.

In 1915, then, the nascent middle Defiance Draw outfit included four households in two residence groups: the parental household of Smiley and those headed by three daughters and their respective spouses. Each residence group had its own customary use area, system of homesites, and herd of 600 sheep and goats, but the two areas seem to have overlapped. These people constituted a nascent outfit in winter only. In summer, the different households separated to two different localities, Smiley back to Hunters Point and Blackgoat to Fort Defiance, where each had kin who

presumably formed other outfits. The households exercised their residual rights to summer range elsewhere because water in the lease townships was unreliable.

While two of Smiley's sons-in-law ran their stock on his winter range, the third, Mr. Towering House Clansman, seems to have kept his stock on land that he shared with his maternal uncle and other matrilateral kin. These people belonged to the neighboring outfit in the Eastern Flat–lower Defiance Draw. Mr. Towering House Clansman may have intended to run his stock between the lands of his family and those of his in-laws, or perhaps even to carve out the interstitial range for himself, but evidently did not succeed in making this a regular practice. Perhaps his relationship with Smiley's family became strained when he took a second wife from a family unrelated to Smiley or his wife.

In 1919 Smiley and one of his daughters died in the wake of the Spanish influenza epidemic. At the same time, Blackgoat moved his family farther north of the draw. His new, ostentatious homesite and the possible doubling of his herd suggest sudden new wealth, perhaps inherited from Smiley or realized from the high wool and livestock prices of World War I. Blackgoat's children were growing up, marrying, and either moving in with their spouses' families or poised to partition the range. By the early 1920s, the number of households occupying the middle Defiance Draw had grown to five (not counting Blackgoat's hired herders), sometimes concentrated in two homesites and sometimes dispersed among four. South of the draw in one homesite were the households of Smiley's widow, who stayed there all year, and her daughter, They Are Raiding Along Behind Each Other, who spent the winter there and in summer took the stock of both households to Hunters Point. North of the draw were Blackgoat's household and those of a married son and married daughter, who sometimes shared Blackgoat's homesite and at other times dispersed to two or three sheep camps. The daughter and possibly the son, if not Blackgoat himself, stayed all year.

On December 10, 1923, Blackgoat's wife died in Fort Defiance, and the next year Blackgoat himself perished in an accident, perhaps at the sheep camp where his son was staying. After the accident, the son moved to the home of his wife's people. Blackgoat's

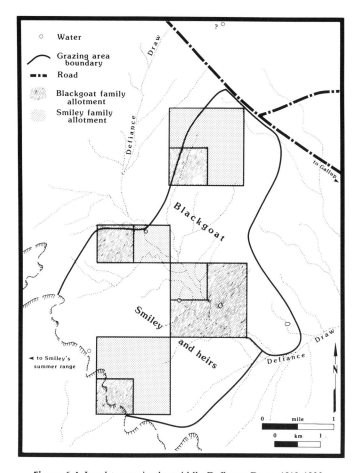

Figure 6.4 Land tenure in the middle Defiance Draw, 1910–1930.

daughter and her husband, however, stayed at the main Blackgoat homestead until 1930. By 1927, another son, who had been living with his wife's family in the lower Black Creek Valley, had started herding in the middle Defiance Draw again in winter, returning to his wife's family home during the summer. His main winter homesite was south of the draw near that of his grandmother and aunt, but he also maintained a sheep camp north of the draw, near his sister. In 1930, then, the outfit consisted of four households in three residence groups. Two of the residence groups (that of Smiley's widow and daughter and that of Blackgoat's daughter) had customary use areas respec-

tively south and north of the draw, while the third (that of Blackgoat's son) straddled the two sides.

Land Tenure in the Eastern Flat-Lower Defiance Draw

The first users of the Eastern Flat, the related women of the Towering House clan and their husbands, at first reportedly moved through the tract from the Puerco north to the reservation line and beyond. They did not use the land in any particular

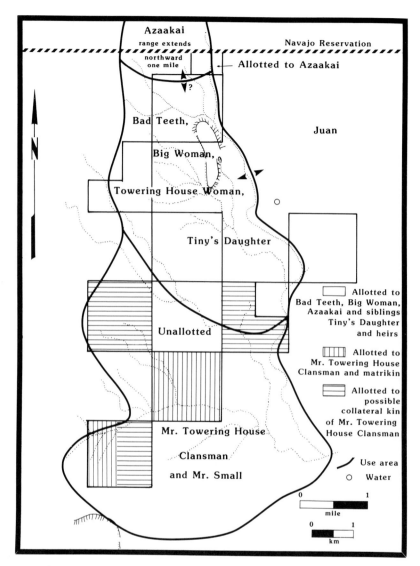

Figure 6.5 Land tenure in the Eastern Flat–lower Defiance Draw, 1910–1920.

season, but moved opportunistically through it with several thousand sheep and goats.

By the early twentieth century, however, descendants of the original claimants were using the range regularly in winter or even all year. They had perhaps segmented the Eastern Flat into three or four customary use areas (see Figure 6.5), although they still may have constituted one outfit. In the far north-

east corner of the lease townships was the allotment of Azaakai, an original claimant who ranged northward into the reservation. Immediately south were the allotments of Azaakai's sister, Big Woman; Big Woman's husband, Bad Teeth; two stepbrothers of Big Woman; Azaakai's daughter, Towering House Woman; and the daughter's husband and children. The stepbrothers may simply have kept sheep camps in the area for occasional use, but the others ranged there most, if not all, of the year. The central segment of the Eastern Flat was allotted to, and used by, Tiny's Daughter, a clan relative whose daughter was a cowife of Towering House Woman, and other members of Tiny's Daughter's household. This family was evidently poor; Tiny's Daughter reportedly wandered around the region selling rugs and left her oldest daughter to raise the younger children. In the southern segment of the Eastern Flat were the allotments of Mr. Towering House Clansman, his father, and several relatives on his mother's side, together with those of other clan (and probably genealogical) relatives. The wealthy Mr. Towering House Clansman and his mother's brother, Mr. Small, evidently dominated the area but used it only sporadically when their range near Oak Springs was poor. They did not live in the southern segment themselves, but rather sent their hired herders there. Some of the matrilateral relatives with allotments may have herded for them.

By World War I, use of the Eastern Flat had intensified and its users had probably split into at least two outfits, one in the northern segment and the other in the southern (the affiliation of the central segment is unclear). In the northern segment, Azaakai was sharing her range all year with her granddaughter (the daughter of Towering House Woman whom Azaakai had raised) and the granddaughter's new husband, Tom Sharp, an in-law of the Damons. Tom Sharp's father was one of the He Walks Around clan settlers north of Tse Bonita Wash who kept a late-winter lambing camp there near Coyote Drinking Water and who thus may have provoked the building of Gray-Eyed Woman's fence. Sharp was also a matrilateral relative of Chee Dodge and reportedly brought his wife some cattle that Chee Dodge had given him. During droughts, Tom Sharp exercised residual land rights by moving to his parent's range near Fort Defiance, which had greater access to water. Big Woman and Towering House Woman continued to share the land south of Azaakai, perhaps year-round by this time.

Land tenure in the central segment around World War I is less clear. The households of Tiny's Daughter and her daughter may have spent the winters in the wooded hills on the western edge of the flat. In 1915, Tiny's Daughter owned no sheep, and her daughter owned only 20. The family may have herded for Juan, a wealthy stockowner, originally from Mexican Springs, who held the neighboring range to the east. Juan had a sheep camp in Tiny's Daughter's use area, and presumably was allowed to use the land through an arrangement such as farming out some of his sheep to the family of Tiny's Daughter. Eventually, Juan's son married one of Tiny's Daughter's daughters, and the families were perhaps linked earlier through another marriage. Another Towering House person maintained a sheep camp in the central-segment cluster of sheep camps that Juan and perhaps Tiny's Daughter or her daughter also used: Mr. Tall, a clan relative of both Azaakai and Big Woman, in the north, and Mr. Towering House Clansman and his uncle, in the south. Mr. Tall had secured allotments in the names of his sons and a stepson near the other sheep camps but apparently used his camp only infrequently (when his land in the Black Creek Valley became poor). Perhaps, therefore, the central segment's inhabitants were part of the outfit in the southern segment, which Mr. Towering House Clansman and Mr. Small dominated. On the other hand, land-use patterns of the 1930s suggest that ties between the central and northern segment families remained strong, so perhaps the central segment's inhabitants were part of the northern segment outfit during the railroad era.

These two outfits persisted through the 1920s, and their members intensified their use of the land. Most inhabitants of the northern segment apparently were already staying there most or all of the year. After 1921 the brothers Tom and John Dixon, sons of Tiny's Daughter, did the same in the central segment. Similarly, soon after his uncle, Mr. Small, died in 1923, Mr. Towering House Clansman began to spend the entire colder half of the year in the southern segment, overseeing his hired herders and his reported 2000–3000 sheep and goats.

Conclusion

In this chapter I have described a nested series of land-using groups, from the household up to the outfit, that inhabited the lease townships during the railroad era. Because each household ideally supported itself with its herd, households tended to disperse over the range. The plethora of productive and domestic chores, however, held the households with the fewest able-bodied members, those of old people and couples with young children, together in residence groups. The great demand for labor within the family also perhaps induced women to produce many children throughout their childbearing years. Whatever the reason, having many children enabled the households of most middle-aged couples to be self-sufficient in terms of daily labor and to live apart as single-household residence groups.

Because of the availability of simple technology (described in Chapter 8) and trading post credit, the residence group was able to supply itself with all the labor it needed in daily production and domestic maintenance. All the residence group needed for short-term self-sufficiency was, therefore, its own land. Land-use rights had indeed become more individualized since the pre–Fort Sumner times, passing from individual parents to their children. Navajo ideology favored matrilineal inheritance, although that principle was not clearly evident in the lease townships (but perhaps only because land still belonged to the original claimants).

In the long run, then, the residence group could not be self-sufficient on this inherited land, partly because mercantile capitalism encouraged some families to amass large herds at the expense of others and partly because of frequent localized droughts. The largest land-using unit, the outfit, therefore coalesced, as individuals asserted residual rights to lands held by collateral, especially matrilateral, relatives in neighboring residence groups. The historical root of this behavior was the pre–Fort Sumner communal tenure of range and matrilineal inheritance of farmland. The outfit was unstable, however, because wealthy stock owners sought to monopolize the land and push the poorer members out, and because people from neighboring outfits intermarried, used the interstitial land, and then tried to separate it from the claims of relatives on both sides. The history of land tenure in the three major drainages of the lease townships illustrates the formation and disintegration of outfits.

Chapter 7

Spatial Aspects of Land Use during the Railroad Era

The spatial aspects of land use are the number, size, and distribution across the landscape of grazing tracts, fields, and homesites. As this chapter shows, changes in the spatial aspects of land use during the railroad era resulted mainly from the subdivision of land through inheritance, both inside and outside the lease townships.

Mercantile trade encouraged land subdivision in two ways. First, as we have seen, it caused people to fill previously unused range, such as the lease townships. After filling the land, the continually multiplying families had to start subdividing it. They split not only the original claims in the lease townships, but also the lands outside the townships that they used in summer. Mercantile trade may even have encouraged the population growth that drove this process, as was mentioned in Chapter 5. Second, as noted in Chapter 6, mercantile trade had undermined communal tenure and continued to undermine its vestigial form, the outfit. Mercantile trade encouraged couples, especially the wealthy, to isolate their customary use areas from the residual claims of their collateral relatives.

Inside the lease townships, the subdivision of original claims into successively smaller customary use areas increased the total number of grazing tracts, which in the lease townships are almost synonymous with customary use areas. At the same time, the size of each grazing tract diminished, and the smaller the tract, the less likely it was to encompass either a reliable water source or the large tracts of sage-grassland that exist only below 6800 ft.

The result was twofold. First, families whose customary use areas covered mainly uplands could not keep large herds there. Second, many families, whether they had upland or lowland range, were forced either to share natural water sources with their neighbors or to build reservoirs. The lack of natural water in the individual customary use areas became even more critical as families subdivided the summer range outside the lease townships and relegated a growing number of their members to the townships all year. Only by building reservoirs could these families use the range there in summer. The mounting numbers of year-round residents then planted more fields; available data unfortunately are inadequate to show whether the sizes of fields and their distribution over the landscape also changed.

One would expect the growing number of families to have built a growing number of homesites. Many families, however, may have used fewer homesites during the year and settled down longer on each one as their grazing areas shrank. These expectations are likely but cannot be confirmed. Diminished household mobility did enlarge dwelling sites, because people needed more work and storage space during the longer periods during which they lived on each site. Changes in the distribution of homesites across the landscape show that families were forced to use the less desirable upland range more intensively as population grew.

To understand these changes and their relationship to the process of land subdivision more completely, one must understand the nature and functioning of the customary use area. Again, this is the contiguous area that a residence group (or a few residence groups in cooperation) monopolized for its own production and domestic maintenance, either in a particular season or all year. I describe the customary use area in general and offer examples of the range of variation in the management of such areas during the railroad era.

Customary Use Areas

In 1910–1915, the lease townships were partitioned into customary use areas. One or more residence groups monopolized each area and used its various parts for a season or even all year. The heads of households in the residence groups that shared a customary use area usually consisted of parents and their grown children, and after the parents died, the surviving children often partitioned it. Again, I emphasize that these customary use areas are not the same as the lands occupied by the outfits, land-use communities, or CKGs mentioned in Chapters 1 and 6. They may, however, be the same as those used by the smaller "cooperating groups" mentioned in Chapter 1 (see Collier 1951), which may have consisted of two or more residence groups sharing land, often because they also shared a herd.

Figure 7.1 shows the 1910–1915 customary use areas; a comparison of this figure with Figure 4.2 reveals their difference from the original claims. In the lease townships there were probably five original claims (see Figure 4.2: Blackgoat's claim is considered an extension of Smiley's, and Gray-Eyed Woman's claim, an extension of those to the east and west). In

1910–1915, however, there were more than five customary use areas, which consisted of parts of original claims. One customary use area, moreover— that of Cornmerchant and Whitegoat Curly—seems to have consisted of parts of two neighboring original claims; its users were the intermarried descendants of the two original claimants. The same may be true of the claim of Lefthanded Slim and Gray-Eyed Woman, for the tract's users seem to have been the intermarried relatives of the claimants on both sides and may simply have spread into the buffer between the two neighboring claims.

That most customary use areas in the lease townships were, in 1915, occupied only in winter is clear from both the recollections of today's local Navajos and the "addresses" at which census enumerators recorded lease-township residents in the summer of 1915. These people lived outside the lease townships in the Black Creek and Puerco valleys (see Table 7.1). According to the census, only the households of Gray-Eyed Woman, her daughter, and her sister (who shared one use area) were inside the townships; local Navajos named two other year-round resident households, those of Tom Sharp and Smiley (see Table 7.2), although Smiley's household appeared in the census outside the lease townships. At least one household in every use area, moreover, moved outside the townships for the summer.

The management of the 1915 customary use areas varied considerably. Similarities and systematic differences in the inventories of both natural resources and sites in these use areas nevertheless exist and are analyzed here. The claim of Mr. Whitegoat is excluded from my analysis of the spatial aspects of land use in this and the next two chapters, because most of it lies outside the lease townships in the Black Creek Valley. The claim north of Tse Bonita Wash is also excluded from this chapter, because sites dating to the 1910–1915 interval have not been recorded there, but the claim is included in later chapters because later sites were recorded there. The customary use area of Cornmerchant and Whitegoat Curly, however, is included here, even though the small part of it used in the winter, which extends into the Black Creek Valley, has not been mapped. Thus, the inventories of resources and sites analyzed are conservative approximations of what each use area contained.

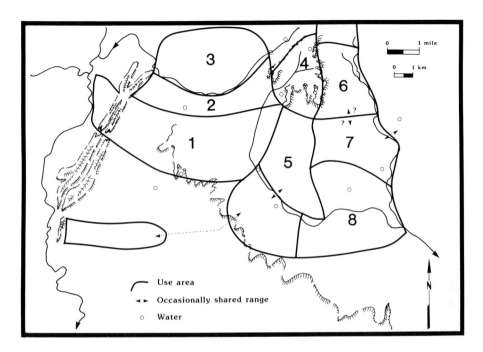

Figure 7.1 Customary use areas in the lease townships, 1910–1915.

Table 7.1
Homes of Lease-Township Residents outside the Lease Townships, 1910–1915[a]

Location	No. of households with summer homes	No. of households with winter homes	No. of households with year-round homes
Hunters Point	3	—	—
Fort Defiance	2	—	—
St. Michaels	13	—	—
Rock Springs	2	—	—
Oak Springs	1	—	—
Five Mountains	1	—	—
No home outside	—	—	3

[a]From Paquette (1915); USDI, BIA, Eastern Navajo Agency (n.d.b).

Each customary use area encompassed most resources that Navajo families needed for herding, farming, and domestic maintenance. As mentioned in Chapter 3, the amount of annual moisture and the length of the growing season are adequate for dry farming throughout the lease townships, and lands with suitable soils and slope are widespread. In fact, these cultivable zones coincide with the best areas for grazing, the open sage-grass plains. Each customary use area contained such open lands, as well as the wooded mesas that supplied each family's fuel and building materials.

Table 7.2

Inventories of Sites in Customary Use Areas in the Lease Townships, 1915

Use area	No. of residence groups[a]	Season	No. of stock[b]	No. of homesteads[c]	No. of sheep camps	No. of campsites[d]	No. of fields
Tse Bonita Wash–upper Defiance Draw							
1	2	winter	900	1 & OLT?	2	2	OLT
2	2	variable (1)	50	1 & OLT?			
		winter (1)	U		other sites not positively identified		
3	1–2	winter	U		sites not positively identified		
4	3	all year (1–2)	230+	2–3	2–3	3	2
		winter (1–2)					
Middle Defiance Draw							
5	2	winter	1400	1–2	0–1	1	1
Eastern Flat–lower Defiance Draw							
6	3	variable (2)	400+	1 & OLT	4[e,f]	1[f]	1 & OLT
		all year (1)	500				
7	3	winter	65+	0–1 & OLT	2–3		
8	1	variable	1000	OLT	1	1	1?

[a]Number of residence groups exceeds total for the lease townships given on Table 6.1, because 2–3 residence groups had homesites only on adjacent tracts outside the lease townships, not inside the lease townships.

[b]According to 1915 census or local Navajos. U = unknown.

[c]OLT = site outside the lease townships used during the same season as those in the lease townships.

[d]Includes isolated corrals.

[e]Includes a sheep camp in upper Tse Bonita Wash.

[f]Includes 1 site on north McKinley Mine lease not counted in south lease sample.

Water, however, was not as widely available. Local Navajos have named only three more-or-less permanent natural water sources and four or five more that sometimes flowed even during the dry season, although more may have existed. Figure 7.1 shows the locations of these sources. Only the use areas in the Eastern Flat are depicted without reliable water sources within or along their boundaries. The inhabitants of these areas perhaps used Wildcat Spring on the east side of the Eastern Flat and possibly dug wells in the Eastern Flat Arroyo itself. The users of the central and southern segments in the Eastern Flat each had a reservoir, as did Smiley and Blackgoat in the middle Defiance Draw and Whitegoat Curly and Cornmerchant south of the Tse Bonita Wash. Some people also ran herds to water in the use areas of neighbors and then took them elsewhere to graze. This extra trekking ruined the range surrounding water sources and was to become a significant cause of its deterioration (Zeh 1932:9125).

The inventories of sites in each use area were more varied than the resource inventories, for users differed in the sizes of their herds and in their access to summer range outside the lease townships. Tables 7.2 and 7.3 tabulate the sites that local Navajos identified with each customary use area around 1915. Almost every use area included at least one homestead and one sheep camp. The one use area without a homestead belonged to Mr. Towering House Clansman and Mr. Small, probably the largest stock owners in the townships. In the other use areas, one family usually kept a homestead, while related families merely built sheep camps and maintained homesteads, other sheep camps, or both outside the lease townships. Families with homesteads in the lease townships also used sheep camps to exploit range far from their homesteads.

Campsites and isolated corrals were not as common as homesites. Most customary use areas with isolated corrals and campsites belonged to the wealthy, that is, owners of 500 or more sheep. All three such sites

Table 7.3
Types of Sites
Identified by Local Navajos and Used in 1915

Type	Number
Homestead	6
Sheep camp	7
Homesite of unknown annual occupation span	6
Campsite and isolated corral	7
Isolated sweathouse	4
Fields	5
Improved water sources	5

Table 7.4
Distances from Homesites to Satellite Sites
in the Same Customary Use Area, 1915 and 1940

mi.	Type of satellite site	mi.	Type of satellite site
<0.25	winter corral	1.0	sheep camp
0.25	winter corral	1.0	sheep camp
0.5	winter corral	1.25	sheep camp
0.5	corral	1.5	sheep camp
0.5	farm camp(?)	1.5	sheep camp
0.75	corral(?)	1.5	farmstead
1.0	winter corral	1.75	corral(?)
1.0	corral	2.0	farm camp
1.0	corral	2.0	sheep camp
1.0	corral	3.0	sheep camp
1.0	corral	3.0	sheep camp
1.0	sheep camp	~4.0	sheep camp
		4.5	sheep camp

belonging to families with smaller herds were corrals in sheltered spots that two families on the highest range in the townships used when bitter winter weather lashed at their homesites. None of the other families needed this type of corral, because their homesites were at lower elevations.

The purpose of the isolated corrals, except for the winter corrals, was the same as the purpose of camp- sites and sheep camps: to minimize the trekking of the herd and the travel of the herders. People tended to keep the herds in isolated corrals and campsites on range about a mile from the homesite where they were based (see Table 7.4). Presumably the herders either returned to the homesite after penning the herd in the corral at night or camped near the corral but fetched provisions from the homesite. When they moved the herd to range more than a mile from a homestead, however, the herders, if not the entire family, would then move to a sheep camp with their own provisons.

Cornfields appeared only in customary use areas with year-round residents. The one exception belonged to Mr. Towering House Clansman and Mr. Small and may have produced food for their hired herders, which would have been stored in the forked-stick hogan at the nearby sheep camp.

Between 1915 and the end of the railroad era more households began to stay in the lease townships all year, so that the inventories of sites in the customary use areas changed somewhat. The number of households staying all year grew from four or five in 1915 to at least nine by the early 1920s. Most heads of the new year-round households—the Dixon brothers, Blackgoat's daughter, a niece of Charley

Boyd, and Towering House Woman—were people whose parents still spent their summers outside the lease townships but shared the summer range with their other children or with collateral relatives, who, in turn, would take control of it when the parents died. Old and new year-round residents alike built additional reservoirs and were mainly responsible for increasing the number of reservoirs in the lease townships from five to ten between 1915 and 1920. All ten reservoirs provided stock and domestic water but only two irrigated fields. Most of the year-round households probably continued to share their use areas with parents (and possibly siblings) who spent the summers outside the townships. Even the year-round residents themselves did not spend the whole year at one homesite. Although each family may have lived most of the year at one homestead, it also spent a few months during the late winter at a sheep camp, perhaps for lambing. According to local Navajos, reasons for such moves included the need for more wood and the need to let the grass sprout around the homestead.

The next two sections of this chapter offer case histories of two very different customary use areas of the railroad era. One is the earliest known area in the lease townships to be used year-round: It belonged to the medium-scale stock owners Gray-Eyed Woman and her husband. The other is the winter range of the large-scale stock owner Blackgoat.

Gray-Eyed Woman's
Year-Round Customary Use Area

By 1910, Gray-Eyed Woman and her husband were living all year in the upper Defiance Draw, which they shared with Gray-Eyed Woman's daughter, Warrior Woman, and Warrior Woman's husband and children. Gray-Eyed Woman and her family ranged all year around the sage basin that lies between the arms of the yellow sandstone mesa curving around the head of the draw (see Figure 7.2). At this time, the 20-ft.-deep chasm that drains the land today was no more than a series of rivulets flowing along the surface. The households of both Gray-Eyed Woman and her daughter lived at the homestead LA 12803 (see Figure 7.3), built in a small grove on a bench that extends into the sage flats. The site consisted of two cribbed-log hogans, two corrals, and possibly a *ramada*. The family's main cornfield, C71, lay at the

foot of the bench on which the site was built, covering an area through which the Defiance Draw has now cut. The family probably got water from a currently undetected spring just north of the Gallup road that would have been about half a mile from the homestead.

Gray-Eyed Woman had another cornfield, C07, with an accompanying windbreak about half a mile southeast of LA 12803. About the same distance south she had another corral and windbreak below a pinnacle on the yellow sandstone mesa (PM 937), where she would run the sheep in summer so they could enjoy the breezes and probably also get away from the gnats in the sage that in early summer torment sheep and humans alike.

Unlike her mother and stepfather, who lived all year at LA 12803, Warrior Woman and her husband spent the late winter about a mile up the draw, during which time they took the herd of 180 to the sheep camps PM

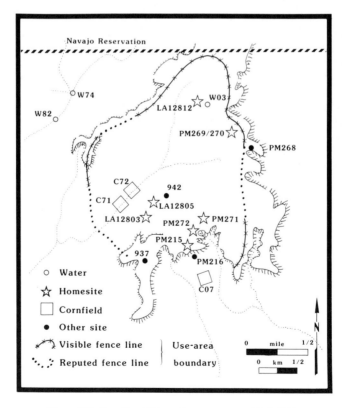

Figure 7.2 Gray-Eyed Woman's use area, ca. 1910–1916.

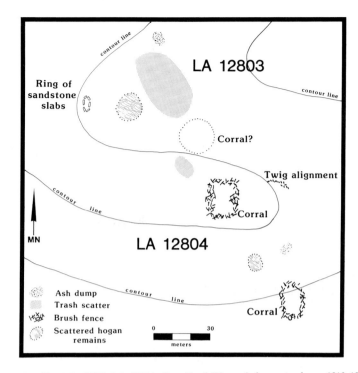

Figure 7.3 Site LA 12803–LA 12804, Gray-Eyed Woman's homestead, ca. 1910–1916.

269–270 and LA 12812. From PM 269–270, they herded in the open sage of the draw's northeastern fork. The sheep camp was built in the trees along the base of a low, southeast-facing sandstone bench and consisted of a cribbed-log hogan, a corral, and a sweathouse (see Figure 7.4). About a quarter of a mile from PM 269–270 stood a winter corral, PM 268, of logs stuffed between boulders below a south-facing ledge, in which they penned the herd when the snow in the upper draw drifted deep. From there the herd could also descend to the lower pastures of the Eastern Flat.

From site LA 12812, the family ran the herd into the northwest fork of the Defiance Draw, mainly in warm weather. To judge from the sparseness of trash remaining, they seem to have used site LA 12812 less often than PM 269–270. The site once consisted of a hogan and a corral in the open near Dripping Spring (W03) and, in the trees perhaps 50 yards away, a windbreak, corral, and sweathouse; only the last feature is now clearly visible. The family sometimes stayed at this site during dry spells in the summer because, in

addition to Dripping Spring, it is near Bubbling Spring (W82) and Coyote Drinking Water (W74), the most reliable summer water sources around, although both were outside Gray-Eyed Woman's claim (see Figure 7.2). The family would run the herd to a well, then back to their own range for grazing.

The fence that the husband of Gray-Eyed Woman built around their customary use area, mentioned in Chapter 6, consisted of piñon and juniper trees and brush that he had dragged into position with a horse, because he had no wagon. He left a gap in the fence where his own allotment extended below the mesa into the Eastern Flat, probably because Gray-Eyed Woman's sister, Margaret Thompson, and father, Fuzzy Face, shared this part of the claim. Margaret Thompson and her three sons had allotments near Rock Springs, and Fuzzy Face seems to have married into an Eastern Flat family after his marriage to the mother of Gray-Eyed Woman and Margaret Thompson. These households therefore may have stayed in the Eastern Flat in summer and used the upper Defiance Draw only in winter, although by 1915

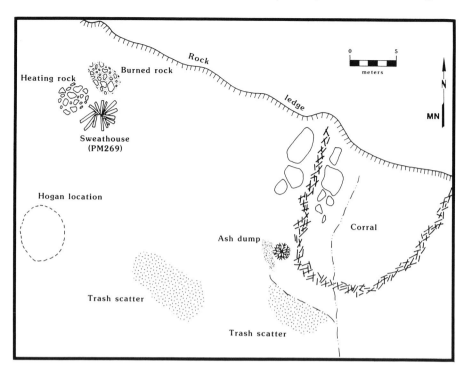

Figure 7.4 Site PM 269–PM 270, Gray-Eyed Woman's winter sheep camp, ca. 1910–1916.

Margaret Thompson may have been staying there all year. Their sites formed a cluster on the mesa top between the Eastern Flat and upper Defiance Draw (see Figure 7.2). Fuzzy Face's winter home, the later component of site PM 215, consisted of one cribbed-log hogan, a lamb pen, and one or two corrals, as well as a winter corral and lamb pen at the foot of the mesa. A sweathouse was about 500 yards southwest of the site, high above a steeply cut arroyo where Margaret Thompson's teenage sons used to drive "wild" horses into a corral. Fuzzy Face may have shared the hogan at PM 215 with a stepdaughter and her children, or with Margaret Thompson's oldest son, Curly Tallman, who presumably herded for his grandfather.

Margaret Thompson lived nearby with her husband Frank and two younger sons at site PM 272, where they had two cribbed-log hogans, two windbreaks or lamb pens, a small corral that was probably for lambs, and, slightly removed from the rest of the site, a sweathouse. Their winter corral, PM 216, was mid-way between PM 272 and PM 215—a situation like that of the winter corral of PM 215, which earlier may

have been dismantled and rebuilt at PM 216. The relative locations of these sites and the relationships among their users suggest that the families of Margaret Thompson and Fuzzy Face ran their livestock together. The stock numbered only 50–70 in 1915, but the many corrals and their large sizes suggest that the herd had once been bigger. Perhaps the aging Fuzzy Face had distributed his stock among his descendants.

Between 1915 and 1918, death struck these households repeatedly and forced them to combine. Fuzzy Face died sometime between 1915 and 1918. In 1916, Warrior Woman died, her husband apparently left, and Gray-Eyed Woman adopted their children. Gray-Eyed Woman had recently moved her field, C71, a short distance up the drainage to C72, apparently dismantling the juniper fence around the old field to fence the new one. She had therefore shifted her homestead from LA 12803 to a similar situation a few hundred yards north at LA 12805. Although the site is sheltered by trees, its slope exposes it to the prevailing southwesterly winds, so that Gray-Eyed Woman built a winter corral, site PM 942, in a sheltered spot closer to the yellow sandstone mesa. Gray-Eyed Woman continued to use the sites up the draw, but less regularly than Warrior Woman had. Two years later, Gray-Eyed Woman also died, presumably of the Spanish influenza. Margaret Thompson adopted her sister's five young grandchildren. She herself left site PM 272 at the same time because of a miscarriage. Abandoning the Defiance Draw for all purposes but herding, she moved with her new charges south of the yellow sandstone mesa.

Blackgoat's Winter Customary Use Area

Between the sudden increase in Blackgoat's wealth in 1918 and his death 6 years later, Blackgoat's winter range in the middle Defiance Draw centered on his homestead, PM 48–49, which he built well up in the wooded hills north of the draw. The site consisted of a stone-based, two-room house with corrugated tin walls, two or three hogans, four or five corrals, a windbreak, a storage cellar, masonry ovens, a large barn with palisaded sides, two sweathouses, and a garage near the barn in which Blackgoat kept his Model-T Ford (see Figure 7.5). The vehicle, in fact, may help to explain the location of the site, which was not far from what was then the main road to Gallup (see Figure 7.6). Probably all of Blackgoat's 1200–1600 sheep and goats were penned on this site during shearing, and the wool was stored in the barn until it could be hauled to Gallup. Blackgoat and his wife began living here with five of their six children, but as the children grew up and married, only the daughter, Mary Tinhouse, brought her spouse to stay most of the time at PM 48–49.

In summer, Blackgoat probably continued to send his sheep to the vicinity of Fort Defiance, but his wife and some of the children may have stayed around PM 48–49 all year. It is not clear how the winter range, which seems to have encompassed about 4 mi.^{2} north of the draw, could have supported 1200–1600 sheep and goats. The 1941 carrying capacity for the middle Defiance Draw, as estimated in Chapter 5, was at most 150 sheep and goats (including lambs and kids) per square mile for 6 months, whereas Blackgoat ran at least twice as many. Probably he was also at times using his mother-in-law's customary use area south of the draw.

Blackgoat maintained isolated corrals around his winter range so that he could move the stock successively from one pasture to another (see Figure 7.6). He also had to divide the herd into several flocks, probably because the rugged, wooded terrain north of the draw does not offer wide expanses of forage in which a big herd can spread out. A flock would be penned in an isolated corral at night and allowed to graze away from it during the day, tended by one of Blackgoat's children or hired herders who stayed nearby in a tent. Such sites include PM 50, a large isolated corral and scatter of trash probably left by the occupants of a tent; PM 54, a rather small corral; and an early component of PM 81 that consists of a large corral and a sweathouse.

Blackgoat also maintained various permanent sheep camps around the range. These included site PM 106—two hogans and two sweathouses occupied by "hired hands," perhaps poor relations—and PM 91, where Blackgoat's son, Descending Orator, lived with his wife and child. PM 91 is about a mile downhill from PM 48–49, on the edge of the trees near Defiance Draw, and consisted of three cribbed-log hogans (two are paired with windbreaks), two or three small corrals, and one large corral (see Figure 7.7). Other members of the family, including Blackgoat and perhaps hired herders, also stayed there. The site may have been a lambing camp where Blackgoat probably practiced drop-bunch lambing, a technique for tending lambing ewes in large herds described in Chapter 8. The windbreaks may have penned orphaned or rejected lambs that no ewe would feed, although the entry in each windbreak also suggests that they sheltered the extra herders that drop-bunch lambing demanded.

Some of the sheep may have lambed instead at site PM 57, not far uphill from PM 48–49, where the Tinhouses would move in January and stay for 3 or 4 months (see Figure 7.6). The site consisted of a hogan and three small (70–80 m^2) corrals, which could have held 100–200 ewes and lambs. Blackgoat also used a hogan at site PM 46 just down the hill east of PM 48–49, but the site may actually have been a precursor of PM 48–49. Several other dwelling sites north of the middle Defiance Draw that date to the early twentieth century were not identified by local Navajos but may have been sheep camps used by Blackgoat's family or hired herders.

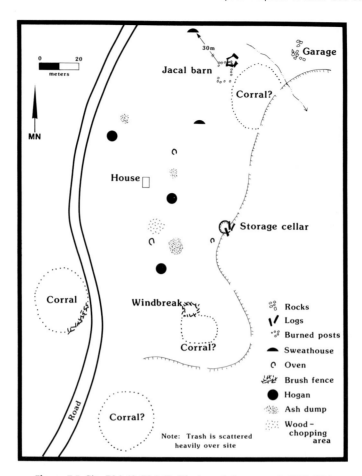

Figure 7.5 Site PM 48–PM 49, Blackgoat's homestead, 1918–1924.

The clustering of sheep camps and corrals at the northern end of Blackgoat's range and, to a lesser extent, the southern end may reflect moves between uplands in late winter and lowlands in late spring. If so, water sources should be clustered at both ends, and indeed they seem to be (see Figure 7.6). When staying at PM 48–49, Blackgoat watered his stock at W85, a small reservoir that he had built close by to catch melting snow. He also probably used the unlocated spring north of the Gallup road. Another small reservoir, W26, supplied water for the stock when they were at PM 91. Blackgoat may also have used the big dam, W20, that he and his father-in-law had reportedly built, although perhaps only for flocks south of

Defiance Draw. The dug well in Defiance Draw, W81, may have supplied water when the sheep were penned at the corral PM 81 about half a mile away.

Grazing Tracts

Both the number and size of grazing tracts in the lease townships, that is, customary use areas, changed as families filled and subdivided the range. The number of tracts increased from the five original claims of the late nineteenth century. Two original claims extended far outside the lease townships: the claim of Whitegoat, which reached into the Black

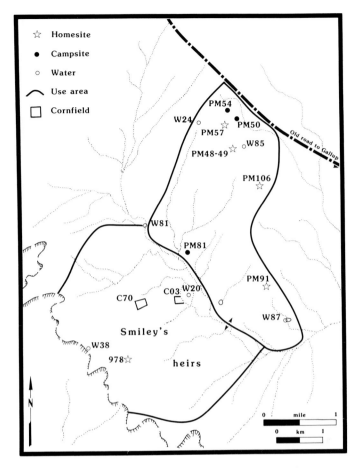

Figure 7.6 Blackgoat's customary use area, 1918–1924.

Creek Valley, and the claim of the He Walks Around clan people, which reached toward the Fort Defiance coal mine. I do not know how Whitegoat's claim was subdivided. The part of the He Walks Around claim that lies inside the townships and the three other claims had been subdivided into nine customary use areas by 1915. This increase was due to the subdivision of land among the children of the original claimants, Tall Salt Clansman in the Tse Bonita Wash and the Towering House people in the Eastern Flat.

The number of grazing tracts per household (or residence group) is harder to determine. Some households used summer range outside the lease townships that seems to have been contiguous with their winter range inside the lease townships. Others used summer range outside the lease townships that was not contiguous. (These summer lands, however, are not considered here.) And in the lease townships, families had not subdivided the range so greatly that they were forced to use discontiguous tracts. As mentioned in Chapter 6, several couples did use lands in the customary use areas of both spouses. Two of the 1915 use areas, moreover, seem to have been consolidated from adjacent parts of two original claims, or, perhaps more accurately, encompassed a little-used, upland buffer zone between the two claims that the intermarried heirs of the original claimants colonized. These consolidated customary use areas, however, include only contiguous lands. Only one household, that of Tom Sharp in the Eastern Flat,

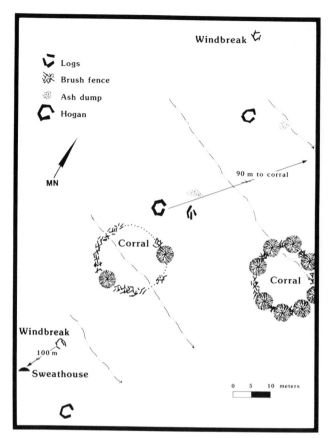

Figure 7.7 Site PM 91, Blackgoat's sheep camp, ca. 1918–1924.

seems to have made regular use of two discontiguous tracts in the lease townships.

Because the use areas in the lease townships covered basically the same area as the original claims, the average size of each grazing tract clearly shrank.[1] As one would expect, the sizes of the customary use areas corresponded, at least roughly, to the number of livestock each supported in 1915 (see Table 7.5). The figures on Table 7.5, however, suggest that overstocking had already begun in some of the tracts: The density of stock in Gray-Eyed Woman's area, which lay entirely in the poor range above 6800 ft., is only

[1]The seven customary use areas that lay entirely or mostly within the lease townships averaged 5.4 mi.[2] if the two discontiguous tracts used by Tom Sharp are counted as one and 4.8 mi.[2] if Tom Sharp's tracts are counted separately.

exceeded by the density in Tom Sharp's area, a large proportion of which was above that elevation.

In their distribution over the landscape of the lease townships, the first grazing tracts may have covered both lowlands and uplands, but people may have herded mostly in the sage–grass plains below 6800 ft. This zone, according to the figures in Chapter 5, has a higher carrying capacity than the uplands. At the time of the allotments, therefore, one might expect that the oldest generation of allottees would have received more than its share of allotments in the sage-grasslands. That was not the case, partly because some of the original claimants had already died by the time of the allotments, and the allottees who were their heirs had begun to subdivide the land. The actual allotment pattern is more interesting.

Table 7.5

Number of Small Stock, Size, and Physiographic Characteristics of Customary Use Areas in the Lease Townships, 1915

Use area no.	No. of small stock (annual equivalents)[a]	Area (quarter sections)	Small stock per quarter section[b]	Range elevation		Water[c]	
				Above 6800 ft.	Below 6800 ft.	Natural	Improved
5	700	36	20	x	x	x*	x*
8	500[d]	30	17+	x	x	x*	x*
1	500	34	15	x	x	x*	x*
6	500[e]	20[f]	25+	x	x	near*	—
7	U	14	U	—	x	near*	x*
4	230	10	23	x	—	x	—
3	U	U	U	x	—	x	—
2	55[g]	8	7+	x	—	x	—

[a]Total number of stock that regularly used the tract multiplied by the fraction of the year that the tract was used. The part of the Black Creek Valley that takes up the southwestern corner of the townships, and the stock of the families that used it, are excluded from this table. U = unknown.

[b]Small stock in annual equivalents divided by tract sizes.

[c]Water inside or on boundary of tract. *Includes water sources below 6800 ft.

[d]An additional 95 animals used the tract occasionally.

[e]An additional 400 animals used the tract occasionally.

[f]Includes acreage in the upper Tse Bonita Wash.

[g]Number of stock given in 1915 census is probably too low, according to statements of interviewees.

Most of the large herds of 1915 (four of the five with 400 or more sheep) belonged to the oldest generation of allottees, and all but one of the three largest stock owners held allotments in the sage-grass zone below 6800 ft. The one exception is an allotment in a zone of mixed sage-grass and piñon–juniper above 6800 ft., but it is situated at the head of a big, low-lying sage-grass basin. This allotment pattern supports the notion that the wealthy tended to monopolize the best range and to force other, especially younger households, into the poorer upland range, where they could not maintain large herds. Indeed, this process is evident in the subdivision of Tall Salt Clansman's claim, where most of the new grazing tracts developed between the original settlement and 1915. Thus, the market-fostered range subdivision and the tendency of the rich to monopolize the best range doomed many households to a life of poverty unless they could find land elsewhere.

Nevertheless, as Table 7.5 shows, even the lowland grazing tracts also extended into the uplands, probably because only there could the herds and their owners find adequate water in middle or late winter. Lowland playas sometimes form today and probably formed in the past where reservoirs are now. Such playas are less likely to form in the colder, often drier months of January and early February than in November and December or late February through April (U.S. Weather Bureau 1919–1978), because less snow melts and drains into the lowlands. The snow accumulates in the uplands under the trees and rocks. Thus, families probably wanted to move to the uplands during these months, where they could melt big chunks of snow for themselves and where their herds could quench their thirst with the unmelted snow. That the water supply was less reliable in the lowlands than in the uplands is evident from Table 7.5. Four of the five reservoirs in 1915 were below 6800 ft. Table 7.5 shows that the customary use areas with land both above and below 6800 ft. supported much more stock than did use areas that lay entirely above 6800 ft.

Fields

Farming, although not important to most lease-township residents in 1915, seems to have become more widespread after that time. Of the 15 fields identified with the railroad era, 5 were probably farmed in 1915, and at least 7 of the rest were first farmed after that year. In addition to 4 of the 5 fields in 1915, most of the other fields belonged to families who spent all or most of the year (including the summer) in the lease townships. With one possible exception, these other fields belonged to families that had owned the 1915 fields or to households that had started to live in the townships all year after 1915. The number of fields therefore depended mainly on the number of year-round resident households and grew after 1915 as the number of such households grew. The range subdivision outside the lease townships that deprived these households of their former summer range, then, ultimately caused the number of fields to grow in the lease townships.

The 1915 census contains information about the size of fields that lease-township residents farmed, although most of these fields were probably outside the lease townships near the summer homes of their owners. The 10 households to which the census attributes fields farmed a total of 27.5 acres (assuming that no two households shared acreage), or 2.75 acres for each farming household[2] and 1.1 acres for each household. This last figure is well below the average of 3 acres for each household in the Southern Navajo Agency jurisdiction (Paquette 1915:7), as well as the reservation averages of 2.5 in 1890 (USDI, Commissioner of Indian Affairs 1890:468) and 1.5 in 1930 (U.S. Senate 1932:8937, 9141, 9461, 9750). The lack of any other data on field sizes prevents one from seeing trends that might be related to the market involvement of the households.

The distribution of railroad-era fields across the lease-township landscape does not seem to exhibit a trend. Nevertheless, for comparison with later distributions, I describe the railroad-era field locations in terms of four zones that differ in the slope of the land. Nelson and Cordell (1982) partitioned the lease and surrounding area into these zones to see if Anasazi sites were situated in cultivable areas. Their analysis assumes that the slope of the land in the lease townships affects both its soil composition and its drainage, and therefore its agricultural potential. The partitioned area does not cover the entire lease

---

[2]$SD = 1.65$, $n = 10$.

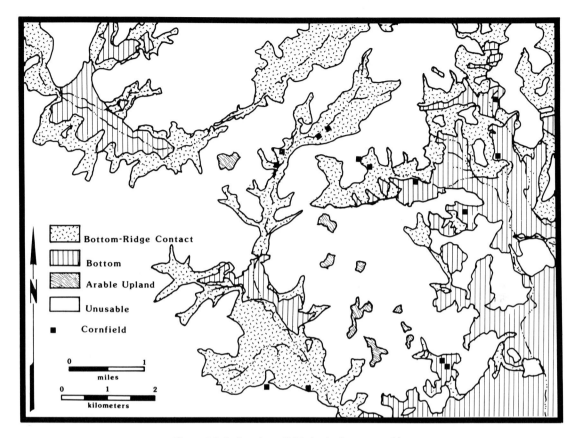

Figure 7.8 Railroad-era fields in the lease townships.

townships, but it does encompass 14 of the 15 railroad-era fields. Figure 7.8 shows the locations of the 14 fields within the zones. The unusable zone consists of shallow, sandy soils in steeply sloping uplands with a few cultivable pockets. The two large cultivable zones are bottom-ridge contact and bottomland. The bottom-ridge contact has slightly more slope, better drainage, and less clay in the soil than the bottomland.

Of the 14 railroad-era fields, 2 were in the unusable zone and the rest were evenly divided between bottom-ridge contact and bottomland (see Table 7.6). Nearly half of the fields lay at the junction of two or more zones, most in flattish areas below steep slopes. Several fields not at zonal junctions also lay below slopes. Abrupt changes in slope, of course, are common on the boundary between slope zones. In a widely used typology of field locations developed by Hack (1942),

Table 7.6
Distribution of Railroad-Era Fields by Slope Zone

	N
Total number of fields	14
Fields by zone	
bottom-ridge contact	6
bottom	6
unusable	2
Fields by zonal junction	
fields at junction of two or more zones	6
slope-wash fields	5
fields not at zonal junction	8
slope-wash fields	3
Proximity to dams	
located next to dams	3
not next to dams	11

fields in such situations are called *slope-wash* fields. Farmers commonly chose slope-wash situations for dry farming, because the flow of rainwater down the hillside hits the flat surface of the field and slows so that the earth can absorb it. Half of the fields in the lease townships not placed below hill slopes lay alongside earthen dams, from which they absorbed moisture. These were also the only irrigated fields.

The two cultivable zones in the lease townships encompass the lowland and the sage-grass plains, and the elevations of the fields and vegetation zones in which they were situated reflect this fact. The average 1915 field lay at an elevation of 6810 ft., and the average railroad-era field, 6800 ft.; all fields were situated in either the sage-grassland, the sage-grassland and piñon–juniper boundary, or the saltbush zone on the lip of the deeper arroyos.

Homesites

During the railroad era, grazing and the subdivision of the range strongly influenced the spatial characteristics of homesites of in the lease townships. As Table 7.3 shows, local Navajos have positively identified 19 such sites in the lease townships. Members of 15 residence groups used these sites, so that the average residence group inhabited 1.3 sites. The average number of sites for each residence group is higher, of course, if one includes the summer homesites that most families maintained outside the lease townships. The changing distribution of stock water and new plant growth dictated the moves of each residence group: If people moved the herd less than a mile, they ordinarily did not change homesites. The number of homesites each family used therefore depended on how often it moved the herd more than a mile.

As the number of families living in the lease townships grew, one would expect the number of homesites to reflect that increase. As families became confined to smaller areas that they could exploit without moving so often, however, one would expect the number of homesites for each family to drop. Unfortunately, the available data are inadequate to show the interaction of these opposing trends, because most dating methods favor later sites. Local people are more likely to know about recent sites, on which

datable artifacts are also more likely to have been discarded during the longer annual occupation spans. Tree-ring dates are not so biased, but relatively few structural wood specimens have been collected, and many have not yielded cutting dates.

The sizes of homesites, however, do show that, as time passed, families were staying longer during the year on more sites. These sizes therefore indirectly reflect the filling and subdivision of the range. In the next chapter I discuss the technology related to the sizes of homesites, including the sizes of dwellings and corrals, the spacing of dwellings and ash dumps, and the variety of other types of facilities. Here one need only know that the sizes, spacing, and variety of these facilities are greater on sites where families spent more of the year and on later sites. Homesites therefore grew bigger during the railroad era as families filled the range and subsequently moved less often.

A more obvious measure of a site's size is the total area it covers. Reliable figures, available only for the excavated sites on the lease, appear in Table 7.7. Identifications by local Navajos and archaeological dates suggest that the earliest homesites in the lease townships are probably the 28 with forked-stick hogans, a dwelling form (to be described in the next chapter) that people did not build in the lease townships after about 1920; most such dwellings probably antedate 1910 or 1900. As Table 7.7 shows, these sites tend to cover smaller areas than do the other, generally later sites of the railroad era.

According to the early railroad era observer, A.M. Stephen,

> [The] spot chosen for a dwelling place is either some sheltering mesa nook or southward hill slope in the edge of a piñon grove, securing convenient fuel, and not too far from water. But the Navajo seldom lives very close to a spring, a survival of an old habit of their former hunting life when they kept away from the springs much as possible so as not to disturb the game when coming to water. (Stephen 1893:348)

Throughout the railroad era, homesites in the lease townships occupied similar situations. The household's unchanging need for shelter and warmth in winter, and for fuel and water all the time, probably explains the constancy of these locational patterns.

Most sites with forked-stick hogans in the lease townships lie in the piñon–juniper woodland or where the woodland gives way to the sage-grasslands. About

Table 7.7

Areas of Excavated Homesites
on the Lease and Annual Occupation Span, All Historical Periods

Area size class m²	Site no.	Period	Annual occupation span
0–2000	42	1880–1930	forked-stick hogan[a]
	73	1880–1950	less than 6 months
	96	1880–1930	unknown
	135	1880–1930	less than 6 months
2000–4000	39	1880–1930	forked-stick hogan
	40	1880–1930	forked-stick hogan
	202	1930–1950	less than 6 months
	243	1880–1930	unknown
	12809	1880–1930	unknown
	12814	1880–1930	unknown
4000–6000	60	1880–1930	unknown
	91	1880–1930	less than 6 months
	124-125-131	1880–1930	less than 6 months
	12808	1880–1930	unknown
6000–8000	7	1930–1979	less than 6 months
	80	1880–1930	unknown
	115	1930–1950	6 months
	201	1930–1950	all year
14,000–16,000	1	1930–1979	all year
18,000–20,000	59	1930–1950	6 months
	225	1880–1930	unknown
26,000–28,000	81	1930–1950	6 months
over 30,000	33	1880–1979	6–9 months

[a]Assumed to have been occupied for less than 6 months.

the same proportion of the 1915 homesites have the same situations.[3] The trees offered inhabitants of the sites both fuel and shelter from raging winter storms. People with wagons could haul a stockpile of wood, but families without wagons needed dead wood near the homesite. Even those with wagons often found hauling impossible through the mud of late winter, when they moved to a sheep camp or ran out of wood.

Both early and late in the era, families tended to place their homesites with a landform on the west and an exposure to the south (see Table 7.8). This type of situation offers both shelter from the prevailing westerly winds and exposure to the winter sun. That large numbers of people also built their homes on ridge tops seems surprising until one realizes that the ridge tops, too, offered shelter if they were heavily wooded.

[3]Twenty-two out of 28 sites with forked-stick hogans and 16 out of 19 homesites occupied in 1915.

Most of these ridge-top sites were sheep camps, which families that herded on different sides of a ridge may have built in a cluster so that they would have help and companionship within easy walking distance.

Similarly, homesite locations seem not to have changed with respect to water. Figure 7.9 shows the locations of all forked-stick hogan sites in the lease and all known water sources of the railroad era. Most such sites are within a mile of a water source, and nearly all are within 1-½ miles. The same is true of the 1915 homesites (see Figure 7.10). If 1-½ miles seems far, the reader should remember that people used these sites mainly during late winter, when only a few steps from the doorway they could find snow for melting. People perhaps avoided living right next to water because of some vestige of "the hunting life," as Stephen suggests, for we have seen that lease-township residents ate some wild game. Probably the main reason, however, was that many families shared

Table 7.8
Situations of Sites on Landforms, Early Railroad Era and 1915

Topographic situation	Number of sites with forked-stick hogans (early RR era)	No. of homesites, 1915
Sheltered on west; exposed on south	16	7
Sheltered on west and south	2	2
Exposed on west and south	1	2
Exposed on west; sheltered on south	0	1
Ridge	8	7
Flat	1	0
	28	19

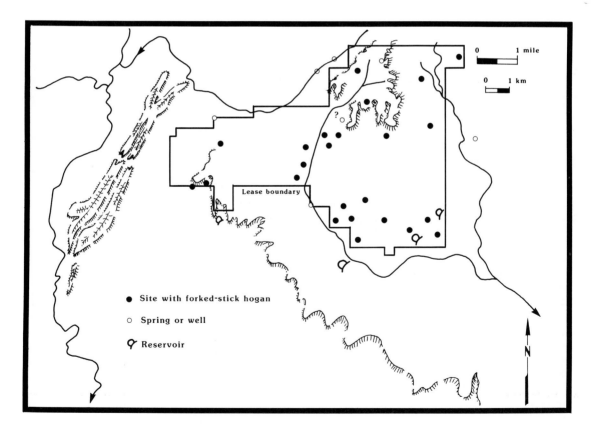

Figure 7.9 All sites with forked-stick hogans inside the South McKinley Mine Lease (sites outside were not recorded systematically).

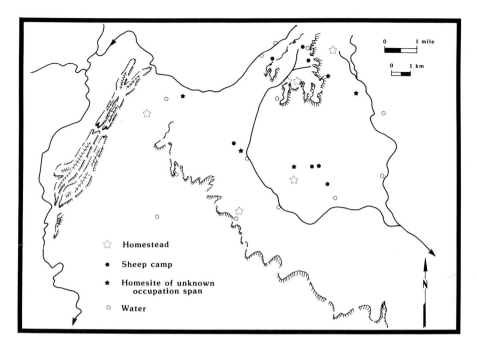

Figure 7.10 Homesites in the lease townships in 1915.

the few reliable water sources. To live close to water was thus to risk both invasions of privacy and the mingling of herds.

The locations of homesites may not have changed with respect to vegetation, landform, and water during the railroad era, but they did change in elevation. The average elevation of the supposedly earlier forked-stick hogans, 6870 ft., is significantly lower than that of the 1915 homesites, 6950 ft.[4] This shift probably reflects range subdivision, which confined a growing number of households to the uplands. That both forked-stick hogans and 1915 homesites tend to be above 6800 ft.[5] shows that families needed shelter and fuel from the groves of trees that are widespread only above that elevation. Perhaps people also wanted to herd in both uplands and lowlands without having to move themselves.

[4]Standard deviations are 120 for the forked-stick-hogan sites ($n = 28$) and 150 for the 1915 homesites ($n = 19$); $t = 2.02$ and $p < .025$ for a one-tailed test.

[5]Of the forked-stick-hogan sites, 64% of the 1915 homesites, 79%.

Conclusion

Statistics on the various spatial aspects of land use aggregated for all lease-township families show that, as the railroad era advanced, families used the land more intensively for stock raising, farming, and their own maintenance. Thus, grazing tracts both proliferated and shrank, the number of fields grew, and the average homesite expanded as people moved less often during the year—a sign that they were filling and subdividing the range. Intensification is especially evident in the uplands, where new grazing tracts tended to develop and where the number of homesites grew the fastest.

These aggregate statistics, however, do not show variations among families in the use of space. Yet, because families decided to change their use of space independently, one must look at variations in the use of space among them to see why they might have intensified their use of the land. Families, moreover, exploited the land through systems of various types of sites, so that a change in the use of one type of site may have affected the use of others and thus the aggregate statistics on the use of space. To show both the variation in the use of space among families and the systematic interrelation of types of sites, I have described the customary use areas of lease-township families—the contiguous areas, each monopolized by one or more cooperating residence groups for production and their own maintenance, that are parts of the land bases of the outfits. This body of information, together with the land-tenure histories in Chapter 6, shows that, while all families intensified their use of the lease townships during the railroad era (probably because of human and livestock population growth on the ancestral summer range outside the lease townships), the poorer families used the lease townships most intensively and were relegated to the uplands by the richer families.

Chapter 8

Technology of the Railroad Era

It is widely known that the railroad and the trading posts brought new tools and equipment to Navajo families; that Navajos were eager for new items is even an anthropological cliché. Less widely recognized, however, is the fact that these changes mark the mounting demand imposed by market production on household labor. The growing demand may also have altered the division of labor within the family.

Railroad-era observers have described a family division of labor that suggests many households were supplementing livestock and crops with handicraft production for trade. Having questioned both Anson Damon and Chee Dodge, the traveler Lieutenant John G. Bourke reported from Fort Defiance in 1881 that

> Young girls assist their mothers in all home duties; women cook, clean "hogan," weave blankets and "tilmas," make their own clothes, (the men make *their* own clothes just as the Apache braves do). The men do most of the knitting [of leggings], but the accomplishment is also shared by the gentler sex. Boys and girls herd the flocks of sheep and goats, the care of which is almost wholly under control of the old women. Shearing is done by all hands. . . . Such little farming as is possible in the arid country of the Navajos is performed by the men, that is the hard work of plowing is their special business, but in this, as

in everything else, the women assist. (Bloom 1936:227–228)

The men also made silver jewelry and cared for the horses and cattle (Franciscan Fathers 1910:271–285; Stephen 1893:354).

Later in the railroad era, however, women and teenage girls may have participated less in daily herding as they stepped up their weaving for the market. In 1910, the Franciscans mentioned "the now vanishing tradition that weaving should be done with proper moderation" and "the custom of withholding maidens from weaving before marriage, which was *formerly* observed" (Franciscan Fathers 1910:222; emphasis added). Neighbors (usually relatives) helped each other when work reached its seasonal peaks during lambing, shearing, planting, and harvesting (Franciscan Fathers 1910:257, 265; Reichard 1928:51–52; Stephen 1893:354–355).

Domestic Technology

Changes in domestic facilities, tools, and equipment during the railroad era suggest that families both

Figure 8.1 A forked-stick hogan of 1892–1893, with a silversmith and his forge outside. The forge is almost as long as the dwelling is wide; smiths needed bigger dwellings if they were to work indoors. (Photograph from Smithsonian Institution, National Anthropological Archives, Bureau of American Ethnology Collection).

stepped up craft production and moved less often during the year. These technological changes therefore reflect indirectly the market-induced filling and subdivision of the range.

All datable dwellings built in the lease townships before World War I were traditional Navajo hogans. They took two basic forms: conical and many-sided. The *conical*, or *forked-sitck,* type had a framework of four or five forked timbers set into a shallowly excavated floor and interlocked at the top. The builders laid shorter timbers against this framework and then plastered the entire exterior with earth (see Figures 8.1 and 8.2). *Many-sided* hogans varied more in construction. Probably the most common construction involved straight-sided walls of horizontal logs that interlocked at the corners (*cribbed logs*), surmounted

by a domed, corbeled-log, earth-covered roof (see Figure 8.3). Many-sided hogans outnumber forked-stick hogans by 55 to 11 on sites on the ease that local Navajos identified.

Rectangular houses did not appear in the lease townships until around World War I, when at least three of the four such railroad-era houses were built. According to the census of 1915, three lease-township households did have rectangular houses, but those houses were probably on summer range outside the townships. By this time, forked-stick hogans were obsolescent; none of the forked-stick hogans either ethnographically or archaeologically postdates 1920.

These changes in dwelling form suggest that, as time passed, people needed roomier dwellings. The many-sided hogans and rectangular houses offered more

Figure 8.2 A forked-stick hogan as it appears archaeologically.

standing room than did the forked-stick hogans, and the rectangular houses tended to have larger floor areas than either type of hogan.[1] Households may have built larger dwellings because they needed more space indoors for work and storage. This need, in turn, stemmed partly from range subdivision, which forced

families to spend longer portions of the year on fewer homesites. The floor areas of homestead dwellings are significantly larger than those of sheep-camp dwellings.[2]

The household's need for more space may also

---

[1]Two of the houses could not be measured, because they were not on archaeological sites on the lease. The other two, with floors of 30 and 48 m², respectively, covered much larger areas than did any hogans but the three largest on the lease (26.2, 28.3, and 33.0 m²).

[2]The average floor area of 12 measurable dwellings on sites that interviewees identified as homesteads, 23.1 m² (SD = 9.9), is significantly larger than that of 10 measurable sheep camp dwellings, 16.0 m² (SD = 5.7), and that of 20 measurable dwelling sites for which the length of occupation is unknown (SD = 6.1; t = 9.72; $p < .001$).

Figure 8.3 A cribbed-log hogan as it appears archaeologically. It once had a dome-shaped, earth-covered roof.

indicate that some families had accumulated wealth and possessions, and others had increased craft production. Roomier dwelling shapes seem to reflect wealth, because three of the four rectangular houses in the lease townships belonged to families with herds above the average size. The families to which the 1915 census attributes rectangular houses were not wealthy, it is true, and their dwellings may have fit the description of most rectangular houses given in the census: "one room houses without windows and with one door, dirt floor, and board or dirt roof" (Paquette 1915:5). If it is true that these dwellings were so constructed, the only attribute to distinguish them from many-sided hogans was their rectangular shape, which may indicate simply that their owners got from the

agency sawmill large pieces of lumber needed to make fewer, longer walls. The Fort Defiance agents had actively encouraged the construction of rectangular houses by supplying the Navajos with lumber after the sawmill was built in 1889 (USDI, Commissioner of Indian Affairs 1889:258, 1890:164). The rectangular houses in the lease townships, however, were not of this hoganlike type; they were big buildings of rock or even tin siding as well as logs.

At the same time, forked-stick hogans may have become obsolete because households produced more handicrafts (see Figure 8.1). The conical shape of these hogans cannot readily accommodate the upright Navajo loom and, during the period when women wove mainly to clothe their families, reportedly forced

Table 8.1
Sizes of Railroad-Era Dwellings and Selected Variables on the South McKinley Mine Lease[a]

Site no.	Area of largest dwelling (m²)	Total dwelling area on site (m²)	Area per occupant (m²)[b]	Maximum small stock of occupants	Resident silversmith	Resident weaver
Homesteads						
48*	48.0	87.2	12.5	1200	U	x
13*	30.0	30.0	6.0	200	U	later[c]
179*	23.7	23.7	4.7	U	U	U
74	19.6	48.1	3.0	800	U	later[c]
272*	15.9	31.8	8.0	50	U	later[c]
Other sites[d]						
124	22.1	38.0	U	1000	—	—
91	19.6	46.4	5.3	600	U	U
135	12.6	25.2	6.3(?)	1000	U	U
46	12.6	12.6	6.3(?)	600	U	U
80[e]	17.7	63.7	4.3	800	U	later[c]
243[e]	9.6	9.6	4.8	400	U	U

[a]U = unknown; x = present; * = year-round occupancy.
[b]Total dwelling area divided by maximum number of occupants.
[c]Female occupants are known to have been weavers in later times.
[d]Includes sheep camps and homesites of uncertain occupation span.
[e]Homesite of uncertain occupation span, probably less than 6 months.

them to confine their work to nice weather and weave outdoors (USDI, Commissioner of Indian Affairs 1890:161). When women plied the loom more steadily for trade, however, they needed dwellings with more rounded ceilings to accommodate the loom indoors, at least in winter. In the early 1930s, Amsden (1934:235) remarked, "Traders long ago noticed that most of their rug purchases are made in the spring, because most weaving is done during the long, idle days of winter."

Although wealth and craft production may have influenced the shapes of dwellings, these two factors do not seem to have affected a family's total dwelling area (see Table 8.1). I have eliminated "noise" from differences in the length of the annual stay by separating homestead dwellings from sheep-camp dwellings. I have shown both the aggregate area of all dwellings on each site and the area of the largest dwelling, because for most sites I do not know which household used which dwelling. Perhaps clear links between dwelling area and wealth or handicraft production do not show up because so few sites have measures of dwelling size, inhabitants' wealth, and

craft production. At any rate, the wealthy or craft-producing families represented did not necessarily occupy dwellings with larger areas.

The table does suggest, however, that the number of inhabitants at least sets a lower limit on the total area of all dwellings combined. A statistical analysis of these sites (together with later ones) shows a significant positive correlation between the total number of inhabitants and the total area of all dwellings combined on all sites not occupied year-round. The correlation does not hold for sites occupied all year (Camilli 1984:66). Dwellings on these year-round sites generally provide more area for each person than do dwellings on sites occupied for shorter spans. These larger areas, again, are probably due to the greater range of indoor activities and items stored on year-round sites. The year-round homesteads that provided very small areas for each person housed adults with many small children.

Other data indicate that larger households of the railroad era tended to use more indoor space by increasing the number of dwellings rather than their sizes. The average number of dwellings per household is 1.2, both on sites identified ethnographically in the lease townships and according to the 1915 census. The average exceeds 1 because, in both samples, four of the five households with more than one dwelling included either an elderly parent of one of the household heads or teenaged children.

A factor that affected the dwelling floor areas of individual dwellings was the age–gender composition of the group of inhabitants. This factor imposed a minimum, which for hogans of households seems to be about 12.6 m^2 (4 m interior diameter; all dwelling floor measurements given in this chapter are interior). The reason for this limit may be in sleeping arrangements. Navajos in general commonly reserve the back of the hogan for sleeping and the front for cooking, eating, and working (Bailey and Bailey 1980:1502; Brugge 1977:213–223; Kent 1983; Tremblay, Collier, and Sasaki 1954:195–197). In the lease townships, most many-sided hogans of the railroad era had six sides, each of which would measure about 2.3 m outside and 2.0 m inside, or just long enough for a grown man. The back of such a hogan therefore would have provided at most one or two sides for married couples or single adults and one or two sides for children. An apparent anomaly is that solitary people, usually the elderly, also had dwellings of 4 m or more in diameter. These dwellings, however, probably also often accommodated younger relatives visiting or helping out and earlier may have sheltered the spouses and children of their lone occupants.

Several sites on the lease identified by local Navajos and dating to the railroad era have shelters like cribbed-log hogans but smaller—2.5–3.5 m in diameter. These *herding hogans*, each of which sheltered teenage boys or hired herders on distant range, are the exceptions that prove the rule. The minimum diameter of the shelters on these various sites, 2.5 m, only slightly exceeds the minimum length of a side of a family dwelling. The herders slept and perhaps cooked inside but did not need to huddle along one wall to give others sleeping room, to reserve the front of the dwelling for domestic activities, or to store their belongings. Herders probably cached food and equipment in some of these shelters.

While the age–sex composition of the group of inhabitants may have determined the minimum viable dwelling size, another factor probably encouraged people of the railroad era not to exceed that size: the need to conserve fuel, because most people lived in the lease townships only during the winter half of the year. As families stayed longer at each homesite during the year, the consequent proliferation of indoor activities and items to be stored in each dwelling exerted a countervailing outward pressure on floor area, which, in turn, affected the choice of a heating device. The heating device then affected the volume of the resulting ash, the number of ash dumps, and the dumps' distance from the dwelling doorway. The types of heating devices and the number, volume, and distance of ash dumps therefore are correlated with dwelling floor areas. Like floor areas, ash dumps reflect the length of time within a year that a family stayed at a homesite. Heating devices and ash dumps therefore also indicate indirectly the extent to which the family found its range restricted through filling and subdivision.

The relationships among the size of a dwelling, the type of heating device, and the various characteristics of ash dumps proposed here are as follows. The two main types of heating devices in Navajo dwellings of the railroad era were open hearths and stoves. Open hearths provide light as well as heat but cannot warm a large dwelling without producing intolerable amounts of smoke. When people needed larger dwellings, they therefore bought stoves or made them out of cans, metal drums, or sheet-metal scraps. People were also forced to buy kerosene lanterns when they replaced the open fire with stoves, which gave no light. By burning more wood, however, the stoves produced more ash than did hearths, for which the scoops (often just pieces of cedar bark) used to remove hearth ash were inadequate. By using the buckets that they needed for the greater amount of stove ash, people could also carry the ash farther before dumping it; this would limit mess in front of the dwelling, where they often worked to have easy access to items kept inside.

Because of these relationships, one would expect the disposal of ash to differ between homesteads and sheep camps. First, ash dumps should be farther from homestead dwellings than sheep-camp dwellings, partly because stoves were more common on homesteads, and partly because work areas in front of homestead dwellings, like the area inside, were probably bigger. Second, homesteads might have fewer ash dumps (but of larger volume) than sheep camps because of the greater need for outdoor work space.

Figures that support this formulation appear on

Table 8.2. The table lists all dwellings in the lease that were measured and have heating devices identified archaeologically or ethnographically. All measurable forked-stick hogans with ash dumps are also listed on the assumption that stoves would have been rare in such hogans, although Young (1955:105) shows an undated photograph of a forked-stick hogan with a stovepipe. Of the dwellings with hearths, all but the last one listed date to the railroad era, whereas only the first two dwellings with stoves date to that time. The two railroad-era dwellings with stoves, moreover, were relatively large, rectangular houses on homesteads, whereas the dwellings with hearths were smaller hogans, located on sites that local people either identified as sheep camps or could not identify in terms of the annual occupation span.

With two exceptions, the dwellings with hearths have floor areas of 19.6 m^2 (5 m diameter) or less, whereas floor areas of all but two dwellings with stoves from all periods exceed 19.6 m^2. Also, with two exceptions, each dwelling with a hearth has its largest ash dump within 11 m of the front of its doorway, whereas all but one of the dwellings with stoves have the largest ash dumps beyond that distance. More dwellings with hearths have multiple ash dumps than do those with stoves. The combined total volumes of all dumps associated with each dwelling are significantly lower for dwellings with hearths than for dwellings with stoves. The measurable dwelling on site PM 225 is noteworthy, for the site is the only one in the hearth group that is likely to have been a homestead; the dwelling is one of the two with hearths that exceeded 19.6 m^2 and the dwelling's heating device was not a simple hearth, like the others, but a masonry fireplace, that is, a homemade type of stove. This dwelling is the exception that proves the rule that larger dwellings were more likely to have stoves.

On the other hand, ash dumps are about the same distances from dwellings on all homesteads and sheep camps identified ethnographically (including dwellings with unidentified heating devices), even though the homestead dwellings are bigger than the sheep-camp dwellings.[3] The reason for this similarity is probably that most dwellings on both homesteads and sheep camps had hearths during the railroad era. Homestead and sheep-camp dwelling areas could differ significantly and still fall within the range of 4.0–5.0 m in diameter characteristic of hearth dwellings. Longer annual stays and larger dwellings may have encouraged people to buy stoves but did not force them to do so. Evidently, if larger work areas were actually needed in front of homestead dwellings, people preserved them by restricting the number of ash dumps rather than their distance from the dwelling.

A final characteristic of ash dumps may be related to the use of stoves: the range of variation in the direction of ash dumps from the doorways of the associated dwellings. On railroad-era sites on the lease, ash dumps commonly are located northeast of the corresponding (usually nearest) dwelling or at least northeast of the doorway orientation, which, according to Navajo tradition, is supposed to be east and may vary from northeast to southeast.[4] Ash dumps may favor the northeast, not only because the prevailing winds come from the southwest but also because most people, being right-handed, throw things in that direction from east-facing doorways, and people who carried the ash out in a bucket would have dumped it in the same place to restrict the mess. One would then expect ash dumps southeast of the doorway mainly when a left-handed person scooped ash from a hearth and tossed it from near the door. Northeastern dumps, then, are likely to fall within or beyond 11 m of the doorway, because they could have come from either stoves or hearths, but southeastern dumps should tend to fall within the 11 m of the doorway common to hearth dumps. Most of the southeastern dumps on the lease are associated with dwellings the heating devices of which have not been identified and the areas of which could not be measured. Five of the six southeastern dumps lie within 11 m of the corresponding dwelling, however, whereas the northeastern and eastern dumps lie both within and beyond that range. Also noteworthy is the fact that four of the six sites with southeastern dumps belonged to two families, and one such dump was on a site belonging to daughters and a granddaughter of a Mrs. Left-Handed.

Still another type of feature on railroad-era

---

[3]Among the 14 homestead dwellings, the average ash dump was 13.8 m distant (*SD* = 6.6), and among the 13 sheep-camp dwellings, the average dump was 11.5 m distant (*SD* = 7.9).

[4]Of the 17 ethnographically identified railroad-era dwellings with measurable doorway orientations, 8 had the largest dump northeast of the doorway, 6 had the largest dump southeast of the doorway, and 3 had the largest dump east of the doorway.

Table 8.2
Heating Devices and Ash-Dump Characteristics
on South McKinley Mine Homesites, 1880–1979

Site no.	Dwelling no.[a]	Distance to ash (m)[b]	Dwelling area (m²)	No. of ash dumps	Volume of ash dumps (m³)[c]
Dwellings with hearths					
124	2	4	22.1	1	0.3
80	1	U[d]	17.7	0	—
80	2	U[d]	15.9	0	—
80	3	U[d]	15.9	0	—
80	4	U[d]	14.2	0	—
60	1	14[e]	19.6	3	2.0
96	1	10	19.6	2	0.3
135	1	11	12.6	1	0.1
135	5	9	12.6	1	0.1
225	1	11[f]	26.2	2	1.9
12[g]	—	3	15.9	1	U
40[g]	1	5	12.6	2	0.2
215[g]	10	3	9.6	1	U
215[g]	11	1	U	1	U
39[g]	1	6	12.6	2	0.3
115[h]	6	29	19.6	1	0.3
N	16	12	15	18	15
$\bar{X}$[i]	—	8.8	16.4	—	0.4
SD	—	7.5	4.4	—	0.5
Dwellings with stoves					
13	1	12	30.0	1	U
48	18	18	48.0	1	U
1	5	28	28.3	1	U
1	9	13	28.3	1	U
1	3	22	16.4	2	U
59	1	30	19.6	1	7.5
81	10	30	28.3	4	5.5
115	1	22	28.3	1	4.4
182	1	21	U	1	U
212	5	14	44.2	1	U
212	1	25	31.5	1	U
7	4	12	28.3	1	U
7	2	11	15.8	1	U
33	4	14	U	3	7.3
N	14	14	12	17	6
$\bar{X}$[i]	—	19.4	28.9	—	4.1
SD	—	6.9	9.6	—	3.2

[a]Provenience number.
[b]Distance to largest dump on sites with more than one dump.
[c]Total volume associated with the dwelling.
[d]No ash dumps observed.
[e]A smaller dump lies 8.0 m from the hogan.
[f]A smaller dump lies 9.0 m from the hogan; the heating feature is a small masonry fireplace.
[g]Forked-stick hogans with ash dumps recorded; heating device is assumed to be a hearth.
[h]Associated dwelling was used for storage and work only.
[i]Difference between ash distance means: $t = 3.89$, $df = 24$, $p < .001$; difference between dwelling area means: $t = 4.68$, $df = 25$, $p < .001$; and difference between ash-dump volume means: $t = 4.90$, $df = 19$, $p < .001$.

Table 8.3
Percentages of Railroad-Era Homesites
in the Lease Townships with Selected Types of Features[a]

Feature type	Homesteads	Sheep camps	Homesites of unknown occupation span	Sites with forked-stick hogans
Dwelling	100	100	100	100
Windbreak, *ramada*	44	20	7	0
Sweathouse	50	72	36	33
Oven	50	0	0	0
Ash dump	100	90	57	44
Woodpile	63	20	0	0
Storage	50	0	0	11(?)
Corral	100	92	67	44
Lamb pen	43	36	38	11(?)
No. of components[b]	(8–10)	(10–22)	(14–16)	(9)

[a]Includes all sites positively identified by interviewees.

[b]Number of components on which presence or absence of a particular type of feature was noted (not all types were noted on sites off the lease).

homesites related to the use of stoves is the woodpile, that is, a bed of chips where people chopped wood stockpiled on a homesite. None of the sites with hearth-heated dwellings listed on Table 8.2 have woodpiles, whereas all of the sites listed with stove-heated dwellings do. One might object that stoves and woodpiles are correlated simply because both are recent: Most sites with hearths antedate 1930, whereas most with stoves postdate that year, and the more recent the site, the better preserved the woodpile. Six pre–1930 sites, however, have stoves known or inferred from ash-dump distances, and all have woodpiles. Apparently railroad-era people used, and perhaps stockpiled, much more wood on homesteads than on sheep camps, probably because they stayed longer on the homesteads.

A final attribute of railroad-era homesites in the lease townships reflects the length of the inhabitants' annual stay: the variety of features on a site. Table 8.3 shows that homesteads tended to have a wider range of features (besides dwellings) than did sheep camps. Most sites in the lease townships with forked-stick hogans, moreover, lack such features. In the early part of the railroad era, to which the forked-stick hogans date, people evidently moved among homesites more often and performed fewer activities at any one site.

Besides dwellings, common types of features on the homesites are corrals and pens, windbreaks, *ramadas*, ovens, ash dumps, woodpiles, storage facilities, and sweathouses. These features are more common on homesteads than on sheep camps, probably because people engage in more activities outside the dwelling the longer they stay on the site. Some of the features are also labor-saving devices, the proliferation of which may also reflect the growing demands on family labor.

Corrals and pens and their functions as labor-saving devices are discussed in the next section of this chapter. Windbreaks are unroofed, round shelters of stacked brush, and *ramadas* are rectangular, roofed brush shelters; both accommodate people working outside in warm weather. The ovens, a meter or so in diameter and made of rocks laid in a beehive shape, save work, at least in cooking for many people, by allowing the cook to make bread of store-bought wheat flour and to do other things while the food bakes. Storage features include a garage for Blackgoat's Model-T Ford, barns in which people stored hay and tack, bell-shaped pits, and rectangular cellars. The cellars are 2–4 m on a side and perhaps 1-½–2 m deep, dug into a hillside or the flat ground, and surmounted by a flat roof or lean-to of earth-covered logs. In the pits and cellars people stored sacked corn and beans, dried squash, store-bought potatoes, and even melons over the winter. Sweathouses are miniature forked-stick hoganlike structures about 1.5 m high and 1.5–2.5 m in diameter, usually built slightly removed from the homesite to give the bathers privacy.

Railroad-era Navajos furnished their dwellings inside with a rather sparse collection of domestic tools and equipment. At the beginning of the railroad era, these included many items of native manufacture, as mentioned in Chapter 5. In the hogans around Fort Defiance that Bourke visited in 1881, he saw

> rugs of sheepskin, blankets, and coverlets of wool woven in bright colors, . . . crockery "ollas" and dishes from the Pueblo tribes of Zuni, Moqui [Hopi], Laguna, Acoma, or the Rio Grande, and the elegant baskets from the Apaches. A fire in the center [of the hogan] is a *sine qua non*. (Bloom 1936:87)

By 1910, however, these items had given way to a greater variety of more specialized, mass-produced items. The Franciscan Friars reported a few "American beds and mattresses", along with the sheepskin bedding, and even tables and chairs in cabins, although not in hogans. Tin and china cups had replaced gourds, and "modern pans, pots, and skillets, too, are quite general," although some women still cooked on stone griddles. Some families even owned coffee mills, but most people ground coffee, as well as corn, with a mano and metate (Franciscan Fathers 1910:219, 328, 467).

Domestic tools and equipment on sites in the lease townships identified by local Navajos include dishes, pots and pans, utensils and small tools, manos and metates, wash tubs and basins, pails, a kerosene lamp, stoves, water barrels, furniture, wagon and horse gear, and even auto parts, as discussed in Chapter 5 (see Table 5.4). Most of these items, other than the small technology (the culinary items, tubs, basins, and pails), appear only on sites that postdate 1910. This difference may show that people were using more mass-produced, often labor-saving devices, as the above quotations suggest. Auto parts are a good example. In 1915, only five Navajos families in the entire Southern Navajo Agency jurisdiction owned automobiles (the families of Chee Dodge, which owned a Dodge, and two of the Damon brothers, who owned Fords, are included in the five) (Paquette 1915). None of these families actually lived in the lease townships, where the first automobile owner seems to

have been the wealthy Blackgoat. (He seems to have bought his Model T Ford around World War I, when high wool and lamb prices supplied extra cash.) Again, however, the proliferation of mass-produced items on later sites may also reflect the probable higher ratio of homesteads to sheep camps in the lease townships after 1910 and therefore the filling of the range.

Stock-Raising Technology

Stock-raising technology in the lease townships during the railroad era seems to reflect most clearly the filling of the range. Its labor-saving aspects may also signal the growing strain on the household's labor power as families turned to commercial handicraft production to make ends meet.

I have mentioned that children during the railroad era were responsible for most daily herding. Large-scale stock owners, however, often deployed teenage boys and hired herders for the task. I did not make systematic inquiries about either daily or seasonal herding practices in the lease townships during the railroad era, but the spontaneous remarks of interviewees suggest that these practices differed little from the general Navajo pattern of the time (Franciscan Fathers 1910:257–258; Kelley 1982c:235–248). Most families took the herd out on the range during the day and returned it to the homesite every night, where they penned it in a corral. The men who herded for the large stock owners moved around the range among sites where they may have spent anywhere from a few days to a couple of months. Some of these sites had all-weather dwellings large enough to house families and therefore belong to the site category of sheep camps. Others had only the smaller herding hogans or windbreaks for shelter, and still others had no remains of shelters at all, because the herders pitched tents there. These sites are not in the sheep-camp category and are here called *campsites*. Many campsites also had corrals, sweathouses, or both, but others did not. The herders grazed the sheep away from these sheep camps and campsites every morning and led them back at night, where they penned the sheep in a corral or bedded them on the ground. Sometimes herders with two separate flocks shared a camp and ranged in opposite directions during the day.

Usually the herders grazed the sheep only 1–3 mi. from the homesite or campsite. In summer they herded the sheep to water every day. In winter, the trek occurred every 2 or 3 days unless snow lay on the ground, in which case the sheep could eat the snow instead. In the broken, wooded country that covers most of the lease townships, the largest number of sheep herded together seems to have been about 200–300; bigger herds were broken up, because they may have been too large for the small open pastures.[5] In the broad sage flats of the Eastern Flat and lower Defiance Draw, however, rich owners reportedly ran flocks of 1000 head.

The annual stock-raising cycle began with lambing, which lasted from January to May. The duration of lambing in any one herd depended on whether the family regulated the breeding period by separating the bucks from the ewes between midsummer and late fall or early winter. Lambing time demands much work if the herd was large and the lambing season compressed. The main problem is that some ewes reject their lambs, especially one of a pair of twins, while other ewes die and leave orphans. The attendants must maneuver the ewes into accepting rejects. They must either pair orphans with ewes whose lambs have died or separate the orphans for bottle feeding—often, during the railroad era, with goats' milk (U.S. Senate 1932:9121).

To save labor in seeing that all the lambs were fed, people isolated the problem animals in special facilities. One type was a round or rectangular pen of cribbed brush or rocks, 1 or 2 m across, that would hold one or two lambs, with or without a ewe. Another special facility was the twin corral, although local Navajos do not identify such features on railroad-era sites, and the only evidence of them is archaeological. People kept all twin lambs in a corral of their own during the day, when the herd was grazing, and penned the mothers of the twins with these lambs at night. The other lambs stayed in the main corral during the day, where their mothers rejoined them at night. People reportedly did not let the lambs run with the herd until early or mid-summer, at least in the smaller herds,

because they did not consider the lambs strong enough.

These methods of caring for lambs are evident on sites of most families with medium-sized herds and may have characterized at least one large-scale operation. Archaeological evidence suggests, however, that other large-scale owners may have maintained special lambing camps where their herders may have practiced a variant of the drop-bunch lambing common at the time to commercial herds elsewhere in the West. In drop-bunch lambing, one herder tends the main herd while that day's lambing ewes and their newborn are separated from the herd and given to different herders, each of whom may or may not have a pen for his small flock (Lobato 1974; Wallach 1981:56). Usually the pens were dispersed around the lambing grounds, although they seem to be clustered on the possible lambing camps in the lease townships, perhaps to save labor in getting food to the herders. The sites that I suspect were for drop-bunch lambing have one–three "family-sized" hogans (either forked-stick or cribbed-log), three or four cribbed-log windbreaks of 2.5–3.5 m diameter (often roofed or half-roofed, that could have sheltered extra herders or lambs or both), and one to three corrals. The family-sized hogans on at least one of these sites housed the owner and his grown children with their families. Figure 8.4 shows the plan of one such site, which accommodated the hired herders of Mr. Small and Mr. Towering House Clansman between about 1905 and 1920. Another possible lambing camp is Blackgoat's sheep camp, PM 91, described in Chapter 7.

In May the traders have always bought wool, and lease township residents of the railroad era left for their summer homes. Apparently they sheared at either winter or summer homesites. People sheared with hand clippers in a corral and packed the wool in sacks, which they would then haul in wagons to various trading posts. (Families with weavers kept part of the clip.) I did not find out how large-scale stock owners organized shearing. Probably all the stock and herders assembled at the homesteads of these owners, where the sacked wool possibly was stored in barns or large houses to keep it from getting wet and rotting before it could be sold.

In July, some stock owners may have removed the bucks from the herd to prevent early breeding. Although today's lease-township Navajos did not mention this practice in connection with the railroad era, many Navajos in other places are reported to have

---

[5]This maximum size has been noted elsewhere in the Navajo country in more recent times (Lamphere 1977:112; Ruffing 1973:71; Shepardson and Hammond 1970:110) and even in western Iran, where 200 is reportedly the largest number that a "typical family" can manage (Hole 1978:146).

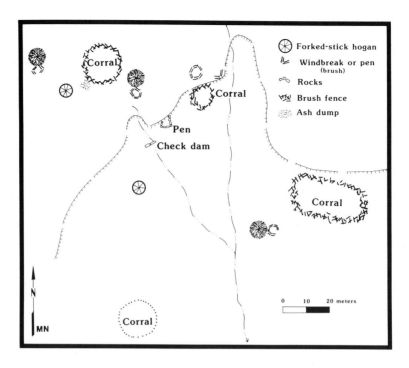

Figure 8.4 Site PM 124–125–131, Mr. Towering House Clansman's sheep camp, ca. 1910.

separated bucks, and the government agents particularly encouraged the large stock owners to set an example by doing so (Brugge 1980:266, 275–276). Controlled breeding may have been more common among large-scale owners than small-scale owners. By causing all the lambs to be born at once, the practice forced people to get extra help during lambing, which the large-scale owners could hire but which the small-scale ones could not afford. (The overworked small-scale owners seeking help from nearby relatives might have found them busy with their own lambs.) Controlled breeding enhances the survival of the lambs by postponing their birth until the cold weather is over and minimizing the number of early lambs that must be sheltered to survive. A small-scale stock owner, however, could easily have sheltered the few early lambs that a small herd produces and therefore did not need controlled breeding. Finally, controlled breeding creates a more uniform cohort of lambs for sale, but the small-scale stock owners probably sold few, if any, of their lambs. Herds grew faster when breeding was not regulated, because the ewes could

breed at intervals less than a year apart (Dyk 1938:67; Hanley 1977:26). This increased rate of breeding may have induced small owners to forego controlled breeding.

Middle or late summer was the time for dipping, although local Navajos did not mention sheep-dipping in connection with the railroad era. Dipping controls scabies, a skin parasite that diminishes the weight and quality of the fleece. After the Fort Defiance agent set up the first dips in 1896 (Brugge 1980:154), Navajos would trek their herds to various centrally located vats, where they would submerge the animals one at a time under the supervision of the agency farmer. Because the agents were zealous in promoting dipping, and because most lease-township residents spent the summer within 10 or 15 mi. of the Fort Defiance Agency and its dip, most lease-township families undoubtedly dipped their sheep.

People have sold their lambs in late September and October since the railroad era, because that is when feedlot operators in neighboring states buy lambs to fatten over the winter (Kelley 1982c:137, 169, 174–175;

Figure 8.5 A lamb pen, measuring about 1.5 m² with a living juniper for shelter overhead.

Youngblood 1937:18104). The sale of lambs is another annual event that interviewees did not mention in regards to the railroad era, and, as discussed in Chapter 4, sales were probably low. Nevertheless, large owners, at least, undoubtedly sold many of their lambs. The large-scale owners in the lease townships probably trekked their lambs to traders in Gallup. Government agents (USDI, Commissioner of Indian Affairs 1889:256, 1890:162, 1892:209) and the Franciscan Fathers (1910:258) also mention a second episode of shearing in the fall that was not mentioned by local Navajos. Presumably people sheared a second time to get credit for winter provisions. The traders may have used this clip mainly to supply weavers who ran out of wool during the winter or lacked it entirely. The manufacturers seem to have bought raw wool only after the spring shearing, and the fall wool might have spoiled if stored all winter for sale the next spring.

In November, most families left their summer homes and moved back into the lease townships. Those who regulated breeding restored the bucks to their herds, and, with breeding, the herding calendar ended.

As the foregoing account shows, the main types of facilities that people used in stock raising during the railroad era were sheep corrals and pens. The construction of lamb pens was described above and is illustrated by Figure 8.5. Sheep corrals of the railroad era in the lease townships consisted of round, oval, or rectangular fences of interwoven piñon and juniper trunks and branches stacked horizontally and other branches leaned vertically against the outside of the fence to form a sheltering overhang (see Figure 8.6).

A statistical analysis of corrals and pens on lease-township sites shows how they reflect the family's need to save labor, its settling down, and its herd size. Nearly

Figure 8.6 A brush corral.

all railroad-era homesites identified by local Navajos have at least one corral. Corrals are less common on sheep camps and sites of unknown occupation spans (probably most of which were sheep camps), however, than on homesteads, and still less common on the sites with forked-stick hogans that I take to represent the early railroad era (see Table 8.3). Railroad-era inhabitants of the lease townships therefore apparently used corrals more on the sites where they spent most of the year than on those where they stayed for short stints. In addition to providing shelter, corrals save labor by keeping the herd from straying while its caretakers are doing other things. Because people performed a wider range of such activities on homesteads than on the other types of sites, their need for corrals on homesteads was correspondingly greater.

Twin corrals and lamb pens also save labor by isolating the problem animals so that the herder need not pick them out of the group at every feeding. Table 8.3 shows that, like corrals in general, lamb pens are less common on early sites (those with forked-stick hogans) and sheep camps than on later sites and homesteads and probably for the same reasons.

Twin corrals seem evident archaeologically on several sites and also seem less common on both sheep camps and early sites. Table 8.4 lists all the railroad-era sites identified by local Navajos that also have measurable corrals and possible twin corrals. The archaeological evidence of twin corrals is as follows. A local Navajo whose family has used a twin corral until recently estimated that about 25% of the females in the herd might have twins. Assuming the Navajo historical average of 64 lambs per 100 mature animals

Table 8.4
Possible Twin Corrals
on Railroad-Era Sites on the South McKinley Mine Lease

Site no.[a]	Area of all corrals combined (m²)	Ratio of smallest corral area to area of all other corrals
Homesteads		
48	1827	0.3
74	927	0.3
12803	510	0.4
12805	414	0.1
Other sites[b]		
124	603	0.1
135	1282	0.6
91	966	0.9
225[c]	2247	0.1
80[c]	920	0.2
243[c]	565	0.4

[a]Includes only sites with measurable corrals for which an estimate of herd size was also available.

[b]Includes sheep camps and homesites of unknown annual occupation span.

[c]Homesite for which annual occupation span is not known.

(Young 1961:173), twins and their mothers would number about a third of the rest of the herd. (The proportion would probably vary, depending on the proportion of goats and old ewes in the herd, because twinning is more common among these animals.) The areas of twin corrals that local Navajos identified on the 1930s–1960s sites range between 20 and 40% of the areas of all other corrals on the site combined. Table 8.4 shows that the ratios of the smallest corral on each railroad-era site to the combined area of all other corrals on the site also lies in or near these percentages.

The foregoing discussion implies that the size of the corral is correlated with the size of the herd, or at least that the area of all corrals on a site combined is correlated with the total number of sheep and goats kept there. Van Valkenburgh (1956:40–41) has also implied this relationship by estimating herd sizes from corral areas, apparently using a rule of thumb of 2 m² per animal. According to the one lease-township resident questioned on this matter, people did not use such a rule of thumb when they built corrals, although intuitively they might have hit on a roughly standard

ratio. The areas of corrals on sites identified by local Navajos on the lease do seem to reflect the numbers of animals penned, but other factors seem to distort or even mask this relationship.

Table 8.5 lists all the railroad-era homesites and campsites identified by local Navajos for which I could estimate herd size. It shows the ratio of the largest number of animals penned on the site (according to ethnographic sources) to the combined area of all corrals on the site. With few exceptions, these ratios vary between slightly less than 1 m² animal, or about the size of a reclining sheep or goat, and slightly more than 2 m² per animal.

One would not expect corrals in the lease townships to have exceeded the minimum of 1 m² per animal, because sheep and goats tolerate crowding, and because the construction of most lease-township corrals required much woodcutting to make them sturdy enough for winter. Two other factors, nevertheless, seem to have encouraged the larger corrals: the weather and the annual length of occupation on the site. Table 8.5 suggests that isolated corrals used in winter and those on homesteads tended to afford more space for each animal than those on sheep camps and nonwinter campsites. The reason for the larger area per animal on sites used in winter or for several months at a time is undoubtedly that corrals used for long periods, especially in winter, cannot dry out quickly; the longer the sheep stay in them, the muckier they become. Local people today, therefore, not only use large corrals but also alternate corrals on the same homesites.

The few sites that afforded less than 0.7 m² for each animal belonged to large-scale stock owners who ran sheep in at least two flocks. Some of the corrals, however, are too small even for half the total stock of these owners, who may therefore have divided their herds into more than two flocks or used the corrals only for lambing ewes, lambs, or twins and their mothers.

Another aspect of the relationship between corrals and herd sizes is the number of corrals for each homesite. Table 8.5 shows that homesteads of the railroad era tended to have more corrals than did sheep camps or campsites. One possible reason is the greater muck problem on homesteads mentioned above. Another is that, if people divided herds that exceeded 200–300 for grazing in the broken uplands of the lease

Table 8.5
Corrals on Railroad-Era Sites on the South McKinley Mine Lease

Site no.[a]	Maximum herd size[b]	No. of corrals	Total corral area on site (m²)	Total corral area per animal (m²)
Homesteads				
48	1200	5	1827	1.5
74	800	3	927	1.2
12803	180	2	510	2.8
12805	180	2	414	2.3
272	50	1	38	0.8
Sheep camps and homesites of unknown occupation span				
215[c]	50–70	3	272–452	3.9–9.0
124–125–131	1000	3	603	0.6
135	1000	2	1282	1.3
91 and 57	1200	2	1186	1.0
73	350	1	672	1.9
269	180	1	144	0.8
225.1[c]	1000–2000	2	2247	1.1–2.2
80[c]	800	3	920	1.2
243[c]	400	2	565	1.4
12812	180	1	314	1.7
118	≥492	1	1800	≤3.7
121	492	3	452+	≥1.0
Winter isolated corrals				
12.2	262–564	1	600	1.1–2.3
268	180	1	352	2.0
942	180	1	130	0.7
216	50–70	1	195	2.3–3.9
Other isolated corrals and campsites				
54.1	600	1	225	0.4[d]
81.1	600	1	720	1.2[d]
108	65	2	252	3.9
113	500	1	168	0.3[d]
64	500	1	707	1.4[d]
36	500	1	254	0.5[d]
937	180	1	177	1.0

[a]Includes only sites with measurable corrals for which an estimate of herd size was also available; component number is to the right of the decimal point.

[b]Largest number of sheep either owned by the occupants around the time they used the site or indicated by local Navajos as likely to have been kept on that site.

[c]Homesite for which length of annual stay is unknown.

[d]Corrals of large-scale owners who split herds into at least two flocks. Herds on sites with one corral are therefore assumed to be at most half the owners' total small stock.

townships, they may have penned the flocks separately at night. Such flocks may thus have been moved to separate sheep camps. When their herders were staying on the family's homestead, however, either for family activities or for such tasks as shearing, the flocks were likewise gathered on the homestead, where each might have had its own pen.

Of the families with two or more corrals on their homesites, then, those who divided their herds into two or more flocks may have used all the corrals at the same time, whereas those with smaller, undivided herds may have used the corrals sequentially. If these two different patterns characterized the large and small owners, respectively, then the sizes of the individual corrals on railroad-era sites show that, in building corrals, the families did aim for about 1 m^2 per animal if they kept the stock on the site for less than 6 months and about twice that area if they kept the stock on the site for 6 months or more (see Table 8.6).

The abundant structural manifestations of herding in the lease townships during the railroad era unfortunately have no parallel in the inventories of artifacts related to stock raising recorded on archaeological sites (see Table 5.4). The only such artifacts recorded were a salt trough and *sheep rattles* (pebble-filled cans strung on wire and used to hustle the herd out of the corral) on the lease and a broken pair of sheep shears outside the lease, where systematic artifact inventories were not taken. Other items probably related to herding include the pots, pans, pails, or basins often found in corrals. People may have used them for milking goats and discarded them on the spot when they started to leak.

Farming Technology

Little is known of farming technology in the lease townships during the railroad era, and how household market involvement affected it is therefore not clear. People seem to have adopted mass-produced, possibly labor-saving technology (the plow) and invested in more facilities to intensify production (reservoirs). These two changes may have been responses to, respectively, the growing demand for labor that producing for the market placed on families, and the market-induced filling and subdivision of the land.

The main crop that people grew in the lease townships was corn, supplemented by beans, squash, and melons. They probably scheduled planting, cultivating, and harvesting as they did in the 1930s–1940s and as they do today (see Chapter 13). In the early part of the railroad era, people in the lease townships reportedly planted with the digging stick (*gish*). Lease-township residents, at least those who lived around St. Michaels in the summer, probably practiced the planting methods that the Franciscan Fathers described in 1910:

> In sandy soil corn is planted by means of a planting stick. . . . The small opening is made to preserve as much moisture as possible. The holes are dug by men, followed by the women, who drop the kernals into and close the holes with their feet.

> Where the soil is loamy the holes are now dug with a mattock. The value of plowing the ground is also being more appreciated. (Franciscan Fathers 1910:265–266)

In 1918 a plow was reportedly used in the lease townships for the first time, perhaps bought with money from the high wartime wool and livestock prices. The plow saved labor if a family could plant a field with it faster than with a digging stick, or if they could plant the seeds more easily behind the plow than behind the *gish*. The easier the planting, the more likely that children would do it.

Most fields were unirrigated, but three received seepage through neighboring earthen dams. One of the fields was irrigated by a reservoir of a family that had lost its summer range outside the townships. The other two were irrigated by a reservoir of Mr. Towering House Clansman, who was now spending the whole winter in the lease townships rather than staying there irregularly, as in earlier times, when he had never bothered to plant there. Whether irrigated or unirrigated, most (nine) of the fields belonged to people who spent all or most of the year, including summer, at a nearby homesite. Smiley and his wife, who planted two fields, summered in Hunters Point in 1915 but apparently stayed all year in the townships later, when they farmed there. At that time, they continued to haul produce by wagon into the lease townships for the winter from a field in Hunters Point. The intensification of farming that these reservoirs indicate therefore resulted from the filling and subdivision of land outside the lease townships.

Table 8.6

Corrals Used by Individual Families during the Railroad Era

Site no.	Occupation span of site	Length of time stock kept on site	Area of each corral (m²)	Corral area per animal (m²)
Gray-Eyed Woman's family[a]				
12803	homestead	9 months	360	2.0
			150	0.8
12805	homestead	all year	378	2.1
			36	lamb corral(?)
12812	sheep camp	3 months	314	1.7
269	sheep camp	3 months	144	0.8
937	campsite	infrequently	176	1.0
268	winter corral	infrequently	352	2.0
942	winter corral	infrequently	177	1.0
Margaret Thompson's family[b]				
215	unknown	unknown	180	2.6–3.6
			177	2.5–3.5
			97	1.4–1.9
272	homestead	unknown	38	0.8
216	winter corral	unknown	195	2.8–3.9
Blackgoat's family[c]				
74	homestead(?)	unknown	400	1.0
			300	0.8
			227	lamb corral(?)
80	unknown	unknown	442	1.1
			348	0.9
			130	lamb corral(?)
Blackgoat's family[d]				
48–49	homestead	less than 6 months	660	1.1
			615	1.0
			360	0.6
			192	lamb corral(?)
91	sheep camp	less than 6 months	504	0.8
			462	0.8
57	sheep camp	3 months	70	lamb corral(?)
			70	lamb corral(?)
			80	lamb corral(?)
54.1	corral	infrequently	225	0.4
81.1	corral	infrequently	720	1.2

[a]180 small stock.
[b]50–70 small stock.
[c]800 small stock run in at least two flocks.
[d]1200 small stock run in at least two flocks.

Conclusion

I have discussed domestic, stock-raising, and farming technology in so much detail here because, together with the spatial distribution of sites, it is the main archaeological manifestation of land use. Observations made during the railroad era suggest that the family's burden of labor grew as the growth of weaving took old women away from herding and replaced them with children. Changes in domestic, stock-raising, and farming facilities, tools, equipment, and techniques in the lease townships seem to reflect both the growth of craft production and the ongoing quest for devices to mitigate the family's growing labor burden. They also reflect the the permanent settling down of most families as they filled and subdivided the range.

Chapter 9

The Great Depression
and Grazing Regulation, 1930–1950

Historical Background

In 1928, an engineering survey determined that sediments in the Colorado River would quickly inundate Boulder Dam and jeopardize the electrical power the dam was to generate for the booming city of Los Angeles. The survey blamed overgrazing on the western ranges, which included the Navajo country (Fonaroff 1963; U.S. Senate 1937:17445). The federal government therefore decided to regulate grazing on public and Indian lands. This regulation filtered and distorted the effects of the Great Depression and World War II on Navajo family land use.

Federal officials first broached the subject of stock reduction to the Navajo Tribal Council at its November, 1928, meeting. The Commissioner of Indian Affairs had created the council almost 6 years earlier, after federal legislation of 1918 and 1920 opened reservation lands to mineral leasing. Tribal council approval of such leases was required by statute of 1891 (Kelly 1968:39; Young 1978:53–54). A single "Commissioner of the Navajo Tribe" was to arrange the leases in all Navajo agencies, subject to council approval. Because grazing regulation also involved the

disposition of Navajo lands, grazing policy also required tribal council approval.

The council in 1928 endorsed the collection of grazing fees from owners of 1000 head or more, but the council and federal officials at first did little to regulate grazing. In 1930, the Director of Irrigation of the Indian Service (as the BIA was called between 1929 and 1947) proposed to wrest 900,000 of the estimated 1.3 million sheep and goats from the Navajos but offered no meaningful plan to accomplish this feat. Southern Navajo Agency jurisdiction Forest Supervisor Donald Harbison wrote prophetically,

> The problem of conserving and restoring the range to its potential productive ability is a difficult one. It is easy to say "reduce the numbers of grazing stock." This, however, is easier said than done. . . . To propose cutting the numbers of his flock, without providing some other source of income to replace his lost income from livestock, is sure to meet with failure. Relief for the range must come through breeding up of a better grade of stock which will provide a greater income from fewer numbers. This process is a long one. (Harbison 1932:9203)

Between 1930 and 1933, the Indian Service also commissioned several studies to estimate the magnitude of overgrazing and to recommend measures to reduce it. A preliminary study in 1931 showed that the Southern Navajo Agency jurisdiction, of which the lease townships were still part, carried almost twice the number of stock that it should have carried (Beck 1937:17908; Kelly 1968:114; Young 1978:71).

Federal officials did establish the political infrastructure through which they hoped to enforce grazing regulation: the grid of local community organizations, or chapters, that covered most of the Navajo country by the early 1930s (U.S. Senate 1932:8943, 9134, 9787). The turn-of-the-century demise of the agent's informal councils of headmen had left a political vacuum at the local level that the tribal council could not fill with only 12 delegates and 12 alternates to represent all agency jurisdictions. First introduced in the Navajo country in 1927, the chapters did not become widespread until after federal authorities decreed grazing regulations, and the tribal council began to allocate money (presumably from oil royalties) for chapter-house construction and other local projects (Young 1978:66–67). By 1930, chapters had been organized at Fort Defiance, St. Michaels, and Oak Springs. Each had elected officers and met once a month in the presence of a government representative (U.S. Senate 1932:9133–9137). Many lease-township residents probably attended meetings at these chapter houses until the Tsayatoh chapter was organized a few years later.

The Navajo Tribal Council and the chapters provided part of the machinery through which the federal government could regulate grazing. The government itself, however, was not organized to regulate grazing effectively until the advent of Franklin D. Roosevelt and the New Deal in 1933. Only the New Deal made available government staff to plan grazing regulation and jobs and relief for Navajos forced to give up livestock. Early in 1933, Roosevelt appointed as Commissioner of Indian Affairs John Collier, a former social worker, officer of the Indian Rights Association, and defender of Pueblo Indian land rights. Collier immediately launched a program of voluntary stock reduction, land expansion, and legislation enabling tribal economic development programs. The range-improvement program of the Soil Conservation Service complemented Collier's efforts.

In November of 1933, Collier persuaded the Navajo Tribal Council to endorse a government purchase of a flat percentage of the livestock in each agency,

later set at 10%. Chapter officials, local headmen, and traders arranged the sales, while government workers, including Navajos enrolled in federal work programs, actually collected the stock and drove them to the shipping points (Parman 1976:48). The effort, however, did not reduce livestock by the intended amount. The large owners pressed small owners to sell breeding stock while they themselves merely culled their flocks, the reproductive capacity of which therefore ballooned (Beck 1937:17986). As Collier himself would later testify,

> When a fellow owns a lot of sheep, by the Navajo custom, he controls the range that the sheep graze,. . . and there is a battle going on between the proletariat, if you like, and the rich fellows on the Navajo Reservation. (U.S. Senate 1937:17468)

Two more purchases in 1934 and 1935 met with similar results. By that time, the grazing surveys begun in 1933 were complete and showed that the Navajo range as a whole was 100% overstocked.

All this time, Collier had been promising wage work, range and water development, and more land if Navajos would reduce their herds, and he had begun to deliver on the first two counts. The U.S. Civilian Conservation Corps (CCC) and Soil Conservation Service (SCS) had special Indian divisions, and Navajos received a large share of the wages budgeted. Indeed, Collier seems to have used the implied threat of withdrawing these jobs to make the tribal council cooperate in stock reduction (Parman 1976:46, 53). Between 1930 and 1936, wage income in the southern jurisdiction leaped from 23 to 55% of all personal income and came mainly from CCC and SCS jobs (Kunitz 1977:188; U.S. Senate 1932:9135, 1937:17447). During the same period, especially after 1933, the government developed 1800 water sources throughout the Navajo country on and off the reservation—three times the number developed during the previous 60 years (Young 1961:168–178).

Collier, however, could not entirely fulfill his promise of land. Early in 1934, his allies in Congress had introduced two bills to extend the boundaries of the Navajo Reservation. Congress speedily enacted the Arizona boundary bill and added about a million acres of land to the reservation, including the land in the lower Black Creek Valley. The New Mexico boundary bill would have added the lease townships and most of the rest of the eastern Navajo country. Besides providing more land, the annexation would have brought under Indian Service control an area that large-scale Navajo stock owners had been using to escape reduction by entrusting some of their stock to poor relatives there (Parman 1976:172; U.S. Senate 1944:3171).

The bill, however, was never reported out of committee because of opposition from an unlikely coalition of Navajos and non-Navajo stockmen who used some of the land in question. The Navajo opposition was organized by Jacob C. Morgan, a tribal council delegate whose constituency in Shiprock adjoined the Eastern Navajo jurisdiction. Morgan advocated investment in water development for small stock owners rather than in unimproved land, which he thought large owners would monopolize. He also expected New Mexico's Senator Dennis Chavez, a spokesman for the non-Navajo stockmen, to get Congress to exempt the New Mexico part of the Navajo country from stock reduction, although Chavez did not deliver this result (Parman 1976:132–159, 170–177; U.S. Senate 1937; Young 1978:82–86, 102–105).

Morgan also opposed the boundary bill, because he disliked both Collier and the Wheeler–Howard bill, another part of Collier's legislative package that Congress passed at the same time as the Arizona boundary bill (Young 1978:82). The Indian Reorganization Act (IRA), as it was then called, was a statute enabling tribally directed economic development. Each tribe that chose to accept the statute in a plebiscite was to elect a representative tribal council and adopt a constitution. Thus chartered, the tribe could operate much like a municipality and include in its functions many that the Indian Service had previously handled; it would also become eligible for credit from a revolving fund to start tribal businesses. In addition to all these benefits, the IRA stopped the allotting program, prohibited the unregulated sale of remaining allotments, and directed the Secretary of the Interior to regulate the use of tribal lands to prevent erosion and deforestation.

Collier saw the IRA as the legislative prerequisite to his goal of self-sufficient Indian reservations. As land-management planners soon calculated, however, "self-sufficiency" for the Navajos meant that two-thirds of all households would have to get along on

herds with a mere 57 mature ewes, while the rest would be doomed to lives of weaving and silversmithing, farming, or government work (Parman 1976:51–52, 118–119). Morgan vehemently opposed Collier's "anti-assimilationism" on ideological perhaps as much as economic grounds, for Morgan was a missionary of the Christian Reformed Church and a former teacher whose belief in progress included formal education, wage work, and Protestantism (Parman 1976:18–19, 28).

Morgan campaigned against the IRA itself before the Navajo people were to vote on whether to adopt it in 1935. He pointed out that, by voting for the IRA, with its soil conservation provisions, people would be voting for stock reduction. The vote was close enough for Morgan's supporters to have swayed it: Only in the Shiprock and Eastern jurisdictions, where Morgan had the most support, did the majority vote against the IRA (Kelly 1968:169; Young 1978:86).

Stock reduction, however, did not end when the Navajos refused to adopt the IRA. After 1935, forced sales officially began. Perhaps to minimize the prospect of organized opposition from Morgan or others, the Collier administration also altered the tribe's political institutions. The once-popular chapters were now seen as hotbeds of opposition to government policies. After 1935, the Indian Service therefore withdrew financial support from the chapters (Young 1978:154). Collier also redoubled his efforts to consolidate the five Navajo agencies (together with Hopi), a process he had started in 1934, because he thought he needed a central authority to get the Navajos to accept his programs (Parman 1976:91). The headquarters for the consolidated Navajo Agency were to be a mile outside the northwest corner of the lease townships at Window Rock.

In 1936, at Collier's urging, the tribal council voted for its own reorganization through a constitutional assembly of headmen (Young 1978:89). A panel consisting of Navajo Agency superintendent E. Reeseman Fryer, the Franciscan Father Berard Haile, Chee Dodge, and another prominent councilman, Deshna Clah Chischillige, chose 70 headmen from names that various communities submitted. The 70 were apportioned—1 representative to roughly 500 people—among the 18 land management units into which the SCS had recently divided the Navajo country. Geographical subdivisions of the land management units have been represented in the tribal council ever since. The chosen men met in April of 1937 and voted themselves the new council (Young 1978:99). Although Morgan was one of the chosen, he and his followers pressed the government into holding a general election in 1938 to form a more truly representative council (Parman 1976:178–179, 190).

While clearing away the organized political opposition, the Collier administration also decreed mandatory stock reduction. Between 1935 and 1940, the number of Navajo mature small stock was reduced by more than a third. The land management units, created in 1935–1936 to encompass both physiographic provinces and the trade areas of groups of trading posts, were the administrative units for the new reduction programs (Parman 1976:112). In Land Management Unit 18, the Black Creek Valley and the lease townships, livestock holdings reportedly plunged from 70,591 sheep units (mature sheep and goats or the equivalents in cattle and horses) in 1936 to 52,121 only a year later—a figure that includes seasonal use of stock from the lease townships (Young 1961:171).

In the spring of 1937, the Indian Service hired range riders, mostly unemployed cowboys from Arizona and New Mexico cattle ranches, to help with stock reduction. They took detailed stock censuses at dips and at roundups of horses and cattle for branding. Horses were impounded and their owners were forced to sell them. A maximum herd limit was established for each land management unit based on the unit's carrying capacity and the requirement that herds smaller than the average be frozen at their current size. The Indian Service then planned to issue permits to owners of herds below the maximum for the number of stock that they dipped in 1937, whereas larger owners would receive permits only for the maximum. Most permits were not distributed until 1940, however, and forced stock sales were mostly of horses (Parman 1976:114–115, 172–183, 240–280; Ward 1951). Between 1939 and 1943, the Indian Service secured court judgments against several Navajos accused of violating the grazing regulations, and those judgments broke the Navajo resistance (Parman 1976:238–242). As a result, in Land Management Unit 18, after the dramatic reduction between 1936 and 1937 came more reduction, so that in 1942 the unit held only 30,017

sheep units, a cut of almost 60% since 1936. This figure is below the official carrying capacity of the unit, which in 1943 was set at 33,008 sheep units (Young 1961:170–171).

After 1940, World War II depleted the ranks of government workers, including federal agents to enforce stock reduction (Adams 1963:46). Because federal officials were being drafted, the Indian Service charged the tribal council with enforcing the permits on the reservation. In 1941 the council petitioned the Indian Service for special grazing permits above the maximum, which were extended in 1942 and have not been revoked to this day (Young 1961:155–156). Nevertheless, many Navajos who left their herds with family or friends to work in wartime industry or the armed forces returned to find that federal agents had seized their stock (Boyce 1974:147).

The lease townships remained part of Land Management Unit 18 until about 1940 (USDA, SCS 1938, 1940). By the time the first permits were issued in that year, however, the lease townships and other off-reservation portions of Land Management Unit 18 had been added to a district in the Eastern Navajo Agency jurisdiction. Grazing in the Eastern Navajo jurisdiction, both on public domain and on non-reservation Indian lands, was regulated by the U.S. Grazing Service, which the USDI had created to administer the Taylor Grazing Act of 1934. In accordance with that statute, the public domain was divided into grazing districts, each under the charge of Grazing Service officials and a land board of local ranchers (Stout 1970:318–319; USDI, Grazing Service 1940–1946).

The first permits that these authorities issued to Navajos allowed each owner the number of sheep units that, according to his or her 1940 permit application, he or she owned in 1938. Those who did not apply for permits were cited for trespassing (USDI, Grazing Service 1940–1946). The Grazing Service planned to change the permits after the off-reservation district carrying capacities had been set (U.S. Senate 1944:3062), and the permits were reduced accordingly in 1943.

The numbers of livestock on the reduced permits were supposed to reflect the total acreage, regardless of ownership, that each permittee reported on his or her permit application. Permittees who continued to run stock seasonally between the lease townships and the Black Creek Valley on the reservation also received permits for the reservation land. Because the numbers permitted on the reservation often exceeded those permitted off the reservation, Grazing Service officials often harassed permittees who conformed to their on-reservation permits (USDI, Grazing Service 1940–1946).

Although the government continued forced reduction into the 1940s, war preparations induced Congress to cut the government work program funds that helped make the stock reduction bearable for many families. Congress halved the CCC appropriation in 1938 and eliminated it altogether in 1941, while the SCS lost two-thirds of its funding (Parman 1976:270–281). After 1940, however, labor recruiters sought many Navajos for jobs outside the reservation, not only in the armed forces and war production, but also in agriculture and on the railroads to replace other workers who had been drafted (Boyce 1974:130). Another source of income, although meager at first, was federal welfare, for which Navajos became eligible in 1941 (Young 1961:296).

The substitution of wage work for livestock production also undermined the power of the traders over Navajo household subsistence, because wage work became an alternative to sales of wool, livestock, and handicrafts to the traders. Navajos, moreover, were spending their wages in the border towns, where prices were lower and the selection of goods wider, even though the traders had tried to persuade the government during the 1930s to disburse all payments through the trading posts (Parman 1976:35, 72–73). As a result, the number of trading posts in the Navajo country did not grow after 1935, even though population did. In the vicinity of the lease townships, the number of trading posts grew only around Window Rock and Fort Defiance and only because government jobs increased there (Kelley 1977:251). Because most families still could not depend on wages, however, the traders kept some of their power. Indeed, many families needed more credit than they could get with their wool, livestock, handicrafts, and pawned personal jewelry. They began to pawn large numbers of saddles, bridles, harness, and even wagons (Counselor and Counselor 1954:370).

After World War II, the contracting national economy rejected the Navajo workers whom it had absorbed during the war. The tribal council persuaded the BIA virtually to stop enforcing stock reduction, so that some Navajos were able to rebuild their ravaged herds. Some also kept working on the railroads and in the crop lands of the West, but many were destitute. To meet this emergency, Congress increased the federal relief appropriation for Navajos tenfold in 1948 and doubled it again 2 years later. In 1949, the states of New Mexico and Arizona agreed to administer the Indian case load (Young 1961:292–301).

During that same year, administration of the livestock permits in some parts of the Eastern jurisdiction, including the lease townships, shifted from the stringent Bureau of Land Management, as the Grazing Service had become in 1946, to the more lenient BIA (Plummer 1966). Apparently at this time, or shortly thereafter, the BIA entirely dispensed with permits in the lease townships. According to range-management officials, the BIA allowed chapters in which almost all the land was allotted or privately owned to vote on whether to abolish the permit system. Evidently Tsayatoh chapter members voted for the change in the lease townships. This decision did not affect the whole Tsayatoh chapter, for permits are still in effect in the two townships south of the lease townships (USDI, BIA, Eastern Navajo Agency 1978).

In retrospect, the 1930–1950 period reveals an irony. The Great Depression, which called forth the federal mechanisms that could regulate grazing, also probably would have reduced livestock eventually even without an organized program. It would have forced many Navajos, especially the poor, to eat their own breeding stock. The grazing regulation program, by providing jobs through the CCC and SCS, actually may have retarded reduction by giving people cash income; they were then able to buy food instead of slaughtering their own stock, which they could keep for future periods of unemployment. This is not to say, however, that the grazing regulation program was a waste. For all its inequities, it surely reduced Navajo livestock more equitably than the so-called free market would have done in its absence.

Trends in Family Land Use

The Depression and grazing regulation perpetuated, even accelerated, the changes in most aspects of land use that household production for the market had started during the railroad era. Two outstanding mechanisms through which household production for the market changed family land use during the railroad era were (1) the growing amount of labor that market production demanded from the household and (2) the filling and subdivision of the land. Both mechanisms resulted from the household's need to pay its trading-post debts by increasing its volume of production, diversifying production, or both. I suggest that the Depression and grazing regulation increased the labor burden on households still more and failed to deter land subdivision, because most households were still depending heavily on production marketed through the trading posts and therefore remained in debt.

Because wool and livestock prices fell more than did the prices of staple foods during the Depression (see Table 4.1), income from wool and lamb sales dropped, even for households that had not reduced their herds. Most households consequently needed other sources of income, the main ones being the expanded production of crops and handicrafts. Households that had reduced their herds suffered even greater losses of income, as well as losses in their meat supply. The extra labor that farming and handicrafts demanded probably was not matched by reductions in herding labor, because a herd of 50 needs as much daily attention as a herd of 250. Most households that found their herding labor reduced may have been those with little or no stock of their own, whose members had worked for the big owners until stock reduction. These households could enjoy their new-found leisure at the price of starving. The lucky households with wage earners may have relaxed their handicraft production, but probably not their stock raising or farming, because even during World War II most jobs were temporary.

I suggest that, in most parts of the Navajo country, the Depression and grazing regulation in themselves did nothing to stop land subdivision. As long as most households depended at least partly on livestock production, people had to keep dividing the land into more and more customary use areas. The process was to stop only when most households could either depend mainly on wage work, alone or combined with relief, or band together in stock-raising cooperatives. During the 1930s the government tried but failed to provide dependable wage work for most adults, and the high employment during World War II did not last. Collier supported the idea of cooperatives, but

neither the government nor the Navajos themselves organized any, at least for livestock raising. The traders opposed cooperatives of any kind, because producers' cooperatives would have bypassed them in marketing, and because consumers' cooperatives would have weaned Navajo families from trading-post credit. The traders therefore exerted their waning, but still strong, influence with the government to forestall any possible development of cooperatives (Parman 1976:67).

In the next four chapters I try to show that, by perpetuating the two railroad-era mechanisms that drove changes in land use—the growing labor burden on the household and range subdivision—the Depression and grazing regulation also perpetuated, or even accelerated, most of the changes in each aspect of land use that had begun during the railroad era. The Depression and grazing regulation did, however, diminish, stop, or even reverse a few railroad-era trends, including the declines in farming and in the consumption of home-produced crops, the growing stratification of households according to livestock wealth, the degradation of the range, and the proliferation of homesites in the marginal uplands.

Stock reduction diminished, but did not eliminate, livestock–wealth stratification, so that family land-use patterns continued to reflect the practices of the large stock owners, including the hiring of herders and the attempts to monopolize range. In the sphere of land tenure, however, both the number of virilocal households and the number of households that used lands of the parents of both spouses declined with the dwindling number of large owners. Stock reduction also minimized but probably did not eliminate overgrazing, so that range carrying capacity probably continued to fall. The Depression and stock reduction did, however, reverse the family's trend of doing less farming and thereby also reversed its tendency to substitute more trading-post food for home-produced crops. Because of this reversal, families considered field locations more than they had before in placing their homesites on the landscape and thus reversed the railroad-era trend at having more homesites in the uplands. These reversals, although only temporary, do distinguish family land use of the grazing-regulation era from what it had been and what it was to become.

Chapter 10

Family Economy
and the Local Environment
during the Era of Grazing Regulation

Family Sources of Livelihood

The Great Depression, grazing regulation, and World War II affected the livelihood of lease-township inhabitants as it did that of other Navajo families. The number of small stock plunged, and people tried to fill the gap with other sources of livelihood. Wage jobs, however, were inaccessible to most residents of the lease townships, so people turned to farming and handicrafts. Land-based production by families thus remained the main form of land use, and the labor that production demanded from the family probably increased.

Although the number of small stock clearly fell in the lease townships, the magnitude of the drop is unclear. Table 10.1 shows a reduction in mature small stock of almost 40% between 1936 and 1941, and this figure is probably fairly accurate. Except for the Human Dependency Survey figure for 1939, which reflects the numbers of stock dipped, figures for 1936 through 1941 are supposed to be the actual numbers of livestock that each family owned. Each document source excludes a few of the families that, according

to interviewees or the other document sources, used the lease townships, although the 1936 source excludes more families than do the sources for any of the following years. The 1936 livestock figure probably is not much farther off than the others, however, because all the missing families were small owners.

On the other hand, the precipitous drop in livestock numbers after 1941 shown on Table 10.1 reflects only the decline in the number of livestock that the government permitted. The actual numbers may have stayed closer to the 1941 figure. The number of permitted small stock fell between 1941 and 1942 because the Grazing Service stopped issuing permits for the number that each applicant requested and evidently used dipping records instead.[1] That the actual

[1]The absence of applications for most 1942 grazing permits suggests that the Grazing Service simply issued permits without applications. Officials singled out permittees for whom no dipping records existed and pointedly issued them permits only for the horses and cattle declared on earlier permit applications. This use of dipping records suggests that the numbers of small stock on the other permits may also have been taken from dipping records.

Table 10.1
Number of Small Stock Owned by Lease-Township Residents, 1936–1946[a]

Year	No. of owners	Total permitted small stock (mature)	Mean small stock per owner	Range of small stock per owner
1936[b]	11	2448	223	46–661
1938	19	3095[c]	163	35–720
1938–1939 winter	19	2413[c]	127	20–620
1939[d]	18[e]	1753	97	0–200
1940	19	2000[c]	105	20–590
1941	19	2101[c]	111	19–490
1942	18	1517	84	0– 482[f]
1943	14	920	66	0–309[f]
1944	19	1484	78	0–448
1945	18	1201	67	0–260
1946–1947	17	1238	73	0–320

[a]From USDI, Grazing Service (1940–1946) unless noted otherwise.

[b]From 1936 livestock registry (USDA, SCS 1936); "number of permittees" is actually the number of heads of households listed.

[c]Declared by permittee on 1940 application; 1941 figure is permitted number, which was the same as the number declared on most permits.

[d]Dipping records from 1939, as reproduced in Human Dependency Survey household schedules (USDA, SCS 1940).

[e]Number of residence groups.

[f]Some permittees had only horses.

numbers of small stock tended to exceed the number dipped is evident from both the recollections of interviewees and archaeological evidence in the form of corral sizes.

After 1942, the number of permitted stock continued to fall. The 1943 permits for most people were even lower than the 1942 permits, because the Grazing Service had finally estimated the carrying capacity of the Tsayatoh chapter area and was now able to peg the permits to carrying capacity (USDI, Grazing Service 1940–1946). In autumn of 1943, the Grazing Service admonished each permittee to sell stock in excess of the permit by the end of the buying season (December 1) or to buy or lease more land. In early December, however, permittees were allowed to apply for war emergency licenses for their excess stock. In 1944 and 1945, the Grazing Service issued similar admonitions about excess stock.

In 1944, the railroad sold most of the odd-numbered sections in the lease townships to a trader and land speculator named Gib Graham. Grazing regulation throughout the West probably encouraged such speculation by pegging the number of livestock on an operator's permit to the amount of land the operator owned or leased. This purchase at first caused further cuts in the permits, but ultimately it contributed to the abolition of permits from the townships. In 1944, Grazing Service officials informed many permittees that their 1945 permits were being cut because of Graham's purchase. Since 1940, if not earlier, the railroad had leased all of its lands in the lease townships to the Indian Service for Navajo use. Because Graham discontinued the Indian Service leases, those sections were to be closed to the permittees, and the permits cut in proportion to the reduction of the corresponding land bases. Grazing Service officials urged some Navajos to buy land from Graham if they wanted to keep their stock. One official even patronizingly advised one man to "go back to work" and save his money until he had enough to buy one section of land. Many local Navajos did contract to buy land from Graham, and their permits were adjusted accordingly (see Chapter 11 for details). Although people who used privately owned range did not need permits, the Grazing Service required those who used a combination of private land and land under federal jurisdiction (the allotments) to hold permits for their entire land-use areas. Because the owners who bought land from Graham also used allotted land, their permits remained in effect.

In 1946, the government extended the permits indefinitely, because it was making the Grazing Service into the Bureau of Land Management. The transfer of grazing permit regulation to the BIA and the subsequent abolition of these permits (described in Chapter 9) occurred 3 years later. Apparently the BIA had decided to treat the allotments as private holdings in the regulation of grazing.

Although the literature on the stock-reduction program tends to emphasize its unfair impact on small stock owners, the evidence available suggests that in the lease townships the relatively large-scale owners bore the brunt. One reason for this pattern is that the evidence postdates 1935, the year when the Indian Service was already imposing its more equitable forced-reduction policies. Smaller owners may have been hit earlier, although interviewees seemed to date the beginning of significant reductions in the lease townships to the forced-reduction period.

Of all the document sources on the period, the 1940 Human Dependency Survey provides the best information on the various household sources of livelihood—especially when the other documents are used to correct the livestock figures (see Appendix A). The group of households in the Human Dependency Survey, however, excludes two that both local Navajos and the grazing-permit records show were the largest stock owners in the lease townships: Whitegoat Curly and Mr. Towering House Clansman. The livestock that these two owners declared on their 1940 permit applications has been added to the numbers in the Human Dependency Survey, based on 1939 dipping records, for a still slightly underestimated total number of livestock in the lease townships in 1940. These figures, inflated to include lambs and kids for comparison with 1915 figures, are shown on Table 10.2.

The results of this comparison are startling. The number of livestock in the lease townships, even after the brunt of stock reduction, exceeded the number in 1915, but the average number per household and per person had not changed. Moreover, as Table 10.3 shows, the number of herdless households in 1939 was lower than it had been in 1915. The actual number of herdless households in 1939, however, perhaps was

Table 10.2
Number of Livestock
Owned by Lease-Township Households, 1939[a]

	Sheep and goats	Cattle
Total no.[b]	4790	71
No. per household	165	3
No. per residence group	228	4

[a]From USDA, SCS (1940); USDI, Grazing Service (1940–1946).
[b]Includes 2875 small stock of households recorded by the Human Dependency Survey and 1915 of households either not recorded by the Survey or recorded but lacking the 1939 dipping record. Young are included in small stock figures.

Table 10.3
Distribution of Sheep and Goats
among Lease-Township Households, 1939[a]

No. of sheep and goats	No. of households	% of all households
0	3	10
1–25	1	3
26–50	5	17
51–75	7	23
76–100	1	3
101–200	4	13
201–300	4	13
301–400	2	7
401–500	—	—
501–600	—	—
600–1100	2	6
Unknown	1	3
	30	100

[a]From USDA, SCS (1940); USDI, Grazing Service (1940–1946). The few herds that sources indicate were shared by households have been divided evenly among those households. Figures include young.

not as low as the table shows. Some of the households enumerated in the Human Dependency Survey consisted of young, collateral relatives of long-term lease-township residents; they may actually have been tending animals that belonged to the large-scale owners—especially Whitegoat Curly and Mr. Towering House Clansman.

Although the average number of livestock per lease-township household in 1940 was well above the subsistence minimum of 100, as it had also been in 1915, more than half of all households owned fewer than 100 small stock, including lambs and kids. Of the 17 poor households, 7 were parts of multiple-household residence groups, only 3 of which, however, owned in aggregate enough small stock to average 100 per household. Just as in 1915, therefore, almost half of the households in the lease townships lacked access to enough small stock for their own support. Cattle did not fill the gap, for only 5 households owned cattle, and most of these also owned more than 100 small stock. The number of cattle had changed little since 1915 (see Table 10.2).

If neither the average number of small stock per household nor the distribution of small stock among households had changed much in the lease townships since 1915, one may wonder what all the fuss over stock reduction was about. First, the number of large stock owners, the sizes of the largest herds, and the total number of livestock in the lease townships grew after 1915, probably peaking around 1930. These large owners subsequently bore the brunt of reduction. Second, wool prices, in particular, had been higher in relation to the prices of staple consumer goods from 1910 to the 1920s than they were during the 1930s (see Table 4.1); for example a pound of wool bought only three-quarters to four-fifths as much flour in 1930 as it did in 1910 and during the 1920s. By 1940, wool and lamb prices were rising faster than those of consumer goods and remained relatively high through most of the decade, but by that time the Grazing Service was demanding further reductions. Third, the parents of 1915 could look forward to giving their children the increase from their own flocks, whereas the parents of 1940 could only expect to divide herds of fixed sizes among their children. I also emphasize that stock reduction did not necessarily affect the lease townships in the same ways as it affected other parts of the Navajo country, where small owners were hurt both before and after forced reduction began. The lease townships had exceedingly high proportions of herdless households and very small owners as early as 1915, and in a sense had already undergone, more gradually, the trauma that stock reduction inflicted on more remote parts of the Navajo country.

In contrast to livestock, access to cornfields was rather evenly distributed in 1940 and had changed dramatically since 1915. The Human Dependency Survey shows that at least 26 of the 30 households had access to a field. The acreage per family, according to grazing permits, ranged from 4 to 40 acres.

Although data are available for only seven permittees, it is worth noting that four of the seven owned less than 100 small stock, and that one of these small owners, the local delegate to the tribal council, John Dixon, cultivated the largest number of acres (40)—almost half the total acreage. John Dixon was the only person to sell his produce; the rest consumed their entire crop. This widespread dependence on farming contrasts sharply with dependence in 1915, when half of all households lacked access to a field and the largest stock owners cultivated the most acreage.

The most likely reason for the increase in farming is the drop in wool and livestock prices relative to those of consumer goods; when people were only able to buy three-quarters of the flour they had previously bought with their wool clip, they probably tried to grow corn and other vegetables to make up the difference. That the number of fields in the lease townships increased after about 1934, as I show in Chapter 12, also suggests that the Depression encouraged more farming.

At least one third of all adult lease-township residents in 1940 also turned to non–land-based production for their livelihood (see Table 10.4). Most of these producers were self-employed weavers, and all but one of the rest were men who worked as silversmiths for Gallup traders. These silversmiths probably outnumbered those of the railroad era, for the earliest local smiths whom local Navajos mentioned were those of the 1930s. Some Navajo smiths did actually work in shops maintained by traders. Navajos from the lease townships, however, often worked for more than one trader and were probably subject to the *putting-out* system common at the time: They received the tools, silver, and settings on credit, made the pieces at home, and were paid for the finished pieces less the cost of the tools and raw materials. Often the payment itself was simply credit with which the smith could buy general merchandise from traders, or part credit and part cash, but it was seldom entirely cash (Adair 1944:203). The Human Dependency Survey records no other forms of self-employment. Fred Tinhouse, however, did blacksmithing and cut hay for people in the surrounding region, while Tom Sharp and his in-laws, the Damons, bartered trade goods from Gallup stores for livestock throughout a large part of the reservation.

The Human Dependency Survey recorded only one true wage worker: a man who earned $50–$80 a month

Table 10.4
Employment in the Lease Townships, 1940[a]

	No. of workers	% of all workers
Total employed	22	100
men	6	27
women	16	73
Self-employed craftworkers	16	73
silversmithing	—	—
weaving (all women)	16	73
Employed by others	6	27
mines (man)	1	4
Gallup businesses[b] (all men)	5	23
Number of adults 18 and older	66	100
employed adults	22	33

[a]From USDA, SCS (1940).
[b]All employees worked as silversmiths for Gallup traders.

as a miner at the old Fort Defiance coal mine. The Indian Service may have employed as many as 50 miners there, but most were Navajos who lived nearer to the mine. The Ganado Mission and St. Michaels Mission mines continued to operate and contract with Navajo haulers, but they apparently did not employ lease-township residents. Owing to the unpaved roads and rarity of motor vehicles, Window Rock, the new Navajo capital, was too far for most lease-township residents to hold government jobs there. At least one lease-township resident, Fred Tinhouse, however, had worked as a stonemason in building Window Rock 4 years earlier. By 1940 the CCC and SCS had also fallen by the wayside.

One might expect higher proportions of wage or craft workers among households with small herds than among those with large herds. Table 10.5, however, shows that households with herds both above and below the subsistence minimum included such workers in about the same proportions. The households with larger herds were simply better off, because they derived more income from wool and livestock sales to add to their wage and craft income (and because they had more meat to eat).

Finally, even though more adults worked in livestock production than in wage and craft work, the latter two sources yielded a much larger share of money income for all households, excluding those of the two largest stock owners, for whom income data

are not available (see Table 10.6). An estimate of the income that these two households derived from wool and lamb sales (assuming they sold half of their lambs), however, would inflate the total income for all households about a third again, raise the proportion contributed by wool and livestock to slightly over half, and reduce the share of wages and crafts to slightly under half.

The average lease-township resident was poorer than Navajos in general and those in the Black Creek Valley in particular. In the lease townships, the $62 average annual income per person (excluding the value of livestock and crops produced and consumed at home) was only about two thirds the average for the entire Navajo country. It was less than one third of that in the Black Creek Valley (Land Management Unit 18), where wages alone contributed $135 per person (USDA, SCS 1939:Table III). The difference is probably due to the high ratio of craft workers to wage workers in the lease townships, because handicraft production, especially weaving, paid less than did wage work (Indian Rights Association 1944:6).

Consumption Patterns

Together with archaeological data, the Human Dependency Survey shows that people continued to use the mixture of mass-produced and home-produced

Table 10.5

Household Livestock Holdings
and Income by Source in the Lease Townships, 1940[a]

	No. of sheep and goats		
Source of most income	100 or less	More than 100	Unknown
Wage work[b]	4	2	0
Weaving	5–6[c]	3–4[c]	1
Livestock and wool sales	1–2[c]	3–4[c]	0
No income	2	0	0
Unknown	4	1	0
	17	10	1

[a]From USDA, SCS (1940).
[b]Includes silversmiths.
[c]One household had half weaving sales and half livestock and wool sales.

Table 10.6

Money Income by Source for Lease-Township Households, 1940[a]

	Source					
	Any[b]	Wages	Weaving	Livestock sales	Wool sales[c]	Other
No. of households with income from source	22	6	16	12	21	1[d]
No. of households without income from source	2	18	8	12	3	23
No. of households with unknown income sources	4	4	4	4	4	4
Aggregate income	$7885	$4164	$630	$1043	$1928	$120
Income per person	$62[e]	33	5	8	15	1
Income per household	$328[e]	173	26	43	80	5
% of aggregate income	100	53	8	13	24	2

[a]From USDA, SCS (1940). Excludes two largest stock owners.
[b]Figures given are less than the sum of households with income from each source listed because most households derived income from more than one source.
[c]Figures not given in Human Dependency Survey; estimated from number of mature sheep and goats, assuming an average fleece weight of 5 lb. and 1940 reservation average price of 22[c] per lb.
[d]Corn sales.
[e]Omits four households with unknown income, totalling 17 people.

foods and other items that had characterized the railroad era. They may, however, have consumed more of their own crops than before.

People also continued to lean heavily on trading-post credit. Table 10.7 shows where each household traded. If the households spent equal shares of income at every place they either owed money to or said that they traded with, Gallup stores should have made about half of all store sales to lease-township residents. Even without good roads or motor vehicles, people were shopping in town, with its greater range of goods and lower prices. People also traded in a variety of stores around the edge of the lease townships and at the one store in the lease townships, the Divide Trading

Table 10.7
Household Trade and Debt in the Lease Townships, 1940[a]

Household	Total debt ($)	Where owed	Where traded	Total income ($)	Debt per income (%)
343	50.00	local	Gallup	780	6
347	4.25	Gallup	local, Gallup	205	2
348	—	—	Gallup	15	—
349	3.60	Gallup	Gallup, local	80	5
354	0.75	Gallup	local	—	—
355	—	—	Gallup	52	—
356	45.00	Gallup	Gallup	775	6
357	—	—	local	20	—
359	—	—	Gallup	60	—
360	—	—	Gallup	60	—
361	60.00	local	local	184	—
362	?	?	Gallup	?	?
363	—	—	Gallup	20	—
367	?	local	Gallup	624	?
364	—	—	Gallup	20	—
365	—	—	Unknown	—	—
366	?	?	local	?	?
368	5.00	local	local	100	5
370	?	?	local	?	?
372	36.00	local	Gallup, local	1779	2
375	—	—	Gallup	24	—
374	23.00	local	local	20	115
377	?	?	local, Gallup	?	?
379	—	—	Gallup	20	—
378	?	local	Gallup	650	?
381	50.00	local	no special place	35	143
384	20.00	local	Gallup	384	5
389	—	—	Gallup	50	—
	297.60			5957	5

[a]From USDA, SCS (1940).

Post. Some later traded at a second store in the lease townships, Wildcat Trading Post, which the land speculator Gib Graham built in November of 1945 and which probably absorbed the clientele of the defunct Rock Springs store (Kennedy 1965). Whether families traded in town or locally, however, the recollections of local Navajos show that they continued the railroad-era practice of buying consumer goods on credit and paying their accounts seasonally with land-based products: wool and, sometimes, lambs. Between these major seasonal trading periods, most paid for goods with rugs.

Of the 24 households on which the Human Dependency Survey gives trade information, half owed various amounts of money, all to trading posts (see Table 10.7). For most, the debt ranged between 2 and 6% of total money income. The remaining households owed between 33 and 143%. Total aggregate debt was only 6% of total aggregate income. The level of indebtedness is surprisingly low, especially because wool payments are missing from income estimates, and the time of the survey (early May) suggests that people had not yet traded their wool. Whether the traders or the families themselves supplied the information on indebtedness to the Human Dependency Survey interviewer, both groups may have wanted to understate the amounts of indebtedness: Most households probably owed more money than the survey shows.

The Human Dependency Survey does not tell what people bought at the trading posts but does suggest that people produced most of their own meat and a large share of their own vegetables. With the likely

Table 10.8
Consumption of Livestock in the Lease Townships, 1940[a]

No. consumed per person per year	No. of sheep and goats in herd		
	100 or less	More than 100	Unknown
Less than 1.5 animals	7	2	1
1.5 or more	5	7	0
Unknown	5	1	0

[a]From USDA, SCS (1940).

Table 10.9
Faunal Remains from
Excavated Sites of the Era of
Grazing Regulation on the South McKinley Mine Lease

Taxon	No. of elements	MNI
Sheep and goat[a]	144	32
Horse	7	2
Cow	3	3

[a]Includes unidentified Artiodactyla.

exceptions of the wealthy Whitegoat Curly and Mr. Towering House Clansman, lease-township households sold comparatively few sheep, evidently preferring to slaughter them for themselves. Of the 24 households on which the Human Dependency Survey gives income data, over half (13) sold no livestock at all, and those that did sold in aggregate only 27% of their lambs. Indeed, excluding the lambs of Tom Sharp (which evidently included lambs he bought from others on the reservation), the number sold was only 18% of the lamb crop. Yet, if they did not consume any of their own animals, these households could have sold three-quarters of their lambs, assuming the commercial rule of thumb that only a quarter of the lamb crop (half the females) is needed for replacement.

Each household with sheep slaughtered between 4 and 13 animals per year and averaged about 9. All lease-township households together therefore slaughtered only about 250, or less than a quarter of the lamb crop (and not all animals slaughtered were lambs). People must have been holding the uncounted half of the lamb crop for ceremonies, exchanges with other Navajos, and additional replacement.

As one would expect, livestock-poor households probably slaughtered fewer of their own animals than did wealthier households (see Table 10.8). The animals most likely to have been slaughtered, according to one interviewee, were old animals and lambs too puny to make sale weight. Archaeological evidence tends to support this statement.[2] According to interviewees, the herd also yielded another source of food, milk, which people commonly mixed with blue cornmeal to make gruel for breakfast.

Other animals that interviewees mentioned eating are rabbits (in summer as well as in winter, despite the risk of both tularemia and bubonic plague), horses (mainly in winter), cows, and chickens. Archaeological evidence is confined to sheep and goats, with a few horses and cows; no small domesticated or any wild forms are represented (see Table 10.9). Remains of wild forms, even small ones, have been found on sites used before 1930, even though the earlier remains have had more time to decay. This difference therefore suggests that lease-township residents ate less wild game during the era of grazing regulation. Perhaps the wild game had diminished as year-round grazing in the lease-townships became common late in the railroad era and during the Great Depression.

Available sources, then, indicate that lease-township residents produced almost all of their own meat. They do not show, however, the proportion of the diet that home-produced crops supplied. Because most families had access to fields, crop production was clearly significant. That crops were much less dependable than livestock is also clear: About half of the families with fields recorded in the Human Dependency Survey, and

[2]On sites that postdate 1930 and from which faunal collections were made, the minimum numbers of sheep and goats represented in various age categories were 8 immature/young, 5 near-adult, 16 adult (including elements of unknown age), and 3 old. Because one could only distinguish elements of younger adults from those of old animals on the basis of tooth wear, any adult elements that were not mandibles, maxillae, or individual teeth could have been from old individuals.

all but one of the permittees who reported fields on their original 1940 permit applications, said that their crops had failed in the drought of 1939. Botanical samples from three homesteads (Toll and Donaldson 1982:772–776) and the recollections of interviewees show that lease-township residents grew and ate not only corn, beans, and squash, but also watermelons, cucumbers, and other garden crops. People dried and stored for the winter not only the corn and beans, but also the squash. They were even able to keep watermelons through December.

Local Navajos also recalled a few wild plants that people gathered for food: pigweed (*Amaranthus*), purslane (*Portulaca*), wild potato (*Solanum*), ground-cherry (*Physalis*), and tansy mustard (*Descurainia*). Archaeological evidence that these plants may have been eaten—burned seeds in hearths or ash dumps—indicates only purslane and pigweed but also adds goosefoot (*Chenopodium*) to the list. All but the tansy mustard grow in cornfields and therefore would have been easier to gather than other wild plants (Knight 1982:676–683; Toll and Donaldson 1982:722–728, 772–779). The lack of archaeological evidence of most of these plants suggests that people ate them as greens in spring, before the plants produced seeds (Knight 1982:676–683). (The seeds in the archaeological samples may have come in by accident with corn.) That people favored wild plants from cornfields may explain why sites of the railroad era exhibited almost no evidence that wild plants were eaten. People farmed less in the lease townships, and fewer people lived there in the late spring and summer, when they would have gathered such plants. The one railroad-era site on which burned seeds were recorded had an associated cornfield, and the seeds were from the goosefoot plant (Toll and Donaldson 1982:770–771, 774, 778–779).

Nevertheless, lease-township residents also bought much food from the trading posts. The food that Fred and Mary Tinhouse bought for themselves and their six children during the late 1930s was supposed to last about 4 months (supplemented by small purchases in exchange for rugs). It consisted of four 100-lb. sacks of flour for bread; one 50-lb. sack of potatoes; salt pork to cook with beans that they grew in their field; and jelly, salt, sugar, baking powder, and lard. The Tinhouses had a herd of 145 animals and a cornfield where they grew all the vegetables listed above; their purchases are probably typical of lease-township families.

Inventories of artifacts found on archaeological sites show the less important items on this food list, because those items came in jars or cans; the more important items, such as the staple flour or potatoes, are not shown, because they came in sacks (see Table 10.10).

Table 10.10
Functional Types of Artifacts
on Sites on the South McKinley Mine Lease, 1930–1950

	N	%
Total no. of components[a]	18	100
No. of components without artifacts	5	28
Artifacts of production		
lamp nipples	—	—
sheep rattles	1	6
salt troughs	1	6
arms/ammunition	2	11
agricultural implements	1	6
silversmithing anvil	1	6
Food		
baking powder can	5	28
vegetable/fruit can/jar	4	22
milk can/bottle	2	11
lard can	4	22
meat can	3	17
jelly can/jar	—	—
syrup can/jar	—	—
Indulgences		
coffee/tea	3	17
pop	6	33
liquor	3	17
tobacco	2	11
Domestic small technology		
dishes	8	44
pots/pans	5	28
utensils	1	6
mano and metate	5	28
wash tubs/basins	3	17
pails	5	28
Household equipment and furniture		
kerosene lantern	1	6
other light	2	11
stove and parts	6	33
water barrel	2	11
furniture	3	17
House construction and maintenance		
locks/chains/hinges	1	6
ax/shovel/large tools	5	28
boards	9	50
tar paper	2	11

(*continued*)

Table 10.10 (*continued*)
Functional Types of Artifacts
on Sites on the South McKinley Mine Lease, 1930–1950

	N	%
Personal effects		
patent medicine/cosmetics	11	61
clothing/buttons/buckles	1	6
shoes	4	22
Entertainment		
toys	7	39
musical instruments	—	—
Transportation		
wagon parts/supplies	4	22
auto parts/supplies	9	50
horse gear	2	11

[a]Includes all sites identified by interviewees on which systematic observations of artifacts were made.

Table 10.10 lists the wide range of other mass-produced items evident on homesites of the period. This inventory resembles closely that of homesites of the 1910–1930 period except in a few respects (compare Tables 10.10 and 10.11 with Tables 5.4 and 5.3, respectively). These differences, like those between the pre-1910 and post-1910 sites, probably reflect the settling down of the later households. In the 1930–1950 sample, homesteads outnumber sheep camps about two to one, whereas the ratio is reversed in the 1910–1930 sample. Lease-township families, moreover, used their sheep camps for more years during the era of grazing regulation than during the railroad era, although for some reason they did not also use their homesteads for more years.[3] Other possible explanations exist for the increase in "consumer durables" after 1930 and are discussed in Chapter 13.

The Environment

The resources that lease-township households needed for production and domestic maintenance in the era of grazing regulation were the same as those of

[3]Eight grazing-regulation-era sheep camps averaged 13 years, as compared to the 8-year average of the railroad era; 30 homesteads averaged 10 years, as compared to 9 years during the railroad era.

Table 10.11
Artifacts on Grazing-Regulation-Era Homesites on the South McKinley Mine Lease[a]

Site number	Dates[b]	Native historic ceramics	Mass-produced Household items[c]	Food Glass	Food Cans	Auto parts	Building materials[d] Lumber	Building materials[d] Other
59[a]	1930–1935	—	x	x	x	x	x	—
212	1931–1963	—	x	x	x	x	x	—
115	1934–1940	—	x	x	x	x	—	—
81[b]	1935–1940	—	x	x	x	x	x	—
202	1935–1941	—	x	—	—	—	—	—
122	1935–1945	—	—	x	x	—	—	—
7	1935–1960	—	x	x	x	x	x	x
1	1935–1974	—	x	x	x	x	x	x
59[b]	1936–1941	—	x	x	x	x	x	—
182	1936–1945	—	x	x	x	x	x	—
24–25	ca. 1940–1960	—	x	x	x	—	x	—
201	1945–1950	—	x	x	x	x	x	x

[a]All sites listed are dwelling components on the lease that were positively identified by interviewees and on which the presence or absence of artifacts was sytematically recorded.
[b]Based on both interviewees' statements and archaeological data.
[c]Small housewares.
[d]Excludes nails.

Table 10.12
Actual 1940 Stocking and Estimated 1941 Carrying Capacities of Subdivisions of the Lease Townships

Small stock per mi.^{2}	Tse Bonita Wash–upper Defiance Draw	Middle Defiance Draw	Eastern Flat–lower Defiance Draw
Actual number of SUYL, 1940^a	74	80	63–100^b
Adjusted 1941 carrying capacity, SUYL^c	54	75	75

^{a}SUYL = Mature sheep units year long; adjusted to include lambs and kids (see Table 5.8).
^{b}Lower figure assumes 6-month use for largest owner; higher figure assumes year-round use.
^{c}Adjusted to include lambs and kids (as on Table 5.8) but not doubled to give 6-month equivalents.

the railroad era, but the natural environment had changed. Because of the population and livestock increases of the railroad era, especially outside the lease townships, a growing number of families lived and kept their stock in the townships all year. These families were able to withstand the dry summers by building reservoirs. Therefore, not only did the number of livestock in the townships increase, but more livestock stayed on the range for the entire year, and it became overgrazed. Overgrazing continued even after stock reduction, because the number of livestock that remained in the lease townships still exceeded the carrying capacity.

The best range in the lease townships remained the sage flats of the middle Defiance Draw and Eastern Flat–lower Defiance Draw. Actual 1940 stocking does not seem to reflect the differences in range quality among the three divisions of the townships as closely as did actual stocking in 1915, and 1940 stocking probably exceeded carrying capacity in all three divisions (see Table 10.12). Of the three divisions, the Tse Bonita Wash–upper Defiance Draw was the most grievously overstocked. Even after the peak of stock reduction, then, the lease townships remained overstocked. The reason is not hard to find: The employment figures show that wage work was not able to replace livestock as a source of income. Most households, which had

less than the critical minimum of 100 sheep, would not have voluntarily parted with any more of their sheep.

Conclusion

In the lease townships, then, grazing regulation did little to change the families' dependence on livestock production for trading-post credit or its consequence, overgrazing. Those forced to sell livestock evidently were mostly the large stockowners, perhaps because so many others had little left to give up. Even if the small owners gave up little or no stock, however, they, together with the large owners, received less from the traders in exchange for their wool and livestock as the Depression brought prices of these commodities down faster than the prices of consumer goods. To make ends meet under adversity, as they had done during the railroad era, people turned to more craft production, notably silversmithing. Finally, when even craft production did not fill the gap between their needs and their livestock income, they planted more crops. The brunt of stock reduction was then to fall on the next generation, which could only divide their parents' herds, never to be allowed any increase.

Chapter 11

Family Demography and Land Tenure during the Era of Grazing Regulation

Family Demography

Because most lease-township households continued to depend on livestock and handicraft production, the family remained the basic production unit, and dispersed residence remained necessary. Production and domestic maintenance chores changed little, except possibly to increase. Therefore, the demographic characteristics of lease-township households and residence groups in 1910–1915 endured through 1940.

The 1940 households were of essentially the same size and age–sex composition as the 1910–1915 group, and (reconstructed) residence groups also remained about the same size (see Table 11.1). Two thirds of all residence groups continued to consist of only one household, and plural-household residence groups usually had two households whose heads were of an older and a younger generation. As before, old people and young adults presumably stayed together to help each other with production and domestic chores. The low sex ratio, like that of 1915, suggests that some men were away working (or looking for work).

Astonishingly, population did not grow very much in the lease townships (only 11%) between 1910–1915 and 1940. Yet the prodigious growth rate of the

Table 11.1
Demographic Characteristics of
Lease-Township Households and Residence Groups, 1940[a]

Total population	157
No. of households	30
No. of residence groups	21
No. of single-household residence groups	14
Population per household	5.2
Population per residence group	7.5
Households per residence group	1.4
Mean age per resident	20.1
% of population under age 18	54
Ratio of males to females	90:100

[a]From USDA, SCS (1940); USDI, BIA (1940); figures include two households not enumerated by the Human Dependency Survey but indentified by local Navajos.

Navajo population as a whole is almost a demographer's cliché. The net natural increase rate for the entire Navajo population was about 2.6% per year in 1954 (Young 1961:88), and lease-township women continued to bear as many children as had their predecessors. The eight women over age 40 in the Human Dependency Survey for whom I know the total number of children averaged seven apiece. The lease townships thus were not the island of demographic stability that the low historical rate of population increase might suggest.

The reason for the seemingly low population growth in the lease townships is as follows. In 1910–1915, residents used the lease townships mainly in winter, and their summer area was probably of an equal size. In 1940, however, most people stayed in the townships all year, while other members of the same families stayed all year in the former summer range. In the combined summer and winter ranges occupied by the 1915 residents of the lease townships, the population probably had almost doubled.

Land Tenure

The character of traditional land tenure in the lease townships did not change dramatically between 1910–1915 and 1940. Heads of households still held land through original claim or kinship (usually descent). These sources of traditional tenure persisted partly because the family remained the basic unit of production, and its land needs persisted. In addition, most land in the townships before 1940 remained unavailable for either local families or outsiders to buy, because it was protected by new forms of legal tenure. The IRA protected the allotments by indefinitely extending their 25-year inalienable status. The Indian Service, furthermore, protected Navajo use of most railroad lands by leasing those lands. During the mid-1930s, two traders each bought a section in the Tse Bonita drainage, but only one seems to have closed his section to Navajos. These purchases, however, may have prompted Whitegoat Curly to secure his hold on his winter range in the Defiance Draw by leasing a railroad section there (USDI, BIA, Eastern Navajo Agency n.d.b).

Legal forms preserved traditional forms of land tenure until 1940, but the protective system started to fall apart when the government issued grazing permits. The permits barred from future use anyone who had not kept stock in the lease townships since 1938, including many people with residual rights there. Five years later, moreover, when Gib Graham bought the railroad lands and the Indian Service lost its leases, many families were forced to validate their traditional rights by buying the land. Grazing Service authorities

told local Navajos either to buy the land they had been using or to have their herds reduced. Five local Navajos with four distinct customary use areas therefore made agreements to buy a total of 14½ sections from Graham, at least according to the grazing-permit records. None of the plat books, however, records these lands in the names of any of these men except Whitegoat Curly; perhaps for some reason the titles were never transferred. Around 1950, Graham fled to Mexico to avoid federal prosecution, reportedly on several charges related to his trading-post practices. The owners of almost all sections recorded after Graham are Gallup-area traders and land speculators.

In the realm of traditional tenure, slight shifts away from tenure by original claim toward matrilocal residence, and away from residence in the lands of families of both spouses, also characterize the era of grazing regulation. These changes probably resulted from the filling of the range and from stock reduction. A comparison of Table 11.2 with Table 6.2 shows that, not surprisingly, the number of sites that people held through original claim diminished, whereas those that people held through descent increased. As in 1915, the sites on land claimed through descent were about evenly divided between those on lands of the husband's family and those on land of the wife's family. Nevertheless, a tendency toward matrilineal inheritance is evident. Use rights to 60% of the sites descended through the mother of one spouse or the other, whereas use rights for only 18% of the cases descended through a father (the rest descended directly from original claimants, who I consider to have transmitted the use rights jointly).

Postmarital residence choices in 1940 also resemble those of 1915 (see Table 11.3). All of the junior-generation households in plural-household residence groups were uxorilocal, whereas senior-generation and solitary households tilted slightly toward virilocality, as they had in 1915. Uxorilocality thus was more prevalent among the junior households than among the others, also as in 1915. Uxorilocality was probably more pronounced among the junior households than among the others because the young wives were still learning housekeeping as sort of "apprentices" to their mothers. When these junior households later moved to homesites of their own, some would move to land

Table 11.2
Land Tenure in the Lease Townships, 1940[a]

Source of use rights	Number of sites			
	Homesite	Campsite or isolated corral	Water source	Field
Original claim	1	—	2	1
Descent	20	4	21	14
Other	3	1	3	2

[a]If a site was used by more than one household, only the rights of the senior-generation household are counted.

Table 11.3
Residence Rights of Households to Main Homesites in the Lease Townships, 1940

Source of residence rights	Junior-generation households	Senior-generation households	Solitary households	Total
Wife's mother	6	1	5	12
Wife's father	2	—	2	4
Wife's parents	1	1	1	3
Wife's family	—	1[a]	—	1
subtotal	9	3	8	20
Husband's mother	—	2	5	7
Husband's father	—	—	—	—
Husband's parents	—	1	—	1
Husband's family	—	—	—	—
subtotal	—	3	5	8
Other	1[b]	—	1[c]	2
	10	6	14	30

[a]Wife's sister and brother-in-law.
[b]Original claim.
[c]Unknown.

of the husband's family (usually of the husband's mother).

True matrilocal residence also prevailed among both groups of households: Almost two thirds of the households were matrilocal. In 1915, the number of matrilocal households was second to the number of households of original claimants plus those of the children of original claimants. The passage of time and the filling of the range made original claimants rare by 1940, however, and matrilocal households therefore became the most common type of households by default. Also worth noting is that, although virilocal residence predominated slightly among the older-generation households of 1915, patrilocal residence was uncommon among their children. This pattern indicates that the children of virilocal couples ordinarily did not stay on the land of their fathers—another testament to the operation of the matrilineal principle in the transmittal of land-use rights.

Between 1915 and 1940, dual residence seems to have diminished. Probably 5 or 6 of the 30 households of 1940 maintained homesites on the lands of the families of both spouses, compared to a somewhat higher proportion (at least 6 out of 25 households) in 1915. As in 1915, the 1940 households with dual residence tended to own more small stock than average or to be the children of the large stock owners of 1915. Only 2 of these households had their main homesites in the lease townships on the husband's land. These 2, and 3 more of the 8 lease-township households classified as virilocal, were among the largest stock owners or the children of the largest stock owners in 1915. Dual residence, virilocality, and livestock wealth therefore continued to be associated in 1940. Probably, fewer households maintained dual or virilocal residence because, after stock reduction, fewer needed the extra land that these residence choices gave them.

Outfits likewise existed in 1940, as they had in 1915. The 1940 outfits were perhaps less obvious, however, because their members may have lacked the extensively overlapping or interlinked customary use areas of the 1915 outfits. The main reason for this change is probably the same as the reason that virilocality and dual residence diminished: the reduction of the largest herds. What remained after the reduction were groups of households using, in severalty, contiguous lands that corresponded roughly to the original claims.

As the land-tenure histories in the following sections show, these groups of households seem to have functioned as outfits even if the customary use areas of their members did not extensively interlock. People seem not to have formalized the boundaries between most customary use areas. Collateral relatives, moreover, seem to have shared, or even transferred among one another, customary use areas or parts thereof. This sharing can also explain why, of all adult lease-township residents identified by local Navajos or any 1936 or 1940 document, one third were not mentioned by local Navajos. These unnamed households tended to be only distantly related to the direct descendants of the original claimants and descendants of the siblings with whom some original claimants shared their claims. Many were nonresident users who must have pooled their herds with those of their resident relatives. Others may have lived in the lease townships, but probably only expediently and for short periods, perhaps while herding sheep that actually belonged to wealthy relatives trying to evade reduction. The data in the next three sections suggest that long-term residual use rights tended to accrue to the matrilineal descendants of the original claimants and of any siblings with whom the latter shared their claims.

The members of these outfits may have shared residual rights to range, but all did not share herds, cornfields, or water sources any more than all shared an undivided range. These resources usually were shared among only a few of the households in each outfit. Small groups of households in two neighboring outfits sometimes shared water and, less often, fields. I discuss the sharing of these resources in more detail in Chapter 12.

Land Tenure in the
Tse Bonita Wash–Upper Defiance Draw

Around 1935, when Cornmerchant died, Whitegoat Curly began to monopolize most of his late father-in-law's range. The families of Fat Salt, Chopped Hair, Tall Red Streak Clansman, and Chee Jim, however, also occupied small parts of the tract (see Figure 11.1). Except for the family of Fat Salt, Cornmerchant's brother, all of these families seem to have moved in when Cornmerchant died. Chopped Hair and Tall Red Streak Clansman were Fat Salt's in-laws (Tall Red Streak Clansman was also married to a matrilateral relative of Whitegoat Curly), and Chee Jim was probably Tall Red Streak Clansman's sister's son. Several other young couples identified with the tract by various documents from the 1940s, but not mentioned by local Navajos, were matrilateral relatives of Whitegoat Curly and Tall Red Streak Clansman or his wife. They may have herded the several hundred sheep that Whitegoat Curly and Tall Red Streak Clansman each owned, possibly to remove the sheep from the threat of reduction on the reservation.

The five men named above and their households, each in a separate residence group, together with the various younger households constituted an outfit, which Whitegoat Curly dominated. In summer, Whitegoat Curly, Tall Red Streak Clansman, and Chopped Hair herded in the part of the Black Creek Valley that adjoins the lease townships east of Black Creek—land that may still have belonged to another outfit or outfits. In winter, Whitegoat Curly moved to Cornmerchant's former range on the ridge south of Tse Bonita Wash and in the Defiance Draw, a small part of which he shared late in the season with Tall Red Streak Clansman and Chee Jim (see Figure 11.1).

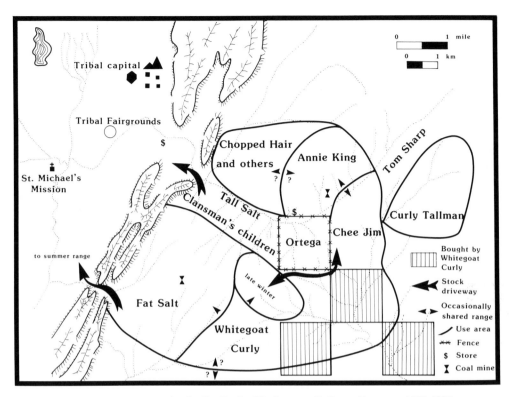

Figure 11.1 Land tenure in the Tse Bonita Wash–upper Defiance Draw, ca. 1937–1945.

Until 1945, Whitegoat Curly leased from the railroad the section where his Defiance Draw sheep camp was. Then he agreed to buy from Gib Graham this section and four others in the winter range, three of which he actually bought and then probably barred once and for all from others in his outfit. Fat Salt, meanwhile, ran his much smaller herd in the lease townships all year on a tract that overlapped Whitegoat Curly's range. Chopped Hair sometimes shared this area and perhaps also used adjoining land north of the Tse Bonita Wash in the He Walks Around clan claim where his mother lived. Whitegoat Curly's outfit and the interlinked herding patterns of its members seem to have persisted until Whitegoat Curly died in 1951.

Meanwhile, sons of Tall Salt Clansman and their wives, the daughters of Little Warrior, retained their hold on the sage flats south of the Tse Bonita Wash, into which Cornmerchant and Charley Boyd had squeezed them during the railroad era (see Figure 11.1). They shared one winter sheep camp on the tract,

which was now merely an extension of their customary use area in the Black Creek Valley (and perhaps annexed to the land base of the outfit to which they belonged there). Perhaps they started spending more of the winter in the lease townships when the Indian Service took some of their Black Creek Valley land for the new Navajo capital. One of Tall Salt Clansman's sons, Tall Mexican Clansman, had thumbprinted the agreement on behalf of his in-laws, reportedly in exchange for a farm wagon (with or without horses) and several cords of wood. At the time, this man may have been working for the George Damon family, which also claimed the land on which the new compound was built (*Navajo Times*, January 26, 1983, p.1; Gallup *Independent*, January 18, 1983, p.1).

To the north, meanwhile, the part of the He Walks Around clan claim between the Tse Bonita Wash and the reservation line had become the province of an outfit dominated by Charley Boyd, who had taken over the east end of Tall Salt Clansman's claim around World War I. Charley Boyd's wife belonged to the He Walks Around clan, and the households of the couple's daughters and daughters' daughters completed the outfit. After Charley Boyd died in 1934, his widow evidently gave her stock to two of her daughters. The outfit then consisted of three or four residence groups, each with its own set of homesites and herd: the households of the widow, her daughter Sadie, Sadie's daughter Annie King, and one of Annie King's daughters, in one or two residence groups; the household of another daughter of Annie King in a separate residence group; and the household of the widow's other daughter and stepson in another residence group. This second daughter was the wife of Chee Jim, who used the land that Charley Boyd had taken from Tall Salt Clansman's daughter most of the year but joined Whitegoat Curly's outfit in late winter. Two other households related to Charley Boyd's widow might also have used the area briefly, although they owned few or no stock and perhaps herded for Chee Jim.

In December of 1937, Lotario Ortega, owner of the nearby Divide Trading Post, which stood at the east end of this outfit's land, bought a railroad section where Annie King was living south of Tse Bonita Wash (see Figure 11.1). He evicted Annie King and fenced the section so that none of the Navajos could use it. Chee Jim was forced to skirt this tract when he moved into the winter range that he shared with Tall Red Streak Clansman. Indeed, he may have started to use the latter's range only after Ortega fenced him out. The herds dwindled with this loss of land and with stock reduction, but the outfit retained the remaining land until Chee Jim died in 1946.

Apparently Chee Jim's widow could not then resist the incursions of others who wanted to graze her late husband's customary use area. One was her half-brother, Chopped Hair, who in 1945 had won a court judgment against their mother for a share of the mother's permit and of his deceased stepfather's sheep. The action was timely, because the next year Gib Graham bought the land near the state line that Chopped Hair had been using. Chopped Hair seems to have exercised his residual rights to shift his winter range to the upper Defiance Draw. He died soon afterward. Another newcomer was Chopped Hair's own son by Tall Salt Clansman's daughter, Zonnie. The

son had spent his adulthood working as a miner and agricultural laborer outside the reservation. When this mother died, also in 1946 or 1947, he discovered that she had an allotment in the upper Defiance Draw. His wife and he therefore moved onto the tract, using Chee Jim's former range southeast of Tse Bonita Wash in winter and moving to the Defiance Plateau in summer. By the early 1950s, Tall Salt Clansman's grandson was sharing this range, as I describe in Chapter 16.

Meanwhile, in the far upper Defiance Draw, Gray-Eyed Woman's claim remained isolated from those of its neighbors (see Figure 11.1). Curly Tallman, the oldest son of Margaret Thompson, monopolized most of the claim, and had Gray-Eyed Woman's grandson, whom his mother had adopted, to tend his herd of several hundred. Two adopted granddaughters lived with their husbands at Margaret Thompson's homesite and ran their small herd in the southern corner of the claim. This group of people made up a nascent outfit of three or four households in two residence groups. Even after Margaret Thompson died in 1943, and Curly Tallman in 1948, the families of the older adopted granddaughter and Curly Tallman's widow continued to share the area.

Land Tenure in the Middle Defiance Draw

Smiley's widow, daughter, and the daughter's children continued to share the middle Defiance Draw during the era of grazing regulation, constituting one outfit (see Figure 11.2). These people made up 6 residence groups with a total of 12 households. Two of the households, however, may not have lived on the land, only pooling their stock with that of residents.

The three customary use areas that emerged at the end of the railroad era remained until the late 1930s. South of the draw were the households of Smiley's widow, her daughter They Are Raiding Along Behind Each Other, and the latter's married daughter and son, all in one or two homesites; and, in another homesite after 1935, the household of one of Smiley's sons, Billy Smiley. Before 1935, this last household had lived near Hunters Point on land of the wife's family, matrilateral relatives of Whitegoat Curly. When the Indian Service appropriated the land for the new

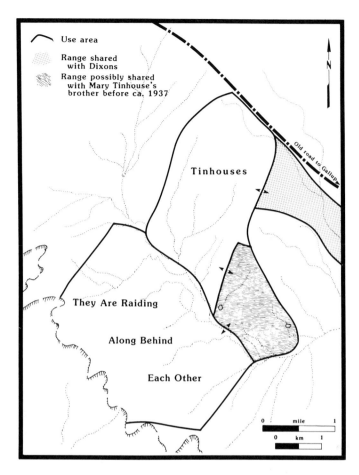

Figure 11.2 Land tenure in the middle Defiance Draw during the 1930s.

Hunters Point boarding school, both spouses exercised their residual land rights by moving into the middle Defiance Draw along the boundary between Smiley's original claim and that of Mr. Whitegoat. They moved back and forth across this boundary and kept their few stock in the herd of They Are Raiding Along Behind Each Other while Billy Smiley was working in a coal mine at Mentmore and his family was staying with him. As in earlier times, the pooled herds of these families, which numbered several hundred mature animals, were taken to Smiley's old range in Hunters Point during the summer.

Meanwhile, Blackgoat's son Turning Warrior continued to move between the two sides of the draw in winter. He sometimes let his impoverished younger brother, Descending Orator, live north of the draw as well, possibly to herd for him. These families had evidently quit using the land north of the draw by 1937. In summer, Turning Warrior went to his wife's family range in the lower Black Creek Valley, as he had done since the 1920s.

Most of the land north of the draw before the late 1930s, and all of it after about 1936, belonged to the Tinhouses, who used the area all year. For a couple of winters during the late 1930s, they also used the neighboring part of the Eastern Flat, because the grass north of the draw was scanty. The Tinhouses would have gained access to this land (and thus become temporary members of the corresponding outfit) through Fred Tinhouse's half brother, who had married into one of the Eastern Flat families.

Land Tenure in the
Eastern Flat–Lower Defiance Draw

During the era of grazing regulation, the three segments of the Eastern Flat seem to have become more rigidly bounded as the two large stock owners at its north and south ends, Tom Sharp and Mr. Towering House Clansman, sought to consolidate their monopolies. Mr. Towering House Clansman had evidently approached this result by the beginning of the era; Tom Sharp succeeded by the end. Squeezed between these two, the families of the Dixon brothers, Towering House Woman, and her children perhaps formed an outfit or perhaps were part of Mr. Towering House Clansman's outfit (see Figure 11.3).

When his wife's grandmother, Azaakai, died in 1933, Tom Sharp gained sole use of her reservation land. He also spread southward within the land base of the same outfit into the former customary use area of Big Woman, where he soon succeeded in eliminating from the land all but his wife's twin sister (raised by Big Woman). During the early 1930s, this sister married and moved to Mexican Springs, and another sister, Violet Brown, took over her niche along Tom Sharp's southern border. Violet Brown and her married daughter used the land for a small herd that evidently included, at least sometimes, a few animals belonging to two of Violet Brown's sons by Chee Jim.

Although his wife died in 1935, Tom Sharp remained on the land with their teenage children, even after he married a woman unrelated to his first wife and continued to crowd his first wife's relatives. His last effort to do so began in 1945, when Gib Graham built the Wildcat Trading Post near Violet Brown's homestead and evicted her from the surrounding tract. She then moved to the west end of her tiny use area, only to be evicted again 5 years later when Tom Sharp was fencing his range and found her on the allotment that his first wife had received in what was then Big Woman's use area.

All this time, the brothers Tom and John Dixon were sharing the Eastern Flat's central segment with

Towering House Woman and her children and with Juan and his son, their brother-in-law (who then let the Tinhouses use their sheep camp there for a couple of years). Towering House Woman and her children evidently owned only a few sheep and goats, which they kept in Juan's son's herd and which they had perhaps received in payment for herding. Towering House Woman or one of her daughters may also have kept some of Mr. Towering House Clansman's stock there (or at least had them on their permit). In 1940, the central-segment outfit, if it was one, consisted of six to nine households in four or five residence groups.

Mr. Towering House Clansman continued to monopolize the southern segment of the Eastern Flat, which he shared with his hired herders and later with the households of his two grown daughters. In the early 1930s he may have run as many as 2000 or 3000 head (including young) in his use area in winter, although by 1938 he was evidently reduced to 1000 (probably including young). In 1945, to avoid further reduction, he arranged to buy 3½ railroad sections from Gib Graham, but he never completed the purchase. One day soon after he had arranged the purchase, as his wife and he crossed the railroad tracks on a return trip from Gallup, a train hit their car and killed them both. His daughters then took over the southern segment and used it year-round through the end of the grazing-regulation era.

Conclusion

Between the railroad era and the era of grazing regulation, although the total population of the lease townships grew little, the length of residence for most families lengthened from 6 months to a full year. The various land-using groups, however, changed little. Residence groups continued to coalesce to supply enough labor for family production and domestic maintenance. Residence groups continued to gain land mainly through the rights inherited by their individual members. By this time, most families had inhabited the lease townships long enough for matrilineal inheritance to appear as the favored type of land inheritance. The outfit, too, persisted as people continued to need alternative lands and therefore to assert residual rights to lands of matrikin. Indeed, as the

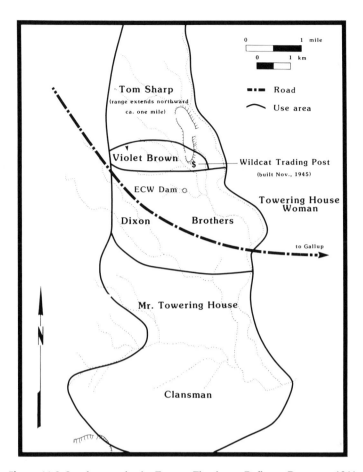

Figure 11.3 Land tenure in the Eastern Flat–lower Defiance Draw, ca. 1944.

government land withdrawals in the Black Creek Valley and speculators' purchases of railroad land displaced many families, people may have exercised these rights more often.

Grazing regulation did, however, change some aspects of land tenure. By cutting down the holdings of the large owners, it reduced the number of households that lived virilocally or on lands of both the husband's and the wife's families. By forcing large owners to buy land that they had previously used for free, moreover, the land speculation that the permit system encouraged may have reinforced the desire of large owners to monopolize land. Thus did speculation undermine the outfit.

Chapter 12

Spatial Aspects of Land Use during the Era of Grazing Regulation

The woodland range consists mainly of piñon and juniper. These areas afford very little forage and in general are very short of water. Much of the stock which use these areas are watered from small springs or seeps which do not have flowing water, and it is necessary for the herder to dip the water from depressions made in the rock and pour it into troughs. To see a herder attempting to water his flock from such a meager supply is to be impressed with the great demand for water development.

Throughout the entire reservation, the Indians have collectively and individually done a great amount of work to improve the water supply, mainly by building earthen dams and reservoirs. (Harbison 1932:9200)

Although the above passage refers to the Southern Navajo Agency jurisdiction in general, its author might have had the uplands of the lease townships specifically in mind. The surge in reservoir construction that had started in the lease townships during the railroad era continued into the era of grazing regulation. It is a symptom of the ongoing range subdivision and restriction of more families to the lease townships for the entire year that had begun in the railroad era and that continued to change the spatial aspects of land use.

Customary Use Areas

By 1940, most families occupied their customary use areas in the lease townships year-round. We can therefore get an idea of how families managed their use areas in summer as well as in winter. Figure 12.1 shows the customary use areas of 1940. Less than one third of the households that used these areas moved outside the lease townships. Those that did so returned to the same summer places as had their predecessors during the railroad era (see Table 12.1).

All customary use areas continued to encompass the woodlands that people needed for fuel and building materials and the open patches of sage–grassland used for grazing and farming. Many areas, however, lacked the wide expanses of sage–grassland that occur only below 6800 ft. Like the customary use areas of 1915, most of the 1940 areas lacked a reliable natural water source, and more families were perhaps forced to use such water sources in neighboring areas. Unlike the 1915 use areas, however, all the 1940 areas also had reservoirs (see Figure 12.1). As in the railroad era,

Table 12.1
Homes of Lease-Township Residents outside the Lease Townships, 1940

Location	No. of households with summer homes	No. of households with winter homes	No. of households with year-round homes
Hunters Point	2	—	—
St. Michaels	2	—	—
Tsayatoh	1	—	—
Houck	2	—	—
Rock Springs	—	1	—
Oak Springs	1	—	—
No home outside	—	—	21

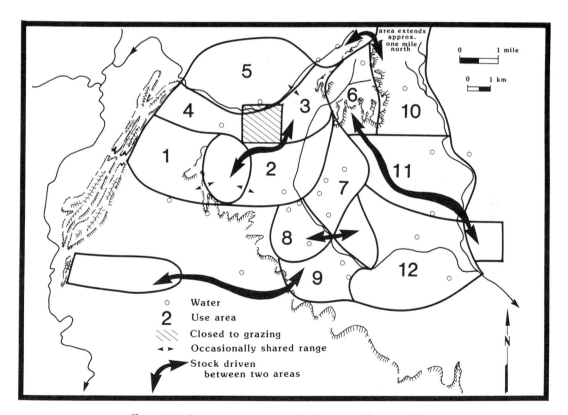

Figure 12.1 Customary use areas in the lease townships, ca. 1940.

Table 12.2
Inventories of Sites in Customary Use Areas in the Lease Townships, 1940

Use area	No. of residence groups[a]	Season	No. of stock[b]	No. of homesteads[c]	No. of sheep camps	No. of campsites[d]	No. of fields
Tse Bonita Wash–upper Defiance Draw							
1	1	all year	100	1	—	1	?(Arizona)
2	2	winter	700	OLT	1	2	?(Arizona)
			60		sites not positively identified		
3	2	winter	400(?)		sites not positively identified		
			240	—	2	1	—
4	1	winter	152	OLT	1	—	?(Arizona)
5	3	all year(2)	73		sites not positively identified		
		summer	240	1	—	—	1
6	2	all year	375	2	OLT	2(?)	1
Middle Defiance Draw							
7	1	all year	145	3	—	—	2
8	2	winter(1)	563	2	—	—	2
		all year(1)					
9	3	all year	472–800	3[e]	2[f]	—	4
Eastern Flat–lower Defiance Draw							
10	2	all year	400	2	3[g]	1	3
11	2	all year	357	2[h]	1	—	2
12	1	winter	968	1	1(?)[i]	1+(?)[i]	1

[a]Number of residence groups exceeds total for lease townships given on Table 11.1 because some residence groups had land in more than one use area.

[b]Maximum combined holdings of all users according to Human Dependency Survey, local Navajos, or 1940 grazing-permit applications.

[c]OLT = site outside of the lease townships used during the same seasons as sites inside the lease townships.

[d]Includes isolated corrals.

[e]Includes one homestead outside the lease townships not counted in South Lease sample.

[f]Farmsteads.

[g]Includes one sheep camp in upper Tse Bonita Wash within a customary use area that lies mostly outside the lease townships and one on the North McKinley Mine lease not counted in South Lease sample; sites used by Tom Sharp.

[h]Sites not positively identified.

[i]Mr. Towering House Clansman's area; sites not positively identified.

most water sources (13 of 22) were mainly for stock and domestic use; the rest also irrigated fields. I had originally assumed that these reservoirs owed their existence to the government water-improvement program, but interviewees mentioned only 4 reservoirs that the government had built. Many lease-township families were already living in the townships all year before the government expanded its water-improvement program, and they evidently needed water so much that they built most of the reservoirs themselves.

Besides reservoirs, the typical customary use area of 1940 had two or three homesteads and two to four fields (see Table 12.2). About half of these fields were shared, either by households with a common homesite or, more often, by households in different homesites but with a common customary use area. Three or four fields in the middle Defiance Draw even yielded crops for all but one of the households in the outfit there. Unlike the fields and homesteads, sheep camps and campsites were less common than in 1915, because people moved the herds less often and over shorter distances. As shown in Chapter 7, people did not use isolated corrals or campsites for moves of less than half a mile and did not use sheep camps for moves of less than a mile. A comparison of Tables 12.3 and

Table 12.3
Types of Sites Identified
by Local Navajos and Used in 1940

Type	Number
Homestead	15
Sheep camp	8
Farmstead	1
Campsite and isolated corral	5
Isolated sweathouse	4
Field	17
Improved water source	22

7.3 shows these changes in the number of each type of site. The changes are more typical of the small owners than the large (compare Tables 7.2 and 11.2), however, because the large owners were not suffering from reduced land bases.

Most people moved their herds over these shorter distances because range subdivision had shrunk grazing tracts, because the herds were smaller, and because the new reservoirs furnished water more reliably. Most families moved their herds only twice a year within the townships or between the townships and areas outside. Some moved between winter and summer homesteads, in which case they moved to the summer site in May and back to the winter site in November. Others moved between a homestead that they occupied all year (or nearly so) and a winter sheep camp, in which case all or part of the family stayed at the sheep camp from about January to April or May. Families that did not follow either of these patterns were the very large and very small owners. The largest owners, Whitegoat Curly and Mr. Towering House Clansman, moved their herds among a series of sheep camps or tent camps inside the lease townships in winter and outside them in summer. Small owners, such as Fat Salt, simply herded within a mile or two of the homestead where each lived all year. Most small users occupied corners of the customary use areas of larger owners.

After 1940, the building of reservoirs that accompanied these changes seems to have slowed. Of the 22 known improved water sources used in 1940, as many as 15 were probably built between 1930 and 1940, compared to the 10 built during the railroad era. After 1940, people built only an estimated 7 more reservoirs. This pattern shows that the lease townships were

essentially transformed from mainly winter to year-round use during the first half of the era of grazing regulation. In the second half, the new year-round use of space in the customary use areas stabilized.

The next two sections illustrate the changes in the management of customary use areas between the railroad era and the era of grazing regulation. To show how sharply family land management could change, I discuss the two customary use areas that also furnished examples for the railroad era: those of Gray-Eyed Woman and of Blackgoat. Both areas were still intact; Gray-Eyed Woman's use area had passed to the families of Margaret Thompson and Curly Tallman, while Blackgoat's area had passed to the Tinhouses.

The Customary Use Area
of Curly Tallman and His Mother

After Gray-Eyed Woman died in 1918 and her sister Margaret Thompson took the orphaned grandchildren south of the yellow rock mesa, the family settled at site LA 12820 (see Figure 12.2). In 1931, the Thompsons' oldest son, Curly Tallman, removed his sheep from the Thompsons' herd, moved across the neighboring meadow to a grove of trees, and built a new homestead, PM 212, for his family. One of the Thompsons' adopted grandsons quit boarding school and accompanied his "uncle" to herd. By this time, only the Thompsons' two adopted granddaughters remained: the older one married and living in a hogan of her own and the younger not married until the late 1930s, when she and her husband shared the Thompsons' hogan. The homestead consisted of three hogans (one was perhaps for work or storage), corrals, a sweathouse, and a small reservoir (see Figure 12.3).

The Thompsons and their granddaughters shared only a small herd—50 mature animals in 1936 and 79 in 1940. They therefore were able to stay all year at their homestead and herd within a mile radius of it (see Figure 12.2). The herd drank at the small, earth-dammed reservoir on their homestead (W83) or at the log-dammed pool (W04) that Curly Tallman had built about a mile north of the mesa. In very dry spells they even trekked their sheep to the big dam that the SCS had built near the homes of the Dixon brothers in

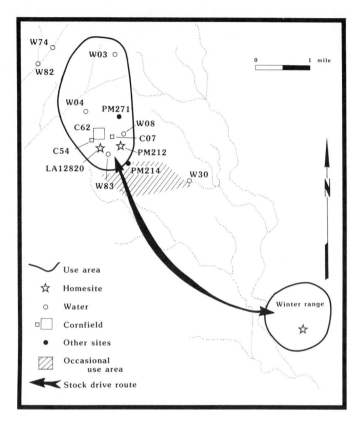

Figure 12.2 Customary use area of Curly Tallman and his mother, 1931–1948.

1934. They hauled their own water from Dripping Spring (W03), where a spring house had been built. At the base of two hills in a *rincon* just north of their homestead they planted two fields, C56 and C62.

Whereas the Thompsons used mainly the corner of Gray-Eyed Woman's customary use area south of the mesa, Curly Tallman covered the entire area with his large herd, which numbered about 300 mature sheep and goats in 1936 and 185 4 years later. His family also kept 25 cattle and 10 horses. He and his wife had three daughters, the oldest of whom seems to have married and had two children of her own while she lived at PM 212. The homestead consisted of the rock house of Curly Tallman and his wife, a hogan for the oldest daughter, several corrals, a *ramada*, and two ovens (see Figure 12.4). The shell of a Model A on the site attests to one of the family's modes of transportation. Almost half a mile south, Curly Tallman had a sweathouse, PM 214.

Curly Tallman's family lived and kept at least part of their herd at their homestead all year. In winter, the family grazed half the herd around the homestead and just north of the yellow rock mesa. Curly Tallman's "nephew" took the other half of the herd to the Rock Springs allotments of Margaret Thompson and her sons, where he lived by himself in a small hogan.

The herd usually drank at a reservoir, W08, tucked beneath a rock tower near the homestead. During dry spells, however, the herd was trekked about 2 mi. to Coyote Drinking Water or Bubbling Spring (W74 and W82), although Curly Tallman may also have had a corral somewhere near the wells. In extreme droughts, the herd was run about 2 mi. in the other direction to the SCS dam, W30. With a wagon, Curly Tallman hauled his family's water in barrels from Dripping Spring. He shared his mother's cornfield, C62, at the foot of a hill between the homesteads.

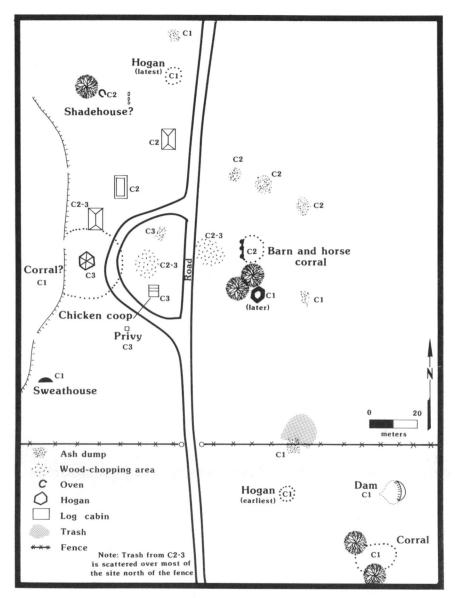

Figure 12.3 Site LA 12820, Margaret Thompson's homestead, noting masking by material from later occupations. Temporal components: C1, 1918–1943; C2, ca. 1950–1970; and C3, ca. 1975–present.

Curly Tallman received a permit in 1940 for 151 sheep units but saw it reduced to 105 by 1945. The Thompsons and their older granddaughter evidently lacked permits of their own. When Margaret Thompson died in 1943, the younger granddaughter's household left, and the older granddaughter moved to a hogan just north of Curly Tallman's homestead, where she probably put her few sheep in Curly Tallman's herd. In the next few years, the "nephew" married and moved in with his wife's family, and Curly Tallman died. His widow remained at PM 212, and the older granddaughter took charge of the herd.

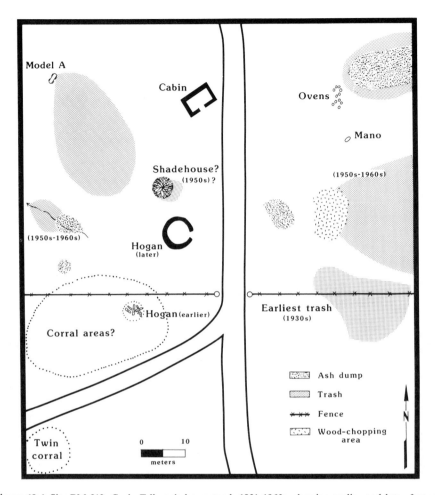

Figure 12.4 Site PM 212, Curly Tallman's homestead, 1931–1960s, showing earlier and later features.

Apparently the widow left the Rock Springs land for one of her daughters to use and ran her own reduced herd in the upper Defiance Draw all year according to the patterns established in Curly Tallman's time.

During the era of grazing regulation, then, the families of Margaret Thompson and Curly Tallman managed Gray-Eyed Woman's claim somewhat differently than had Gray-Eyed Woman and Margaret Thompson. They did so because together they had more sheep, and because Curly Tallman had a full-time herder. Although Margaret Thompson and Curly Tallman seem to have kept to separate herding areas north and south of the yellow rock mesa, as had Gray-

Eyed Woman and Margaret Thompson, they used the upper Draw in summer rather than in winter and took part of the stock outside the lease townships in winter. Also unlike Gray-Eyed Woman, they confined their fields and homesites to the area south of the mesa, where they consequently built new reservoirs. The confinement of homesites and fields south of the mesa may have started after Gray-Eyed Woman's death simply because Margaret Thompson continued her own pattern: intensive use of the land south of the mesa and sporadic use of the land to the north. By 1931, however, when Curly Tallman was using the land north of the mesa rather heavily, he may have chosen not to move there because the channel of the Defiance Draw had cut deeper into the alluvium and farming was no longer possible. Furthermore, he did not need to maintain sheep camps there, because his full-time herder had time to trek the sheep farther to pasture and because he used the extreme upper draw only in warm weather, when all-weather shelters for herders were unnecessary.

The Customary Use Area of the Tinhouse Family

Fred and Mary Tinhouse and their children had finally moved from Blackgoat's homestead, PM 48–49, to a new place about half a mile up the drainage (see Figure 12.5). They stayed all year at their new homesite, PM 59, until the middle 1930s, when they began to move seasonally between the upper and lower parts of Blackgoat's former winter range. They spent the summers near the Defiance Draw at PM 81, where Blackgoat had kept a corral for a tent camp. In the winter they moved about a mile and a half back up the hill to PM 59, where they had torn down their hogans and corrals (perhaps to renew them) and rebuilt them a short distance north. For a couple of winters they stayed at PM 115, about a mile east of PM 59, instead of at PM 59. This pattern persisted through 1940. The Tinhouses may have begun to move seasonally, because Mary Tinhouse's two brothers had stopped using the land along the draw around the middle 1930s.

The Tinhouses chose between their two winter homesteads on the basis of grass and water availability. The area around PM 115 was the land (mentioned in Chapter 11) that belonged to in-laws of Fred Tinhouse's half brother. The half brother and his wealthy father, Juan (who was not Fred Tinhouse's father), may have been running more than 300 mature sheep and goats in this area during the late 1930s and evidently were willing to share it with the Tinhouses. The corrals on both PM 115 and the northern part of PM 59, being excessively large for the Tinhouses' 145 mature animals and young, suggest that the Tinhouses may even have kept the half brother's herd at times. Another possible reason for the excessive size of these corrals, however, is simply that the Tinhouses

salvaged corrals built for the bigger herds of Blackgoat and Juan from earlier sites nearby and rebuilt these corrals at their original size to minimize the mud problem.

The Tinhouses stayed at either PM 59 or PM 115 from November to May and at PM 81 from May to November. When they stayed at PM 59, they got stock and domestic water from snow-fed reservoirs that Fred Tinhouse had built, W24 being next to the site and W84 about half a mile southwest (see Figure 12.5). The Tinhouses also used W84 when they stayed at PM 115. Another source was Mr. Towering House Clansman's large reservoir, W28, in the Eastern Flat, about the same distance in the opposite direction. When the Tinhouses lived at PM 81 they got water from other sources: a dug well, W81, in the bottom of Defiance Draw near PM 81, and two reservoirs, W22 and W37, that Fred Tinhouse built within half a mile north of the site. Sometimes they also hauled water from Smiley's Spring, W38. Seepage from the reservoir W22 watered their two fields, C05 and C29.

All of the Tinhouses' homesteads were large and complex (see Figures 12.6, 12.7, and 12.8). On site PM 59 were two hogans (one not visible archaeologically) and, in a cluster, two sheep corrals, one horse corral, a hay barn, and a garage. Fred Tinhouse had hauled the last structure on skids from Blackgoat's homestead to house the family's Model T (presumably also inherited from Blackgoat). Nearby, Fred Tinhouse had set up his forge, a sheet-metal drum and, mounted on a cable spool, a sort of super-bellows that Fred Tinhouse had ingeniously fashioned from heavy-equipment parts salvaged from the Mentmore mine dumps. Nearer to the hogans was a storage cellar and adjoining *ramada*. Fred Tinhouse's sweathouse, out of sight among the trees, completed the homestead.

Site PM 81 had only one hogan, a cribbed-log type; a large, domed masonry oven, and a *ramada*. In the hogan was a stove made of half an oil barrel. Like PM 59, the site also had in a cluster a sheep corral, horse corral, hay barn, and forge, but this forge was of sandstone masonry and employed a conventional bellows. In another part of the site was a second sheep corral with a small pen attached where the Tinhouses would keep overnight two or three kids whose nannies they were planning to milk for breakfast. Near the field, C05, was another pen where the Tinhouses kept the horses at midday when they were plowing or

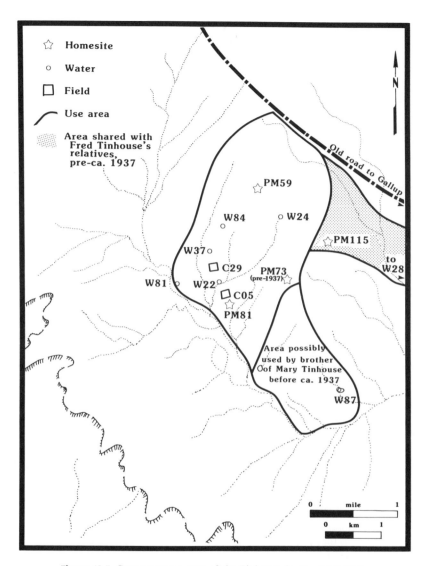

Figure 12.5 Customary use area of the Tinhouse family, 1930–1941.

hauling the crops from the field. A fenced patch of bare sandstone nearby was used for drying corn. Fred Tinhouse's sweathouse was out of sight beyond a hill just north of the rest of the homestead.

Like PM 59, PM 115 had two hogans: The family ate and slept in one, and in the other they stored food and did such work as laundry, for which they had an old-fashioned, hand-operated washing machine. Both

hogans were of cribbed-log construction, and the work hogan was plastered with earth from ground to smokehole. The living hogan was heated with an oil-barrel stove, but the work hogan had only a hearth, which may explain why it was plastered. Kerosene lamps provided light for both hogans. Probably the Tinhouses found a second hogan necessary at the two winter sites but not at PM 81 because they could do

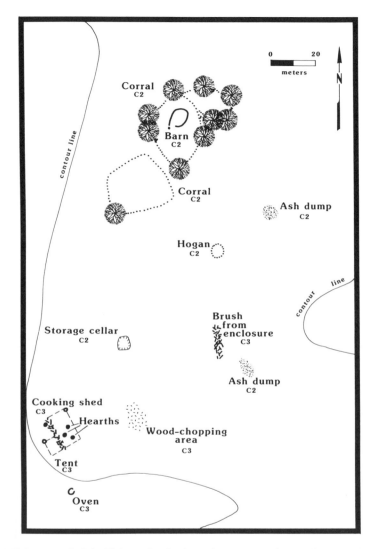

Figure 12.6 Site PM 59, homestead of the Tinhouse family. An early component just south was used all year, ca. 1930–1934; middle component (shown) was used in winter ca., 1935–1941; and later component (also shown) was used for a squaw dance, ca. 1960. Temporal component: C2, 1935–1941; C3, ca. 1960.

more work outside in warm weather; for example, Mary Tinhouse laundered in the *ramada* at PM 81. Site PM 115 also had a horse corral, a double sheep corral with lamb pens, and a single sheep corral, but no hay barn or forge. The Tinhouses stored hay for the horses on a platform in a tree, where they also preserved foods, such as cornbread, in the cold air.

When Fred Tinhouse wanted to do some blacksmithing, he would ride over to PM 59 and use the forge there. The Tinhouses hauled wood home from the surrounding groves in a riding wagon with the sides folded down flat.

The Tinhouses' management of their customary use area during the late 1930s, then, differed from

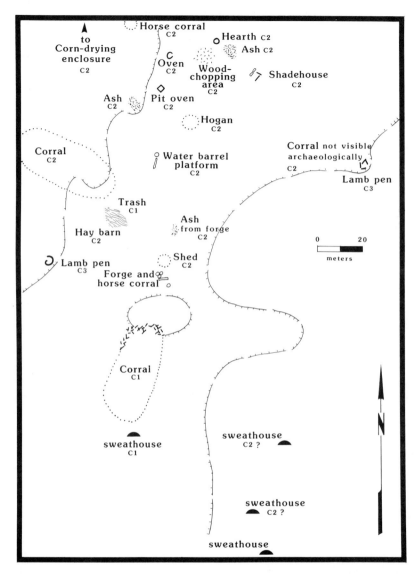

Figure 12.7 Site PM 81, summer homestead of the Tinhouse family, ca. 1935–1941, showing features of earlier component, a campsite of Blackgoat, and later component, a recent pen for lamb born on range. Temporal component: C1, ca. 1918; C2, 1935–1941; C3, post-1959.

Blackgoat's management of the same area 15 or 20 years earlier. The main differences were that the Tinhouses used the area all year and that they kept a smaller herd, which they did not need to divide into flocks or move more often than every 6 months. Like Blackgoat, however, they used the lowlands along the draw in warm weather and the uplands in cold. Indeed, two of the Tinhouses' homesteads were on or near sites that Blackgoat had used earlier. The reason for this coincidence may be that the Tinhouses were using

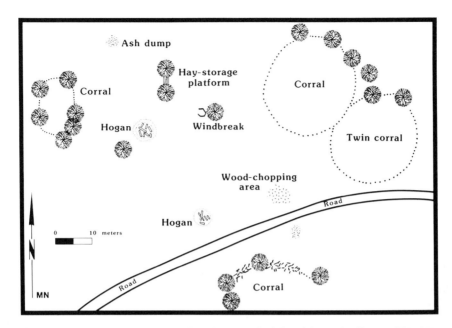

Figure 12.8 Site PM 115, alternate winter homestead of the Tinhouse family, ca. 1935–1941.

almost the same water sources in the late 1930s that Blackgoat had used earlier.

After 1940, the Tinhouses abandoned all three homesteads. They abandoned PM 59 because a hand trembler (a person who diagnoses illness) told them that someone had bewitched the site, and they abandoned PM 81 because another medicine man told them that it was too close to one of the antelope corrals in the Defiance Draw (contact with abandoned hunting corrals is considered dangerous). They moved about a mile down Defiance Draw from PM 81 to a site where they would stay year-round. The move, however, did not place the family beyond the dangerous forces that the medicine men had tried to address, for Mary Tinhouse died in the spring of 1941.

Grazing Tracts

The Tinhouses and Curly Tallman had not divided the customary use areas of their forebears, but other families divided the land of their own forebears. Between 1915 and 1940, the ongoing subdivision of the range caused grazing tracts to grow in number and diminish in size. The number of customary use areas in the lease townships increased from 8 in 1915 to at least 12 in 1940. This subdivision occurred because the heirs of Smiley split his claim into two parts and because Cornmerchant's area had been divided into three parts (see Figure 12.1). The growth in the number of tracts was accompanied by a reduction in size from an average of 4.8 to 3.0 mi.[2] The fragmentation of the range also shows in the growing number of families that used discontiguous tracts. These users were relatively large-scale stock owners whose main grazing tracts lay mostly above 6800 ft. and were too small to accommodate the stock all year.

As in 1915, most grazing tracts were distributed over the lease-township landscape to include range both above and below 6800 ft. (see Table 12.4). Nevertheless, almost half of the grazing tracts lay entirely above 6800 ft., as in 1915, and most of these tracts accommodated only the smallest herds. Also like the 1915 tracts, most of the 1940 tracts had no natural water sources inside their boundaries. Unlike the 1915 tracts, however, all of the 1940 tracts had their own reservoirs. That most grazing tracts had natural water sources on their boundaries both in 1915 and 1940 sug-

Table 12.4
Number of Small Stock, Size, and Physiographic Characteristics of Customary Use Areas in the Lease Townships, 1940

Use area no.	No. of small stock (annual equivalent)[a]	Area (quarter sections)	Small stock per quarter section[b]	Range elevation Above 6800 ft.	Below 6800 ft.	Water[c] Natural	Improved
1	100 ⎱	—	—	x	—	x	x
2	380 ⎰ 36	36	17	x	x	x	x
3	160 ⎱	—	—	x	—	x	x
7	145 ⎱	24	22	x	x	x	x
8	350 ⎰			x	x	x	x
12	484	23	21	x	x	—	x
10	400	18[d]	22	x	x	near	x
11	357	17	21	—	x	near	x
6	288	12	24	x	—	x	x
9	236–400	10	24	x	x	x	x
4	76	6	13	x	—	x	near
5	U	U	U	x	—	x	x

[a]Total number of stock that regularly used the tract multiplied by the fraction of the year that the tract was used. The part of the Black Creek Valley that takes up the southwestern corner of the townships, and the stock of the families that used it, are excluded from this table. U = unknown.

[b]Small stock in annual equivalents divided by tract sizes.

[c]Water inside or on boundary of tract.

[d]Includes acreage in the upper Tse Bonita Wash.

gests how the boundaries of customary use areas evolved: Two families would herd from separate homesites toward a shared natural water source. Nearly all customary use areas thus gave access to natural water sources both in 1915 and 1940. Reservoirs therefore did not proliferate because families had lost access to natural water sources; they proliferated, instead, because more families needed to store water for the summer, since they were staying in the townships all year.

Fields

Changes in grazing tracts may have progressed smoothly from the late railroad era through the era of grazing regulation, but some changes in fields seem more abrupt. In addition to the steady growth of population, range subdivision, and year-round residence that affected both grazing tracts and fields, the unfavorable prices for wool and lambs goaded more families to plant more and perhaps bigger fields.

An aerial photograph of the lease townships that was probably taken in 1934 (USDA, SCS 1934) shows 12 fields—about the most that were under cultivation at any one time during the railroad era. This was a big increase over the 5 fields of 1915, of course, but between 1934 and 1940 the total number of fields grew to at least 17 and possibly to as many as 22.

Between 1915 and 1940, fields may have grown bigger as well. In 1915, the average household with a farm planted only 2.75 acres (mainly in the Black Creek Valley). Unfortunately, acreage planted in 1940 is recorded for only seven families, covering probably 12 fields; the average is 12.4 acres per family or 7.2 acres per field. Even excluding John Dixon's family, who farmed 40 acres, the average acreage per family was 8.4, or 5.2 acres per field.

Undoubtedly the acreages in both the 1915 source (Paquette 1915) and the 1940 source (USDI, Grazing Service 1940–1946) were estimated, not measured. It is hard to believe, however, that different observers would make eyeball guesses that vary so widely. Another possible reason for the difference is that the aridity of the lease townships, the widespread use of the plow, or both, induced people to space plants farther apart in 1940 than they had done in 1915, when most fields were in the moister Black Creek Valley and were planted with the *gish*. Lease-township residents, however, recall planting corn in clumps about every two paces behind the plow and spacing the furrows about two paces apart (Knight 1982:709). Various descriptions of the *gish* method of planting specify the same spacing (Bingham and Bingham 1979:24; Hill 1938:30–31). If the 1940 fields were genuinely bigger than those of 1915, and the plants spread the same distance apart, then lease-township families were raising more crops in each field in the later interval than in the earlier interval.

The distribution of fields across the landscape of the lease townships had not changed after the railroad era, despite the increase in farming and the development of reservoirs that could have irrigated fields. To water their fields, people still relied mainly on natural runoff. Altogether, people farmed 32 fields in the lease townships at various times during the era of grazing regulation, 26 of which lie within the area zoned for slope analysis as described in Chapter 7 (see Figure 12.9). These fields, like those of the railroad era, tended to cluster along the junctions of two slope zones, and almost half were in the slope-wash locations common to the zonal junctions (see Table 12.5). About a third of the fields not in slope-wash settings were next to dams, which, however, irrigated only 6 of the total 32 fields. I do not know why people did not use their new reservoirs for irrigation. Remarks by local Navajos suggest that the best spots for reservoirs often have soil with too much clay for successful farming.

People placed their fields in the same open vegetation zones as they had in the railroad era, and the average elevations of the fields of the two periods, 6800 ft. for the earlier period and 6740 ft. for the later one, do not differ significantly.[1] The unchanged aridity, vegetation, and topography still restricted successful farming to the lowland sage–grass plains.

Homesites

Population growth in the lease townships caused the number of sites to increase from 19 in 1915 to 24 in 1940. This increase is proportionally almost the same as the increases in the number of households and residence groups. The average family therefore may

have used the same number of homesites in the lease townships in 1940 as in 1915. Most of the 1915 households, however, had other homesites outside the lease townships, whereas most of the 1940 households did not. Therefore, families actually maintained fewer homesites overall in the later period but stayed longer on each one.

As families became confined to shrinking use areas in the lease townships and stayed longer on each homesite, the number of homesteads grew in relation to the number of sheep camps; the average homesite therefore enlarged. The number of homesteads more than doubled between 1915 and 1940, whereas the number of sheep camps (assuming that homesites of unknown occupation span were also sheep camps) fell by about a third (compare Tables 7.3 and 12.3). The resulting size increases show in the total areas that homesites covered (see Table 7.7) and in the inventories and spacing of features on homesites, as I show in Chapter 13.

The growing numbers and sizes of homesites during the era of grazing regulation continued trends that had started in the railroad era, just as did the underlying causes: increases in population, range subdivision, and the number of year-round residents. In contrast, some changes in the environmental distribution of homesites reversed the trends of the railroad era. In particular, families began to build homesites at lower elevations.[2] The reason for this change is probably that people were farming more and therefore wanted to be near their fields, which were best situated in the lowland sage–grass plains.

The locations of homesites in relation to water also changed after the railroad era. Most homesites were now within only half a mile of a water source, and

[1]Standard deviations are 160 ft. for the railroad-era figures and 120 ft. for those of the grazing-regulation era.

[2]As a consequence, the average 1940 homesite, at 6879 ft. ($SD = 130, n = 24$), was significantly lower than its 1915 counterpart (6950 ft.: $SD = 150, n = 19, t = 1.87, p < .05$ for a one-tailed test). This difference also distinguishes the homesteads of the two eras: the average elevations of 1915 homesteads (6970 ft.: $SD = 125, n = 6$) and 1940 homesteads (6860 ft.: $SD = 110, n = 15$) differ significantly ($t = 2.02, p < .05$ for a one-tailed test). Moreover, in 1915, all the homesteads and 71% of the sheep camps, plus sites of unknown occupation span, were situated above 6800 ft.; in 1940, about the same proportion of sheep camps (66%) were at the higher elevations, but more than half of the homesteads (53%) were now below 6800 ft. These figures show that people would not build a homesite below 6800 ft. unless they were going to farm when they stayed at that homesite.

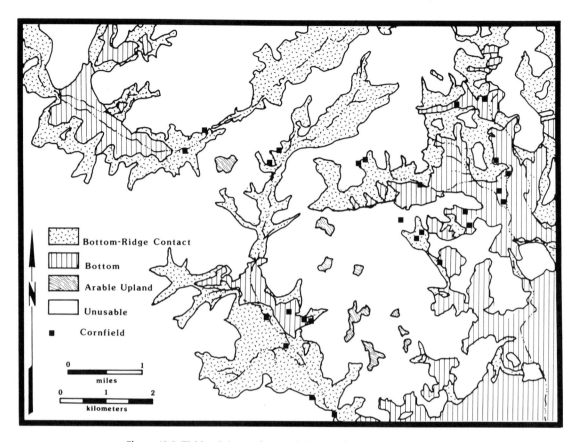

Figure 12.9 Fields of the grazing-regulation era in the lease townships.

almost all were within a mile (see Figure 12.10). These distances are about half the distances common during the railroad era, and many homesites were even right next to water. The reason for the change, of course, is the building of reservoirs, which many families did not share and therefore did not need to live apart from.

In some respects, homesite locations did not change between the railroad and grazing-regulation eras. I could not determine the vegetative and topographic settings of 3 of the 24 homesites, because strip-mining has altered the terrain. Of the remaining 21, the great majority (15) were still situated in the piñon–juniper woodland or on the boundary of the woodland and the sage–grasslands. People had built more than half of their homesites with sheltering landforms on the

west and often with southern exposures (see Table 12.6). Ridge-top locations were not so common as during the railroad era, however, perhaps because wagons and motor vehicles had become more common.

Families sited their homes near wood and sheltering landforms, as they had done in the railroad era, for they needed wood and shelter, especially in winter, as much as before. One might expect wood and sheltering topography to have mattered less to lease-township families in the era of grazing regulation than in the railroad era, because during the later period more families stayed in summer; few families, however, had special summer homesites in the lease townships. Most families in both eras used their homesites either in winter or all year, when wood and shelter were important.

Table 12.5
Distribution of Fields
by Slope Zone in the Era of Grazing Regulation

	N
Total number of fields	26
Fields by zone	
bottom-ridge contact	9
bottom	13
unusable	4
Fields by zonal junction	
fields at junction of 2 or more zones	14
slope–wash fields	9
fields not at zonal junction	12
slope–wash fields	3
Proximity to dams	
located next to dams	6
not next to dams	20

Table 12.6
Situations of Homesites on Landforms, 1940

Topographic situation	No. of sites
Sheltered on west; exposed on south	6
Sheltered on west and south	6
Exposed on west and south	2
Exposed on west; sheltered on south	4
Ridge	3
Flat	0
Other[a]	3
	24

[a]Topography altered by mining.

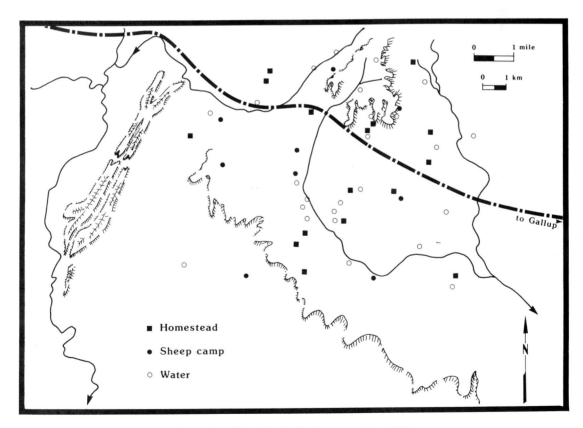

Figure 12.10 Homesites in the lease townships, 1940.

Conclusion

Grazing regulations neither stopped the subdivision of land nor enabled many families to make a living in ways other than stock raising and farming. Most families, therefore, were forced to coax an undiminished amount of product from shrinking land bases. They therefore built more reservoirs, farmed more and bigger fields, and stayed in the lease townships all year. Most families also kept more than one homesite, but, as their grazing tracts shrank, they spent half the year or more at one homesite, thus needing fewer sheep camps and campsites to exploit distant range. These trends dominate the aggregate statistics on the number, size, and environmental distribution of grazing tracts, fields, and homesites, and they are most evident among the small owners, whom larger owners had relegated to the uplands during the railroad era. In contrast, by continuing to squeeze their neighbors in this way and having money to buy land back from speculators, large owners, such as Tom Sharp and Mr. Towering Clansman, lost little of their land. They were forced to sell some of their livestock, moreover, and were actually producing less from the land. They therefore continued to exploit their lands much as they had done during the railroad era.

Chapter 13

Technology of the Era of Grazing Regulation

The division of labor within the Navajo family in general did not change between the railroad and grazing-regulation eras, probably because families continued to produce the same things and to face the same domestic chores. Women still wove, kept house, and helped their children tend the sheep. Men usually hauled the wood and water, worked the farms, and did the silversmithing and wage work. When the men worked away from the home, the women assumed their domestic chores. Neighbors still helped each other during lambing, shearing, planting, and harvesting (Collier 1951:27, 64; Hill 1938:36; Kluckhohn and Leighton 1947:102; Landgraf 1954:61).

The division of labor within lease-township families undoubtedly followed this general pattern. Many lease-township families, however, may have spent more time in productive tasks than before, particularly in craft work and farming. And as the burden of labor continued to grow, families continued the quest they had begun in the railroad era for labor-saving tools, equipment, and techniques. The technology of the grazing-regulation era manifests this quest, as well as increased craft and crop production. Technological changes reflect more strongly, however, another trend that carried over from the railroad era: the settling down of most households, which had resulted from still another holdover, range subdivision through inheritance.

Domestic Technology

Lease-township families continued to build progressively bigger, roomier dwellings, as they had done during the railroad era. Although the dome-shaped, cribbed-log hogan was the most common form in both periods, the more constricted forked-stick hogan had already disappeared by the end of the railroad era, and the roomier cabin was becoming more common. Of the 90 dwellings recorded on the lease-township sites identified with the era of grazing regulation by local Navajos, 22% (20) were cabins, as compared to 6% (4) during the railroad era. These cabins may have exceeded, on the average, the size of the hogan, although the available data do not show a clear difference.[1]

The households that owned cabins were among those that needed the most living and storage space: households with silversmiths and year-round residents. Four of these households, moreover, included weavers, and three included both silversmiths and weavers.[2] Wealthy households, however, evidently did not favor cabins. Whether cabins or hogans, the 22 measured dwellings of the grazing-regulation era were significantly larger than their railroad-era counterparts.[3] The average sizes of dwellings on homesteads, however, do not differ significantly between the two periods.[4] The main reason for the increase in the overall average size, therefore, is that homestead dwellings were in the minority during the railroad era but in the majority later.

In contrast to homestead dwellings, the average sheep-camp dwelling of the grazing-regulation era was bigger than its average precursor.[5] Families perhaps were staying longer during the year on sheep camps; they were certainly using them for a greater number of years. (The grazing-regulation era sample of measurable sheep-camp dwellings may not be representative, however; it consists of only four dwellings.) Dwellings, therefore, became larger in the era of grazing regulation mainly because more dwellings were built to accommodate people for 6 months or even all year, rather than just for stints of a couple of months.

[1]Most of the cabins were on sites outside the lease, so that the dimensions of only four are available. Two of these cabins were occupied year-round and, at 44.2 and 30.0 m², exceeded the area of the average dwelling (24.2 m²). The other two, however, were much smaller (15.8 and 16.4 m²). One was built on a sheep camp; the other was originally intended as a sheep-camp shelter but came to be occupied year-round by a dependent herder of Fat Salt's family.

[2]Conversely, of the six silversmiths that the Human Dependency Survey or local Navajos identified, three had cabins, one had a hogan, and two had dwellings of unrecorded forms.

[3]The grazing regulation era mean is 24.2 m² ($SD = 7.5$, $n = 22$); that of the railroad era is 18.4 m² ($SD = 7.7$, $n = 42$); $t = 2.91$ and $p < 0.01$.

[4]The means are 23.1 m² for the railroad era and 25.7 for the grazing-regulation era.

[5]The average is 21.0 m², but n is only 4.

Individual dwelling sizes also vary, of course. These variations seem not to reflect wealth so much as the number of occupants, year-round residence, and craft work. The six sites listed on Table 13.1 are all the sites for which all the variables can be evaluated. Together with Table 8.1, Table 13.1 shows that the number of occupants noticeably influenced the sizes of dwellings used for 6 months or less (sheep camps and 6-month homesteads) but not the sizes of dwellings used for most or all of the year. When people built a house in which they would live the entire year, they evidently allowed room not only for a certain family size, but also for a wide range of indoor activities and storage of possessions. Table 13.1 also hints at a relationship between dwelling size and craft work: The largest dwellings on the five sites with craft workers exceed the average homestead dwelling size, whereas the largest dwelling on the one site without craft workers is below average.

As during the railroad era, larger households tended to have more dwellings. Five of the seven households with more than one dwelling enumerated by the Human Dependency Survey were larger than average (one was smaller). The average number of dwellings per household, 1.4, differed little from that of the railroad era. All dwellings exceed the 12.6-m² minimum for dwellings occupied by households of the railroad era. The itinerant herders, who had used the smaller shelters in the railroad era, were not as numerous and, in any event, were probably using tents by the time of grazing regulation.

During the railroad era, the few dwellings that had stoves were the bigger, homestead dwellings. Stoves became more common during the era of grazing regulation and not just because homesteads were more common; stoves began to appear on sheep camps as well (this change may explain why sheep-camp dwellings grew bigger). The proliferation of stoves after 1930 was mentioned in Chapter 8 and is evident on Table 8.2. The growing use of stoves, especially on homesteads, is one reason that the biggest ash dumps on homesteads of the grazing-regulation era are farther from the dwellings than those on sheep camps or those on railroad-era sites.[6] (Another reason for the distance is that people needed more clear space in front

[6]Grazing-regulation era homestead dumps averaged 22.3 m from the dwelling ($n = 17$), while sheep-camp dumps averaged only 11.0 m ($n = 9$).

Table 13.1

Sizes of Dwellings on Grazing-Regulation-Era Homesteads and Selected Variables on the South McKinley Mine Lease

Site no.	Area of largest dwelling (m²)	Total dwelling area on site (m²)	Area per occupant (m²)[a]	Maximum small stock of occupants	Resident smith	Resident weaver
1[b]	28.3	73.0	12.1	100	—	x
81	28.3	28.3	3.6	145	—	x
201[b]	21.2	40.8	3.7	100	—	—
212[b]	44.2	75.7	9.5	296	x	x
115	28.3	47.9	6.2	145	—	x
33[b]	33.2	33.2(?)	12.6(?)	262	—	x

[a]Total dwelling area divided by maximum of occupants.

[b]Homesite occupied for most or all of the year.

of homestead dwellings in which to perform the greater range of tasks that accompanied longer stays.) The growing use of stoves also explains why woodpiles are more common on sites of the grazing-regulation era than on earlier sites. I defer the question why more households had stoves during the era of grazing regulation until the end of this chapter.

People left more ash dumps and woodpiles, windbreaks and *ramadas*, sweathouses, ovens, storage features, corrals, and lamb pens on railroad-era sites as they filled the range and settled down on fewer homesites. Families also might have used more ovens, corrals, and lamb pens because these devices saved labor. During the era of grazing regulation, people continued to build more facilities on sheep camps, but not on homesteads (compare Table 13.2 with Table 8.3).

On homesteads, only sweathouses and woodpiles became more common. I have already mentioned that woodpiles increased along with stoves. The increase in sweathouses may be more apparent than real: The sweathouses that inhabitants of earlier homesites used may have stood farther from the homesites and therefore were recorded archaeologically as separate sites. A possible reason for this separation is that, in the earlier period, fewer families owned wagons in which to haul the necessary wood and rocks, therefore placing their sweathouses where both of these materials were plentiful.

On sheep camps of the grazing-regulation era, sweathouses probably became more common for the same reason. The increase in woodpiles and ash dumps on these sites probably also reflects the growing use

of stoves. People may have built more windbreaks and *ramadas*, storage features, and corrals because they were staying longer on each sheep camp, either within the year or for a greater number of years. The possible enlargement of sheep-camp dwellings mentioned above is consistent with this notion.

Like the features on sites, the movable domestic tools and equipment that people discarded on homesites of the grazing-regulation era were more numerous and varied than those on earlier homesites. A comparison of Tables 5.5 and 10.10 shows that the following items were much more common on sites of the grazing-regulation era than on earlier sites: artifacts of production in general; manos and metates; washtubs, basins, and pails; stoves and parts; furniture; axes, shovels, and other large tools; boards and tar paper; patent medicines and cosmetics; toys; wagon parts and supplies; and auto parts and supplies.

The domestic tools and equipment actually observed on "typical" sites of the grazing-regulation era, however, do not differ much from items typical of the late railroad era. The following description of the Navajo hogan in general differs from those of earlier observers mainly in its greater detail; it also offers a picture of the inside of a cribbed-log hogan and shows that this type offered storage space in the ceiling not available in the obsolete forked-stick type:

> Goods have a fixed disposal which utilizes all available space. Herbs and some types of dried foods, ceremonial equipment, guns and bows and arrows, hats and articles of clothing in current use, are stowed away in corners of the rafters or suspended from beams by thongs or nails. Reserve clothing and bedding, prized jewelry and

Table 13.2

Percentage of Grazing-Regulation-Era Homesites
in the Lease Townships with Selected Types of Features[a]

Feature type	Homesteads	Sheep camps	Homesites of unknown occupation spans
Dwelling	100	100	100
Windbreak, *ramada*	48	0	60
Sweathouse	73	67	67
Oven	46	0	0
Ash dump	100	100	100
Woodpile	92	75	50
Storage	53	0	67
Corral	100	100	100
Lamb pen	54	40	20
No. of components[b]	(12–34)	(4–10)	(2–6)

[a]Includes all sites positively identified by interviewees.

[b]Number of components on which the presence or absence of a particular type of feature was noted (not all types were noted on sites off the lease).

ceremonial articles are stored in trunks or suit cases, which are stacked against the wall where the roof is lowest. Pots and pans are stacked near the central fire or placed with the spoons and supplies of flour, lard, coffee, and sugar in crude cupboards made of boxes nailed to the wall by the door. . . . Ordinarily there are no heavy or bulky pieces of furniture. Stoves and beds are very much on the increase but are much more apt to be placed in the supplementary cabins [workplaces] than in hogans. The same may be said for tables. (Kluckhohn and Leighton 1947:47)

The Tinhouses used a similar inventory of domestic items on both summer and winter homesteads, although many items did not enter the archaeological record (see Table 13.3). The medium size of this family and of its herd makes it typical of lease-township households.

As mentioned in Chapter 10, families did not necessarily use more of certain items just because they are more commonplace on later archaelogical sites. Most of these items may be more common simply because people tended to discard them on homesteads, the sites on which they stayed the longest, and because homesteads were much more common during the era of grazing regulation than in earlier times. That these items are more commonplace is therefore more evidence that families were settling down.

As Kluckhohn and Leighton suggest, however, families may actually have used more of certain durable goods, such as stoves, furniture, wagons, and automobiles. These goods may have become cheaper and more available to Navajos by the era of grazing regulation. During the railroad era, a supply of these items would have accumulated slowly in Gallup and in the government compounds, where white people, who were better off than most Navajo families, lived. As these items grew old and were replaced, they may have been sold secondhand to Navajos. Thus, the items "trickled down" and appeared among lease-township families sometime after they had first appeared on the local market.

Stock-Raising Technology

By the later half of the railroad era, stock-raising technology in the lease townships had reached a state that persisted, with few changes, through the era of grazing regulation. Like the more dramatic changes in stock-raising technology between the early and late parts of the railroad era, these changes reflect the settling down of more families and the continued increase in the work they had to do.

Table 13.3

Comparison of Functional Types
of Artifacts on the Tinhouses' Winter and Summer Sites, 1935–1940

	PM 115, Winter homestead		PM 81, Summer homestead	
	Used on site[a]	Remains present	Used on site[a]	Remains present
Artifacts of production				
sheep rattles	x	x	x	—
agricultural implements	—	—	x	x
arms/ammunition	x	x	x	x
Food				
meat, fresh	x	x	x	x
corn	x	x[b]	x	x[b]
beans	x	—	x	x[b]
squash	x	—	x	x[b]
melons	x	—	x	x[b]
other fruits/vegetables (fresh)	—	—	x	x[b]
baking powder	x	x	x	x
vegetables/fruits, canned	—	x	—	x
milk, canned	na	x	na	x
lard, canned	x	x	x	x
meat, canned	—	—	—	x
Indulgences				
coffee/tea	x	x	x	x
pop	x	x	x	x
liquor	—	—	—	x[c]
tobacco	x	—	x	x
Domestic small technology				
dishes	x	x	x	x
pots/pans	x	—	x	x
utensils	x	—	x	x
mano/metate	na	—	x	x
washtubs/basins	x	x	x	x
pails	x	x	x	x
Household equipment, furniture				
kerosene lamp	x	—	x	x
other light	na	x	na	x
stove and parts	x	—	x	x
water barrel	x	x	x	—
House construction, maintenance				
locks/chains/hinges	na	—	na	x
ax/shovel/large tools	x	—	x	x[d]
boards	na	x	na	x
Personal effects				
patent medicines/cosmetics	x	x	x	x
clothing/buttons/buckles	x	—	x	x
shoes	x	x	x	x

(*continued*)

Table 13.3 (*continued*)
Comparison of Functional Types
of Artifacts on the Tinhouses' Winter and Summer Sites, 1935–1940

	PM 115, Winter homestead		PM 81, Summer homestead	
	Used on site[a]	Remains present	Used on site[a]	Remains present
Entertainment				
toys	x	x	x	x
other (shot-put stone)	x	x	—	—
Transportation				
wagon parts/supplies	x	—	x	x
auto parts/supplies	x	x	x	x
horse gear	x	—	x	x

[a]According to a former occupant interviewed on both sites; items listed include all types observed on the sites.
na = not asked.
[b]Evidence consists of remains in flotation samples.
[c]Liquor bottle fragments do not date to the 1935–1940 occupation.
[d]A shovel was present but may not date to the 1935–1940 occupation.

This chapter began with the observation that children still did the herding in most families. The histories of land tenure and customary-use-area management in previous chapters show that large-scale stock owners still hired herders, although the number may have diminished as stock reduction struck the large owners.

The daily herding regime of the railroad era continued into the era of grazing regulation. In the Southern Agency jurisdiction, Harbison reported,

> I do not know of but two owners that practice a bedding-out system of handling sheep and goats. The general practice is for the family to follow the herd from one locality to another year after year as water and feed conditions demand. They always return to the same area, and have built a string of hogans and corrals at each place. These hogans and corrals are used as headquarters and the sheep and goats are trailed to and from the range to the corrals. This is usually done twice a day as the herder comes back to the hogan for lunch. This practice certainly is very detrimental to the range as it causes so much trampling. (Harbison 1932:9201)

The bedding-out system to which this passage refers would have been feasible only for large owners, for only they had full-time herders. Commercial non-Navajo sheep ranchers in the Southwest used the bedding-out system: Pairs of men lived in tents on the open range while tending herds of thousands or more sheep, which they moved to new pasture every few days (Kelley 1982c:148–170). The bedding-out system was probably uncommon among even large-scale Navajo owners, including those of the lease townships, for at least two reasons. First, these owners often seem to have simply parceled their sheep out to other families, who herded them as they would have herded sheep of their own. Second, in the bedding-out system someone had to check on the men to tell them where to move every week and to bring them fresh provisions every 3 or 4 weeks. To save this work and its expense, many large-scale Navajo stock owners probably simply maintained a string of line camps out on the range to house their hired herders until provisions were depleted. Mr. Towering House Clansman seems to have used this method, at least during the railroad and early grazing-regulation eras. By the late 1930s, however, the recollections of local Navajos suggest that he had adopted the bedding-out system. I do not know the reason for this alleged change.

The annual stock-raising schedule differed little from that of the railroad era. After forced stock sales began, the traders probably bought more lambs in the fall than during the railroad era, but they no longer bought wool at that time. If the fall clip was mainly to supply weavers, the traders may have quit supplying them with wool for rugs that the traders could not sell.

More families may have controlled the breeding time of their sheep when the government induced the chapters to organize community buck herds. Chapter members pooled their bucks and turned them over to one family between July and November, a service for which each buck owner paid the caretakers one sheep or goat. This program was supposed to increase the income that each family gained from its (reduced) herd by postponing lambing until after the bad weather was over and thereby insuring that more lambs survived until sale time. Fat Salt, for example, took one of the buck herds in the lease townships.

Another change from the railroad era was that fewer households moved as often as every few weeks. Yet another seasonal practice that was not common until the era of grazing regulation was the cutting of wild hay for storage over the winter as horse feed. Fred Tinhouse even owned a horse-drawn rake and cutter, with which he not only cut hay for his own stock, but toured the neighboring countryside as far north as Wheatfields, north of the Black Creek Valley, to cut hay for others.

The facilities that families used in stock raising seem to reflect their settling down and their constant need to save labor. As already mentioned in this chapter, the labor-saving corrals were slightly more common on sheep camps in the era of grazing regulation than in earlier times. This change may mean that families were spending more time on their sheep camps, that they engaged in a wider range of productive and domestic chores there, or, most likely, both (because a wider variety of chores inevitably accompanied longer stays). Many families used two other labor-saving devices, lamb pens and twin corrals, during the era of grazing regulation, as they had evidently done earlier.

Most corrals of the grazing-regulation era, like those of the railroad era, still provided 1–2 m^2 for each animal (see Tables 13.4 and 13.5). Some of these corrals, however, may have afforded much more room. I initially thought the main reason for this increase was that families of the grazing-regulation era had more corrals, originally built for the big herds of the past, available for salvaging than their railroad-era

predecessors (Kelley 1982a:322). Although this difference still explains some of the excessively large corrals,[7] another reason for the increase in size emerged after analysis of the grazing permits and livestock registry. These documents suggest that some families with excessively large corrals temporarily took in herds of others and combined them with their own. This pooling seems to have been far more common during the era of grazing regulation than during the railroad era and may show that some families were avoiding reduction by hiding their stock with other families, or that they were leaving the lease townships to find work.

This farming out of herds may also explain why most sheep camps of the grazing-regulation era had more than one corral, as did homesteads, but not railroad-era sheep camps. Another possible reason is that more corrals became irremediably mucky during the greater number of years that people used their sheep camps during the grazing-regulation era. More corrals were consequently rebuilt elsewhere on the various sites, so that two corrals are evident archaeologically but only one was used at any one time.

I have already mentioned the steady growth in the number of reservoirs, the other important type of stock raising facility (Figure 13.1). These numbers grew from the late railroad era throughout the Depression, as more families settled down to living all year in the lease townships.

Artifacts used in stock raising are hardly more evident on sites of the grazing-regulation era than they are on sites of the railroad era (see Table 10.10). The inventory of artifacts that people actually used in stock raising was not particularly extensive, however; it included a few mass-produced, specialized items, mainly hand shears and sheep bells, which rarely wore out beyond repair and therefore were rarely discarded. The items more likely to have worn out and to have been discarded are those fashioned from other, recycled artifacts: the sheep rattles made from cans, pop bottles topped with either store-bought or homemade rubber nipples for feeding lambs, and milking pans of old pots, pans, or basins.

[7]For example, Tall Salt Clansman's grandson salvaged the corrals that Chee Jim had previously built at site PM 33 for a bigger herd.

Table 13.4
Corrals on Grazing-Regulation-Era Sites on the South McKinley Mine Lease

Site no.[a]	Maximum herd size[b]	No. of corrals	Total corral area on site (m²)	Total corral area per animal (m²)
Homesteads				
1	100–140 + bucks	2	477	≤3.4–4.8
33.2	160	2	665 +[c]	4.2+
182	80–100	1	200	2.0–2.5
201	80–100	1	240	2.4–3.0
59.1	145–637	3	1292	2.0–8.9
59.2	145–637	3	1088+	1.7–7.5+
115	145–637	3	1104+	1.7+–7.6+
Sheep camps				
7	131–206	2	408	2.0–3.1
202	250	1	320	1.3
121	492	3	452+	1.1+
122	115–372	2	254+	0.7+–2.2+
73	350	1	672	1.9
Winter corrals				
182	80–100	1	177	1.8–2.2
12	262–564	1	600	1.1–2.3
23	1084	1	2000	1.8
Other isolated corrals and campsites				
917	1084	1	1256	1.2
271	296	1	500	1.7
24–25	82–242	1	504	2.1–6.1

[a]Includes only sites with measurable corrals for which an estimate of herd size was also available; component number is to the right of the decimal point.

[b]Largest number of sheep either owned by the occupants around the time they used the site or indicated by local Navajos as likely to have been kept on that site.

[c]Plus sign indicates additional corrals were too deteriorated to be measured.

Farming Technology

The farming technology used by families in the lease townships probably continued to evolve along lines that had started in the railroad era. Information on farming during the era of grazing regulation, however, is more detailed.

The growing season in the lease townships begins around the middle of May and ends around the middle of October. People therefore planted around May 15. Corn remained the main crop, and beans were secondary. Squash and watermelons were also common, and some families planted other vegetables as well. By this time, most families used the plow rather than the *gish*. They hoed the fields, preferably twice during the summer. Neighbors helped each other harvest in mid-October.

The harvest regime of the Tinhouses was probably typical. They would pick the ears of corn, pile them in a wagon, and haul them from the field to their homestead, where they dried the ears on a bald patch of sandstone fenced to keep out livestock. They first set aside the wormy ears for the horses, then husked the rest and laid them out to dry. (Other families probably dried their corn on the flat roofs of *ramadas*, which was a common Navajo practice.) They later shelled the ears into a gunnysack, probably with pegs, and stored the sacks of corn in hogans or a cellar. They gave the cobs to the horses. The Tinhouses usually did not set seed aside, except when the crop was scanty. Ordinarily they just planted whatever was left in the spring.

Families with fields more than a mile from their summer homesites maintained shelters near the fields.

Figure 13.1 A stock reservoir in the lease townships. The original dam, the wall of rock and earth in the foreground, was built in the 1930s and later breached. The new dam was built in the 1960s, a short distance down the drainage. The fence keeps unattended cows from wandering into the pool and getting stuck in the mud.

Table 13.5
Corrals Used by Individual Families during the Grazing-Regulation Era

Site no.	Annual occupation of site	Time stock kept on site	Area of each corral[a]	Corral area per animal
The Tinhouse family, 145–637 small stock				
59.1	homestead	all year	646	1.0–4.5
			646	lamb corral
59.2	homestead	6 months	780	1.2–5.4
			308	lamb corral
			U	—
115	homestead	6 months	594	1.0–4.1
			510	lamb corral
			U	—
Violet Brown's family, 80–100 small stock				
182	homestead	all year	200	2.0–2.5
182	winter corral	infrequent	177	1.8–2.2
201	homestead	all year	240	2.4–3.0

[a]U = unknown.

Some of these were windbreaks and *ramadas*, but others were cribbed-log hogans. This innovation suggests that some families were spending more time at their fields and therefore needed more substantial shelters in which to store domestic equipment instead of moving it back and forth from other homesites. Plows and other new, expensive farm equipment were likewise kept safe from theft and the weather in these shelters.

More families used plows during the era of grazing regulation than during the railroad era; twice as many reservoirs, moreover, were used to irrigate twice as many fields. These trends carried over from the railroad era because of two familiar underlying causes: the family's quest for efficient technology to relieve its labor burden and the intensifying land use owing to land subdivision.

Conclusion

Changes in domestic and stock-raising, as well as farming, technology during the grazing-regulation era reflect most strongly the intensification of land-based production that had started in the railroad era and, especially, the setting down of the families. This intensification, in turn, was caused by land subdivision, which resulted from the families' continuing subsistence on mainly land-based production. Some technological changes also may reflect an increase in craft production (silversmithing) and the family's perpetual search for labor-saving devices to reduce its labor burden.

Chapter 14

The Industrial Era, 1950–Present

Historical Background

The events of the era of grazing regulation did not by themselves transform Navajo family land use; trends that had started in the railroad era were continuing to unfold. The programs that the federal government had developed during the era of grazing regulation did, however, guide the transformation during the most recent period of Navajo history, the industrial era. And it was during this period that the draglines finally came to the lease townships.

Once the hectic days of World War II were over, Navajos found that they could subsist neither on livestock nor on wage work. Industry remained conspicuously absent from the Navajo country because the traders and wholesalers, who for years had profited from Navajo livestock, wool, and handicrafts, had not invested in any local industries (Kelley 1977:162–172; Weiss 1984). The post–World War II recession further discouraged industrialization, for industry tends to stay in cities during recessions, where cheap, unemployed labor is concentrated, and expands into the countryside mainly during booms. Since World War II, these downturns in the business cycle have also stimulated congressional sentiment toward terminating federal trusteeship of Indian lands (Kelley 1979:41). The federal government had been propos-

ing to terminate particular tribes as early as 1947 (Tyler 1973:163).

Congress, however, also recognized that each reservation needed an economic base to keep its citizens off the state welfare rolls. Therefore, for the Navajos and Hopis, Congress passed the Navajo–Hopi Long-Range Rehabilitation Act early in 1950. The act authorized more than $88 million over 10 years to finance "infrastructure": health services, education, "industrial and resource development," and road construction. The act also authorized the tribal government to lease tribal lands and budget its own U.S. Treasury funds (mainly from land claims and oil and mineral leases and royalties), with the approval, of course, of the Secretary of the Interior (Young 1978:132, 136–137). In other words, Congress provided money to groom the Navajo country for private industry, then allowed the tribal government to manage this "grooming process" and carry the Navajo labor force through recessions.

In 1953, Congress adopted House Concurrent Resolution 108, a policy statement that advocated termination of all tribes but required a separate bill for the termination of each tribe. Congress then directed the BIA to schedule the termination of various tribes. The Navajo Tribe was not terminated, but was prepared for an eventual termination that has not materialized. Between 1953 and 1958, the federal government encouraged the tribal government to take on many BIA services: the reservation police, irrigation projects, water wells, and various welfare programs (Young 1978:143–145). The Long-Range Rehabilitation Act and federal termination policy thus cemented relationships among the federal government, the tribal government, and private industry that have dominated Navajo history since 1950.

The Long-Range Rehabilitation Act funded massive school construction. Federal termination policy also encouraged the states to use federal Johnson–O'Malley funds, available since 1934, to finance state public schools on Indian reservations. Arizona and New Mexico undertook such contracts in 1952 (Young 1961:52–54). Navajo parents had come to view schooling more positively since stock reduction had transformed children from an economic asset as herders into an unproductive liability (Young 1961:132). Therefore, school enrollment in the Navajo country, which had inched upward from about 3000 students in 1930, surged to over 22,000 in 1954, an increase of over 7000 in one year alone (Young 1961:18, 24). Until 1958, lease-township children of all ages, if they went to school at all, attended various boarding schools, including the one in Fort Defiance and a new "dormitory" school in Gallup. In that year, however, the Gallup–McKinley County Public Schools opened the Tse Bonito Elementary School in the lease townships for kindergarten through fifth grade.

The federal, state, and tribal governments also paved roads and financed soil-conservation and water projects. In 1950, the only paved roads were around the edges of the reservation, including the road north from Gallup to Shiprock and Route 66 south of the lease townships. Around 1951 or 1952, the state paved a road from the Shiprock–Gallup highway through the northern part of the lease townships to Window Rock. By 1960, another several hundred miles had been paved within the reservation (Young 1961:133–137). Between 1953 and 1960, soil-conservation projects throughout the Navajo country affected 20 times the acreage covered between 1930 and 1953, although the rate of water development lagged behind that of the 1930s (Young 1961:169–178). The lease townships had no soil-conservation projects, but instead received several windmills and shallow wells.

Meanwhile, the Navajo country's natural resources began to attract mining, oil, and gas companies, which remain the foundation of private-sector employment to this day. These industries are capital intensive and therefore have furnished few jobs, leaving the title of major employer to the public sector. The resulting lease payments, royalties, and bonuses, however, constitute a large share of tribal-government revenues (Benson 1976:51–52).

Between 1950 and 1954, the northern Navajo country around Shiprock and Farmington, New Mexico, enjoyed the first of several booms in oil and gas production. In 1954, the wells on the reservation pumped several million dollars into the tribe's U.S. Treasury account (Young 1978:152). At the same time, the tribal government sought to transform these returns on its nonrenewable resources into a wide variety of self-sustaining businesses. In 1951, it even took over the old Fort Defiance coal mine north of the lease townships (Young 1961:190). Four years later, however, the tribe was forced to liquidate many of these enterprises, probably because oil and gas revenues had fallen by more than two thirds that year (Young 1961:190, 1978:152). Apparently the tribe lacked the capital to see its small-business ventures through the inevitable first unprofitable years. The tribe, however, did not close the Fort Defiance mine.

Oil royalties remained low until 1957 (Young 1978:152) and forced the tribe to lure more private industry to the reservation instead of creating its own. Unfortunately, most firms proved to be small, short-lived plants seeking cheap labor (Young 1961:192). Just in the nick of time, the Four Corners oil field burst on the scene in 1957, and tribal revenues soared. The tribal government soon became among the largest employers in the Navajo country and also provided various social services and supplementary welfare (Young 1961:217).

Navajo workers flocked to the various reservation administrative centers, including Window Rock and Fort Defiance, where, by 1970, more than 8000 people lived, most of them government workers and their families (U.S. Commission on Civil Rights 1973:968–995).

With its new revenues, the tribe redoubled its effort to attract manufacturing firms and to develop some of its own. The Long-Range Rehabilitation Act had not brought electricity, running water, or other infrastructure to reservation communities, even though such infrastructure is basic for manufacturing. The tribal government immediately sought remedies, first in 1959 by arranging to buy electricity from Farmington. It created the Navajo Tribal Utility Authority (NTUA) to distribute the power, as well as to build water and sewage systems, first at Window Rock and a couple of other reservation communities (Young 1961:194–195). Nevertheless, electricity did not reach the homes of lease-township residents until after 1970, and then it was a privately owned company in Gallup that offered the service. Everyone still lacks running water.

Around 1960, electric-power production from coal also began to generate jobs and tribal revenues. Before this time, coal mining had waned as the natural-gas boom made that fuel available in large centers like Gallup, Window Rock, and Fort Defiance. In the vicinity of the lease townships, the result had been the closing not only of the St. Michaels and Ganado coal mines, but also of the coal mines around Gallup (Ximenes 1958:69; personal communications from Mike Andrews and Father John Lanzrath, 1978). The old Fort Defiance mine persisted under tribal management until the late 1960s, when the tribe pulled out.

Meanwhile, however, people had been swarming into Phoenix, Tucson, and southern California, where the skyrocketing demand for electricity was pushing utility companies far afield in search of power sources (Kelley 1977:151, 176). To meet this demand, the Arizona Public Service Company built two power plants in the Navajo country, one of which, the Cholla plant, was built between Winslow and Holbrook in 1961. The McKinley Mine was opened that same year to supply the plant with coal from private lands and leased allotments in the western part of the lease townships. The owner of the mine, the Pittsburg and Midway Coal Company, was a wholly owned subsidiary of Spencer Chemical Company until Gulf Oil Company bought it in 1964 (Dames and Moore 1974:2–4;, Wilson 1977:253).

The flurry of new oil and gas development, mining, and power plant revenues settled down to a steady stream in the 1960s. The BIA usually negotiated these leases at terms widely considered favorable to the companies (Robbins 1978:36; Ruffing 1979:99; U.S.

Commission on Civil Rights 1982:95). Tribal revenues stagnated, as did employment in the new industries, while the Navajo population and labor force (mainly unemployed) kept growing. The tribal government, therefore, established the Office of Navajo Economic Opportunity (ONEO) in Fort Defiance, which funneled the federal money to local Navajos through the recently revived chapters (Young 1978:163–164). Since the mid-1960s, ONEO and other disbursements to individual chapters have employed people in Tribal Works, Comprehensive Employment and Training Act (CETA), Navajo Pre-Vocational Training Program (NPVTP), and other projects (Bingham and Bingham 1976). The tribe disbanded ONEO in 1981, but many of its programs continued under the tribe's divisions of Chapter Development and, later, Community Development (*Navajo Times*, September 14, 1983, p. 1).

The tribal government also stepped up its quest for manufacturing firms to occupy tribally financed plants during the 1960s. Unfortunately, "footloose industries," mainly defense contractors like General Dynamics in Fort Defiance, were the main occupants (Ruffing 1979:105; *Navajo Times*, February 2, 1978, p. 415). The tribe also continued to develop its own business enterprises, the largest of which include the tribal sawmill near Red Lake and the Navajo Tribal Utility Authority and the Navajo Engineering and Construction Authority in Fort Defiance. Except for the sawmill, however, these enterprises have been undercapitalized and therefore marginal (Henderson 1979:115). To make matters worse, by the early 1970s tribal leases and royalties had dipped again (Benson 1976:11-12, 51–52). At the same time, the post–Vietnam War recession had thrown many Navajos out of work and doubtless increased the tribe's social-services burden. Casting about for a way to keep itself afloat, the tribe considered taxing coal, uranium, and electrical power projects, and renegotiating some of the 1960s mineral leases (Robbins 1978; Ruffing 1979:102).

At the eleventh hour, the so called Arab oil crisis of late 1973 set off a new flurry of plans for mining and power production. The McKinley Mine began to expand from a capacity of 400,000 tons a year to 4 or 5 million (Wilson 1977:253), and therefore bought or leased much of the remaining land in the lease townships. The Indian Self-Determination and Education Act of 1975 has also provided new jobs by enabling the tribal government to assume more BIA functions on contract. As a result, the tribal government has become the largest employer of Navajos in a public sector that employs three quarters or more of all working Navajos (Navajo Tribe, Office of Program Development [OPD] 1974; 24–25, 1977:20–21; Navajo Tribe, Division of Economic Development [DED] 1978:24–25). At the time of this writing, minerals and related revenues contributed about one third of the tribal government's annual budget, while federal grants and contracts contributed nearly all of the rest; about one third of the federal monies went for general assistance and employment assistance (*Navajo Times*, September 14, 1983, p. 1).

Even the growing energy industries and government have not, however, been able to absorb many employable Navajos. In 1979, according to the *Navajo Times*, with unemployment hovering between 40 and 50%, and a third of all reservation Navajos receiving tribal or state welfare,

> The absence of jobs on the reservation lies at the root of Navajos' need for welfare, Lillie Footracer, Fort Defiance Agency manager for TAPP, says.
>
> "People really think of welfare as a hand-out. But it's not a hand-out. Its a substitute for something they can't have anymore," Footracer says, adding that sheepherding was once a way of life for the Navajos, but that the reservation land cannot support sufficient livestock for most families. (*Navajo Times*, April 5, 1979, p. 1)

As if that economic picture were not bleak enough, federal budget cuts and the economic slump in 1981 reduced Navajo per-capita income by almost 25%, raised the unemployment rate from an already astounding 38% in 1980 to an estimated 72% in 1982, and simultaneously cut the budgets of the social-service programs to which the growing numbers of unemployed were turning for help (Navajo Tribe, Division of Community Development [DCD] 1982, based on figures from the U.S. Census, the BIA, and Arizona Department of Economic Security). Matters have become worse since then.

Land problems have accompanied industrialization, and, especially, the recent minerals development. In localities like the lease townships where the surface rights to much land are in trust allotments but where

the federal government has retained the rights to minerals (or at least to coal), the conflicting interests of the Navajo surface users and the federal government perhaps pose the biggest problem. The BIA's leasing policy, as a BIA official described it to the *Navajo Times* in 1978, does not ordinarily involve the allottees until after the lease has been negotiated.

> "That's right. We don't notify the allottees before their land is offered for bid," said Andrew Latham, Assistant Director of [BIA] Real Property Management.
>
> "Some of those tracts have as many as a hundred owners [heirs of the original allottee]. They are scattered all over. We prepare the lease and accept the bids and bonuses from the companies. Then it is up to the companies— most of whom have Navajos working for them—to make the contact with the allottees to get their signatures on the leases." (*Navajo Times*, November 16, 1978, p. C-1)

Sometimes allotments have even been leased without the consent of the allottees (*Navajo Times*, November 16, 1978, p. C-1; Gallup *Independent*, June 28, 1979, p. 1; Moore 1976; U.S. Commission on Civil Rights 1982:94–104).

Since 1950, then, private industry, especially mining, has dominated the Navajo economy directly, and also indirectly through its support of the tribal government. In turn, the tribal government, which was federally instituted to smooth the path of private industry, has tried to amplify industrialization by turning royalties from mineral extraction into self-sustaining agriculture and manufacturing. The mercantile economy before 1930 and the subsequent grazing regulation, however, left widespread poverty that industrialization has been too limited to alleviate. The tribal government is forced to beat the clock of dwindling natural resources by cranking up a self-sustaining economy with one hand, while the other is tied behind its back, dispensing welfare and jobs.

Trends in Family Land Use

In the railroad and grazing-regulation eras, family production for the market led to an increased family workload and the subdivision of the land through inheritance. These two forces, in turn, changed many aspects of land use. In the industrial era, too, the work of production and domestic maintenance may have grown more, at least for many families, and land subdivision continued, at least in some localities. The workload may have grown in some families because for the first time many children went to school, and young, able-bodied adults went away to work, leaving the elderly behind with most of the stock raising, farming, and domestic chores. Land subdivision continued as land was withdrawn for private industry, such as the McKinley Mine lease, and for public uses, such as the expanding government compounds in Window Rock and Fort Defiance.

Yet the growing workload and land subdivision did not affect family land use in the industrial era as they had before. Families no longer supported themselves mainly by production from their own land, but by the wage and welfare payments that their members received for being part of the national labor pool. This is not to say that stock raising and farming have not remained important to many families, for they offer a much-needed supplement to the other sources of income. In addition, these are the only useful activities open to many elderly people, who have spent most of their lives farming and raising livestock, and who without them feel useless and demoralized. Finally, people still need livestock for feeding guests at ceremonies.

In the next four chapters I show that industrialization has transformed family land use in the lease townships as grazing regulation was supposed to do, but did not. Industrialization cut the number of households engaged in stock raising and farming, eliminated all large-scale owners, and forced everyone to depend mainly on wages, welfare, or both. The worsening terms of trade between livestock products and consumer goods also eroded the family's dependence on livestock; by 1974, a pound of wool would buy only half of what it had bought even in 1930, the previous low point in the terms of trade (see Table 4.1). Families once able to subsist from a herd of 100 therefore could no longer do so. Diminishing herds and the new sources of money income also led families to stop producing things for their own consumption, even food.

Despite the eventual reduction in livestock in the lease townships, however, overgrazing continued. One reason is that, when industrialization had brought in the McKinley Mine, many families had lost grazing land. Another reason is that stock raising is still the only productive activity that engages many older people, and many want to make the most of it. Industrialization and the corresponding growth of the tribal government in Window Rock provided enough jobs near the lease townships to keep many young wage workers from moving away, so that the resident population could grow (in more remote parts of the Navajo country, however, many young people must leave to work). Residence groups enlarged because younger people no longer raised stock and therefore did not need to leave the homesites of their parents for herding space of their own.

Land tenure has also changed. The land withdrawals, especially those in Window Rock and the McKinley Mine, together with the wage workers' need to live near their jobs, have forced people to make more opportunistic residence choices. As a result, the transmission of residence rights may be moving toward bilateral inheritance. The same changing residence needs have probably helped extend the life of the outfit, although bilateral inheritance of residence rights, if it replaces matrilineal inheritance, may create conflicts that will undermine the outfit in the long run. Present-day outfits are hard to discern, for the large stockowners, who in the past linked most members of an outfit through shared grazing rights, are no more. Only recent land transfers among collateral relatives show the persistence of the long-term residual land-use rights that I believe are the foundation of the outfit. Industrialization and land withdrawals have also forced families to safeguard their traditional rights with new forms of legal tenure. As a result, people have begun to invoke their legal rights even in disputes among themselves over traditional rights.

Industrialization has also changed the ways that families use space in the lease townships. Two main agents have changed the environmental distribution of grazing tracts, fields, and homesteads: the intrusion of the McKinley Mine and the need of families to live near the paved road now that they depend so thoroughly on the outside world. Wage earners obviously need to live near the paved road so that they can get to work. In addition, all families need to live near the paved road so that they can reach schools, stores, hospitals, the food-stamp office, and so forth.

Families started gravitating to the paved road after

declining wool and livestock markets, among other factors, put the old, general-merchandise wholesalers out of business and new, specialized wholesalers began to supply the trading posts. These new wholesalers would not carry the traders' accounts over several months or accept payment in wool or livestock; they insist on monthly or even biweekly money payments and have forced traders to follow suit in extending only short-term credit to their customers (Kelley 1977:37; Sears 1954:7). Therefore, families can no longer get enough food on credit in the fall to carry them through the winter. By issuing stamps for only short periods (until recently), the food-stamp program, started after 1962, also has forced people to make short-term purchases and thus more frequent visits to the store.

By moving near the paved road, families have altered the shape and locations of their grazing tracts, which they have also had to change to make way for the McKinley Mine. They have not altered the distribution of homesites and grazing tracts in relation to natural resources, however, for their resource needs have changed little. Nor have they changed the situation of their fields much, for the optimal farming zone covers a large portion of the lease townships.

The number of grazing tracts, meanwhile, has grown little, for few younger-generation households have taken up stock raising, and the McKinley Mine has eliminated some tracts. The sizes of the tracts have diminished because families lost parts of many tracts to the mine. I have the impression that families plant less acreage, and they certainly plant fewer fields, now that wages, public assistance, and food stamps allow

them to buy all their food. The number of homesites has grown but has not kept pace with population growth for two reasons: one, because the lack of livestock has caused more and more families to stay all year on one homesite and, two, because younger people lack the stock that, in the olds days, by multiplying, eventually forced younger people from the parental home. The resulting increase in the number of households in each residence group also has probably enlarged the homesites. As family production dwindles, however, so does the number of facilities on the homesite. This reduction might counteract enlargement from the increase in households.

Industrialization has unleashed much spending on bigger, more comfortable dwellings and labor-saving domestic, farming, and even herding technology. Multiroom houses of mass-produced frame-and-siding construction, rather than hogans, are now the norm. Everyone heats, cooks, or both with wood- or coal-burning stoves, if not with those that burn butane. Most households have electricity, although none yet have running water. Pickup trucks have replaced wagons for all-purpose hauling, and almost every residence group has one. Tractors have replaced plows. Barns and stalls of mass-produced lumber have replaced winter corrals and twin corrals. Finally, the ultimate labor-saving "device" for several families has become the hired herder, even though no herd in the lease townships is large, even by the modest standards of the grazing-regulation era.

Family Economy and the Local Environment during the Industrial Era

Family Sources of Livelihood

Between 1950 and 1978 in the lease townships, as in the Navajo country generally, wages and welfare replaced stock raising, farming, and handicraft production. Although the lease-township population continued to grow, the land available for stock raising had actually diminished by over 20% when the McKinley Mine evicted local Navajos from its lease. At the same time, deteriorating terms of trade meant that, by 1974, a family would have needed a herd of 200 or 300 to buy what the minimum subsistence herd of 100 formerly would have bought. Even in 1940, two thirds of all lease-township households had fewer than 200 small stock, and by 1978 only one household kept a herd of more than 200. Even that family could no longer live off its herd; the 6-month trading-post credit that allowed people to live by trading lambs and wool was no longer available, and family expenses were rising as motor vehicles, clothing and equipment for school children, as well as other new items, became necessities.

Because of the deteriorating livestock markets and the land withdrawals for the mine, then, lease-township families simply could no longer hope to support themselves by stock raising. Therefore, both the number of livestock and the number of households that raised livestock dwindled. The decline in stock raising is clearly due to the two causes just mentioned, and not to grazing regulation, for the lease townships were exempt from the permit system.

The statistics throughout this chapter and the next three, unless specified otherwise, cover 62 households that actually lived in the lease townships in 1978 and 5 that did not, but maintained houses there. In 1978, the number of small stock in the lease townships, including lambs and kids, was only one eighth of the 1940 average (see Table 15.1). These animals were, as always, unevenly distributed. In 1978, however, 2 out of 3 households lacked livestock entirely, compared to only 1 in 10 in 1940 and 1 in 4 in 1915. The number of stock-owning households, moreover, was actually slightly lower in 1978 than in 1940, although the total number of households had more than doubled (see Table 15.2).

Table 15.1
Number of Livestock
Owned by Lease-Township Households, 1978[a]

	Sheep and goats	Cattle[b]
Total no.[c]	1434	U
No. per household	21	U
No. per residence group	48	U

[a]From field census.
[b]U = unknown.
[c]Includes lambs and kids.

In other parts of the Navajo country, families have started to raise more cattle, but I do not think that lease-township families have done so. Although I did not take a cattle census, most families seem to keep no cattle, a few own a small number apiece, and only one owns more than 10 or 12.

Farming has dropped as abruptly as stock raising. Two thirds of all households (42) lacked access to a field in 1978, whereas nearly all households in 1940, and even about half in 1915, had access to fields. Nearly all of the 1978 households with fields also kept livestock, which were the main consumers of the corn crop. Rising money incomes and, especially, food stamps made farming for food superfluous.

Craftwork, especially weaving, had also declined. The number of craftworkers and the type of items that they make vary tremendously, however, according to the state of the craft markets and the availability of better-paying jobs (see Table 15.3). In 1978, only two women wove regularly on their own, although three more received wages through CETA to weave at the chapter house (the chapter then sold the rugs and kept the proceeds). Two of these CETA weavers had previously made their living at silversmithing, but could not do so in 1978 because the Hunt brothers' speculation in the international silver market had priced the metal beyond the reach of most smiths. A few lease-township residents nevertheless continued to get along as best they could on silverwork. Unlike the 1940 smiths, most of these producers were women. Men can leave home for a job every day more easily than can women with small children, but such women can make jewelry at home if they have bought their own equipment. Craftworkers, however, made up less than one sixth of all workers in 1978, whereas weaving alone employed three-quarters of all workers in 1940.

Table 15.2
Distribution of Sheep and Goats
among Lease-Township Households, 1978

No. of small stock[a]	No. of households	% of all households
0	42	63
1–25	7	10
26–50	5	7
51–75	2	3
76–100	4	6
101–200	4	6
201–300	1	1
Unknown	2	3
	67	100

[a]Includes lambs and kids.

Wage work has grown tremendously in contrast to stock raising, farming, and craftwork. During the 1950s, several men from the lease townships started to work as miners at the old Fort Defiance coal mine, and many more took seasonal work on the railroads. The railroads recruited Navajo men through the federal Railroad Retirement Board office in Gallup, which in turn sent work calls through 63 "claims agents," rural traders who received a fee for every man recruited (Sears 1954:7). One former claims agent, whose recruitment area included at least part of the lease townships, estimated that 80% of the able-bodied men in his area worked on the railroad sometime during the early 1950s. These railroad jobs were especially desirable because they paid for up to 130 days of unemployment as well (Sears 1954:7). After 1957, however, automation eliminated three out of every four railroad jobs (Young 1961:224). Other lease-township residents departed in the summer to pick crops in various western states, often leaving their sheep with relatives and taking their children with them. In 1978, however, few lease-township residents worked for the railroad and none, so far as I know, worked as harvest hands.

In 1978, wage jobs employed the great majority of all working lease-township residents (see Table 15.3). Unlike Navajos in general, less than half of the employed lease-township residents worked for the government. A few worked for either the McKinley Mine or the smaller Carbon Coal Company mine that

Table 15.3
Employment in the Lease Townships, 1978[a]

	No. of workers	% of all workers
Total employed	46	100
men	30	66
women	16	33
Self-employed craftworkers	7	15
silversmithing	5	11
men	1	2
women	4	9
weaving (all women)	2	4
Employed by others	39	85
mines (all men)	8	17
government	12	26
men	6	13
women	6[c]	13
Gallup businesses	8	17
men	6	13
women	2	4
Other	11	23
men	9	19
women	2	4
No. of adults 18 and older	108	100
employed adults	46	43

[a]From field census (1978).

[b]Includes families on the lease only.

[c]Includes three weavers employed in a government-funded project.

had recently opened near Gallup. A few grown children of other lease-township residents also worked for the McKinley Mine but had moved to trailer parks in Window Rock and therefore are not counted here. One may be surprised that fewer than eight lease-township residents worked in a mine that was almost in their backyards and employed 250 people, 70% of them Navajos because the United Mine Workers of American union contract with Pittsburg–Midway stipulates Navajo preference in hiring. Most of these jobs, however, require skilled or semiskilled workers who are more likely to live in Window Rock and Fort Defiance than in the lease townships.

Overall, more adults were employed in 1978 than in 1940, and more of the employed worked full-time for a living wage. Nevertheless, over half of all lease-township residents age 18 years and older were not working in 1978, not even part-time (see Table 15.3). The widespread unemployment and underemployment have forced many lease-township residents to depend on welfare.

Unfortunately, I did not find out the degree to which lease-township residents depend on welfare and the other income sources, but two estimates are available. In Land Management District 16, which encompasses the lease townships and many similar rural areas near Gallup and government centers, wages contributed over two thirds of all income in 1973. Welfare plus retirement (mainly from the railroad) contributed most of the rest (see Table 15.4). Livestock and wool sales contributed almost nothing. In 1940, the share of income that livestock products contributed, 38%, was second only to the 52% contributed by wages, almost all of which was actually from silversmithing. I have also tried to estimate aggregate household income in the lease townships in 1978–1979 (see Table 15.5) with essentially the same result as the 1973 study.

Since 1940, wage work and welfare have dramatically increased both the money income and real purchasing power of families. When one converts the annual income figures on Tables 10.6, 15.4, and 15.5 to constant (1967) dollars, the average of $148 per person in 1940 had increased fivefold by 1973 and sixfold by 1978. The recent figures, moreover, do not include the value of food stamps, which have freed even more money income for nonfood items. The growth of money income, however, should not blind one to the fact that the income of the average lease-township inhabitant is only a fraction of the national average. In 1973, for example, per-capita income in the lease-townships was only one fifth of the national figure (USDC, Bureau of Economic Analysis 1975).

Consumption Patterns

During the 1950s, some lease-township families continued the trade and consumption patterns of the previous two decades. Tall Salt Clansman's grandson, for example, would exchange his lambs in the fall at a local trading post for a winter's worth of food. During the winter his household of three consumed 20 sacks of flour, each weighing 25 lbs., and sugar, potatoes, lard, baking powder, salt, and pop. He and his wife would not buy very many canned goods

Table 15.4

Household Income by
Source, Land Management District 16, 1973

	% of total
Source of income	
wages	69
retirement	7
welfare	15
handicrafts	7
livestock and wool sales	2
other	—
	100
Per-capita income	$1003
Median household income	$4098
Mean household size	5.0 persons

From Wistisen, Parsons, and Larson (1975:8, 14).

because they grew their own corn and squash. Their herd of 160 sheep and goats supplied their meat.

Faunal and botanical samples were analyzed from only one site built after 1950. They therefore cannot show whether most families, like Tall Salt Clansman's grandson, consumed their own crops and livestock.

Indirect evidence, however, suggests that many families did not. Except for the Window Rock store, all local trading posts where 1940 lease-township residents traded had closed by 1958. These closings indicate that local people were trading mainly in Gallup and thus already had more money income, for credit was harder to get in Gallup than at trading posts (Sears 1954:7). Moreover, in the following report of a regional business journal in 1954, one can practically hear the Gallup businessmen rubbing their hands at their jingling cash registers as Navajos abandoned home-produced for mass-produced goods.

Jay McCollum, proprietor of Jay's Supermarket, . . . estimates that 50 per cent of his trade comes from Indians. Total Indian trade with his store has about tripled during the last thirteen years.

[M]ost families have no access to gas or electric utilities, or to centrally supplied piped running water . . . but the Navahos are . . . buying self-contained appliances such as gasoline washers and battery radios. . . . In addition the Indian market is very good for oil stoves, linoleum, beds, kitchen cabinets, and general furniture items of all sorts.

Table 15.5

Estimated Aggregate Personal Income
by Source, South McKinley Mine Lease Residents, 1978–1979

Source	Calculation of estimate	Amount ($)	%
Wages	39 employed @ $2.90/hr., 40 hrs./wk., 39 wks./yr.	176,436	62
Craftwork	silver: 5 smiths @ $7,500/yr. weaving: 2 weavers @ $500/yr.	38,500	13
Livestock	wool: 776 mature small stock @ 9.5 lbs.[a] @ 65¢[b] = $4,792[c] lambs: assume sale of half crop from herds 50 and over only; 310 mature animals, 198 lambs, 99 sold @ 50 lbs.[d] @ 70¢[b] = $3,465	8,257	3
	Subtotal	223,193	78
Retirement	assume 7%[e]	—	7
Welfare	assume 15%	—	15
		286,145	100
	per capita[f]	1,693	

[a]From Kelley (1977:248).
[b]Prices offered in and around lease townships in spring (wool) and fall (lambs), 1979.
[c]Excludes USDA wool incentive payment and therefore slightly underestimates total wool income.
[d]From Kelley (1977:247).
[e]Land Management District 16 figure from Wistisen, Parsons, and Larson (1975:8, 14).
[f]Includes 169 residents on lease; 4 households with 22 people surveyed did not specify income sources.

Table 15.6
Household Consumption Expenditures,
Land Management District 16, 1973[a]

Expenditure	% of total expenditures	% spent off the reservation
Housing	3.6	30.4
Household expenses	1.9	64.1
Home repairs	2.6	72.6
Food	35.2	66.9
Clothing	13.0	69.3
Transportation	16.9	67.6
Car or pickup payment	17.1	74.8
Recreation	0.6	64.2
Meals eaten out	1.6	62.4
Livestock supplies	1.7	74.9
Farm equipment	0.1	76.5
Personal care	3.5	64.7
Other	2.2	61.8
	100.0	67.3

[a]From Wistisen, Parsons, and Larson (1975:34, 87).

As the Navajos come closer to the white man's way they are buying lumber and building materials and putting up their own houses. George Bubany, proprietor of Bubany Lumber Company, sells about $100 a day worth of lumber materials and paint to Navajo buyers, totaling about $30,000 a year in such purchases. Mr. Bubany points out that this is an entirely new market which did not exist before the war. He feels that if the trend continues, modern houses with floors, windows, doors, and sinks, containing $1,000 to $1,500 worth of building materials in each, will replace the log and earth and stone hogans for living quarters on the reservation within the next fifteen years. (Sears 1954:5–6)

George Bubany was right. In 1973, the average household in Land Management District 16 spent 4.5% of its annual income, or about $225, on household expenses and home repairs, along with a third of its income on food, another third on transportation and vehicle payments, and the rest on many other goods (see Table 15.6). The average household, moreover, bought two thirds of these goods outside Navajo land, presumably mostly in Gallup. The expenditure patterns of lease-township households probably come close to this average.

The artifacts left on industrial-era archaeological sites on the lease, however, barely suggest this surge in consumerism (see Table 15.7). The reason is that most homesteads of the industrial era are still occupied

Table 15.7
Functional Types of Artifacts on Sites
on the South McKinley Mine lease, 1950–1979

	N	%
Total no. of components[a]	14	100
No. of components without artifacts	4	29
Artifacts of production		
lamb nipples	1	7
sheep rattles	—	—
salt troughs	—	—
arms/ammunition	—	—
agricultural implements	—	—
silversmithing equipment	—	—
weaving equipment	—	—
Food		
baking powder can	—	—
vegetable/fruit can/jar	1	7
milk can/bottle	2	14
lard can	1	7
meat can	1	7
jelly can/jar	—	—
syrup can/jar	—	—
Indulgences		
coffee/tea	2	14
pop	2	14
liquor	4	29
tobacco	1	7

(continued)

Table 15.7 (*continued*)
Functional Types of Artifacts on Sites
on the South McKinley Mine lease, 1950–1979

	N	%
Domestic small technology		
dishes	5	36
pots/pans	3	21
utensils	1	7
mano and metate	2	14
wash tubs/basins	1	7
pails	3	21
Household equipment and furniture		
kerosene lantern	1	7
other light	1	7
stove and parts	5	36
water barrel	1	7
furniture	3	21
House construction and maintenance		
locks/chains/hinges	2	14
ax/shovel/large tools	2	14
boards	7	50
tar paper	4	29
Personal effects		
patent medicine/cosmetics	5	36
clothing/buttons/buckles	3	21
shoes	—	—
Entertainment		
toys	3	21
musical instruments	—	—
Transportation		
wagon parts/supplies	1	7
auto parts/supplies	6	43
horse gear	2	14

[a]Includes all sites identified by interviewees on which systematic observations of artifacts were made.

and therefore, of course, were not recorded archaeologically. Most sites abandoned during the industrial era have been sheep camps, campsites, and isolated corrals. The sample of sites on the lease on which artifacts were recorded reflects this pattern. The sample contains as many campsites, isolated corrals, and other types of specialized sites as it does homesites, and sheep camps outnumber homesteads four to three. The artifact inventory from industrial-era sites therefore resembles the inventory from late railroad-era sites more than from the grazing-regulation era sites.

Because the site samples of the late railroad and industrial eras are similar, differences in their artifact inventories cannot be explained by families settling down, as were differences between the inventories of the railroad and grazing-regulation eras. Instead, these differences probably reflect real changes in consumption patterns. Thus, the absence of baking powder cans from industrial-era sites suggests that people were buying more store-bought bread. And industrial-era sites have more liquor containers, light fixtures, stove parts, house construction and maintenance items, patent medicines and cosmetics, and clothing than do even sites of the grazing-regulation era (also see Table 15.8). Conversely, wagon parts were on the decline. Auto parts are about as common on industrial-era sites as on sites of the grazing-regulation era, despite the less intensive use of the later sites. They therefore reflect the widely known fact that more Navajos used motor vehicles in the industrial era than earlier.

An inventory of artifacts probably typical of industrial-era homesteads was recorded on one currently occupied site (see Table 15.9). An average-size family has always lived there, although for a longer time than that of the average homestead (the average lease-township homestead has been occupied for 16 years, whereas the site described here has been occupied for 30). Most artifacts observed, however, probably date to only the last few years (various structures have been built on top of the earlier parts of the site). The inventory listed here is probably the minimum that one would find on a contemporary homestead; the inhabitants haul their trash away or burn it, and the only items recorded are scattered on the surface and not likely to be removed when the site is abandoned. Unlike earlier sites, this site has artifacts (usually many) in almost every category except artifacts of production. Some of the items, moreover, are much more common than they are on earlier sites: mass-produced building materials in a wide array, patent medicines and cosmetics, toys, and auto parts and supplies. These are the very things that started the Gallup cash registers jingling 30 years earlier.

The Environment

Overgrazing early in the industrial era may have continued to change the physical environment of the lease townships, but its effects were minuscule compared to those of the McKinley Mine. The Pittsburg

Table 15.8
Artifacts on Industrial-Era Dwelling Sites in the South McKinley Mine Lease[a]

Site no.	Dates[b]	Native historic ceramics	Household items[c]	Food		Auto parts	Building materials[d]	
				Glass	Cans		Lumber	Other
212	1931–1963	—	x	x	x	x	x	x
7	1935–1960	—	x	x	x	x	x	x
1	1935–1974	—	x	x	x	x	x	x
21	1951–1961	—	x	x	x	x	x	—
15	1956–1959	—	x	x	x	—	x	x
12804	1963–1971	—	x	x	x	x	x	—
16	1972–1974	—	—	x	x	—	x	x

[a]Abandoned sites only. All sites are dwelling components on the lease that were positively identified by interviewees and on which the presence or absence of artifacts was systematically recorded.
[b]Based on both interviewees' statements and archaeological data.
[c]Small housewares.
[d]Excludes nails.

Table 15.9
Minimal Inventory of Artifacts Observed on a Currently Occupied Homestead in the Lease Townships

Artifacts of production
  arms/ammunition
Food
  baking powder can
  vegetable/fruit can/jar
  milk can/bottle
  lard can
  plastic butter tub
  meat can
  frozen-food foil dishes
  tinfoil
  cow, sheep, and goat bones
  corn cobs
Indulgences
  coffee can
  pop bottles and cans
  beer cans
  tobacco (snuff lids)
  candy packages (plastic)
Domestic small technology
  dishes
  pots and pans
  utensils
  washtubs/basins
  pails

Household equipment and furniture
  stove and parts
  furniture parts
  small-appliances parts
House construction and maintenance
  chains
  large tools
  boards
  tar paper
  cinder blocks
  linoleum
  insulating material
  concrete
  domestic cleaners
  paint thinner
Personal effects
  patent medicine/cosmetics
  clothing
  shoes
  pens, pencils
Entertainment
  toys
  Christmas decorations
Transportation
  auto parts and supplies

Table 15.10
Actual 1978 Stocking and Estimated 1941 Carrying Capacities of Subdivisions of the Lease Townships

Small stock per mi.^{2}	Tse Bonita Wash–upper Defiance Draw	Middle Defiance Draw	Eastern Flat–lower Defiance Draw
Actual number of SUYL, 1978[a]	31+	81	53
Adjusted 1941 carrying capacity, SUYL[b]	54	75	75

[a]SUYL = mature sheep units year long; adjusted to include lambs and kids (see Table 5.8).
[b]Adjusted to include lambs and kids (as in Table 5.8) but not doubled to give 6-month equivalents.

and Midway Company at first closed an area of about eight sections in the western part of the lease townships, south of the paved road and the Tse Bonita Wash. This area constituted the original south mine lease, where strip-mining began in 1961 with a single dragline. The land was then "revegetated" (Wilson 1977:5). According to a mine official, mining moved north of the road in 1968, where another 3 mi.^{2} in the lease townships have since then been closed to grazing. In 1961, the AT&SF Railroad had built a spur from its main line into the south lease. This spur was extended north of the paved road in 1974 as a growing number of draglines clawed their way up the Tse Bonita Wash into the part of the reservation known as the north lease. At this time, the Gulf Oil Company also began to buy and lease the land that forms the rest of today's south lease, eventually covering that area with a network of drilling roads and a grid of drill holes.

In the mid-1970s, bigger draglines and higher coal prices made recovery of the coal deep under the original south mine lease seem profitable, and in 1979 a new dragline began to strip the reclaimed land there. Therefore, in the western part of the lease townships, both north and south of the paved road and the Tse Bonita Wash, some land was in the process of being stripped, some was in the process of being revegetated, and some had been completely revegetated. The revegetated areas are the piles of soil and rock that a dragline has moved to expose the coal. As the environmental planners from both the Navajo tribe and the mine explain, bulldozers grade these piles into gently rolling hills, their topsoil, which has been set aside, is replaced, and a mixture of native grasses (trees evidently cannot be replaced) is planted. According to a tribal official, livestock were allowed very briefly into one small revegetated area that had been mined

in 1961. At this writing, however, that area was being strip-mined again.

Strip-mining, then, has changed the environment available to the lease-township inhabitants by depriving them of most of the Tse Bonita Wash. It has also reportedly fouled one spring south of the wash and cut people off from two reliable wells, Coyote Drinking Water and Bubbling Spring. It has also covered the entire south lease with roads plied by a blue-green drilling rig and its entourage of assorted vehicles. The roads have proved a mixed blessing; they make hauling wood from the uplands easier not only for lease residents, but also for strangers.

Despite the loss of range, the number of livestock in the lease townships has dropped so much that stocking now is below the 1941 carrying capacity in many parts of the townships, including the Tse Bonita Wash–upper Defiance Draw (see Table 15.10). I do not know whether actual stocking is below today's carrying capacity, however, for more recent carrying-capacity estimates are not available. I do know that the range is not used evenly. Some families continue to overstock. Others, especially those with very small herds, keep the stock grazing near their homesites all year so that they need not stay out with the herd all the time. The stock overgraze the land around homesites but seldom visit more remote parts of the lease townships. In some of these remote places neighbors trespass with their stock, but other places remain almost unused for long periods.

By 1978, lease-township households demanded less of both grazing and other resources in the townships than they had in earlier times. Besides range, most households no longer needed farmland. Many were hauling water from wells outside the lease townships, although those without pickup trucks toted their water from the nearest wells and stock reservoirs. Most families were still getting their wood from the uplands of the lease townships but had the trucks to haul wood from elsewhere, if necessary. The resource needs of the stock-raising households, however, had changed little from earlier times. Most lease-township households therefore made little use of the resources of the lease townships other than wood and water and did not demand much even of those, but a large minority continued as before. And the lease townships continued to provide for these needs.

Conclusion

Industrialization has finally transformed the basis of family livelihood in the lease townships, as throughout the Navajo country. Families now support themselves with wages and the welfare payments that maintain the industrial reserve army, rather than by land-based production. Craft production, especially silversmithing, remains important, but only a minority of households in the lease townships farms or raises livestock. Owing to the resulting tremendous growth in both cash income and real purchasing power, local families have freed themselves from dependence on long-term trading-post credit and now use mass-produced food and other goods almost entirely.

The shift from family livestock production to industrial production has also shifted the main cause of environmental change from overgrazing to the effect of industry—which in the lease townships is strip-mining. A large portion of the land is now off-limits to livestock, and the degree to which it will support livestock again is unknown.

Chapter 16

Family Demography and Land Tenure during the Industrial Era

Family Demography

As the family ceased to be the basic productive unit in Navajo society, the household's need for productive labor no longer determined the size or composition of most lease-township residence groups. Instead of shrinking between 1940 and 1978, however, the average residence group grew. This is one of the four or perhaps five major demographic changes in the lease townships between those years. The other three or perhaps four are the doubling of the population, the decrease in average household size, the normalization of the sex ratio, and the possible, but very recent, tendency of women to limit their number of children (see Table 16.1). These changes have various causes, all related directly or indirectly to industrialization.

The population growth is only indirectly related to industrialization. Families had earlier filled and subdivided the range so much that they were confined to the lease townships all year, and therefore so were their children. Industrialization in nearby Gallup and Window Rock–Fort Defiance has simply helped the lease townships to retain this population. The other changes, however, are the direct results of industrialization.

The average residence group was bigger in 1978 than in 1940 for two reasons. First, plural-household residence groups were now in the majority. Second, the biggest residence groups of 1978 were bigger than their counterparts in 1940. The reason for both of these differences is that, since most young adults no longer maintained herds, they did not need to leave their parents' homesites, as they formerly did when their own herds had grown large enough. Seven households in 1978 lived outside the townships for most or all of the year so that their working members could be near their jobs and simply maintained houses on homesites where their parents or siblings also lived. Residence groups that consisted of the households of siblings were rare in earlier times: Only one such residence group existed in 1915 and none in 1940. Yet, because of "absentee residents," four such residence groups existed in 1978, and these were the largest in the lease townships. Another force still encouraging

Table 16.1

Demographic Characteristics of Lease-Township Households and Residence Groups, 1978–1979[a]

	On lease only				Lease townships			
	All-year residents[b]	Summer residents	Non-residents[c]	Total	All-year residents[b]	Summer residents	Non-residents[c]	Total
Total population	191	19	28	238	NA	NA	NA	315[d]
No. of households	47	1	3	51	60	2	5	67
No. of residence groups	24	0	0	24	31	1	0	32
No. of single-household residence groups	10	0	0	10	14	1	0	15
Population per household	4.1	—	—	4.7[e]	NA	NA	NA	NA
Population per residence group	8.0	—	—	9.9	NA	NA	NA	NA
Households per residence group	2.0	—	—	2.1	1.9	—	—	2.1
Mean age per resident	27.8	—	—	25.3	NA	NA	NA	NA
% of population under age 18	51	—	—	55	NA	NA	NA	NA
Ratio of males to females	104:100	—	—	98:100	NA	NA	NA	NA

[a]From field census (1978); Tse Bonito Elementary School (1970–1977).

[b]Those who live on the lease in winter and off the lease in summer are counted on lease all year. NA = not available.

[c]Those who live outside the lease townships all year but maintain houses in the lease townships.

[d]Estimated assuming that the average household outside the lease was the same size as the average household on the lease.

[e]Compare 5.0 persons per household in Land Management District 16, 1974; Wistisen, Parsons, and Larson (1975:8, 14).

households to stick together in residence groups was the undiminished need for domestic labor, since most households still had to haul their own fuel wood and water.

Unlike the residence group, the average year-round resident household of 1978 was much smaller than the average household of 1940. When one counts summer residents and nonresidents, however, the two averages are not much different. The households of year-round residents were smaller because more of them consisted of old people without children. Industrialization has lowered the size of the average household by drawing younger people and their families elsewhere.

The fact that whole families, rather than just men, have gone away to work has also normalized the ratio of males to females in the lease townships. The ratio in 1978 was not so severely skewed in favor of females as it had been in earlier times. Industrialization, moreover, has created more jobs near the lease townships, so that fewer people seeking wage work must leave to find it.

Statistics from the lease townships do not reveal the lower birth rate that I believe is another significant demographic result of industrialization. The women of age 40 years or over in 1978 had an average of six children apiece, a figure that does not differ significantly from the 1940 figure. Most of these women, however, are old enough to have depended heavily on family livestock production throughout most, if not all, of their childbearing years. I think that younger women—those now in their twenties and early thirties—will, on the average, end up having fewer children than did their mothers. Women in this age group elsewhere in the Navajo country are generally in favor of family planning (Ackerman *et al.* 1978). Indeed, the overall annual Navajo birth rate has declined from 48.8 per thousand in 1966 to 34.6 ten years later (*Navajo Times*, November 9, 1978, p. A–9). Many younger women in the lease townships have already allowed more years between births than their mothers did. The reason seems to be partly the expense of supporting more children, although some families minimize this by assigning one or more children to the grandparents. Another, perhaps more important reason seems to be that these younger women do not want infants to care for when they must hold down wage-paying jobs.

Land Tenure

Both legal and traditional forms of land tenure in the lease townships changed in the industrial era. The main trend in the legal sphere carried over from the grazing-regulation era: Individual Navajos either safeguarded their traditional claims through a greater variety of legal forms or lost the traditional claims to outsiders. The trend toward outsiders taking land that local Navajos had been using eventually culminated in the Pittsburg and Midway Company's negotiating with the BIA to lease the allotments without the BIA first consulting local Navajos. A new development is the growing tendency of families to invoke their legal ownership in land disputes among themselves, thereby combining the often contradictory legal and traditional systems.

Changes in the traditional sphere have been more complex. One might have expected industrialization to undermine the outfit because, even in earlier times, certain individuals isolated their customary use areas from the lands of the rest of their outfits by denying the residual rights of matrikin. As industrialization made families depend less on land for survival, one might therefore expect these residual rights to become less important; then more people could get away with denying the residual rights of others. The outcome would be the decomposition of outfits into families that monopolize particular customary use areas. So far, however, the outfit has survived because residual rights remain important to the many families that industrial or public projects have displaced, and to many more that move from job to job. These land withdrawals and job shifts, however, may ultimately undermine the outfit in that they encourage bilateral residence choices and, perhaps, an increasing tendency toward bilateral inheritance of land-use rights. If the number of land disputes escalates as a result, more families may deny the residual rights of all relatives, including matrikin, and the outfit would then disappear.

The particulars of industrial-era land tenure in the lease townships that make up this general picture are as follows. At the beginning of the industrial era, most land legally held by local Navajos was allotted. In addition, several Navajos had bought, or arranged to buy, the surface rights of several railroad sections from

Gib Graham and had lost the use of others to Graham and to other non-Navajos. Finally, the government had legally limited herding on these lands to families with permits, although the permits were soon abolished. After 1950, all but one of Graham's land-purchase agreements seem to have fallen through. In the early 1950s, however, several other local Navajos purchased the surface rights of sections from either Graham's family or from other non-Navajos who had bought the land from Graham. The largest local buyer was Tom Sharp, who promptly sold his four-and-a-half sections to the Navajo tribal government, which still owns the land in fee. The descendants of Juan also sold four allotments to the tribal government. In 1964, the tribe bought surface rights to another quarter section near Window Rock from the State of New Mexico, and in 1975 obtained the entire neighboring section from the Gulf Oil Company in exchange for a section along the reservation boundary that had been previously bought, in part, from Tom Sharp (USDI, McKinley County Assessor's Office 1960–1979, 1983; USDI, BIA, Eastern Navajo Agency n.d.b). Thus, Navajos now own land legally in fee simple as well as through trust allotments; the tribal government's ownership of land also safeguards local Navajo use rights to some degree.

Outsiders bought the rest of the land after 1950 and fenced more of it to keep local Navajos out. One of these buyers was a matrilateral relative of Corn-merchant, who bought three sections in the Eastern Flat where, as far as I can tell, he held no traditional rights. Non-Navajos who bought land from Gib Graham around 1950 also closed several sections to Navajo use. Two sections have been subdivided for the public school and for businesses and houses of outsiders, while other lands have been leased to at least two local Navajo families (USDI, BIA, Eastern Navajo Agency n.d.a, n.d.b). By 1978, the Gulf Oil Company had bought up most of the unallotted land in the townships outside the tribal lands, the two subdivided sections, and a couple of fee sections that local Navajos refused to sell (McKinley County Assessor's Office 1979, 1983).

While local Navajos were seeking new legal safeguards for their use rights, they were finding that the old safeguard, trust allotment, was losing its effectiveness. The BIA first allowed right-of-ways across their allotments for two gas pipelines, an electrical transmission line, an electric power line, a state highway, and the mine railroad spur (USDI, BIA, Eastern Navajo Agency n.d.a). Next, the BIA arranged the terms of two sets of allotment leases with the Pittsburg and Midway Coal Mining Company and Gulf Oil mentioned above. The leases were invalid without the signatures of allotment holders, but many say that, lacking advice from the BIA, they signed only out of ignorance or fear that the government would condemn the land and that they would get nothing. Because of differences between traditional and legal inheritance patterns explained below in this section, moreover, the users of an allotment were not necessarily among the heirs and therefore exerted even less influence on the terms of the lease. The first group of allotments, leased in 1961 in the Tse Bonita Wash, apparently returned little money to their owners. The 25-year lease to at least one allotment reportedly went for $880 ($0.22 per acre per year), which was then divided among 13 heirs. The second group of leases began in 1973 in the Defiance Draw and the Eastern Flat. The payments were higher, although they evidently varied among families. Because people were also compensated for houses and other improvements, moreover, many have never known exactly how much of the money was for the land. In any event, the payments to most families probably reflect roughly what the land would bring if leased for grazing at public-land rates. The Navajo tribal government, however, received more for the section mentioned above that the tribe had received in trade from Gulf in 1975. In 1978, Gulf decided to buy the section back and offered to pay the tribe for grazing land at the going rate. The tribe held out for a higher price on the grounds that the strippable coal underneath enhanced the value of the surface rights. The company eventually raised its offer, agreeing to lease the land for 5 years and then buy it for $150,000 plus a coal royalty (*Navajo Times*, July 19, 1979, p. 1).

Still another form of legal tenure arose in the late 1970s: the homesite lease. On the reservation the Navajo tribal code requires such leases of people without customary use areas (grazing permits) and of permittees who want to build homes with public utilities on their use areas (Thal 1982:31). Homesite leases are also required under analogous circumstances

Table 16.2
Land Tenure in the Lease Townships, 1978[a]

Source of use rights	Number of sites			
	Homesite	Campsite or isolated corral	Water source	Field
Original claim	—	—	—	—
Descent	31	1	18	17
Other	6	—	2	3

[a]If a site was used by more than one household, only the rights of the senior-generation household are counted.

on allotments. The applicant must get the allottee or heirs representing the majority of shares to sign the lease application, and the BIA must approve it. In 1977 the BIA approved four homesite leases in the lease townships, all for the children of heirs of the allotments on which each homesite was to be built. This policy is still too new to have had much effect on land tenure.

These land withdrawals and changes in legal tenure, together with the shifts in homesites that families have made to be near work and the paved road, have altered traditional tenure. In 1978, most land-use rights were transmitted through inheritance, as they were during the era of grazing regulation (see Table 16.2). Residence rights, and the channels through which they are transmitted, seem to be changing, however, in that a trend toward bilateral inheritance of residence rights may be emerging. Among younger-generation households of 1978 (households of people who still share a homesite with their parents), patrilocal residence had become almost as common as matrilocal residence, although it was relatively uncommon among older-generation households (solitary households and senior-generation households in multiple-household residence groups; see Table 16.3). About half of these older-generation households were virilocal, as in the past. For the first time, however, many of their children were staying on homesites with them, because these children could not move readily to the lands of their mother's families since their mothers no longer used the family land (perhaps in many cases because the land has been withdrawn for public or industrial use). Most of these younger-generation households will therefore undoubtedly remain after the parents die if

the mine does not displace them first.

Only five households in 1978 maintained homesites on the lands of both husbands' and wives' families, and only three of these households lived virilocally in the lease townships. The couples with dual residence have almost disappeared because the people of 1978 hardly needed to move their small herds. The past association of virilocal residence with livestock wealth and dual residence rights might lead one to expect a drop in virilocal residence, at least among the older people (one might expect virilocality among younger people because of their frequent moves to live near work). Virilocality did not decline among the older-generation households, however, because many of these people had exercised their residence rights in the past, when they still lived by stock raising, and simply did not revert to uxorilocal residence as the stock-raising life became moribund.

Nevertheless, lease-township families continue to invoke the matrilineal principle of inheritance in land disputes; they often refer to the homestead of their parents as "mother's place," even if it is on land previously used by their father's family. This usage implies that they have received their land rights through their mothers, even if that is not objectively the case. I have the impression that other people sometimes counter this implication by invoking clanship, claiming that land in a particular area belongs to members of a particular clan. This is an effective counterargument, for the children of the women who moved in with their husbands' families would not belong to that clan.

In land disputes of the industrial era, people have also invoked their legal land-use rights to back up their

Table 16.3
Residence Rights of Households to Main Homesites in the Lease Townships, 1978

Source of residence rights	Junior-generation households	Senior-generation households	Solitary households	Total
Wife's mother	8	8	4	20
Wife's father	6	4	4	14
Wife's parents	—	—	1	1
Wife's family	—	—	—	—
subtotal	14	12	9	35
Husband's mother	5	14	2	21
Husband's father	3	1	1	5
Husband's parents	—	1	1	2
Husband's family	—	—	—	—
subtotal	8	16	4	28
Other and unknown	—	2	2	4
	22	30	15	67

traditional rights. The examples that appear in the next three sections involve allotments: Someone wants to build a home or to herd on an allotment in which he or she has inherited an interest but which falls in the customary use area of another, usually collateral, relative. As more people legally back their traditional claims, more disputes are inevitable, because the heirs to allotments determined legally by probate court are not the matrilineal descendants of the allottee, let alone collateral matrikin. Instead, they are the original allottee's spouse and all direct descendants (USDI, BIA, Eastern Navajo Agency n.d.a). Users of allotments who are not heirs sometimes have verbal agreements (or say they have) with one or more of the heirs to "take care of" the allotment. One can easily imagine homesite leases serving as another weapon in future disputes over whether newcomers should be allowed to build homes on particular allotments.

That outfits have so far survived these changes in traditional tenure is evident in the next three sections of this chapter. The outfits of the industrial era, however, are much harder to observe in operation. In the past, large-scale stock owners constantly asserted the residual land rights that I believe define the outfit to gain the use of large blocks of land. These owners no longer exist, and people today exercise their rights only when public or industrial land withdrawals displace them, or when they move to go to work. Even in the absence of strip-mining, which is breaking up the outfits in the lease townships by preempting their lands, displacement and shifts for work might, in the long run, undermine the outfit. These two processes not only encourage people to move among matrikin, but also force many to seek long-term or permanent residence with their fathers' families. In the future, enough of the resulting instances of patrilocal residence might detonate a series of land disputes in which people would increasingly invoke legal tenure. If people come to ignore the traditional tenure on which the outfit is based, the outfit itself seems unlikely to survive.

Land Tenure in the Tse Bonita Wash–Upper Defiance Draw

Between Whitegoat Curly's death in 1951 and the opening of the mine 10 years later, the surviving members of his outfit kept to their own discrete customary use areas, with little overlap or sharing (see Figure 16.1). Whitegoat Curly's widow used the

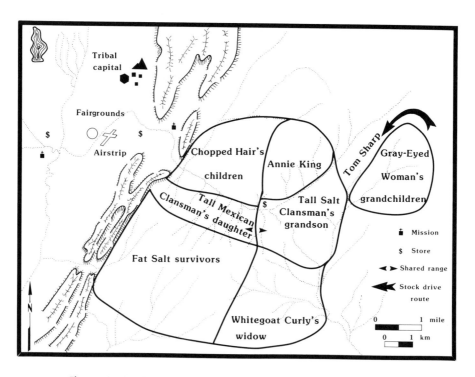

Figure 16.1 Land tenure in the Tse Bonita Wash–upper Defiance Draw, 1950s.

eastern part of her late husband's winter range from a homestead in the Defiance Draw next to Cornmerchant's old sheep camp and returned to the Black Creek Valley in summer. She shared this range for short periods with Mrs. Billy Smiley, a daughter of one of Whitegoat Curly's sisters, who built a sheep camp on an allotment that Whitegoat Curly had secured in Mrs. Smiley's name or in the name of her brother but who spent most of the year in the middle Defiance Draw.

At the opposite end of Whitegoat Curly's winter range, Fat Salt's family remained year round. By the late 1950s, the family was reduced to Fat Salt's widow, Big Woman, her older adopted daughter, and the orphan whom Cornmerchant had adopted long ago as a herder. Between the two of them, Big Woman and Whitegoat Curly's widow seem to have absorbed the land between their respective homesteads that Tall Red Streak Clansman and Chee Jim had shared before the latter died late in the grazing-regulation era.

North of Fat Salt's family land in the flats along

the Tse Bonita Wash was a sliver of land that Tall Salt Clansman's son used in conjunction with adjoining land in the Black Creek Valley. To the east lived Tall Salt Clansman's grandson (daughter's son), who had reclaimed the divide between the Tse Bonita Wash and Defiance Draw from the late Chee Jim. The grandson and his wife spent the entire winter on this tract and shared it for part of the season with two other couples: the grandson's sister and her husband (a son of Little Warrior), and the grandson's wife's sister and her husband (Charley Goldtooth, a son of Cornmerchant). Between 1956 and 1959, Charley Goldtooth leased the section around Divide Trading Post that the trader Lotario Ortega had fenced in 1937, thereby adding to the group's range. The families of Charley Goldtooth and Little Warrior's son had homesteads in the Black Creek Valley, but Tall Salt Clansman's grandson was only allowed to farm, not herd, there. All three households shared summer range on the Defiance Plateau. Together with Tall Salt Clansman's son's daughter and perhaps the other descendants of

Little Warrior who lived in the Black Creek Valley, these three households seem to have constituted a winter outfit.

Northeast of Tall Salt Clansman's grandson, in the far upper Defiance Draw, the successors of Curly Tallman during the 1950s continued to manage their use area independently, perhaps constituting a small outfit. At first the users consisted of Curly Tallman's widow and her children in one homestead, and Margaret Thompson's adopted granddaughter (Gray-Eyed Woman's granddaughter) and her family in another, but the two families seem to have combined their stock into one herd. Soon, however, Curly Tallman's "nephew" (Gray-Eyed Woman's grandson) and his family returned during the winters at the invitation of his sister. This third family spent the summers on land of the wife's family near the Puerco. Curly Tallman's widow and Gray-Eyed Woman's granddaughter together ran one herd, evidently in the southern part of the use area, while the grandson ran another, evidently in the northern part. These families lost range along their southern boundary when sisters of Tom Sharp's deceased wife and their children moved onto their allotments there, and later when a non-Navajo bought and subdivided a former railroad section.

When the McKinley Mine moved into the Tse Bonita Wash–upper Defiance Draw, it disrupted the land-use patterns of all these families. Many lost part, or even all, of their range and water sources and were forced to reduce their livestock or even abandon the area entirely. The mine also destroyed some of the outfits there by taking the land, the rights to which had held the members of the outfit together. The customary use areas that remained in 1978 are shown in Figure 17.1 in the next chapter. I avoid illustrating them in more detail in deference to the privacy of current inhabitants.

Perhaps the families hardest hit by the mine's intrusion were Tall Salt Clansman's grandson and the other two families that shared his range. In 1959, the Ortega family canceled Charley Goldtooth's lease and sold the land to the Pittsburg and Midway Company, forcing Charley Goldtooth to abandon his sheep camp. Little Warrior's son abandoned his sheep camp nearby at the same time, and the two families seem to have confined themselves to their winter homes in the Black Creek Valley. Tall Salt Clansman's grandson,

however, had no other winter range, and his summer range was too high in the mountain for him to use all year. He was also angry that he had regained his mother's allotment from the family of Charley Boyd, only to lose it again. He would not budge from his homestead until the mine forced him out in the early 1960s. Then he sought permission to use the neighboring part of the upper Defiance Draw from Gray-Eyed Woman's grandchildren, who belonged to the same clan as his wife.

The system worked as long as Gray-Eyed Woman's successors could spare some of their range. At first it seemed that the number of users was even diminishing: By the 1960s, Curly Tallman's daughters had married and moved away, and his widow moved in with one of them. That left only Gray-Eyed Woman's granddaughter and grandson, with their two separate herds and homes south of the yellow rock mesa.

Around 1970, however, while some of her herdless children and grandchildren remained south of the mesa, Gray-Eyed Woman's granddaughter and her daughters moved north of the mesa, forcing Tall Salt Clansman's grandson to leave. Because strip-mining had moved northward and the south lease had been revegetated, Tall Salt Clansman's grandson moved back to that area. He set up a sheep camp on a hilltop in an unmined area, only to have his road cut off by the extension of the mine railroad in 1974. For the next few years, he occupied a succession of sheep camps from which mine personnel repeatedly chased him. Between the early 1960s and 1978, his herd dwindled from 160 to less than a third of that size.

The mine also curtailed stock raising among the other residents of the Tse Bonita Wash–upper Defiance Draw, whose fortunes declined as they aged, leaving them little land or livestock to offer to their children. Around 1960, the widow of Whitegoat Curly, whose winter home was on a section that her husband had bought from the railroad, sold the land to the Pittsburg and Midway Company. She built a new homestead about half a mile south, where her husband had previously maintained a corral. At the same time, Mrs. Billy Smiley was forced to abandon her sheep camp. Soon old age caught up with the widow, and she began to stay at her summer place year-round; Mrs. Smiley has since then used what remains of the widow's range outside the mine lease.

The daughter of Tall Salt Clansman's son left her sheep camp south of the Tse Bonita Wash in the early 1960s after strip-mining reportedly fouled the spring nearby. She moved more than 50 mi. east to live with her husband's family.

Big Woman lost the southern half of her range in 1961 when strip-mining began just south of her homestead. As she was now old, her younger adopted daughter came to take care of her. The sheep herd was in decline, as the herder gradually sold the animals to buy wine from the nearby Navajo Inn. When Big Woman died in 1974, the younger daughter moved away, and the herder stayed alone on the homestead until a car struck and killed him near the Navajo Inn. After the herder died, Big Woman's older adopted daughter, who was still living nearby, took the few sheep that remained but soon sold them and began leasing the land to a daughter and son-in-law of Charley Goldtooth for winter range. One night not long after the herder died, some patrons of the Navajo Inn went to his abandoned homesite to spend the night. To keep warm, they holed up in one of the hogans, built a fire, and nodded off to sleep. The unattended flames soon ignited the hogan's dry log walls, and the men only narrowly escaped as the hogan burned to the ground.

This string of misfortune among Fat Salt's successors happened during the time that Charley Boyd's daughters, granddaughters, and great-granddaughters were losing their range north of the Tse Bonita Wash to the expanding McKinley Mine. One granddaughter, Annie King, having sold half of her stock in 1937 when Lotario Ortega had bought and fenced part of her land, was forced to sell the other half because the draglines were eating their way up the Tse Bonita Wash through the rest of her range. In 1978, one of Annie King's herdless daughters and her family lived in a homestead hemmed in by the mine, and another had "relocated" with her grown children to housing the company had built near the old Fort Defiance coal mine.

In the Tse Bonita Wash–upper Defiance Draw, then, only the original claim of Gray-Eyed Woman and its corresponding outfit had survived intact in 1978 (see Figure 16.1). That tract (excluding the allotments belonging to the Eastern Flat people and the subdivided land bought by outsiders) encompassed two customary use areas and four residence groups.

Members of the two older generations of this family had previously spent the summers with their respective in-laws in the lower Black Creek and Puerco Valleys. As they aged and their grown children did not want to assume care of the two herds, however, these people gradually reduced their stock. By 1978, the herds were too small to demand seasonal moves, and the families stayed in the upper Defiance Draw all year.

Land Tenure in the Middle Defiance Draw

Before 1950, the middle Defiance Draw belonged to one outfit but was divided into three customary use areas, one north of the draw and two south, as illustrated in Figure 10.2. After Fred Tinhouse's wife died in 1941, he continued to use the area north of the draw, even though the land belonged to her family. One of the areas south of the draw still served as winter range for Turning Warrior and his household. The other area served as winter range for They Are Raiding Along Behind Each Other and several of her grown children. Her brother, Billy Smiley, and his wife also continued to use the part of the area that adjoined the wife's family's range. They Are Raiding Along Behind Each Other shared a homesite with the households of her two grown sons and a daughter. In 1951, another daughter and her husband bought a railroad section in the family's customary use area and set up their own sheep camp there. Thus, the outfit consisted of at least five residence groups in the three customary use areas.

Then the families south of the draw began to extend their range northward. Probably they wanted to be nearer the newly paved road, even at this early date. They also may have wanted to use Burned Through The Rock Wash, a northern tributary of the draw that Whitegoat Curly's widow seems to have abandoned after her husband died. They Are Raiding Along Behind Each Other and her youngest son built a sheep camp north of the draw, and another son soon built a homesite nearby. Despite this intrusion, Fred Tinhouse continued to herd north of the draw. In 1956 he began to share the area in summer with his oldest son, who had lost to a non-Navajo a railroad section in the Eastern Flat that his wife's family had previously used. By 1960, the middle Defiance Draw outfit had grown to six residence groups. The number of customary use areas had not changed, but their boundaries were different.

After 1960, the intrusion of the McKinley Mine sent ripples through the middle Defiance Draw, even though the area lay outside the mine lease at that time. The outcome of this process, together with the desire of families to move near the paved road, was the reorientation of customary use areas as shown in 1978 by Figure 17.1 (see Chapter 17). The chain reaction to the mine's intrusion started because Mrs. Billy Smiley lost her sheep camp near Whitegoat Curly's widow's place when the mine leased the land. Instead of confining herself to her main range in the middle Defiance Draw, Mrs. Smiley reacted by moving her sheep to the allotment of her father, Mr. Tall, who during the railroad era had gotten land in the uplands between the Eastern Flat and Blackgoat's former use area. This tract was also desirable because it was near the paved road.

In locating the allotment's boundary, and aided by the section corners marked by the cadastral survey that had accompanied mining, Mrs. Smiley discovered that the sheep camp of They Are Raiding Along Behind Each Other and her son was just inside her allotment. She therefore evicted them. The two households then moved north to the paved road, where They Are Raiding Along Behind Each Other's allotment was situated. Eventually they and the households of other sons and daughters began to spend the entire winter north of Defiance Draw, using the range south of the draw most of the summer and Hunters Point only for short periods.

When They Are Raiding Along Behind Each Other and her family moved north, they evidently displaced Fred Tinhouse's younger son Sammy, who had laid the foundation for a cabin there but never finished building it. Sammy Tinhouse seems to have been pushed back to the strip along the north side of Defiance Draw. He and his recently married sister stayed all year at a homesite next to their father's home.

At this time, Blackgoat's son Turning Warrior also built a sheep camp near the paved road. The move may have been partly to ease travel, and partly for access to Burned Through The Rock Wash. As he grew older and his herd declined, Turning Warrior and his family, too, began to spend most of the winter near the road and to use the land south of the draw in summer, instead of moving to the Black Creek Valley as in earlier times. His survivors still follow this pattern.

By 1978, the middle Defiance Draw outfit consisted of eight residence groups and four customary use areas, all oriented much differently from those of earlier times and all used year-round. Not only were the use areas rearranged, but their inhabitants had broken up and recombined into new groups. The inhabitants of two use areas were the children of people who had claimed two of the three customary use areas in 1950: Fred Tinhouse and They Are Raiding Along Behind Each Other. The family that used the third area, that of Turning Warrior, however, had now joined with the children of They Are Raiding Along Behind Each Other to share a customary use area. In contrast, two families that had previously shared They Are Raiding Along Behind Each Other's use area, the family of Billy Smiley's widow and that of a son of They Are Raiding Along Behind Each Other, had carved out their own customary use areas.

Land Tenure in the Eastern Flat–Lower Defiance Draw

The configuration of customary use areas in the Eastern Flat in 1950 had not changed fundamentally from the configuration shown in Figure 11.3. Changes in that configuration after 1950 reflect land purchases of outsiders other than the Pittsburg and Midway Company more than the intrusion of the mine itself. If customary use areas shrank as a result, the sizes of most herds shrank even more. More families therefore each stayed all year on one homestead, and the overlap in customary use areas that resulted from the sharing of range for part of the year almost disappeared. The outcome is shown in Figure 17.1 of the next chapter.

In 1950, when Tom Sharp evicted the family of Violet Brown from the allotment of his deceased wife, Violet Brown moved her family about half a mile west to her own allotment, which extended into the land that Curly Tallman had previously used on the edge of the Eastern Flat. At the same time, two of Violet Brown's sons by Chee Jim built homesteads on this tract. These three homesteads were still occupied in

1978 by these people or their survivors. The families have remained confined to Violet Brown's allotment and the adjoining one, which belongs to her sister. The sister herself moved onto her allotment in the early 1960s after the death of her husband, with whose family she had been living. By 1978, she and Violet Brown's survivors, who occupied four homesteads, pooled their stock into one small herd that they kept all year on the two allotments.

Having finally crowded his late wife's sisters to the very edge of the Eastern Flat, Tom Sharp found himself in control of the rest of the northern segment. Based, as always, at his homestead at the northern end of his land, Tom Sharp also continued to move his herd to his lambing camp in the upper Tse Bonita Wash or to one in Azaakai's former range (until about 1955). Most of the area covered by the three-and-a-half sections he bought from Gib Graham lay outside this customary use area; that he sold the land to the Navajo Tribe almost immediately suggests that he had bought it on speculation. At the same time, the trader A.L. ("Colonel") Springstead bought the section around the Wildcat Trading Post at the south end of Tom Sharp's use area and may eventually have fenced it off.

When Tom Sharp died in the mid-1960s, his grown children abandoned the Tse Bonita Wash camp but agreed to continue collectively operating the "Sharp Ranch" in the Eastern Flat. Since then, most have held jobs and lived elsewhere all year, maintaining houses in their late father's homestead only for visits. The one or two children who actually lived at the homestead in 1978 tended cattle and sheep, the numbers of which had gradually dwindled. One descendant speculated that Tom Sharp was reaching down from heaven and gathering his livestock to him.

The central segment of the Eastern Flat split into two customary use areas after the Dixon brothers divided their herd late in the grazing-regulation era. The residents of the two use areas together might still have constituted one outfit in 1979, however, for their use-area boundaries seemed somewhat flexible. Since the split, the children of the two brothers have expanded into a total of six residence groups, all clustered around the parental homesites near the big ECW dam and, fortuitously, the paved road as well. In 1978, each customary use area supported two herds. One use area accommodated the largest in the lease townships, which had been moved to the Tinhouse family range in the middle Defiance Draw in summer since 1956, when "Colonel" Springstead fenced land in the Eastern Flat. The other use area was also truncated in 1951 when a matrilateral relative of Cornmerchant bought and fenced a section that Mr. Towering House Clansman had previously arranged to buy from Gib Graham.

In the southern segment, the same relative of Cornmerchant bought and fenced another section and a half previously earmarked for Mr. Towering House Clansman. Still another section that Mr. Towering House Clansman had arranged to buy from Gib Graham is also in the southern segment and was bought by a local rancher. It was not fenced, however, and remained part of the area that the daughters of Mr. Towering House Clansman had used year-round since their father's death. In 1978, two daughters in two separate homesites were running two herds there, each smaller than their father's by an order of magnitude.

Conclusion

Industrialization has changed dramatically the demography and land tenure of the lease townships. Jobs nearby have enabled most members of growing families to stay (or at least maintain homes) in the lease townships, so that, given high rates of natural increase, the population of the lease townships doubled between 1940 and 1978. The high rates of natural increase themselves are not products of industrialization, because they characterized earlier eras; some evidence suggests that younger women may limit themselves to fewer children than did their mothers, perhaps because many must work outside their homes.

The various land-using groups have also changed. Households have shrunk as the people who do leave the townships tend to be young adults with children. Residence groups have grown bigger, however, as most young couples, lacking livestock, need not move away from the parental home, and in any event may have nowhere else to go if the family has lost land to the mine or to purchasers from outside. Residence groups still get land for homesites and production through the rights of their individual members, but individuals no longer rely on traditional, matrilineal inheritance as much as they once did. A growing number of people have gained rights through their fathers, often because their mothers' families have lost land to industry or government. Other sources of rights are lines of inheritance established for allotments by probate court, which are bilateral, and lease or purchase. Outfits have survived, even though some are now restricted to unbelievably tiny parcels of land, because land withdrawals by government and industry continually force people to exercise residual rights to their relatives' land. As more people assert rights inherited from their fathers or established legally, however, the conflicts with relatives who consider only traditional, matrilineal tenure valid may in the long run destroy the outfit.

Chapter 17

Spatial Aspects of Land Use during the Industrial Era

As if pushed aside by flat stones dropped into a small puddle, the families of the lease townships were forced into the interstices of lands that the McKinley Mine and others had taken. They situated their homes for the best access to the outside world of jobs and services and adjusted their grazing and farming patterns within the limits of this paramount need.

Customary Use Areas

The customary use areas of the industrial era kept the range of natural resources typical of earlier use areas. The industrial-era use areas, however, lost the specialized sites for grazing and farming from their site inventories. Industrialization had so diminished the importance and scale of land-based production that each family could carry out most production activities from one homestead.

The customary use areas of the lease townships are shown in Figure 17.1. An even greater majority of households stayed all year in these customary use areas in 1978 than in 1940 (see Table 17.1). Most households that did not stay in the townships all year lived out-side to work, rather than to herd. That almost none of the lease-township households herded outside the townships is owing to three factors: first, most households no longer herded at all; second, of those that did, range subdivision during previous eras had eliminated many from range outside the townships; and third, the few people with rights to summer range outside the townships had become old and tired of trying to manage big herds. They had therefore reduced their herds so that they could keep them all year in the lease townships.

Most customary use areas of 1978 kept the same inventories of resources as those of previous years: woodlands, open sage–grass flats for grazing and farming, and water sources. All water sources, mostly reservoirs, were improved. These reservoirs would dry up, but many families had a more dependable source (a well or windmill) in or near their use areas. Families that lacked such watering places either drove their stock far into neighbors' areas or hauled water to their homesteads in oil drums. Most families found the local water unpalatable to drink and hauled their domestic water from wells outside the townships.

Because nearly all households stayed in the lease townships year-round, and because land withdrawals

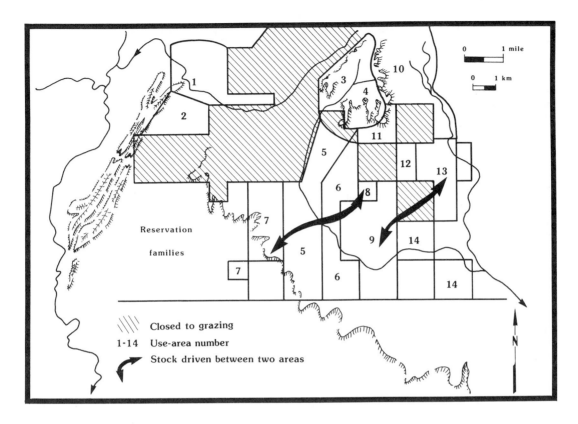

Figure 17.1 Customary use areas in the lease townships, 1978 (all boundaries approximate).

Table 17.1
Homes of Lease-Township Residents outside the Townships, 1978[a]

Location	No. of households with summer homes	No. of households with winter homes	No. of households with year-round homes
Hunters Point	2[b]	—	—
Fort Defiance	—	—	2
St. Michaels	2	—	—
Tsayatoh	—	—	1
Fort Defiance Coal Mine	—	—	1
Other	—	2	1
No home outside	—	—	56

[a]From field census (1978).
[b]Occasional use only.

Table 17.2
Inventories of Sites in Customary Use Areas in the Lease Township, 1978[a]

Use area	No. of residence groups[b]	Season	No. of homesteads	No. of sheep camps	No. of campsites	No. of fields[c]
Tse Bonita Wash–upper Defiance Draw						
1	2	All year	2	—	—	1
2	2	All year(1) Winter(1)	1	1	—	—
3	1	All year	1	1	—	—
4	3	All year	3	—	—	2
No number[d]	1	All year	1	—	—	—
No number[d]	1	Winter	—	1	—	OLT
Middle Defiance Draw						
5	4	All year	3	1	1	3
6	1	All year	2	—	—	1
7	2	Summer(1) All year(1)	2	1	—	—
8	1	All year	1	—	—	—
9	2	All year(1) Summer(1)	1	1	—	3
Eastern Flat–lower Defiance Draw						
10	2	All year	1	1	1[e]	1
11	4	All year	4	—	—	2
12	2	All year	2	—	—	3
13	4	All year(2) Varies(1) Winter(1)	3	1	—	4
14	2	All year(1) Winter(1)	1	1	—	—

[a]Number of stock is not given in deference to the privacy of residents.

[b]Number of residence groups exceeds the total for the lease townships on Table 16.1 because some families maintain homesites in more than one customary use area.

[c]OLT = outside lease townships.

[d]Homesite only; use area completely preempted by mine.

[e]Isolated corral outside lease townships on north McKinley Mine lease; not counted in site sample.

and shrinking herds had restricted household moves even more than in 1940, one might expect a continuation of the grazing-regulation–era trends toward more summer sites (improved water sources and fields) and fewer specialized herding sites (sheep camps, campsites, and isolated corrals). The inventories of sites in the 1978 customary use areas meet these expectations partly but not entirely (see Tables 17.2 and 17.3). Most use areas lacked sheep camps in 1978, while only one had an isolated corral (for cattle), and none had campsites. Two other factors besides restricted ranges have

helped to make isolated corrals obsolescent. In 1978, people had the money to build winter barns and stalls, and most herds were small enough to fit inside such structures. In addition, as population growth and land withdrawals crowded families closer together, their dogs would form packs that roamed the countryside at night and attacked unattended livestock. Fewer use areas had fields than in 1940, however, and the number of use areas with improved water sources had not grown, owing to the dwindling of farming and stock raising.

Table 17.3
Types of Sites
used by Local Navajos in 1978

Type	Number[a]
Homestead	28
Sheep camp	9
Campsite or isolated corral	1
Isolated sweathouse	U
Field	20
Improved water sources	27

[a]U = unknown.

The gradual restriction in the family use of space is evident in the two case histories that follow. The two customary use areas are located in the same parts of the lease townships as were those described for earlier periods: the claim of Gray-Eyed Woman in the far upper Defiance Draw, and the segment of the middle Defiance Draw that Blackgoat originally used. During the industrial era, the herds in these two areas are, respectively, among the smallest and the largest in the lease townships.

The Customary Use Area of Gray-Eyed Woman's Grandchildren

By 1978, Gray-Eyed Woman's original claim had been divided into the two customary use areas shown on Figure 17.1. During the 1960s, after Curly Tallman's widow had left, however, the remaining users, the granddaughter and grandson of Gray-Eyed Woman, seem to have shared it for a few more years, when they replicated the use pattern of Curly Tallman and Margaret Thompson (see Figure 17.2).

The household of Gray-Eyed Woman's grandson spent the entire winter south of the yellow rock mesa, where they had also planted a cornfield. They hauled their drinking water from various improved wells. Not only did they live near Curly Tallman's former homestead, but they also ran their stock where Curly Tallman had run his. The herd of 200 was often divided in two, the children tending half the herd north of the yellow rock mesa, and the parents the other half around the homestead, during which time they also worked at other chores. The stock ordinarily drank at a reservoir on the homestead after the one that Curly

Tallman had built nearby washed out, or at the reservoir with the log dam (W04) about three quarters of a mile north. In dry spells, the family penned the herd overnight about a mile and a half away in an isolated corral against the yellow rock mesa's northern arm (LA 15945) so that they could run it another mile or so to Coyote Drinking Water. In the summer, they trucked the herd to a homesite north of the Puerco.

At the same time, Gray-Eyed Woman's granddaughter had moved back to Margaret Thompson's former homestead, LA 12820, where she stayed all year with the households of two grown daughters (see Figure 17.2). They farmed the field near the homestead that Margaret Thompson had farmed and probably kept their small herd south of the mesa most of the time, as Margaret Thompson had done. One of the daughters had earlier built a winter corral, site PM 913, a short distance up the rincon, but spent most of her time with her husband's people in Black Creek Valley. The southwestern part of the Defiance Draw north of the mesa was where these families allowed Tall Salt Clansman's grandson to herd in winter. He had a small, movable shed at LA 12804 next to the reservoir, W04, and evidently refurbished the corral at Gray-Eyed Woman's railroad-era homestead, LA 12803.

As long as their herds remained roughly the same size as those of their predecessors, Gray-Eyed Woman's grandchildren preserved the land-use regime of their predecessors. This regime ended in the early 1970s, however, as both herds had dwindled and even the two households that had moved away in the summer were joining Gray-Eyed Woman's granddaughter in staying all year. The granddaughter and her daughters moved over the yellow rock mesa into the Defiance Draw, forcing Tall Salt Clansman's grandson back to his old range. Gray-Eyed Woman's two grandchildren then divided the area in two, each centered on a homestead around which the small herds ranged all year. By 1978, the more remote reaches of the upper Defiance Draw were left mainly to cattle.

The Customary Use Area of the Tinhouse Family's Successors

As recounted in Chapter 16, They Are Raiding Along Behind Each Other, her sons, and Turning Warrior displaced the Tinhouse family from

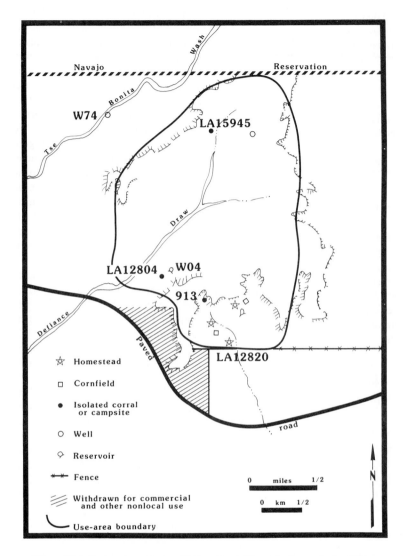

Figure 17.2 Customary use area of Gray-Eyed Woman's descendants, 1960s.

Blackgoat's former range north of the middle Defiance Draw during the early 1960s. During the preceding 6 or 7 years, They Are Raiding Along Behind Each Other and her children had followed an extensive land-management regime south of the Defiance Draw required by their herd of 250 to 450 animals—one of the largest in the lease townships (see Figure 17.3). This use pattern evidently followed that of Smiley several decades before. (Because the summer part of this pattern is the only summer regime that I recorded in detail outside the lease townships, I describe the whole pattern in this section.)

The family spent the winters south of the draw near Smiley's old homestead and moved to Hunters Point in the summer, just as Smiley had done. Their winter homestead, PM 920, stood at the edge of the trees looking down the sage flats into the draw. It consisted of three cribbed-log hogans, a triple brush corral, and a sweathouse, and it housed They Are Raiding Along Behind Each Other and the households of two of her

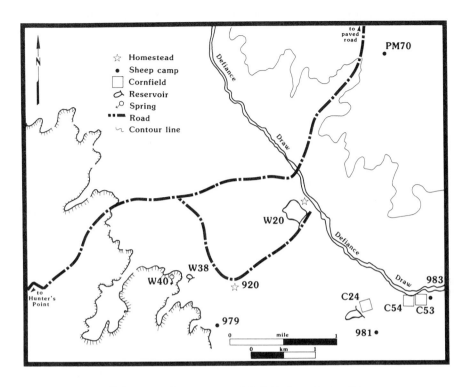

Figure 17.3 Winter use area of Smiley's descendants, 1950s.

sons, Henry and Thompson Wilson. The family watered their stock at Smiley's Spring, W38, and a reservoir associated with it, W40, about half a mile from the homestead. Although PM 920 was their base during the 6-month winter season, they also used two midwinter sheep camps. When They Are Raiding Along Behind Each Other had exhausted the wood supply around PM 920, she and the household of one of her sons would often move half a mile into the hills to PM 979, where they had two hogans, two corrals, and a sweathouse. At other times they would use the two hogans, four corrals, and sweathouse at PM 70, north of Defiance Draw, from which they could more easily reach the paved road in the car or truck that they had on the site. When they moved to the sheep camps, snow supplied the water for both stock and domestic use.

In summer, they also made some slight use of the area south of the draw, where each son maintained a farmstead (PM 981 and 983) consisting of a hogan, *ramada*, and corral, with one or two associated fields (C24, C53, and C54). The two men spent most of the summer, however, herding near Hunters Point (see Figure 17.4). The sites at Hunters Point extended for about 2 miles between two water sources along the sparsely wooded spine of a grassy hill, from which the family could run the herd either north or south. They Are Raiding Along Behind Each Other and her two sons had a homestead (HP3) that consisted of two cabins, two hogans, a storage shed, a shadehouse, and two corrals, all perched atop the red rock bench east of Black Creek's floodplain. Nearby was one daughter's summer sheep camp, HP2. Both families trekked their herds across the floodplain about half a mile to water in Black Creek. When the range around the summer homestead became depleted, They Are Raiding Along Behind Each Other or one of her two sons would move their herd eastward to a tent camp, either HP6 or HP8, from which they grazed the herd a mile and a half north to a government stock dam

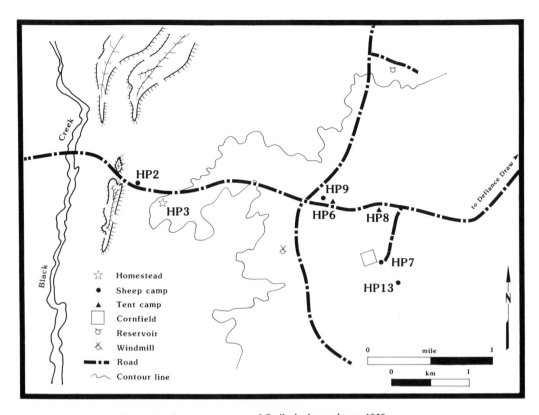

Figure 17.4 Summer use area of Smiley's descendants, 1950s.

and back again. All that remains of each tent camp is a solitary corral and a sweathouse. In 1960, the Navajo tribal government installed a windmill south of these sites, and the family responded by building a sheep camp, HP7—cabin, corral, and sweathouse— about half a mile west. Another son and daughter of They Are Raiding Along Behind Each Other sometimes kept their own separate herds at two sheep camps near these water sources, HP9 and HP13.

Why the Wilson brothers and their mother abandoned this regime after the early 1960s is not clear. A land dispute may have been involved, for the family complained that someone had vandalized PM 920 one summer when they were in Hunters Point. Their herd, moreover, had diminished as both mother and sons aged. In 1978, therefore, this family was herding all year in the lease townships on the combined former ranges of Smiley and Blackgoat, which they shared

with the widow of Turning Warrior (see Figure 17.5). They had not entirely abandoned their land in Hunters Point, but were using it only sporadically.

In 1978, the households of Henry and Thompson Wilson, their mother, and several of their grown children lived all year on a sprawling homestead just south of the paved road, where they also planted a cornfield. The herdless household of their mother's grandniece lived in another homestead nearby, also with a small field. During the winter, the Wilson brothers kept their herd around these homesteads, watering it at two reservoirs filled by snowmelt and sharing the range with Turning Warrior's widow, whose hired herder was staying at her winter sheep camp nearby. The widow herself, however, spent most of the year about 3 miles away on a homestead south of the draw, which she shared with a couple of her grown daughters and their families. During the sum-

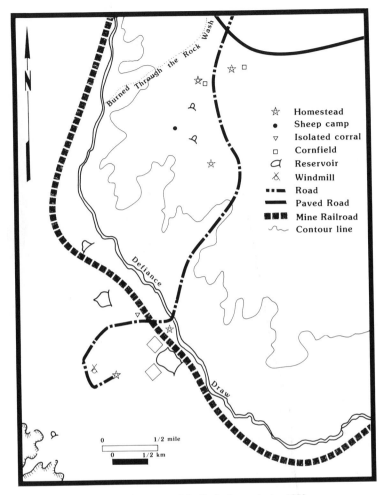

Figure 17.5 Use area of Smiley's descendants, 1970s.

mer, the herder took care of the widow's herd and that of the Wilson brothers combined, since the only dependable water for both herds was the windmill near the widow's homestead. The combined herd was one of the largest in the lease townships in 1978. The widow also had a cornfield next to the big reservoir that Smiley and Blackgoat had built long ago. The dam has washed out, but water still collects there.

The land-use regime of the Wilson brothers and Turning Warrior's widow in 1978, then, combined elements of the regimes of their predecessors, the Tinhouses, and, even earlier, perhaps, Blackgoat. Like the Tinhouses, they herded in the uplands in winter and in the open sage-flats in summer because of the distribution of water. As Blackgoat had probably done, they also used a corridor from the Gallup road all the way south across the Defiance Draw, probably because the relatively large size of their combined herds allowed them to control the big flats along the draw. Unlike the Tinhouses (but perhaps like the Model-T owner, Blackgoat), they situated these homesites to be near the main road; also unlike the Tinhouses, who had about the same size herd, these families had enough money from wages to hire a herder.

Grazing Tracts

The number of grazing tracts increased very little between 1940 and 1978, for range subdivision slowed as younger adults abandoned stock raising for wage work. Although their number hardly increased, the grazing tracts diminished greatly in size owing to the land withdrawals. The tracts were also reoriented on the landscape to bring their users as close as possible to the paved road.

A comparison of Figure 17.1 with Figure 12.1 shows that the number of customary use areas, or grazing tracts, in the lease townships barely increased (from 12 to only 14) between 1940 and 1978. Yet during the same period population more than doubled. The tendency of younger adults to take up wage work (when they were lucky enough to find it) instead of stock raising forestalled a greater increase in the number of grazing tracts. In the grazing-regulation era, moreover, people were subdividing the range faster than they were reducing their herds, so that several large owners were forced to use discontiguous tracts to get enough range for their stock. In the industrial era, the process reversed itself: Range subdivision no longer kept pace with herd reduction. Therefore the number of families that needed to herd on discontiguous tracts was lower (only two) during the industrial era than during the previous period.

Yet that is not the whole story. The land-tenure histories in Chapter 16 describe the subdivision of several customary use areas during the industrial era. These divisions occurred among people who were already middle aged by the early industrial era and were still clinging to the stock-raising life. Two processes offset the increase in grazing tracts that these divisions would have created. First, herd reductions, old age, and the shortage of younger people to herd induced several stockowners to combine both herds and customary use areas. Second, the McKinley Mine eliminated some customary use areas entirely. That their former occupants could subsist without land or livestock is a result of the wage work and welfare that are part of industrialization.

The slowing of range subdivision did not prevent

the average grazing tract from shrinking to little more than half of its 1940 size (1.8 mi.^{2} in 1978, down from 3.0 mi.^{2} in 1940). Land withdrawal by the McKinley Mine and other outsiders is the cause.

Although many grazing tracts had been reoriented to come as close to the paved road as possible, the 1978 tracts lay across environmental zones much as had those of earlier times (see Table 17.4). Most tracts still encompassed both upland and lowland range and water sources. The water sources were different, however, for families no longer used natural sources for their stock. The mine had fenced or fouled some natural sources, while wells and windmills had tapped others. Use areas with lowland range were still necessary to give the larger herds enough room. The density of animals in each tract was generally lower in 1978 than in 1940, but the correspondence between the size of the tract and the number of livestock was not as close in 1978 as it had been in the earlier interval. The highest averages still were in the lowlands, however, which also have had the highest carrying capacity. A few families with lowland range also moved to the uplands in midwinter, just as they had done in earlier times. The reason for these moves, however, was no longer so much to be near stock water as it was to be near the paved road when the dirt roads were at their worst.

Fields

The number of fields in the lease townships barely increased between 1940 and 1978. Indeed, I have already mentioned that the number of families with access to a field dwindled greatly. Fields yielded not so much vegetables for the family table as feed for the stock, and most households lacked stock. Paradoxically, the number of fields that I have dated to the entire industrial era is almost twice the number that I have dated to the grazing-regulation era (see Table 17.5). The difference is probably due to the different sources used to identify fields in the two periods: Local Navajos were the ones to identify most grazing-regulation–era fields, with the one aerial photograph from that period showing only a few others, whereas four sets of aerial photographs are available for the industrial era, adding many fields to those that local

Table 17.4

Number of Small Stock, Size,
and Physiographic Characteristics of Customary Use Areas in the Lease Townships, 1978[a]

Area (quarter sections)	No. of small stock[b]	Small stock per quarter section[c]	Range elevation		Water used	
			Above 6800'	Below 6800'	Natural	Improved
18	274	15	x	x	—	x
13	78–195	6–15	x	—	—	x
11	260	24	x	x	—	x
11	126	12	x	x	—	x
7–11	110	10–16	x	x	—	x
10	110	11	x	x	—	x
8	120	15	—	x	—	x
6–8	190	24–32	—	x	—	x
4	57	14	x		—	Nearby
2–4	80	20–40	—	x	—	Nearby

[a]Use-area numbers are not given in deference to the privacy of lease-township residents; some use areas have been combined owing to overlapping herding patterns, and one has been omitted because the number of livestock is unknown.

[b]Annual equivalent including young; see notes, Table 7.5. Where stocking includes a large number of cattle, the equivalent number in sheep units has been included.

[c]Annual equivalent; see notes, Table 7.5.

Navajos pointed out.

Although I did not record the sizes of the 1978 fields, or acreage per family, I suspect that the average acreage per family diminished, again because farming was no longer important. Most families with fields in 1978 probably planted about the same acreage as did most families of the grazing-regulation era—4 to 10 acres. However, no one planted as much land in 1978 as John Dixon had planted in 1940; several families planted areas of only an acre (kitchen gardens). The average field in 1978, therefore, was probably smaller than the average field in 1940.

In their distribution across the landscape, the fields of the industrial era also differed little from earlier ones, probably because farmland of adequate quality was so widespread. People continued to favor the sage-grass plains, for that is where most arable land is. Local farmers said they chose locations with some slope for drainage and a soil of "silt loam," a mixture of sand, silt, and clay (Knight 1982:708). The average elevation of these fields (6570 ft.) does not differ significantly from the grazing-regulation-era average. The fields had also changed little in their distribution among the various slope zones (see Table

17.5 and Figure 17.6). The fields were still divided about evenly between the bottomland and bottom-ridge contact zones, about half were still at the junction of two or more zones, most remained unirrigated by reservoirs, and a large proportion (especially of fields at zonal junctions) were still slope-wash fields.

Homesites

In 1940, there were 24 homesites in the lease townships, and in 1978 there were 37. This change is proportional to the increase in residence groups. Nevertheless, the average lease-township family today has fewer homesites than in 1940. Only one sixth had additional homes outside the townships in 1978, whereas almost one third had them in 1940. Nearly all homesteads in 1978 were occupied year-round (most people who move seasonally do so between homesteads that their children occupy all year), whereas many homesteads were not occupied all year in 1940. These changes show that industrial-era families continued the settling down that began late

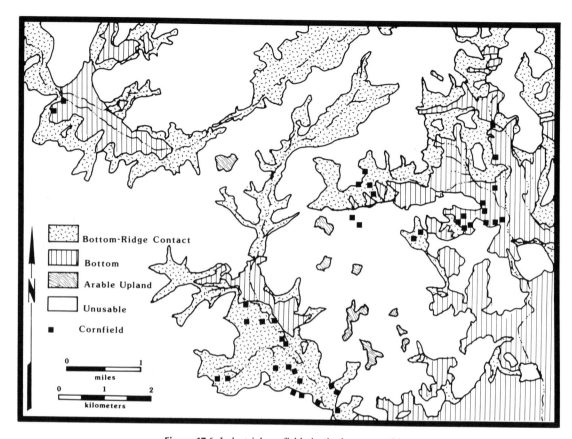

Figure 17.6 Industrial-era fields in the lease townships.

in the railroad era as grazing areas, herd sizes, and the importance of stock raising itself continued to diminish.

Partly because the process of settling down has continued, one would expect industrial-era homesites to be bigger than those of earlier times. Homesteads constituted two thirds of all homesites in both grazing-regulation and industrial eras, but the average industrial-era site might be larger than the average site of the grazing-regulation era because it was occupied for a longer time span, both within the year and over the years.[1] More households, moreover, lived on the

---

[1]The average industrial-era homesite was occupied for 16 or 17 years, depending on whether it was a homestead or a sheep camp, and the average grazing-regulation–era homesite for 10 to 13 years.

Table 17.5
Distribution of Fields
by Slope Zone in the Industrial Era

	N
Total number of fields	45
Fields by zone	
bottom-ridge contact	21
bottom	16
unusable	8
Fields by zonal junction	
fields at junction of 2 or more zones	22
slope-wash fields	11
fields not at zonal junction	23
slope-wash fields	5
Proximity to dams	
located next to dams	14
not next to dams	31

Legend within figure:

Bottom-Ridge Contact
Bottom
Arable Upland
Unusable
■ Cornfield

0   miles   1
0   1   kilometers   2

N

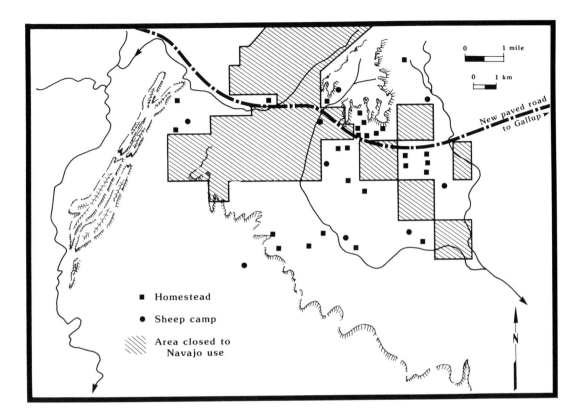

Figure 17.7 Homesites in the lease townships, 1978.

average industrial-era site. Another reason that one would expect industrial-era homesites to be bigger is that people have more money and buy more things. This money could go into bigger houses and perhaps more storage structures on the homesite, and their trash thus become more scattered or dumped over a wider area.

One might just as reasonably expect, however, a decrease in the size of homesites owing to the diminishing number of structures and features related to herding, to the preparation of home-produced foods, and to the storing of all types of foods. As I show in the next chapter, dwellings probably have grown in size and storage features have become more common, but the total number of features may have decreased. Unfortunately, I cannot say whether the net effect of these changes has been an increase, decrease, or no change at all in the size of the

industrial-era homesite. Most homesites, especially homesteads, are still occupied and therefore were not measured.

One might also expect families of the industrial era to situate their homesites on the landscape more in relation to man-made features (especially the paved road) and less in relation to natural features than earlier families had done. Instead, however, families more consistently situated their homesites in relation to both man-made and natural features.

When the average distance of homesites from the old Gallup road in 1915 and 1940 (2.1 mi.) is compared with the average distance of homesites from the new paved road in 1978 (1.5 mi.), the difference is not statistically significant. Figure 17.7, however, when compared to Figure 12.10, shows that homesites increasingly clustered near the paved road. The move of certain families to the new road and the greater

Table 17.6
Situations of Homesites on Landforms, 1978

Topographic situation	No. of sites
Sheltered on west; exposed on south	23
Sheltered on west and south	4
Exposed on west and south	4
Exposed on west, sheltered on south	0
Ridge	5
Flat	1
	37

clustering of homesites may not have produced a significantly shorter average distance because the old road, unlike the new one, passed right through the middle of the lease townships. No site could possibly be as far from the old road as from the new. Figure 17.7 also shows that all homesites had a water source within half a mile, instead of within a mile, as they had had in 1940.

The locations of 1978 sites also were more strongly constrained by natural features that provide shelter, warmth, and light than were earlier homesites. All 1978 homesites were situated in the piñon–juniper woodland or on its edge, as opposed to only three quarters during the grazing-regulation era. And a much larger majority in 1978 were situated with both a sheltering landform on the west and an exposure to the south (see Table 17.6). Most families still heated with wood or coal that they provided themselves. They therefore still tried to derive as much shelter as possible from the trees and landforms, and supplemental warmth from exposure to the winter sun in the south. Earlier families perhaps had adopted a greater variety of situations because their greater involvement in both

herding and farming sometimes led them to choose such situations as ridge tops. Now that herding and farming had diminished so greatly, families could pick homesite locations based on almost purely domestic considerations.

Conclusion

Changes in aggregate statistics on the number, size, and distribution of grazing tracts, fields, and homesites in the lease townships since the grazing-regulation era clearly reflect two results of industrialization. One result, the shift from herding and farming to wage work and welfare as the main sources of family livelihood, has caused the slowing of land subdivision, the redistribution of grazing tracts and homesites for better access to the paved road, and the reduction in the number of fields and specialized herding sites. Land use has therefore become less intensive. This trend would be more obvious if it were not for the other result of industrialization, large land withdrawals by industry and land speculators, which has caused grazing tracts to shrink and homesites thus to crowd together. The distribution of homesites across the landscape also has not changed as much as it might have if industrialization had provided homesites with a full range of public utilities. As it is, lease-township families must still situate homesites to conserve heat and be near fuel wood.

Although these aggregate changes have occurred among the relatively large stockowners as well as among small owners and herdless families, the large owners still approximate the more intensive land-use patterns common to most families in past eras.

Chapter 18

Technology of the Industrial Era

Wage work and the great upsurge in money income during the industrial era have transformed stock-raising, farming, and especially domestic technologies. Wage jobs and the schooling that prepares wage workers of the future have changed the family division of labor by engaging most able-bodied young people away from home. Domestic, stock-raising, and farming chores therefore fall upon old people, who need as never before the labor-saving devices that money can buy. Some people, whose children have moved away to work, are even forced to pay their neighbors for help:

> Yanadesbah Begay puts it this way. "Who has the money to be going to the store all the time. . . . We ask our neighbor over the hill to take us, he agrees, and we buy him gas, likes it better when it's fill up, and on top of that we give him ten dollars in cash. When we get to the store we have to buy food on credit."
>
> Others are paying up to sixty dollars for a load of wood, especially in areas where there is a scarcity. But it is a little different when you ask someone to haul wood or water. They will require gas and cash at the same time before helping anyone. It's hard on those elderly Navajos who do not have children living nearby to help. (Lewis 1979)

Some people hire and board people to herd for them or board their sheep with people whom they also pay to herd. Others pay neighbors who have tractors to plow their fields. Thus, wage relations have penetrated even the domestic, herding, and farming spheres that formerly ran on unpaid family labor.

Domestic Technology

Industrialization has transformed homesites. These changes reflect the growth in money income, the shortage of family labor, and, perhaps, an increase in work performed indoors as wage workers relegate housework to evenings.

Although most homesites still consist of the same types of structures as did the homesteads of the grazing-regulation era, industrial-era homesites tend to have more dwellings and storage sheds, and most structures are now made of mass-produced building materials. Many homesites in the lease townships have electricity, and a few families even have telephones.

Dwellings have grown bigger. Although cabins had become more prevalent in the lease townships between the railroad and grazing-regulation eras, hogans always outnumbered cabins. In the industrial era, however, families came to favor not only cabins, but

Figure 18.1 A modern homesite in the lease townships, with stuccoed frame house, stuccoed log hogan, several sheds, and barrel for ash and trash.

also multiroom houses and trailers. Of the 155 industrial-era dwellings recorded, almost 60% (87) were of these types, and in 1978 the proportion was two thirds. Most hogans and other house types of the industrial era, moreover, had at least roofs of mass-produced building materials: planks covered with tar paper. By 1978, most dwellings also had walls of frame-and-siding construction, or of logs, common also in earlier times, but now covered with stucco (see Figure 18.1). The industrial-era dwellings on sheep camps did include two forked-stick hogans, but they were made of two-by-fours covered with tar paper and insulated with strips of corrugated cardboard.

Dwelling areas also have undoubtedly grown. The increase is difficult to show statistically, however, because the sample of sites on which dwellings were measured is not representative; it excludes all currently occupied sites and includes instead a disproportionate share of sheep camps and "old-fashioned" dwellings that people have abandoned for bigger, more modern

ones. The average area of the dwellings in this sample therefore does not differ significantly from that of the average grazing-regulation–era dwelling, nor do the separate homestead and sheep-camp averages.[1] On two currently occupied homesites, I was able to measure three types of dwellings that are typical of those on most currently occupied sites, and all exceed the archaeological averages.[2] Dwellings also afforded more area per person on most homesites, both homesteads and sheep camps (see Table 18.1). These size increases reflect not only the proliferation of

[1]The average dwelling in archaeological sites of the industrial era is 22.2 m² ($SD = 9.0$; $n = 14$); homesteads averaged 23.2 m² ($SD = 10.0$; $n = 10$) and sheep camps, 19.6 m² ($SD = 6.2$; $n = 4$).

[2]The hogans were 24 m², single-room houses, 24 and 32 m², multiroom houses, 54–64 m², and trailers, 74 m².

Table 18.1
Sizes of Industrial-Era Dwellings and Selected Variables on the South McKinley Mine Lease

Site no.	Area of largest dwelling (m²)	Total dwelling area on site (m²)	Area per occupant[a] (m²)	Maximum small stock of occupants[b]	Resident smith	Resident weaver
Homesteads[c]						
1[d]	28.3	73.0	12.1	100–140	—	x
212[d]	44.2	75.7	9.5	296	x	x
90	23.7	23.7	5.9	U	x	—
Curr. occ.	65.0	183.0	16.6	30	x	x
Curr. occ.	23.7	23.7	5.9	0	—	—
Curr. occ.	54.0	100.0	20.0	0	x	—
Sheep camps						
16	14.5	14.5	14.5	65	—	—
70	12.6	25.2	3.2	250–450	—	—

[a]Total dwelling area divided by maximum number of occupants; excludes sheds and dwellings used for storage but includes those used for work.
[b]U = unknown.
[c]Homesite occupied all year.
[d]Also occupied in 1930–1950 period.

possessions that money can buy, but also the greater amounts of wood to heat them that people can haul with the pickup trucks they can now afford, and the increase in indoor activities as wage workers relegate more domestic chores to evenings.

In 1978, some households still used two dwellings. The extra dwelling served as a silversmithing workshop or home for elderly or teenaged members of the household. Therefore, the average number of dwellings per household, 1.2, was about the same as that of earlier times.

Although dwellings have grown during the industrial era, the number and variety of other features on homesites have diminished (see Table 18.2). I was able to record only large structures on the currently occupied sites. Small structures and nonstructural features were systematically recorded only on sites in the archaeological sample, with its disproportionate share of sheep camps. Even when homesteads and sheep camps are separated, however, most features are less common on sites of both types than they were in the era of grazing regulation. Only storage sheds have become more common.

One reason for the diminishing number of homesite features in the industrial era is the rising proportion of herdless families, which also accounts for the reductions in homesteads with corrals and pens. Another possible reason for the overall reduction is that many activities once performed outdoors, like warm-weather cooking, now occur inside the larger dwellings; this reason could explain the reductions in windbreaks, *ramadas*, and ovens. Ash dumps and woodpiles may be missing from many archaeological sites because more families clean up their homesites and haul the debris away; some even use trash cans. Finally, sweathouses may be obsolescent for two reasons. First, many adults can now shower on the job or pay for public showers in Gallup. Second, and probably more important, men, who traditionally made the sweatbath a social occasion, now have little time for that leisurely pastime. They work a regular week away from home and on weekends usually go to town with their families.

The proliferation of small domestic equipment and large furnishings may be seen in the industrial-era consumption patterns discussed in Chapter 15. In this chapter I emphasize the changes in certain basic pieces of domestic equipment and techniques for domestic maintenance: those that fill the needs for light, heat, cooking, food preservation, water, and transportation.

Table 18.2
Percentage of Industrial-Era Homesites
in the Lease Townships with Selected Types of Features[a]

Feature type	Homesteads	Sheep camps	Homesites of unknown occupation spans[b]
Dwelling	100	100	100
Windbreak, *ramada*	30	0	50
Sweathouse[c]	50	40	U
Oven[c]	22	0	U
Ash dump[c]	89	100	U
Woodpile[c]	67	75	U
Storage	65	27	U
Corral	75	100	100
Lamb pen[c]	0	100	U
No. of components[d]	(9–45)	(3–16)	(3–5)

[a]Includes all sites positively identified by interviewees unless noted otherwise.

[b]U = unknown.

[c]Percentage of archaeological components only.

[d]Number of components on which the presence of a particular type of feature was noted (not all types were noted on sites off the lease or on currently occupied sites).

I have mentioned that most homesites in the lease townships received electricity in 1978. Some entire homesites, however, lacked the service, making kerosene and Coleman lamps widespread. Stoves entirely replaced hearths for cooking indoors, although in hot weather many families often cooked over outdoor hearths because cooking on a stove made the house far too hot. Stoves varied from the primitive oil-barrel type and small mass-produced wood- or coal-burning models to wood-burning and propane ranges. Some families cooked with electric hotplates, frying pans, and so forth. The new cooking devices probably reflect the family's need to save labor. Electricity also induced some people to buy refrigerators, although most probably still lacked these appliances. The dugouts and tree platforms that people used to store food in earlier times nevertheless had all but disappeared, for most people bought food every week or two and therefore did not need to store it over the winter. Food-storage features are the only types of storage to have become less common.

Although a few households heated and cooked with propane, most still depended heavily on wood and coal. Most families had access to a truck in which to haul these fuels. Many even had the labor-saving chain saws. Nevertheless, most families probably still used axes, at least for cutting wood once they had brought

it home. Some families lacked trucks and either paid others to get wood for them or went to the woods with an ax and a wheelbarrow or sled.

Similarly, everyone hauled water. In 1977, the U.S Public Health Service (PHS) planned to run water lines to about 15 homesites in the northern part of the lease townships (Correll 1977). PHS abandoned the project, however, when it found out that the Pittsburg and Midway Company would soon move the families. In 1978 most lease-township families hauled water in army-surplus tanks rather than in the wooden barrels of earlier times. Families without trucks, however, got water in a random collection of small glass and plastic bottles and jugs from whatever water source was nearby, even if it was a scum-filled stock trough or reservoir. People used their domestic water for drinking, cooking, and bathing, although, as I have mentioned, many adults also used public showers; children showered in school. Most people hauled their laundry to laundromats in Gallup.

For most lease-township residents today, the need to haul fuel and water makes a pickup truck a real necessity, and trucks replaced wagons early in the industrial era. Moreover, in 1978 only one very small trading post was operating in the lease townships, and it has since gone out of business. No store has ever been within easy walking distance of most families.

In 1978, everyone therefore depended on motor vehicles even to get food. People without vehicles either paid neighbors for rides or took their chances hitchhiking. Since 1981, the Navajo tribal government has operated a bus line, one route of which connects the lease townships with Gallup and Window Rock. Most passengers seem to be commuters, however, and the buses do not run on weekends.

Stock-Raising Technology

Stock-raising technology of the industrial era reflects mainly three results of industrialization: (1) the shortage of unpaid family labor, (2) the great reduction in herds (itself partly a result of the labor shortage within the family), and (3) the growth of money income.

I have already mentioned that neither children nor most young adults were available for herding, and that families therefore took to paying others to herd. One family that used its own land in herding for another family received about $30–40 a month, whereas other families paid the herders they boarded $100 a month plus board. Despite the demise of the large herds, then, the practice of hiring herders has persisted, even becoming more common. In contrast, some families with very small herds (around 25 or 30 animals) often allow the stock to roam unattended around the homesite.

In 1978, daily herding had changed little since the stock-reduction era; information on herding in 1978 is simply more detailed. In the long, warm days between May and September, people usually took the herd out in the morning, returned it to the homesite at noon, then took it out again late in the afternoon and returned it at dark. During the rest of the year, the herd went out in the morning and came back in the afternoon. As the days grew shorter and colder, the herd left the corral progressively later and came back earlier. People tried to herd their sheep to water every day in summer. In dry spells, however, families without a dependable water source would cross their sheep into a neighbor's range for water or haul water back to the corral, therefore possibly watering the stock as little as every 2 days. In winter the herd only needs water every 2 or 3 days, or even less often if snow is on the ground. Each family sharing a water source tried to schedule its watering for a certain day,

or time of day, when none of the others would be there, so that the herds would not mingle. Small herds got salt by grazing in stands of saltbush along the arroyos. Owners of larger herds often put a block of salt in the corral.

The seasonal herding schedule also changed little after the era of grazing regulation. Although I cannot tell whether fewer families separated the bucks in 1978 than in the past because the practice was hardly universal even in the era of grazing regulation, a few families still took their bucks to a family that agreed to care for them between dipping (July or August) and November and had that fact announced in the chapter meeting or on the radio. The main change since the grazing-regulation era is thus as follows: Because most herds were so small, many families separated the bucks simply by putting them in a pen of their own and letting them range around the homesite when the rest of the herd was on the range. Other families let the bucks run with the herd but equipped them with contraceptive aprons—burlap sacks or big rags tied around their bellies.

Most families had herds of less than 100 head, including young, and these families did not seem to sell their lambs systematically. The larger owners sold a few. They usually trucked the lambs to Gallup and sold them either to traders of general merchandise or to specialized livestock buyers. Some people have sold stock sheep when they have needed money, or have bought stock sheep to replenish or expand their herds. People seem to buy and sell among themselves rather than through trading posts or stock traders.

Finally, winter feeding seemed more common in 1978 than in the past. That many families grew corn mainly for a winter supplement has already been mentioned. Many also bought baled hay at $2.50–3.50 a bale, which they stored in barns over the winter. Some perhaps still cut wild weeds, at least for horses, but this practice was undoubtedly less common than in the era of grazing regulation.

The structures associated with herding in 1978 also reflected both smaller herd sizes and more money income (see Figure 18.2). More corrals were made of milled lumber than in earlier times, although brush corrals were still common. Even the latter, however, were likely to incorporate odd pieces of milled lumber, sheet metal, and springs from beds, chairs, couches, and car seats. The bigger pieces of wood for these corrals were also likely to have come from either earlier

Figure 18.2 A modern corral; fenced cornfield is in background at right.

corrals or hogans that the family had abandoned in favor of larger houses. For this purpose, people salvaged the wood from corrals and hogans on many sites of the grazing-regulation era.

Twin corrals and lamb pens have persisted into the industrial era. Figure 18.3 shows a winter corral, PM 92, that could perhaps be the "type site" for lambing a medium-sized herd. This brush corral includes not only a section for twins and their mothers, but also several lamb pens along one side, some with car hoods or pieces of sheet metal leaned against their outer sides to be laid over the pens as roofs during storms. By 1978, however, few, if any, families were using twin corrals. Most herds were so small that the few twins

they produced could be kept in lamb pens or barns. Bottle feeding of rejects and orphans remained the common way to insure that these animals survived, but canned milk rather than goat's milk was the preferred supplement. Nearly all goats in 1978 were angoras, not milk goats. Few people drank goat's milk, and many owners of small herds allowed the young to run with the herd after they were a few days old, often marking the orphans or rejected lambs with a red thread around the leg.

Industrial-era corrals seem to occur in about the same numbers per site as those of the grazing-regulation era and offer about the same amount of space per animal (see Table 18.3). The corrals that

Table 18.3
Corrals on Industrial-Era Sites on the South McKinley Mine Lease

Site no.[a]	Maximum herd size[b]	No. of corrals	Total corral area on site (m²)	Total corral area per animal (m²)
Homesteads				
1[c]	100–140 + bucks	2	477	3.4–4.8
33.2	160	2	924	5.8
Currently occ.	200	2	346	1.7
Sheep camps				
7[c]	131–206	2	408	2.0–3.1
70	250–450	4	1200	2.7–4.8
12804	100–160	1	360	2.3–3.6
16	65	1	180	2.7
Isolated corrals				
15945	200	1	196	1.0
92	150	2	333	2.2

[a]Includes only sites with measurable corrals for which an estimate of herd size was also available; component number is to the right of the decimal point.

[b]Largest number of sheep either owned by the occupants around the time they used the site or indicated by local Navajos as likely to have been kept on that site.

[c]Also occupied in 1930–1950 period.

offer the most space per animal were made of wood salvaged from earlier corrals that originally accommodated larger herds on the same sites. Corrals built "from scratch" for particular herds still offered 1–2 m² per animal, depending on the season and the length of time within the year that the herd would be in the corral. As one would expect, the corral that offered the least room was an isolated corral used sporadically in warm weather to pen a herd near a water source.

I have the impression that corrals for the comparatively few horses and cattle people kept were more common in 1978 than in earlier times. These corrals were often made of rails or wire and posts. If the increase is genuine, it may be due to the improved roads and motor vehicles that industrialization has brought. In the Navajo country as a whole, these factors have increased both stock theft and the incidence of livestock killed by motor vehicles. Even so, horses and cattle in the lease townships ranged freely around the countryside most of the time, for the cost of penning them and feeding them was prohibitive. Another change in livestock structures that I have already mentioned is the increase in barns and sheds for sheltering both supplemental feed and small herds themselves.

Finally, the improvement of water sources continued. Around 1962, the Navajo tribal government drilled two or three wells (two are at the sites of natural springs) and around 1970 installed two or three windmills. In 1976 or 1977, the Tsayatoh Chapter received some money from the tribal government to improve several earthen dams that had washed out. Families also continued to build their own reservoirs, often with tractors.

Artifacts of industrial-era stock raising, however, remained primitive. In 1978, people still fed lambs with pop bottles to which they attached commercial or homemade rubber nipples. Hand shears were still the rule in shearing. Few, if any, families continued to milk their goats, so that receptacles for milking were less common than formerly. The sheep were branded with paint. Simple contraceptive aprons have been mentioned. Individual sheep and goats that tended to lead or stray wore bells, as they did in earlier times. Thus, the meager inventory of stock-raising artifacts in 1978 hardly exceeded the inventories of artifacts on archaeological sites of earlier times.

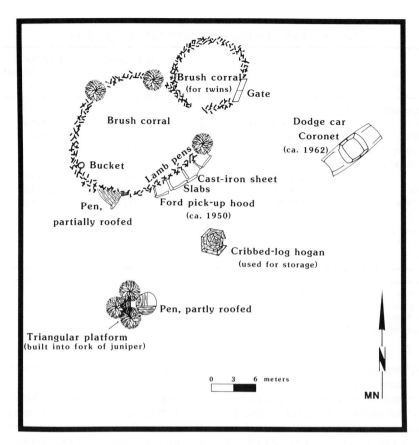

Figure 18.3 Site PM 92, a winter corral with lamb pens and twin corral that was used 1962–1969.

Farming Technology

Farming technology varied tremendously among lease-township families in 1978, as it undoubtedly did earlier. The largest-scale farmer in the townships, John Dixon's successor Robert Lee, was also the most scientific and technologically advanced. Some aspects of farming have changed little since earlier times: Corn, beans, squash, and melons have remained the most important crops, and the various stages of farming—planting, hoeing, harvesting, and processing the crops for storage—have persisted. The equipment used in 1978, however, reflects the same shortage of family labor and increase in money income that domestic and stock-raising technologies do.

Until the 1960s, most families had their fields plowed with a team. Those without a team or plow persuaded a relative or neighbor to do the work, presumably in exchange for either pay or part of the crop. In 1978, however, most families had their fields plowed with tractors. Most did not own the tractors, but paid relatives or neighbors who did to plow their fields. Some people felt that plowing with a tractor caused the topsoil to blow away. These and other people without the means to pay a tractor owner used the *gish* method of planting, although most, if not all, pierced the ground with a spade or trowel rather than an actual *gish*. One farmer used a tractor and trowel in alternate years.

The seeds planted were simply those left over from the previous year's crop. Some people planted corn continuously in rows, but most planted it about two steps apart in clusters that probably retard evaporation. They planted white, yellow, red, and blue varieties, all flint, in separate parts of the field to minimize mixing. They reserved sections of most fields for other crops, usually the beans and squash (yellow, white, and a native dark green variety that, when sliced in half, looks like a clear October sunrise). They planted these crops in clusters, as they did the corn. Robert Lee rotated beans with his corn every third year to maintain soil fertility, but others did not (Knight 1982:709).

Everyone hoed with the simple iron hoe, usually during the cool evening hours. Robert Lee hoed three times: first, about a month after planting, second, when the corn was 2 or 3 ft. tall, and third, when the corn was 5 ft. tall. Others, however, seemed to hoe only once during the summer. One elderly farmer probably expressed a common complaint when he said that one should hoe twice but that he could hoe only once because no one would help him.

Families usually harvested their own crops, hauling the produce from the field in trucks or wheelbarrows. They picked green corn in mid-September, as needed for meals, then waited until mid-October, when the tassels had dried on the corn plants, to harvest the rest. Some pulled the dried stalks off the field to feed their horses in winter, whereas others let sheep or cattle feed inside the stubble fields. The latter practice, incidentally, led to about the only form of manuring that any of these fields received (although one farmer ran a ditch from his corral to his field to channel manure-laden runoff). Robert Lee used his tractor to plow after the harvest so that winter moisture could penetrate the earth more deeply. He plowed across the crop furrows, then plowed in the same direction as those furrows in the spring. Others, however, did not plow in the fall. People dried the corn on platforms or the roofs of *ramadas* and then shelled it, often with hand-cranked shellers. Gunnysacks were still common storage containers; so were steel or plastic garbage cans.

The proportion of fields in 1978 irrigated by seepage from reservoirs, one third, was a little higher than the proportion in 1940, but not by much. The seepage from the big ECW dam allowed Robert Lee to grow a good corn crop in one field for 17 years straight. Many other fields have been used for periods of similar length, but probably were not planted every year. People did not allow their fields to lie fallow intentionally, but the frequent years with early summer droughts imposed an irregular fallowing schedule by preventing the crops from sprouting. Probably about a third of the fields recorded in the lease townships in 1978–1979 had not produced crops for the previous four years, owing to drought. People usually abandon a field if it produces an exceptionally meager crop in a year of normal moisture, but may try it again within a decade or two. An invasion of knotweed (*Polygonum aviculare*) or bindweed (*Convolvulus arvensis*) also forces people to abandon fields, for these weeds strangle crops; 10 or 20 years may elapse before these weeds give way to the normal local vegetation, and the field can be used again (Knight 1982:710). Overall, farming in the lease townships in the 1970s was not grandly successful: Besides the four years of drought that had preceded this study, drought in the next 5 years was to reduce crops once again, and early frosts, twice more.

Conclusion

Industrialization in the lease townships is transforming domestic, stock-raising, and farming technologies just as it has other aspects of land use. The technological changes described in this chapter reflect most strongly the growth of money income, the shortage of unpaid family labor as the able-bodied members go to work or school, and the reduction of herd sizes. The *gish* method of planting and other technological survivals from earlier times are simply the calm eye in the storm of change.

Chapter 19

The Future

The family land-use patterns that I have described here are disappearing from the lease townships. Most families are moving to make way for strip-mining and, when the mine plays out, are not likely to return and replicate their old way of life. The revegetated land will bear little resemblance to the land before strip-mining, and many families may not be able to resume stock raising after having liquidated their herds. In fact, many people may find that a new federal law has deprived them of their legal rights to allotments on the lease.

The Near Future

The near future holds relocation in store for inhabitants of the south McKinley Mine lease, who make up the majority of families in the lease townships. This relocation will take two forms and has already started: A few families are moving individually to their own lands outside the lease, but most are moving into a housing development southeast of the lease that is on Mr. Towering House Clansman's former range. The Pittsburg and Midway Company has built new, multiroom dwellings for all households in both groups and has covered the cost of installing some utilities.

The relocation housing development will accommodate about 30 or 40 households. This development is several miles from the pavement, but the county has graveled the road to make it passable in all weather. The development offers a school-bus service, new to most families. The development itself seems comfortable, with its neat, wood-frame houses set back from curving, graveled lanes under the piñon and juniper trees. Because households were allowed to choose their own lots, the houses are in clusters that correspond roughly to the residence groups on the lease rather than arranged in stark rows. The houses themselves are also more comfortable than those that many families now inhabit. Each house has a living–dining room, bedrooms, a kitchen, and a bathroom; the bedrooms have closets, the bathroom has fixtures, the kitchen has cabinets, the living–dining room has a heating stove that can burn either wood or coal, and all rooms have linoleum floors. Each house is wired for electricity and will have indoor plumbing when the U.S. Public Health Service (PHS) installs the water system that was originally planned for the northern part of the townships in 1977.

But behind this pleasant facade are some unpleasant facts. More than a year after the company had told the families to move into the new houses, the houses still lack running water. The houses themselves are not made of the highest quality materials. In each kitchen counter is a gap where the cook stove should be, for people must supply their own. Most people already have wood-burning or propane stoves, rather than the electric ranges for which the space is designed, and therefore must improvise ways to install their old stoves if they cannot afford to buy new ones. Although the houses are wired for electricity, families without electricity at their old homes must pay the full cost of installation. People who were teenagers when their parents signed the leases, but now have families of their own and want to stay near their parents, as they would have done without the leases, are not allowed housing in the development.

Finally, the housing development offers no land where people can raise livestock. A few families may find other land for their sheep and goats, although they will probably have to pay for boarding their sheep with other families or herding on lands nearby. Most families, however, will have no choice but to sell all their stock unless they are offered more range in the future. In addition to the obvious direct economic cost of this obligatory sale, there will be an indirect economic cost: Families that want to hold ceremonies must buy livestock rather than take it from their own herds. There may also be a psychological cost: Many older people, having lost their productive activity in life, may become depressed and thereby more prone to bodily illness, as others have been in similar circumstances (Scudder 1982:10–16).

The Distant Future

The 25-year leases on most allotments in the lease townships will begin to expire in 1998 (USDI, BIA, Eastern Navajo Agency n.d.a). If the company does not renew the leases, then the relocated families, their children, and others with interests in the allotments, should regain the use of their land. Some families may not want to return to their land, others may only want to live there, and still others may want to raise livestock there. This last group may include some people whose families were forced to sell all their stock when they left the lease and cannot afford to buy new stock. Presumably these people will be out of choices.

Whether they want to live on the land, raise livestock, or farm, however, the returning families will find the topography, vegetation, and probably the distribution of water sources vastly different from their condition before mining. If the already-revegetated areas are any indication, today's country of piñon- and juniper-covered sandstone and shale mesas, interspersed with sage flats along the arroyos, will be transformed into rolling grasslands with only a few islands of trees and rocks that the draglines have avoided. The old dug wells in the arroyos and springs beneath the mesas will have disappeared with the rock strata from which the water seeped. Presumably, if strip-mining disturbs the aquifers tapped by the old drilled wells, most future water sources will be reservoirs in pockets of the grasslands and drilled wells in new places.

If the present pattern of surface ownership is imposed on this future terrain, families may find that they cannot readily reside, farm, or herd there. Houses in the open, without sheltering trees and landforms, may be too cold in winter and too hot in summer. Property lines may deny many families access to the new water sources. People may not be able to drive to their homesites most of the time because the reclaimed land, with its lack of underlying rock, makes mud even worse than before. Moreover, according to one tribal official, the current revegetation plan requires that roads be routed only along natural contours so as to retard erosion. Soon several families living in dispersed homesites on this land may be opportunistically making roads in all directions to avoid muddy areas, hastening the ensuing erosion.

Indeed, if all human use of the land is not carefully regulated, the land might become quickly denuded and gullied. The land lies in a physiographic zone in which the National Academy of Sciences considers revegetation somewhat problematic. Average annual moisture in the vicinity of the lease is not far above the 10 in. that the Academy considers the minimum for successful revegetation and often falls below it (National Academy of Sciences 1974:2–3, 81; U.S. Weather Bureau 1919–1978).

According to one tribal official, environmental planners with both the mine and the Navajo Tribe have already recognized the impossibility of restoring the land-use patterns that existed on the north McKinley Mine lease before strip-mining. These planners have been reportedly considering the Savory grazing method for managing livestock on revegetated land. This intensive technique of range management, developed by a Rhodesian emigrant named Allan Savory, is supposed to promote symbiosis between plants and livestock by moving the animals around the range in relation to plant-growth cycles. It is thereby supposed to increase the carrying capacity of the range (Savory 1983). This method has recently been introduced on Sandia Pueblo land near Albuquerque, New Mexico, and at several places on the Navajo Reservation, where it seems to be used for cattle. These projects control the stock through the *Savory cell*, a series of fenced paddocks that radiate from a central corral and water source. All the stock are concentrated in one paddock for a short time, then moved to the next one. With their hoofs, the animals break the crust of the soil so that more moisture can penetrate and more plants can sprout (Albuquerque *Journal*, February 20, 1983, p. E–16; *Navajo Times*, July 30, 1981, p. 24).

If this method of range management is adopted, stock owners would have to pool their herds and might have to switch from sheep to cattle, if the current preference for cattle in Savory cells is any indication. If grazing on the revegetated land is limited to Savory cells, and the Savory cells are limited to cattle, many people whose families sold their livestock when they left the lease might not be able to afford the cattle they would have to buy to participate in the new method of range management.

If residence on the revegetated land, too, must be restricted, families, like the stock in the Savory cells, might be "closely herded" in housing compounds such as the relocation housing development. There seems to be no guarantee, however, that they would even be able to stay in the relocation housing. The development is on land that the company owns in fee. Presumably the company would sell this land when it closes the mine and moves out. Residents might then be faced with the prospect of either buying (and paying taxes on) the lots and houses, which few could afford to do, or seeing them sold to another private owner who might charge them rent or evict them. Presumably the Navajo tribal government could step in and buy the land if either of these prospects actually materalized. Otherwise, the families would have no place to go but to the allotments in the revegetated strip mine, to which they still hold rights.

But even if residence on the revegetated land is not restricted for environmental preservation, many relocated lease families might find they no longer hold rights there. According to the Indian Land Consolidation Act of 1983, when an heir to an allotment dies, and his or her share in the allotment is 2% or less, having returned less than $100 cash in the year before the death, that share would pass to the Navajo Tribe rather than to the surviving spouse and children (Gallup *Independent*, June 11, 1983, p. 1).

What the distant future could hold in store for many relocatees from the south mine lease, then, is complete expropriation: eviction from their homes, with their former allotments monopolized by a few relatively wealthy cattle owners. Of course, the future may not be so grim. The tribal government could buy the housing development, the Indian Land Consolidation Act might be implemented only very slowly, and an equitable range-management plan might be devised. Nevertheless, that haphazard planning has made the worst case even possible is deeply disturbing.

Chapter 20

Navajo Land Use:
An Ethnoarchaeological Perspective

At the beginning of this book I offered a formulation of the ways in which the gradual ascendance of industrial over mercantile capital in the United States has acted, through federal Indian policy, to change Navajo family land use. Since the United States conquered the Navajos in 1864, Navajo families have seen their main source of livelihood change from land-based production for their own use to land-based production partly for their own use and partly for the market, and then to wages and welfare. I consider familial sources of livelihood to be one of several interrelated aspects of land use, the other aspects being the environment, family demography, land tenure, use of space, and family technology—all of which have undergone change.

The first change, from family production for direct consumption to production for the market, was already well under way when people settled the lease townships, and indeed was the force behind the other forces that had pushed people into the townships. Land use within the townships has manifested the second change, from family production for the market to individual participation in the national labor market for wages and welfare.

The sources of information that I have used to both describe and explain changes in land use in the lease townships include various documents, the recollections of local Navajos, my own participant observations, and the archaeological record. None of these sources is transparently informative; all must be scrutinized for omissions and distortions. The ethnographic sources, however, are less recondite than the others and the process of distilling information from them more straightforward; the scrutiny I have applied to them is thus fairly clear in the body of this work and requires no further comment. The archaeological record, however, is another matter. In this final chapter, therefore, I try to bring out more clearly what the archaeological record alone reveals about changes in land use in the lease townships. This focusing on the archaeological record rather than simply summarizing major results and conclusions also serves to recapitulate the study with what I hope will be a little more novelty.

All the changes in land use shown in this work are the outcomes of the change from market-oriented family production as the economic mainstay of the Navajo family, to wages and welfare, in other words, the class transformation. After the lease townships were settled early in the railroad era, market-oriented family production was the economic mainstay. The class transformation began during the era of grazing regulation but was not complete until the industrial era. Therefore, instead of running down the list of changes in land use and asking how the archaeological record manifests each (if at all), I ask how the archaeological record manifests the class transformation. The class transformation does not, however, necessarily eliminate family production. As this study shows, family production survives, as do many traits of its early stages, including technology. The common occurrence of mass-produced artifacts on archaeological sites shows that the inhabitants were linked somehow to an industrializing political economy, and evidence of production on homesites (especially facilities) shows that families were productive units. The question is how one can tell whether the family was the basic productive unit or only a survival in a system dominated by individual wage work for private enterprise.

I suggest that at least four types of archaeological evidence, taken together, can show whether the class transformation has occurred: (1) evidence, on and around homesites, that the family intensified and diversified production, (2) evidence of environmental degradation, (3) evidence of certain changes in consumption patterns, and (4) changes in recycling and re-use of artifacts.

Throughout this work I have argued that intensified and diversified production is what distinguishes Navajo family production in the railroad era and in the transitional era of grazing regulation from production in the industrial era. The reason for this trend, again, is that families suffer at once from shrinking land bases and a growing burden of indebtedness that forces them to produce goods in greater volume, variety, or both. Through the judicious use of both technology and space, therefore, families must enlarge output in proportion to the land and labor input. If these means do not suffice, families have no choice but to overexploit and degrade their resource base. Industrial-era families feel less pressured to enlarge land-based production because it is not their main source of livelihood.

Archaeological evidence of intensified and diver-

sified use of space includes the following. The number of what many archaeologists call "special-activity" sites—here, sheep camps, campsites, and isolated corrals—diminishes with land subdivision. A family would use these sites to exploit lands far from the homestead where it was based at the time. As its customary use area shrinks, a family needs fewer of these sites. Special sites for exploiting the farthest lands therefore may vanish. (Sites for exploiting lands nearer the homesite—here, isolated corrals—do not entirely disappear, however, for the family must use its land base as evenly as possible.) Another kind of evidence is the increase in the overall size and complexity of homesites. This increase indicates longer annual stays that result from range subdivision. It is correlated with certain technological changes (larger dwellings, more facilities on homesites, and wider spacing of features in front of dwellings) that signal intensified, diversified production. Finally, homesites do not begin to cluster noticeably near major transportation links to the outside world until the class transformation is well underway.

Technological evidence of intensified, diversified production includes the following. Dwelling sizes grow and forms become more spacious as land subdivision forces families to settle down and as they increase craft production. The number and variety of artifacts on sites also increases as families settle down. Other indications of settling down and more production on a homesite are longer distances between the front of the dwelling and other features, especially refuse dumps and more diffuse trash scatters. Artifacts and facilities (such as loom frames) used in handicraft production may become more common on archaeological sites as production intensifies and diversifies, although they did not do so in the lease townships. Of special interest is evidence of crafts such as weaving, which process, and thereby add value to, the raw products of the land.

Still another type of evidence is growth in the number and variety of other production facilities and equipment on the homesite, especially in home-made items. I have argued elsewhere (Kelley n.d.) that homemade items, especially facilities, characterize family production under merchant capitalism because families cannot afford much mass-produced equipment and will substitute homemade, labor-saving facilities such as specialized corrals and pens. When a lot of new, mass-produced equipment becomes evident on sites, the class transformation is probably well advanced. Still other technological evidence of intensified, diversified production includes more storage features, such as barns, for keeping home-produced items, and more improvements of natural features, such as water sources. These facilities suggest that people cannot readily move to where resources are naturally available and therefore signal land subdivision. They also suggest that people are trying to get more out of the land by retarding loss or spoilage.

Intensified, diversified production did not support lease-township families well enough to keep them from overgrazing the land. Archaeological data were not analyzed for evidence of this range degradation. I suggest that such evidence might appear in the remains of livestock if families did not give them supplementary food produced elsewhere. The remains of wild fauna might also testify to overgrazing, as might pollen and macrobotanical samples.

Archaeological evidence of family consumption patterns should also reveal the class transformation. The main change in consumption patterns that accompanied the class transformation in the lease townships was the great surge in the number and variety of mass-produced goods. Of special importance is the change in foods, which most families stopped producing for themselves. These changes appear in the items discarded on sites (when one controls for length of occupation). If faunal and botanical samples had been collected from more sites, those samples might have shown that families ate fewer wild plants, crops, wild game, and domesticated animals (home-produced meat could be distinguished from the store-bought kind through evidence of butchering techniques).

I also suggest that the consumption patterns evident in a group of industrial-era homesites would show differences in wealth among families. These differences would probably be sharper than the wealth differences evident among earlier sites. I suggest that the more interdependent families are, the less obvious their differences in wealth; families either share their wealth or hoard it, but avoid flaunting it through conspicuous consumption. Mercantile trade might diminish family interdependence but does not destroy it. Families must often share labor, if nothing else. Industrialization, however, further diminishes family interdependence, for each family gets its own paychecks or welfare checks and can no longer expect help from others without paying them. Families therefore may be more willing (certainly no less willing) to let differences in wealth show than they were before the class transformation.

Wealth differences among families also may tend to be greater under industrialization, because capitalism imposes a highly variable wage structure on workers and guarantees only their most rudimentary subsistence needs. The contrast between Blackgoat's homestead and those of his contemporaries shows that wealth differences appear in the archaeological record as early as the railroad era. I have not been able to determine such differences in the archaeological record of the grazing-regulation and industrial eras, but only because the relatively wealthy families of both eras inhabited sites where people are still living. I believe that these differences would appear archaeologically if these sites were free to be studied.

Finally, changes in the disposal and recycling of artifacts may reflect the class transformation, although evidence of recycling artifacts was not recorded systematically in the lease townships and has therefore not been discussed in this book. With the class transformation, the growth in the family's disposable income, and the increasing consumption of mass-produced items, people throw away a growing volume of things (especially packaging such as cans and bottles). At the same time, they recycle and repair fewer items because they can readily afford to replace at least inexpensive things. As a result, discarded packaging and broken items may eventually threaten to engulf a homesite. Growing numbers of people may then clean up their homesites and dump the trash far away. The paradoxical outcome may be that the more things people consume and discard, the fewer remain on homesites when the class transformation is well advanced.

Appendix *A*

Methodology

I first discuss the overlap between the lists of lease-township families identified in the documents and named by local Navajos. Then I discuss the overlap between the group of sites that the families named by local Navajos inhabited and the groups of sites in various archaeological samples.

Two sets of documents provide statistical information about the lease townships and their inhabitants between 1910 and 1915: records relating to land allotments made in 1910, and a 1915 census. With the records of these allotments (USDI, BIA, Eastern Navajo Agency n.d.a, n.d.b; USDI, BIA, Navajo Area Office n.d.), genealogical records maintained by the Franciscan Friars of St. Michaels, Arizona (Franciscan Friars n.d.b), and genealogies and oral histories provided by local Navajos, I have reconstructed the households and residence groups that occupied the lease townships in 1910. First, I identified each allottee genealogically by determining the person's parents, spouse or spouses, and children, as well as all clan affiliations and birth and death dates. The resulting list shows each adult allottee in 1910, the spouse or spouses, and all children born as of that year. These groups constitute nuclear families. The procedure also revealed genealogical relationships among allottees. Next, I provisionally aggregated these nuclear families into households and residence groups by applying a

few assumptions about contemporary Navajo household and residence-group structure, based on the ethnographic literature (see Kelley 1982a:385). Local Navajos confirmed the composition of many of these groups and did not disconfirm the rest. Households that local Navajos identified with the block of unallotted sections in the northwestern part of the lease townships I added to the allotted households to give a reconstructed total inventory of households and residence groups in the lease townships.

The 1915 census was commissioned by agent Peter Paquette in the Southern Navajo Agency jurisdiction (Paquette 1915). Of the 29 households that lived in the lease townships in 1910, according to the allotment records and local Navajos, I was able to identify 22 (76%) in this census by a combination of personal names, clans, and names of places of residence. Most of these households consisted of the inhabitants of one dwelling. I assume that these households belonged to the same residence groups in which I placed them in 1910 unless they were not consecutively listed in the census or unless local Navajos provided evidence to the contrary. Some of the (reconstructed) 1910 households seem to have fissioned in 5 years or dispersed temporarily into separate summer sheep camps. Altogether, therefore, the 1915 group includes 25 households in 15 (reconstructed) residence groups.

Paquette's census actually shows 29 households, but 4 of them, each consisting of a single elderly person, are here counted with the household of a grown child assigned to the same residence group. This adjustment was necessary because later censuses do not treat single elderly people as separate households, and all censuses must be comparable for the purposes of this study.

Another contemporary list of lease-township residents consists of the inhabitants that interviewees have identified with homesites dated to around 1915 by interviewees, archaeological evidence, or both. Seventeen such residence groups were identified as users of the lease townships, but only 15 (26 households) maintained any kind of homesites inside the townships. Of these, I failed to identify only 4 households in 4 residence groups in the 1915 census; 2 nevertheless received allotments in 1910. Conversely, of the 29 households in the 1915 census (before single adults were aggregated into related households), 7 were not identified by local Navajos.

Four sets of documents provide information about the lease townships between 1936 and 1946. The first is a 1936 livestock registry (USDA, SCS 1936), a list of livestock owners in Land Management District 18. The second set consists of annual applications for livestock permits made between 1940 and 1946 (USDI, Grazing Service 1940–46). The third set consists of individual family interview schedules from the Human Dependency Survey of 1940 (USDA, SCS 1940). The fourth document consists of the 1940 Navajo Tribal census roll (USDI, BIA 1940), part of the decennial census of the United States but actually taken in 1939. One person may appear in different sources under different names, but each source also gives the corresponding census number, which the federal government has assigned to every Navajo since 1928. Therefore, I was able to identify individuals unambiguously. Again, I determined the genealogical links among virtually all people listed in all sources from the genealogical files of the Franciscans and statements of local Navajos.

The lists of families in these sources overlap extensively, but only the Human Dependency Survey seems to include most households in the lease townships. The designers of that survey called the family groups that they enumerated "consumption groups," an enigmatic term that later scholars have found does not cor-

respond to either the household or the residence group, but to something in between (Henderson and Levy 1975:6, 137). That the survey was designed to rely heavily on data from trading posts suggests that the consumption group might include adults who, together with their dependents, shared a trading-post account. The groups identified in the lease townships, however, correspond to households identified by local Navajos and the 1940 census. I have aggregated these households into residence groups in the same way I did the 1910–1915 households.

The Human Dependency Survey identified 28 households in 19 residence groups. Local Navajos failed to mention 2 of these households, representing 2 residence groups, but added another 2 households representing 2 residence groups and possibly a third household (which, however, may have been part of another household enumerated in the Human Dependency Survey). The 1940 household sample analyzed here therefore includes all households enumerated in the Human Dependency Survey plus the 2 clearly different households added by local Navajos.

In November and December of 1978 I undertook a census of the Navajo residents of the lease townships for information comparable to the 1910–1915 and 1936–1946 documents. Time and weather did not allow me to visit all of the comparatively few households living outside the south McKinley Mine lease, but the public school census, and visits the following summer, filled the gaps. Again, the Franciscan files and local Navajos identified these people genealogically. Thus, there is a perfect correspondence between the census data and the on-the-ground locations of families for 1978 and 1979.

The group of site components that local Navajos identified with particular households links the documentary and archaeological data sets. Through interviews with 87 local people, interpreters and I gathered these oral histories on archaeological sites, together with information on currently occupied sites and on cornfields and water sources of all periods. The interviewees included representatives of 27 of the 32 residence groups in the lease townships. Neighbors, a 1976 aerial photograph (Pittsburg and Midway Coal Mining Company 1976), and simple observation yielded information on the remaining 5 residence groups and on the sites that they use. At homesites occupied by single households, we interviewed the male or female head of the household. At homesites with more than one household, we usually spoke with the male or female head of the senior household, often with a number of junior-household members interpreting or listening in. We also interviewed representatives of most residence groups that were evicted from the part of the lease that was strip-mined after 1960. Interviewees identified both archaeological sites and those currently in use, mainly by visiting them with us. Some interviewees identified sites by recognizing photographs of them or by pointing out their locations either on USGS 7.5′ quadrangle maps or on aerial photographs. I field-checked the locations of sites identified on maps and photographs. The dated aerial photographs (Pittsburg and Midway Coal Mining Company 1976; USDA, CSC ca. 1934; USDI, Geological Survey 1952, 1962, 1973) also showed the locations of, and of course indicated dates for, additional cornfields and water sources that interviewees had not identified.

The past and present site components, the locations of which are unambiguous, constitute the basic sample of site components identified ethnographically. The composition of this sample is shown on Table A.1. The sites in this sample are hereafter called positively

identified sites because interviewees located them unambiguously, thus eliminating uncertainty about which sites an interviewee was talking about. Sometimes interviewees mentioned sites and gave general locations for them that, for one reason or another, I could not substantiate by field observation. These ambiguously located sites, and others located and dated by archaeological means on tracts of land that local Navajos identified with particular users of the same period, constitute a group of tentatively identified sites that I have used only sparingly in this book.

The interpreters and I tried to find out the function of each positively identified site component; the names of its users and their relationships to other lease-township residents; the years and seasons of its use; the sources of livelihood of its users; and the dwelling sites, water sources, fields, range area, satellite herding camps, and other sites that its users maintained at the same time. Interviewees were rarely able to supply all of this information, and for some of the sites could only say that they had been used before a particular time. Thus, the amount of information on positively identified sites varies widely.

The positively identified site components date to various years. Those that date to the three baseline intervals constitute a subset of the positively identified

Table A.1
Site Components by Type in the Positively Identified Sample in the Lease Townships[a]

Type[b]	1880–1930	1930–1950	1950–1979	Total, all periods[c]
Structural components	66	66	76	172[d]
homesteads	14	34	45	
sheep camps	15	10	16	140
homesites of uncertain function, farmsteads	16	6	5	
campsites, isolated corrals	16	11	10	25
isolated sweathouses	5	5	—	
Miscellaneous[e]	NC	NC	NC	7
Water sources and cornfields	NC	NC	NC	134
water sources	NC	NC	NC	63
cornfields	NC	NC	NC	71

[a]NC = not counted separately for each period because a large proportion of components overlap.
[b]Terms are defined in the body of this work.
[c]Detail does not add to total because a few components overlap periods and are counted more than once.
[d]Represents 148 sites.
[e]Includes fences, petroglyphs, antelope-hunting corrals, and Squaw Dance location.

Table A.2
Site Components by Type
in the Limited Site Sample in the Lease Townships

Type[a]	1915	1940	1978
Structural components			
homesteads	6	15	29
sheep camps	7	8	6
homesites of uncertain function, farmsteads	6	1	2
campsites, isolated corrals	7	5	1
isolated sweathouses	4	4	—
Miscellaneous	—	—	—
Water sources and cornfields			
water sources	12	29	20
cornfields	5	17	20

[a]Terms are defined in body of this work.

sample hereafter called the limited site sample (LSS). The composition of this sample is shown on Table A.2. A few components belonging to the residence groups of each baseline interval were not positively identified, but the overlap of positively identified components and residence groups is still respectable in all three baseline intervals. Nine of the 15 residence groups in the 1915 census are represented by 11 main homesites plus associated sites; an additional 2 main homesites and associated sites represent the 2 residence groups among the allottees that were not in the census, and 2 more main homesites and associated sites represent the 2 residence groups that do not appear in any documents. In addition, 1 household in the census is represented only by a campsite in the LSS. In 1940, 17 of the 19 residence groups in the Human Dependency Survey are represented by 19 main homesites and associated sites, while an additional 3 sites represent the 2 or 3 other residence groups mentioned by local Navajos. In 1978, of course, all 32 residence groups are represented by the group of currently occupied main homesites and associated sites. The identification of documented households with each component brings in economic and demographic data on the site that interviewees usually were not able to supply. Therefore the LSS includes the site components with the widest range of reliable information.

The components in the LSS, then, adequately represent the families that both documents and local

Navajos place in the lease townships during the baseline intervals. The lack of documentation outside the baseline intervals prevents a similar assessment of the entire positively identified sample. It seems reasonable to assume, however, that the inventory of sites in the archaeological surveys closely approximates the inventory of the sites (other than water sources and fields) that users of the lease left during all periods. Assuming this, one can see how representative the positively identified sample is by comparing it to the archaeological survey inventory.

The sites in the positively identified sample are located in the lease townships both on and off the lease. If the density of sites on the lease is replicated throughout the unsurveyed remainder of the townships, the structural sites in the positively identified sample probably represent a rather large proportion, 22%, of the structural sites in the lease township (see Table A.3). The 71 positively identified archaeological sites (83 components) on the lease, both structural and nonstructural (but excluding cornfields and water sources), represent about 30% of the 233 site components on the lease.

The positively identified sample probably represents rather accurately the distribution of sites both through time and among various types, at least on the lease, as Tables A.4 and A.5 indicate. The group of dated sites in the archaeological survey inventory may be biased slightly toward sites that postdate 1910. One

Table A.3
Navajo Ethnographic Samples
and Estimated Number of Archaeological Sites, Lease Townships

Site inventory	All sites[a]	Dwelling sites
Archaeological and currently occupied sites, south McKinley Mine lease		
sites recorded by 1975–1977 arch. surveys	233	109
additional sites recorded by OCA[b]	38	20
currently occupied sites	25	24
total no. of sites	296	153
sites per square mile	12.5	6.4
Archaeological and currently occupied sites, lease townships		
projected total no. of sites	663	341
total ethnographic sample		
no. of components	257	178
no. of sites	233	168
sites as a percentage of projected total	35%	49%
Positively identified sites		
no. of components	179	140
no. of sites	155	130
sites as a percentage of projected total	23%	38%
Limited site sample		
no. of components	98	77
no. of sites	98	77
sites as a percentage of projected total	15%	23%

[a]Excludes water and cornfields.
[b]Includes sites recorded in 1978–1979 and 1981 (Eck 1981); OCA = Office of Contract Archaeology.

Table A.4
Navajo Sites
on the South McKinley Mine Lease in
Positively Identified Ethnographic Sample
Compared to Archaeological Survey Inventory by Date

	Archaeological survey inventory		Positively identified ethnographic sample	
	No.	%	No.	%
Total no. of components	261	100	83	100
Pre-1880	2(?)	1	1	1
1880–1930	50	19	42	51
1930–1979	48	18	32	39
Single components counted in two periods	—	—	8	10
Date unknown	161	61	—	—

Table A.5
Navajo Sites
on the South McKinley Mine Lease in
Positively Identified Ethnographic Sample
Compared to Archaeological Survey Inventory by Function

	Archaeological survey inventory[a]		Positively identified ethnographic sample[b]	
	No.	%	No.	%
Total no. of components	237	100	83[c]	100
Homesites	111	47	55	66
Isolated corrals, campsites	56	24	18	19
Isolated sweathouses	63	27	3	4
Miscellaneous sites	7	3	7	9

[a]Includes data from 1975 (Koczan 1977), 1977 (Hartman 1977), and 1981 (Eck 1981) surveys.
[b]Excludes 11 archaeological components on the lease unrecorded by 1975 and 1977 surveys, and 30 components in 24 currently occupied sites; also excludes cornfields and water sources.
[c]Components (represent 71 sites).

reason, as explained in Chapter 5, is that later sites are more likely to have datable artifacts; another is that early structural wood samples offered few cutting dates. The positively identified ethnographic site sample is more biased toward sites after 1910, but not heavily so. Table A.4 shows that, when sites are aggregated into long (50-year) time spans, roughly equal proportions of dated sites in both the ethnographic sample and the survey inventory fall into each time period. Table A.5 shows that the main difference in functional types of sites represented is in the proportion of sweathouses identified. If one excludes sweathouses from the total number of sites, the proportion of the adjusted total that each type of site represents is much the same in both samples, with only a slight bias toward dwelling sites in the ethnographic sample. The reason that so few isolated sweathouses were identified ethnographically is that most are associated with nearby homesites or herding camps and are not in themselves informative about land-use patterns. Therefore, I did not work very hard to overcome the tendency of interviewees not to bother identifying sweathouses, which they probably regarded as parts of the other sites that they did identify.

On the other hand, Table A.6 shows a pronounced geographical bias. The problem is not as serious as it appears on the table, however. On the west side of the lease, where the largest proportion of sites in the survey inventory were identified ethnographically, strip-mining undoubtedly had already destroyed many archaeological sites before the survey. To compensate for this factor, the interpreters and I worked extra hard to identify sites in this area, including locations within the strip-mined tracts where they had once been. Moreover, different groups of families used each of the three sectors of the lease; although sites belonging to families on the east side are underrepresented, the information that I did collect indicates that the range of variability in family land-use patterns there replicates the range of variability among families in the other two segments.

Like the ethnohistorical information, the archaeological information on each site varies in quantity and quality. Only inventories of structural features are available for currently occupied sites and for archaeological sites outside the lease. For each archaeological site on the lease, the surveys specify both structural and nonstructural features and their dimensions, and indicate roughly the artifacts present. An effort was made to record systematically the functional and material categories of artifacts present on 83 components of the 71 sites included in the positively identified ethnographic sample, and to collect potentially datable artifacts. Time and the limits of the laboratory facilities allowed such observations on only 72 components of 60 sites (including those where the

Table A.6
Navajo Sites
on the South McKinley Mine Lease in
Positively Identified Ethnographic Sample
Compared to Archaeological Survey Inventory by Location

	West side of lease	Center of lease	East side of lease	Total lease
No. of sites in survey inventory	33[a]	106	98	237
No. of sites positively identified by interviewees	19	46	14	79[b]
% of survey inventory identified by interviewees	58	43	14	33

[a]No. is lower than for other areas because of previous strip-mining in area.

[b]These sites account for 79 site numbers in the survey inventory but are considered to represent 71 sites in ethnoarchaeological analyses.

complete absence of artifacts was determined)—65 homesite and campsite components and 7 of other types. The greatest amount of archaeological information is available on the 34 sites randomly selected for subsurface testing or excavation. Of these, 24 (mostly homesites) are in the positively identified sample. Data peculiar to these sites include the types of subsurface features, the volumes of certain types of waste deposits, and the faunal and botanical remains present.

Genealogy

The following genealogies are not complete. They show genealogical relationships among people named in the text only. Individuals are grouped by clan. Clans are grouped geographically in each of the three major subdivisions of the lease townships. Clans of in-married people are shown in parentheses after the name. Marriage links are shown as *m*. Children of each marriage are listed below the names of their parents. Clan members mentioned in the text without known cognatic links to other members of the same clan are not listed in this appendix.

TSE BONITA WASH–UPPER DEFIANCE DRAW

Salt Clan

Salt Clan Woman *m*. husband (Towering House)
1. Tall Salt Clansman *m*. Mexican Clan Woman (Mexican)
   children: *see* Mexican Clan
2. Shorthair *m*. daughter of Gray Woman (Red Streak Into Water)
3. Salt Clan Woman *m*. Mr. Howler's Grandson (Charcoal Streak)
   3.1. Fat Salt *m*. 3 daughters (Edgewater) of Bald Head (He Walks Around)
   3.2. daughter *m*. Tall Red Streak Clansman (Red Streak Into Water)

   3.3. daughter *m*. Chopped Hair (He Walks Around)

parentage unrecorded

1. Cornmerchant *m*. Taozba (Edgewater)
   children: *see* Edgewater Clan
   Cornmerchant *m*. Anajiba (Edgewater)
   Cornmerchant *m*. daughter (Edgewater) of Taozba and Bald Head (He Walks Around)

He Walks Around Clan

Bald Head *m*. Taozba (Edgewater)
   children: *see* Edgewater Clan
Bald Head's siter *m*. husband (clan unknown)
   1. daughter *m*. husband (Towering House)
      1.1. Little Warrior *m*. Mrs. Left Handed (Many Goats)
         daughters married into Mexican Clan
      1.2. Old Sally *m*. Good Luck (Many Goats)

         1.2.1. Chopped Hair *m*. daughter (Red Streak Into Water) of Louis Reeder (He Walks Around)
         Chopped Hair *m*. daughter (Mexican) of Tall Salt Clansman (Salt)
         children: *see* Mexican Clan

Chopped Hair *m.* daughter of Salt
Clan Woman: *see* Salt Clan
Old Sally *m.* Charley Boyd (Edgewater)
1.2.2. Sadie *m.* Jeff King (Towering
House)
    1.2.2.1. Annie King
    Sadie *m.* Fat Edgewater Clansman
    (formerly married into Zia Clan)
1.2.3. daughter *m.* Chee Jim (Red Streak
Into Water)
1.3. daughter *m.* husband (Edgewater)
    1.3.1. son *m.* daughter (Mexican) of Tall
    Salt Clansman (Salt)

Edgewater Clan

Little Woman *m.* husband (Within His Cover)
1. Taozba *m.* Bald Head (He Walks Around)
    1.1. Big Woman *m.* Fat Salt (Salt)
    1.2. daughter *m.* Fat Salt (Salt)
    1.3. daughter *m.* Fat Salt (Salt)
    1.4. daughter *m.* Cornmerchant (Salt)
    Taozba *m.* Cornmerchant (Salt)
    1.5. Charley Goldtooth *m.* wife (Red Streak Into
    Water)
    1.6. daughter *m.* Whitegoat Curly (Mountain
    Cove)
Little Woman *m.* husband (He Walks Around)
2. Anajiba *m.* Cornmerchant (Salt)
    Anajiba *m.* Tall Red Streak Clansman (Red
    Streak Into Water)

Mexican Clan

Mexican Clan Woman *m.* Tall Salt Clansman (Salt)
1. Tall Mexican Clansman *m.* daughters (Many
    Goats) of Little Warrior (He Walks Around)
2. son *m.* daughters (Many Goats) of Little War-
    rior (He Walks Around)
3. daughter *m.* Chopped Hair (He Walks Around)
    3.1. son *m.* wife (Red Streak Into Water)
    3.2. daughter *m.* son (Many Goats) of Little
    Warrior (He Walks Around)
    daughter *m.* son of Bald Head's sister's
    daughter's daughter (He Walks Around)

Mountain Cove Clan

Warrior Woman *m.* husband (Edgewater)

1. Whitegoat Curly *m.* daughter (Edgewater) of
    Cornmerchant (Salt)
2. daughter *m.* Mr. Tall (Towering House)
    2.1. daughter *m.* Billy Smiley (Zia)

Red Streak Into Water Clan

Gray Woman *m.* Fuzzy Face (Edgewater)
1. Tall Red Streak Clansman *m.* daughter of Salt
    Clan Woman (Salt)
    Tall Red Streak Clansman *m.* Anajiba
    (Edgewater)
2. daughter *m.* Shorthair (Salt)
3. Gray-Eyed Woman *m.* husband (clan unknown)
    3.1. Warrior Woman *m.* Schoolboy (Towering
    House)
    children: 2 sons and 2 daughters
    Warrior Woman *m.* husband (clan
    unknown)
    children: 2 daughters
    Gray-Eyed Woman *m.* Lefthanded Slim
    children: none
4. Margaret Thompson *m.* Tall Ute (Ute)
    4.1. Curly Tallman *m.* wife (Towering House)
    4.2. Chee Jim *m.* Violet Brown (Towering
    House)
    children: *see* Towering House Clan
    Chee Jim *m.* daughter (He Walks Around)
    of Charley Boyd (Edgewater)
Margaret Thompson *m.* Frank Thompson
adopted Gray-Eyed Woman's grandchildren

MIDDLE DEFIANCE DRAW

Zia Clan

Warrior Girl *m.* Smiley (Many Goats)
1. daughter *m.* Blackgoat (Red Streak Into Water)
    1.1. Turning Warrior
    1.2. Mary Tinhouse *m.* Fred Tinhouse
    (Edgewater)
    1.3. Descending Orator
2. daughter *m.* Fat Edgewater Clansman
    (Edgewater)
3. They Are Raiding Along Behind Each Other *m.*
    Mr. Towering House Clansman, (Towering
    House)
    3.1. Henry Wilson
    3.2. Thompson Wilson

4. Billy Smiley *m.* daughter of Whitegoat Curly's sister (Mountain Cove)

EASTERN FLAT-LOWER DEFIANCE DRAW

Towering House Clan

name unknown *m.* Good Luck (Many Goats)
1. Azaakai *m.* Pete Price
   1.1. Towering House Woman *m.* Lefthanded's Son (Edgewater)
      1.1.1. twin daughter adopted by Azaakai *m.* Tom Sharp (Jemez)
      1.1.2. twin daughter adopted by Big Woman
      1.1.3. Violet Brown *m.* Chee Jim
             children: 3 sons
             Violet Brown *m.* husband (clan unknown)
             children: daughter and son
      1.1.4. daughter? *m.* Juan's Son (Edgewater)

name unknown *m.* husband (clan unknown)
2. Big Woman *m.* Bad Teeth (Many Goats)
name unknown *m.* Tiny (Near To Water)
   1. Tiny's Daughter *m.* Fuzzy Face? (Edgewater)
      1.1. daughter *m.* Lefthanded's Son (Edgewater)
      1.2. Tom Dixon
      1.3. John Dixon
      1.4. Schoolboy? *m.* Warrior Woman (Red Streak Into Water)
      Tiny's Daughter *m.* Galashazh (Edgewater)
      1.5. daughter *m.* Juan's Son (Edgewater)
K'inaba *m.* husband (Black Sheep)
   1. Mr. Tall *m.* sister of Whitegoat Curly (Mountain Cove)
sister of Azaakai? *m.* Mescalero (Mountain Cove)
   1. Mr. Small
   2. Little Woman *m.* Gambler's Son (Tsi'naajinii)
      2.1. Mr. Towering House Clansman *m.* They Are Raiding Along Behind Each Other (Zia)

References

Aberle, David F.
1961   Navaho. In *Matrilineal kinship*, edited by David M. Schneider and Kathleen Gough, pp. 96–201. University of California Press, Berkeley.
1963   Some sources of flexibility in Navajo social organization. *Southwest Journal of Anthropology* 19:1–8.
1980   Navajo exogamic rules and preferred marriages. In *The versatility of kinship*, edited by Linda S. Cordell and Stephen Beckerman, pp. 105–143. Academic Press, New York.
1981a   A century of Navajo kinship change. *Canadian Journal of Anthropology* 2:21–36.
1981b   Navajo coresidential kin groups and lineages. *Journal of Anthropological Research* 37:1–7.

Ackerman, Alan, Klara B. Kelley, Joyce Shohet Ackerman, and Katherine D. Hale
1978   *Family planning attitudes of traditional and acculturated Navajo Indians*. Paper presented at the Population and Food Policy Conference, Capon Springs Public Policy Series No. 2, Washington, D.C.

Adair, John
1944   *Navajo and Pueblo silversmiths*. University of Oklahoma Press, Norman.

Adams, William Y.
1963   Shonto: a study of the role of the trader in a modern Navajo community. *Bureau of American Ethnology, Bulletin* 188. Smithsonian Institution, Washington, D.C.

Allen, Christina G., and Ben A. Nelson
1982   *Anasazi and Navajo land use in the McKinley Mine area near Gallup, New Mexico, Volume 1: Archeology*. Office of Contract Archeology, University of New Mexico, Albuquerque.

Amsden, Charles Avery
1934   *Navaho weaving: its technique and history*. The Fine Arts Press, Santa Ana, California.

Bailey, Garrick A., and Roberta Glenn Bailey
1980   Ethnohistory. In Prehistory and history of the Ojo Amarillo, archaeological investigations of Block II, Navajo Indian Irrigation Project, San Juan County, New Mexico, edited by David T. Kirkpatrick, Vol. 4, pp. 1389–1524. *Cultural Resources Management Division, Department of Sociology and Anthropology, New Mexico State University, Report* No. 276. Las Cruces.

Bailey, Lynn R.
1964   *The long walk: a history of the Navajo wars 1846–1868*. Westernlore Press, Los Angeles.

Bannister, Bryant, John W. Hannah, and William I. Robinson
1966   *Tree-ring dates from Arizona K: Puerco-Wide Ruin-Ganado area*. University of Arizona Laboratory of Tree-Ring Research, Tucson.
1937   History of stock reduction program on Navajo Reservation. In *Survey of Conditions of the Indians in the United States, Pt.* 34. U.S. Senate, pp. 17985–17989. Government Printing Office, Washington, D.C.

Bedinger, Margery
    1973   *Indian silver: Navajo and Pueblo jewelers.*
            University of New Mexico Press, Albuquerque.
Benson, Michael
    1976   *The Navajo Nation and taxation.* DNA-People's
            Legal Services, Window Rock, Arizona.
Binford, Lewis R., and Jack B. Bertram
    1977   Bone frequencies and attritional processes. In
            For theory building in archaeology, edited by
            L.R. Binford, pp. 77–156. Academic Press, New
            York.
Bingham, Sam, and Janet Bingham
    1976   *Navajo chapter government handbook.* Rock
            Point, Arizona, Community School.
    1979   *Navajo farming.* Rock Point Community
            School, Chinle, Arizona.
Bloom, Lansing B., editor
    1936   Bourke on the Southwest. *New Mexico
            Historical Review* 11:77–122, 217–282.
Borgman, The Rev. Francis, O.F.M.
    1948   Henry Chee Dodge: the last chief of the Navajo
            Indians. *New Mexico Historical Review*
            23:81–93.
Boyce, George
    1974   *When the Navajo had too many sheep: the
            1940s.* Indian Historian Press, San Francisco.
Brugge, David M.
    1970   Zarcillos Largos, courageous advocate of peace.
            *Navajo Historical Publications, Biographical
            Series* 2. Research Section, Navajo Tribe Parks
            and Recreation, Window Rock, Arizona.
    1972   Navajo and western Pueblo history. *The Smoke
            Signal* 25. The Tucson Corral of the Westerners.
    1977   Tsegai: an archeological ethnohistory of the
            Chaco region. Ms. on file, Chaco Center,
            National Park Service, Albuquerque.
    1980   A history of the Chaco Navajos. *Reports of the
            Chaco Center* 4. Chaco Center, National Park
            Service, Albuquerque.
Camilli, Eileen
    1984   *Site occupational history and lithic assemblage
            structure: an example from southeastern Utah.*
            Ph.D. dissertation, Anthropology Department,
            University of New Mexico. University
            Microfilms, Ann Arbor.
Carlson, Alvar Ward
    1969   New Mexico's sheep industry, 1850–1900: its role
            in the history of the territory. *New Mexico
            Historical Review* 44:25–49.
Carstensen, Vernon (editor)
    1963   *The public lands: studies in the history of the
            public domain.* University of Wisconsin Press,
            Madison.

Chandler, Alfred N.
    1945   *Land title origins: a tale of force and fraud.*
            Robert Schalkenback Foundation, New York.
Clawson, Marion
    1967   *The federal lands since 1956: recent trends in use
            and management.* The Johns Hopkins Press,
            Baltimore.
Clawson, Marion, and Burnell Held
    1957   *The federal lands: their use and management.*
            The Johns Hopkins Press, Baltimore.
Collier, Malcom Carr
    1951   *Local organization among the Navajo.*
            Unpublished Ph.D. dissertation, Anthropology
            Department, University of Chicago.
Coolidge, Dane, and Mary Roberts Coolidge
    1930   *The Navaho Indians.* Houghton Mifflin,
            Boston and New York.
Correll, J. Lee
    1976   *Through white men's eyes.* (published in 1979
            as Vol. 1 of work of same title) Navajo Tribal
            Museum, Window Rock, Arizona.
    1977   Archaeological clearance survey report of a
            waterline for the Navajo community of Black
            Hat, New Mexico. MC-77-067. Ms. on file,
            Navajo Nation Cultural Resource Management
            Program, Window Rock, Arizona.
    1979   *Through white men's eyes* (6 vols.). Navajo
            Heritage Center, Window Rock, Arizona.
Correll, J. Lee, and Alfred Dehiya
    1978   *Anatomy of the Navajo Indian Reservation: how
            it grew* (rev. ed.). Navajo Times Publishing Co.,
            Window Rock, Arizona.
Counselor, Jim, and Ann Counselor
    1954   *Wild, wooly, and wonderful.* Vantage Press, New
            York.
Dames and Moore Consultants, Inc.
    1974   Environmental assessment, McKinley Coal
            Mine, McKinley County, New Mexico, prepared
            for Pittsburg–Midway Coal Company, Denver.
            Ms. on file, U.S. Department of the Interior,
            Bureau of Land Management, Albuquerque.
Davis, W. W. H.
    1962   *El Gringo, or, New Mexico and her people.* Rio
            Grande Press, Chicago (first published in 1857).
Debo, Angie
    1970   *A history of Indians of the United States.*
            University of Oklahoma Press, Norman.
Dyk, Walter
    1938   *Son of Old Man Hat.* The Dryden Press, New
            York.
Eck, David C.
    1981   An archaeological survey of two parcels of land
            on the McKinley Mine south lease for the

Pittsburg and Midway Mining Company. Ms. on file, Office of Contract Archeology, University of New Mexico, Albuquerque.

Eck, David C., Jeffrey L. Boyer, and Klara B. Kelley
1982   Dating methods and results. In *Anasazi and Navajo land use in the McKinley Mine area near Gallup, New Mexico, Volume 1: Archeology*, edited by Christina G. Allen and Ben A. Nelson, pp. 843–865. Office of Contract Archeology, University of New Mexico, Albuquerque.

Ellis, Florence Hawley
1974   An anthropological study of the Navajo Indians. In *Navajo Indians I*, edited by David Agee Horr. Garland, New York and London.

Fonaroff, L. Schuyler
1963   Conservation and stock reduction on the Navajo Tribal range. *Geographical Review* 53:200–223.

Franciscan Fathers
1910   *An ethnologic dictionary of the Navajo language.* Franciscan Fathers, St. Michaels, Arizona.
n.d.a   Files of Father Anselm Weber.
n.d.b   Genealogical records, census office.

Frazer, Robert W. (editor)
1963   *Mansfield on the condition of the western forts, 1853–54.* University of Oklahoma Press, Norman.

Frink, Maurice
1968   *Fort Defiance and the Navajos.* Pruett Press, Boulder, Colorado.

Gates, Paul W.
1936   The Homestead Law in an incongruous land system. *American Historical Review* 41:652–681.

Greever, William S.
1954   *Arid domain: the Santa Fe Railway and its western land grant.* Stanford University Press, Stanford, California.

Gregory, Herbert E.
1916   The Navajo country, a geographic and hydrographic reconnaissance of parts of Arizona, New Mexico, and Utah. *U.S. Geological Survey Water Supply Paper* 380.

Grubbs, Frank H.
1961   Frank Bond: gentleman sheepherder of northern New Mexico, 1883–1915. *New Mexico Historical Review* 36:138–158, 230–243, 274–345.

Hack, John T.
1942   The changing physical environment of the Hopi Indians of Arizona. *Papers of the Peabody Museum of American Archaeology and Ethnology* 35(1).

Hanley, Max
1977   Untitled. In *Stories of traditional Navajo life and culture, by twenty-two Navajo men and women*, pp. 17–55. Navajo Community College Press, Tsaile, Arizona.

Harbison, Donald E.
1932   Working plan report of the grazing resources and activities of the Southern Navajo Indian Reservation, Arizona and New Mexico (December 24, 1930). In *Survey of conditions of the Indians in the United States, Pt.* 18. U.S. Senate, pp. 9196–9210. Government Printing Office, Washington, D.C.

Hartman, Russell P.
1977   Archaeological clearance survey report of a tract of land in the vicinity of McKinley Mine, McKinley County, New Mexico. MC-77-104. Ms. on file, Navajo Nation Cultural Resource Management Program, Window Rock, Arizona.

Henderson, Al
1979   Tribal enterprises: will they survive? In Economic development in American Indian reservations, edited by Roxanne Dunbar Ortiz, pp. 114–118. *Native American Studies Developmental Series* 1. Native American Studies Center, University of New Mexico, Albuquerque.

Henderson, E. B., and J. E. Levy
1975   Survey of Navajo community studies, 1936–1974. *Lake Powell Research Project Bulletin* 6. Institute of Geophysics and Planetary Physics, University of California at Los Angeles.

Hill, W. W.
1938   The agricultural and hunting methods of the Navaho Indians. *Yale University Publications in Anthropology* 18. Yale University Press, New Haven.
1940a   Some aspects of Navajo political structure. *Plateau* 13:23–29.
1940b   Some Navajo culture changes during two centuries. In Essays in historical anthropology of North America. *Smithsonian Miscellaneous Contributions* 100.

Hoffman, Virginia
1974   *Navajo biographies* (Vol. I). Navajo Curriculum Center Press, Phoenix.

Hole, Frank
1978   Pastoral nomadism in western Iran. In *Explorations in ethnoarchaeology*, edited by Richard A. Gould, pp. 127–167. University of New Mexico Press, Albuquerque.

Indian Rights Association
1944   *Indian Truth* 21(3). Philadelphia.
James, George Wharton
1914   *Indian blankets and their makers*. A.C. McClurg, Chicago.
Jenkins, Myra Ellen
1980   The Pueblo of Zuni and United States occupation, 1846–1868. Ms. on file, Zuni Archaeology Program, Pueblo of Zuni, New Mexico.
Johansen, Bruce
1978   The reservation offensive. *The Nation*, February 25, pp. 204–207.
Kelley, Klara B.
1977   *Commercial networks in the Navajo–Hopi–Zuni region*. Unpublished Ph.D. dissertation, Department of Anthropology, University of New Mexico, Albuquerque.
1978–   Site histories told by the McKinley Navajos. Ms.
1979   on file, Office of Contract Archeology, University of New Mexico, Albuquerque.
1979   Federal Indian land policy and economic development in the United States. In Economic development in American Indian Reservations, edited by Roxanne Dunbar Ortiz, pp. 30–42. *Native American Studies Development Series* 1. Native American Studies Center, University of New Mexico, Albuquerque.
1980   Navajo political economy before Fort Sumner. In *The versatility of kinship*, edited by Linda S. Cordell and Stephen Beckerman, pp. 307–331. Academic Press, New York.
1982a   *Anasazi and Navajo land use in the McKinley Mine area near Gallup, New Mexico, Volume 2: Ethnohistory*. Office of Contract Archeology, University of New Mexico, Albuquerque.
1982b   The Black Creek Valley: ethnohistoric and ethnoarchaeological investigations of Navajo political economy and land use. In Prehistoric and historic occupation of the Black Creek Valley, northeastern Arizona and northwestern New Mexico, by Russell T. Fehr, Klara B. Kelley, Linda Popelish, and Laurie E. Warner, pp. 55–113. *Navajo Nation Papers in Anthropology* 7. Navajo Nation Cultural Resource Management Program, Window Rock, Arizona.
1982c   The Chaco Canyon Ranch: ethnohistory and ethnoarchaeology. *Navajo Nation Papers in Anthropology* 8. Navajo Nation Cultural Resource Management Program, Window Rock, Arizona.
n.d.a   Navajo ethnohistory of the McKinley Mine

north lease. In preparation.
n.d.b   Production and material culture in the Chaco Canyon country. Ms. in author's possession.
Kelly, Daniel T.
1972   *The buffalo head: a century of mercantile pioneering in the Southwest*. Vergara, Santa Fe.
Kelly, Lawrence C.
1968   *The Navajo Indians and federal Indian policy, 1900–1935*. University of Arizona Press, Tucson.
1970   *Navajo roundup: selected correspondence of Kit Carson's expedition against the Navajo, 1863–1865*. Pruett, Boulder, Colorado.
Kennedy, Mary Jeannette
1965   Tales of a trader's wife. Valliant, Albuquerque (privately published).
Kent, Susan
1983   The differentiation of Navajo culture, behavior, and material culture: a comparative study in culture change. *Ethnology* 22:81–91.
Kimball, Solon, and John H. Provinse
1942   Navajo social organization and land-use planning. *Applied Anthropology* 1:18–25.
Kluckhohn, Clyde, and Dorothea Leighton
1947   *The Navajo*. Harvard University Press, Cambridge.
1962   *The Navajo* (rev. ed.). Doubleday, Garden City, New York.
Knight, Paul J.
1982   Ethnobotany and agriculture on the McKinley Mine lease. In *Anasazi and Navajo land use in the McKinley Mine area near Gallup, New Mexico, Volume I: Archeology*, edited by Christina G. Allen and Ben A. Nelson, pp. 668–711. Office of Contract Archeology, University of New Mexico, Albuquerque.
Koczan, Steven A.
1977   A cultural resource inventory of 2.5 sections of land near Tse Bonita School, New Mexico, for Pittsburg and Midway Mining Company. Ms. on file, Contract Archeology Section, Museum of New Mexico, Santa Fe.
Kunitz, Stephen J.
1977   Economic variation on the Navajo Reservation. *Human Organization* 36:186–193.
Lamphere, Louise
1970   Ceremonial cooperation and networks: a reanalysis of the Navajo outfit. *Man* 5:39–59.
1976   The internal colonization of the Navajo people. *Southwest Economy and Society* 1(1):6–14.
1977   *To run after them: the cultural and social bases of cooperation in a Navajo community*. University of Arizona Press, Tucson.

Landgraf, John L.
1954   Land-use in the Ramah area of New Mexico, an anthropological approach to areal study. Reports of the Ramah Project 5. *Papers of the Peabody Museum of American Archaeology and Ethnology* 42(1).

Lewis, Ray Baldwin
1979   Navajos are facing realities of inflation. *Navajo Times*, Oct. 4, p. 5.

Littell, Norman
1967   *Proposed findings of fact in behalf of the Navajo Tribe of Indians in area of the overall Navajo Claim before the Indian Claims Commission, Docket* 229; on file, Indian Claims Commission, Washington, D.C.

Lobato, G. H.
1974   Interviews with G. H. Lobato, Aztec, N.M., October 17-18, 1974, conducted by David M. Brugge. Transcript on file, National Park Service, Chaco Center, Albuquerque.

McKinley County Assessor's Office
1960–   Plat books. Gallup, New Mexico.
1979
1983   Current property maps (by township and section). Gallup, New Mexico.

McNitt, Frank
1962   *The Indian traders*. University of Oklahoma Press, Norman.
1972   *Navajo Wars*. University of New Mexico Press, Albuquerque.

Maldonado, Ronald P.
1981   Window Rock coal mine archaeological survey. CRMP-81-014. Ms. on file, Navajo Nation Cultural Resource Management Program, Window Rock, Arizona.

Mandel, Ernest
1976   Capitalism and regional disparities. Translated from the French by Ted Richmond and Jim Peterson. *Southwest Economy and Society* 1:41–47 (first published in *Socialisme*, April–May–June 1969).

Marx, Karl
1967   *Capital*. (Vol. 1). International Publishers, New York. (First published 1887)

Matthews, Washington
1883   Navajo silversmiths. In *Second Annual Report of the Bureau of American Ethnology*. Smithsonian Institution, Washington, D.C.

Means, Gardiner
1964   Economic concentration. In *Hearings before the Subcommittee on Antitrust and Monopoly of the Committee on the Judiciary, Pt. I: Overall and conglomerate aspects*. U.S. Senate. Government Printing Office, Washington, D.C.

Mera, Harry P.
1947   *Navajo textile arts*. Laboratory of Anthropology, Santa Fe.

Mindeleff, Cosmos
1898   Navajo houses. In *Seventeenth Annual Report of the Bureau of American Ethnology, Smithsonian Institution, Pt.* 2, pp. 469–518. Government Printing Office, Washington, D.C.

Moore, James L. (editor)
1981   *An archeological study of the Catalpa Mine and an ethnographic profile of the Catalpa Canyon Navajo*. Office of Contract Archeology, University of New Mexico, Albuquerque.

Moore, Lewis R.
1976   Title examination of Indian lands. In *Institute on Indian land development: oil, gas, coal, and other minerals*, April 1-2, 1976, Tucson, AZ. Rocky Mountain Mineral Law Foundation, University of Colorado, Boulder.

Morgan, Kenneth, and G. Mark Lathrop
1979   Clan groups and clan exogamy among the Navajo. *Journal of Anthropological Research* 35:157–169.

Mosk, Sanford
1963   Land policy and stock raising in the western United States. In *The public lands: studies in the history of the public domain*, edited by Vernon Carstensen, pp. 411–430. University of Wisconsin Press, Madison (first published 1943).

National Academy of Sciences
1974   *Rehabilitation potential of western coal lands: a report to the Energy Policy Project of the Ford Foundation*. Ballinger, Cambridge.

Navajo Tribe, Correll Collection (CC)
1962   Navajo land claim site reports. On file, Cultural Resources Division, Window Rock, Arizona.
n.d.a   Navajo statements. On file, Cultural Resources Division, Window Rock, Arizona.
n.d.b   Scout records. On file, Cultural Resources Division, Window Rock, Arizona.

Navajo Tribe, Division of Community Development (DCD)
1982   Poverty "profound" on Navajo land. Reprinted in *Navajo Times*, November 10, p. 16.

Navajo Tribe, Division of Economic Development (DED)
1978   *Navajo Nation overall economic development program, 1978 annual progress report*. Window Rock, Arizona.

Navajo Tribe, Office of Program Development (OPD)
1974   *The Navajo Nation overall economic develop-*

ment program, 1974. Window Rock, Arizona.

1977   *Navajo Nation overall economic development program, 1977 annual progress report*. Window Rock, Arizona.

Nelson, Ben A., and Linda S. Cordell

1982   Dynamics of the Anasazi adaptation. In *Anasazi and Navajo land use in the McKinley Mine area near Gallup, New Mexico, Volume 1: Archeology*, edited by Christina G. Allen and Ben A. Nelson, pp. 867–892. Office of Contract Archeology, University of New Mexico, Albuquerque.

New Mexico Department of Agriculture (NMDA)

1962   *New Mexico agricultural statistics* (Vol. I). New Mexico State University, Las Cruces.

Newcomb, Franc Johnson

1964   *Hosteen Klah: Navajo medicine man and sand painter*. University of Oklahoma Press, Norman.

Otis, D. S.

1973   History of the allotment policy. In *The Dawes Act and the allotment of Indian lands*, edited by F. P. Prucha. University of Oklahoma Press, Norman (first published in *Readjustments of Indian Affairs*, U.S. House of Representatives, Committee on Indian Affairs, Government Printing Office, Washington, D.C.).

Papstein, Bob, Barbara Bayless Lacy, Irene Benelly, and Don Callaway

1980   *Pictures of the Navajo: their health and environment in 1980*. Navajo Health Authority, Window Rock, Arizona.

Paquette, Peter

1915   Census of the Navajo Reservation under the jurisdiction of Peter Paquette, year 1915. National Archives, Interior Branch, Record Group 75, File No. 64386-14-034.

Parish, William J.

1961   *The Charles Ilfeld Company*. Harvard University Press, Cambridge.

Parman, Donald E.

1976   *The Navajos and the New Deal*. Yale University Press, New Haven.

Pittsburg and Midway Coal Mining Company

1976   Aerial photographs of South McKinley Mine lease. Gallup, New Mexico.

Plummer, Edward O.

1966   Statement before Public Land Law Review Commission, Nov. 10-11, 1966. Ms. on file, Navajo Tribe, Office of Navajo Land Development, Window Rock, Arizona.

Priest, Loring Benson

1942   *Uncle Sam's stepchildren: the reformation of the United States Indian policy, 1863-1887*. Octagon, New York.

Reeve, Frank D.

1957   Seventeenth-century Navaho–Spanish relations. *New Mexico Historical Review* 32:36–52.

1958   Navaho–Spanish wars, 1680-1720. *New Mexico Historical Review* 33:205–231.

1959   The Navaho–Spanish peace, 1720s–1770s. *New Mexico Historical Review* 34:9–30.

1960   Navaho–Spanish diplomacy, 1770-1790. *New Mexico Historical Review* 35:200–235.

1971   Navajo foreign affairs, 1795-1846. *New Mexico Historical Review* 46:101, 132, 223–251.

1974   The Navajo Indians. In *Navajo Indians II*, edited by David Agee Horr. Garland, New York and London.

Reichard, Gladys

1928   Social life of the Navajo Indians. *Columbia Contributions to Anthropology* 8.

Reynolds, Terry R., Louise Lamphere, and Cecil Cook. Jr.

1967   Time, resources, and authority in a Navajo community. *American Anthropologist* 69:188–199.

Robbins, Lynn A.

1978   Energy developments in the Navajo Nation. In *Native Americans and energy development*, pp. 35–48. Anthropology Resource Center, Cambridge.

Rogal, Kim C.

1976   Bad days on the reservation. *The Nation*, November 20, pp. 525–530.

Ruffing, Lorraine Turner

1973   *An alternative approach to economic development in a traditional Navajo community*. Ph.D. dissertation, Economics Department, Columbia University. University Microfilms, Ann Arbor.

1979   Dependence and underdevelopment. In Economic development in American Indian reservations, edited by Roxanne Dunbar Ortiz, pp. 91–113. *Native American Studies Development Series* 1. Native American Studies Center, University of New Mexico, Albuquerque.

Savory, Allan

1983   The Savory Method or Holistic Resource Management. *Rangelands* 5:155–159.

Scudder, Thayer

1982   *No place to go: effects of compulsory relocation on Navajos*. Institute for the Study of Human Issues, Philadelphia.

Sears, Paul M.
1954   Gallup merchants like it—when Indians come to town. *New Mexico Business* 7(11):2–8.

Shannon, Fred A.
1936   The Homestead Act and the labor surplus. *American Historical Review* 41:637–651.

Shepardson, Mary, and Blodwen Hammond
1970   *The Navajo Mountain community*. University of California Press, Berkeley.

Sjoberg, A. F.
1953   Lipan Apache culture in historical perspective. *Southwest Journal of Anthropology* 9:76–98.

Snyder, Donna, and Paul Fyfe
1983   A San Juan primer, Pts. I and II. *The Chaco–Bisti News* 5 (Summer and Fall). Committee on Coal, Albuquerque.

Stephen, A. M.
1893   The Navajo. *American Anthropologist* 6:345–362.

Stokes, M.A., and T.L. Smiley
1966   Tree-ring dates from the Navajo Land Claim: III. The southern sector. *Tree-Ring Bulletin* 27(3–4):2–11.

Stout, Joe A., Jr.
1970   Cattlemen, conservationists, and the Taylor Grazing Act. *New Mexico Historical Review* 45: 311–333.

Sutton, Imre
1975   *Indian land tenure: bibliographic essays and a guide to the literature*. Clearwater, New York.

Thal, Alexander
1982   *Fairness in compensation procedures: a case study of Navajo tribal land acquisition policies*. Unpublished Ph.D. dissertation, State University of New York at Buffalo.

Toll, Mollie S., and Marcia Donaldson
1982   Flotation and macro-botanical analyses of archeological sites on the McKinley Mine lease: a regional study of plant manipulation and natural seed dispersal over time. In *Anasazi and Navajo land use on the McKinley Mine lease near Gallup, New Mexico, Volume 1: Archeology*, edited by Christina G. Allen and Ben A. Nelson, pp. 712–786. Office of Contract Archeology, University of New Mexico, Albuquerque.

Tremblay, Marc-Adelard, John Collier, Jr., and Tom T. Sasaki
1954   Navaho housing in transition. *America Indigena* 14:187–219.

Trillin, Calvin
1973   U.S. Journal: Gallup, N.M. *The New Yorker* 49 (May 12): 122–132.

Tse Bonito Elementary School
1970–   Enrollment lists.
1977

Tyler, S. Lyman
1973   *A history of Indian policy*. Government Printing Office, Washington, D.C.

U.S. Commission on Civil Rights
1973   *Hearings held in Window Rock, Arizona, October 22–24, 1973*. Washington, D.C.
1982   *Energy development in northwestern New Mexico: a civil rights perspective*. Washington, D.C.

U.S. Department of Agriculture (USDA)
1910–   *Agricultural statistics*. Government Printing
1930   Office, Washington, D.C.

U.S. Department of Agriculture, Soil Conservation Service (USDA, CSC)
1934   Aerial photograph of northwest McKinley County, N.M. On file, U.S. Department of the Interior, Bureau of Indian Affairs, Navajo Area Office, Branch of Land Operations, Window Rock, Arizona.
1936   Livestock registry. Manuscript on file, Arizona State Museum Library, University of Arizona, Tucson.
1938   Watershed plan, land management unit no. 17, Navajo District, Region 8. Ms. on file, U.S. Department of the Interior, Bureau of Indian Affairs, Navajo Area Office, Fort Defiance Agency, Branch of Land Operations.
1939   Statistical summary: Human Dependency Survey, Navajo and Hopi reservations, Section of Conservation Economics, Navajo Area, Region 8.
1940   Human Dependency Survey household schedules. Microfilm, Native American Research Library, Navajo Tribe, Window Rock, Arizona.

U.S. Department of Commerce (USDC), Bureau of the Census
1961–   *Statistical abstract of the United States*. Govern-
1975   ment Printing Office, Washington, D.C.

U.S. Department of Commerce (USDC), Bureau of Economic Analysis
1975   *Survey of Current Business* 55(4).

U.S. Department of Commerce, (USDC), Bureau of Foreign and Domestic Commerce
1913–   *Statistical abstract of the United States*. Govern-
1936   ment Printing Office, Washington, D.C.

U.S. Department of the Interior, Bureau of Indian Affairs (USDI, BIA)
1940   Navajo Tribal census roll. Documents on file, Census Office, Franciscan Friars, St. Michaels, Arizona.

U.S. Department of the Interior, Bureau of Indian Affairs (USDI, BIA), Eastern Navajo Agency

1978   Grazing permit plats, Tsayatoh and Rock Springs chapters. Crownpoint, New Mexico.

n.d.a   Allotment and estate records. Crownpoint, New Mexico.

n.d.b   Eastern Navajo Agency plat book. Crownpoint, New Mexico.

U.S. Department of the Interior, Bureau of Indian Affairs (USDI, BIA), Fort Defiance Agency

n.d.   Fort Defiance Agency plat book. Fort Defiance, Arizona.

U.S. Department of the Interior, Bureau of Indian Affairs (USDI, BIA), Navajo Area Office

n.d.   Allotment schedule, public domain allotments, former "Southern Navajo" jurisdiction, Arizona-New Mexico. Window Rock, Arizona.

U.S. Department of the Interior (USDI), Census Office

1890   *Report on Indians taxed and Indians not taxed in the United States at the eleventh census, 1890.* Government Printing Office, Washington, D.C.

U.S. Department of the Interior (USDI), Commissioner of Indian Affairs

1868–   *Annual report of the Commissioner of Indian*
1920   *Affairs.* Government Printing Office, Washington, D.C.

U.S. Department of the Interior (USDI), General Land Office

1881–   Survey plats of McKinley County townships.
1893   On file, McKinley County Clerk's Office, Gallup, New Mexico.

U.S. Department of the Interior (USDI), Geological Survey

1952–   Aerial photographs of northwest McKinley
1973   County, N.M., Denver, Colorado.

U.S. Department of the Interior (USDI), Grazing Service

1940–   Old Indian case files. On file, U.S. Department
1946   of the Interior, Bureau of Land Management, Farmington, N.M., Resource Area Office.

U.S. Department of the Treasury (USDT), Bureau of Statistics

1901   *Statistical abstract of the United States, 1901.* Government Printing Office, Washington, D.C.

U.S. Senate

1932   *Survey of conditions of the Indians in the United States, Pt.* 18. Government Printing Office, Washington, D.C.

1937   *Survey of conditions of the Indians in the United States, Pt.* 34. Government Printing Office, Washington, D.C.

1944   *Administration and use of Pueblo lands, Pt.* 10. Hearings before a subcommittee of the Committee on Public Lands and Surveys. Government Printing Office, Washington, D.C.

U.S. Weather Bureau

1919–   *Monthly reports for New Mexico stations.*
1978   Government Printing Office, Washington, D.C.

Van Valkenburgh, Richard F.

1941   *Dine bikeyah.* U.S. Department of the Interior, Indian Service, Navajo Agency, Window Rock, Arizona.

1956   *Report of archeological survey of the Navajo-Hopi contact area.* Prepared for the Indian Claims Commission, Navajo-Hopi Land Claims.

Vivian, R. Gwinn

1960   *The Navajo archaeology of the Chacra Mesa, New Mexico.* Unpublished Master's thesis, Department of Anthropology, University of New Mexico, Albuquerque.

Walker, J. G., and O. L. Shepherd

1964   *The Navajo reconnaissance: a military exploration of the Navajo country in 1859,* edited by Lynn R. Bailey. Westernlore Press, Los Angeles.

Wallach, Bret

1981   Sheep ranching in the Dry Corner of Wyoming. *Geographical Review* 71:51–63.

Ward, Elizabeth

1951   *No dudes, few women: life with a Navajo range rider.* University of New Mexico Press, Albuquerque.

Weber, The Rev. Anselm, O.F.M.

1937   The Navajo Indians, a statement of facts. In *Survey of conditions of the Indians in the United States, Pt.* 34. U.S. Senate, pp. 17560–17575. Government Printing Office, Washington, D.C.

Weiss, Lawrence D.

1984   *The development of capitalism in the Navajo Nation: a political-economic history.* MEP Publications, Minneapolis.

Westphall, Victor

1958   The public domain in New Mexico, 1854–1891. *New Mexico Historical Review* 33:24–52, 128–143.

White, Richard

1983   *The roots of dependency: subsistence, environment, and social change among the Choctaws, Pawnees, and Navajos.* University of Nebraska Press, Lincoln.

Wilkin, Robert L.

1955   *Anselm Weber, O.F.M.: missionary to the Navaho, 1898–1921.* Bruce, Milwaukee.

Wilson, John C.

1977   The McKinley Mine. In *New Mexico Geological Society Guidebook, 28th Field Conference, San Juan Basin III,* edited by J.E. Fassett, pp. 253–255. New Mexico Geological Society, Albuquerque.

Wilson, John P.
1967   Military campaigns in the Navaho country, northwestern New Mexico, 1800–1846. *Museum of New Mexico Research Records* 5. Santa Fe.

Wistisen, Martin J., Robert J. Parsons, and Annette Larson
1975   *A study to identify potentially feasible small businesses for the Navajo Nation, phase I: an evaluation of income and expenditure patterns,* (Vol. 2). Center for Business and Economic Research, Brigham Young University, Provo, Utah.

Witherspoon, Gary
1975   *Navajo kinship and marriage.* University of Chicago Press, Chicago.

Ximenes, Vincente T.
1958   *The 1958 directory of New Mexico manufacturing and mining.* Bureau of Business Research, University of New Mexico, Albuquerque.

York, Frederick
1981   An ethnohistory of the Catalpa Canyon Navajo Indians. In *An archeological study of the Catalpa Mine and an ethnographic profile of the Catalpa Canyon Navajo,* edited by James L. Moore, pp. 178–208. Office of Contract Archeology, University of New Mexico, Albuquerque.

Young, Robert W.
1955   *The Navajo yearbook.* U.S. Department of the Interior, Bureau of Indian Affairs, Navajo Agency, Window Rock, Arizona.

1958   *The Navajo yearbook.* U.S. Department of Interior, Bureau of Indian Affairs, Navajo Agency, Window Rock, Arizona.

1961   *The Navajo yearbook.* U.S. Department of the Interior, Bureau of Indian Affairs, Navajo Agency, Window Rock, Arizona.

1978   *A political history of the Navajo Tribe.* Navajo Community College Press, Tsaile, Arizona.

Young, Robert W., and William Morgan (editors)
1952   *The trouble at Round Rock.* U.S. Department of the Interior, Bureau of Indian Affairs, Branch of Education, Washington, D.C.

Youngblood, B.
1937   Navajo trading. In *Survey of conditions of the Indians in the United States, Pt.* 18. U.S. Senate, pp. 18036–18115. Government Printing Office, Washington, D.C.

Zeh, William H.
1932   General report covering the grazing situation on the Navajo Indian reservation. In *Survey of conditions of the Indians in the United States, Pt.* 18. U.S. Senate, pp. 9121–9132. Government Printing Office, Washington, D.C.

Zelditch, Morris, Jr.
1959   Statistical marriage preferences of the Ramah Navaho. *American Anthropologist* 61:470–491.

Index

A

Agency, *see also* Crownpoint; Fort Defiance
  Eastern Navajo, 100–101
  Navajo, 29, 100
  Southern Navajo, 27, 33, 98
Allotments, 14, 29, 46, 102, 168–171, 206–207, *see also*
    General Allotment Act
  leases of, 152–155, 168–171, 200–201
Annuity goods, 23, 29
Antonio El Pinto, 19
Arab oil crisis, 153
Archaeological record, 4, 203–205
Archaeological sites, 1, 3, 208–212, *see also* specific types
  sample, 208–212
Archaeological survey, 3, 4, 208–212
Arizona Public Service Company, 153
Artifacts, *see also* Equipment and tools
  and annual stay, 38, 112–113, 162
  on campsites, 39, 113, 162
  and class transformation, 204–205
  on homesteads, 38–39, 113, 162
  inventories, 35–40, 112–113, 144–145,
    160–162
  and money income, 161–162
  on sheep camps, 38–39, 113, 162
Ash dumps, 84–85, 142, 193
Azaakai, 56–57, 122, 176
  descendants, 57, 122

B

Bad Teeth, 56
Bald Head, 50
Barboncito, 21
Bear Spring, 19, 21, *see also* Fort Fauntleroy

Bedding-out system, 146
Big Woman, Azaakai's sister, 56–57, 122
Big Woman, Fat Salt's widow, 172, 174
Black Creek Valley, 16, 19, 21, 26–27, 29, 50, 55, 101,
    108, 119–121, 136, 172, 174, 175, 181, 183
Blackgoat, 28, 34, 53–55, 60, 62–63, 67–68, 88, 89, 127,
    131, 134, 181, 182
  descendants of, 54–55, 63, 67–68, 131,
    175, 181–185
Blacksmithing, 107, 131, 133
Bonito Canyon, 20, 22
Botanical remains, 16, 35, 38, 112, 160, *see also* Farming
Boulder Dam, 98
Boundary bill
  Arizona, 99, *see also* Navajo Reservation
  New Mexico, 99, *see also* Navajo Reser-
    vation
Bourke, John G., 79
Boyd, Charlie, 29, 53, 119
  family of, 63, 120, 173–174
Brown, Violet, 122, 175–176
Burned Through the Rock Wash, 50, 174–175
Business cycle, 151, 153

C

Camp, 2, *see also* Residence group
Campsite, 62–63, 88, 126–127, 180, *see also* Customary
    use area
Capitalism, *see* Industrial capitalism; Merchant
    capitalism
Carlton, George S., 21–22
Carrying capacity, 101–102, *see also* Lease townships
Carson, Kit, 21–22, 30
Cattle, 34, 104, 107, 128, 158, 176, 197, 202, *see also*
    Livestock; Stock raising

Census, 4–5, *see also* Human Dependency Survey; Population
  field, 5, 207, 209
  Southern Navajo Agency, 33, 206–207, 209, *see also* Agency, Southern Navajo; Population
Chapters, 4, 99–102, *see also* Tsayatoh Chapter
Chavez, Dennis, 100
Checkerboard area, 24, 28–29, *see also* Agency, Eastern Navajo
China Springs, 21
Chopped Hair, 50, 118–120
Chuska Mountains, 16, 19
Cienega Amarilla, 21, 23, 26, *see also* Saint Michaels
Civil War, 21
Civilian Conservation Corps, 99, 102
Clan, 2
Class transformation, 10, 203–204
  and archaeological record, 203–205
Coal mines, *see also* Stripmining
  Catalpa Canyon, 27
  Defiance, 27
  Fort Defiance, 35, 108, 152–153, 174
  Gallup, 27, 153, 158–159, *see also* Coal mines, Mentmore
  Ganado Presbyterian Mission, 35, 108, 153
  McKinley, 1, 3, 50, 153, 155, 157, 158–159, 162–164, 169–170, 173–175, 200–202
  Mentmore, 27, 34, 121, 131, *see also* Coal mines, Gallup
  Saint Michaels Mission, 35, 108, 153
Collier, John, 99–101
Comprehensive Employment and Training Act, 153, 158
Consumption group, 207
Cooperating group, 2, 60, *see also* Customary use area
Cooperatives, 13, 103
Coresidential kin group, 2, 49, *see also* Outfit
Cornmerchant, 50, 60, 62, 118, 172
Corrals, 12, 87, 143, 193, *see also* Facilities, on homesites
  and annual stay, 91, 147, 196–197
  antelope, 16, 135
  and family labor, 91, 147
  and herd size, 91–92, 131, 147, 196–197
  on homesteads, 92, 147, 196–197
  isolated, 62–63, 126–127, 180, *see also* Customary use area
  lamb, *see* Corrals, twin; Pens
  number, 93–94, 147, 196–197
  on sheep camps, 92, 147, 196–197

  size, 93, 105, 147, 196–197
  twin, 12, 89, 149, 196
Credit, *see* Trading posts
Crops, *see* Botanical remains; Farming
Crownpoint, 29; *see also* Agency, Eastern Navajo
Crystal, 27
Curly Tallman, 66, 120, 127–130, 173, 175–176, 181
Customary use area
  defined, 46
  examples, 50–57, 64–68, 118–122, 127–135, 171–176, 181–186
  resource inventory, 61–62, 124, 178
  seasonal use, 60, 124–125, 127, 178–179, *see also* Mobility, seasonal
  site inventory, 62–63, 126–127, 180

D

Damon, Anson, 24, 28
  descendants of, 28, 50, 57, 79, 88, 119
Dawes Act, *see* Allotments; General Allotment Act
Defiance Draw, *see* Lease townships
Defiance Plateau, 16, 120, 172
Demographic transition, 45
Depression, 98–101, 103, 104, *see also* Business cycle
Descending Orator, 67, 121
Deshna Clah Chischillige, 100
Dinetah, 16
Divide Trading Post, 109–110, *see also* Ortega, Lotario
Dixon brothers, 57, 63, 128, 136, 176
Documents, 3, 4, 203, 206–207
Dodge, Chee, 27–28, 57, 79, 88, 100
Dodge, Henry L., 20, 27
Dwellings, 12, 14, 32, 200
  and age–sex composition of family, 84
  and annual stay, 83, 142, 192
  and craft production, 83–84, 142–143, 193
  doorway orientation, 85
  forms, 80–81, 141–142, 191–192
  and fuel conservation, 84, 193
  on homesteads, 83, 142, 192
  and money income, 192–193
  number, 83–84, 142, 192
  and number of inhabitants, 84, 142–143, 193
  on sheep camps, 83, 142, 192
  size, 81, 142–143, 191–192
  and wealth, 83–84, 142–143

E

Eastern Flat, *see* Lease townships
Environmental degradation, *see also* Overgrazing; Strip-
  mining
  and class transformation, 204–205
Equipment and tools, 32, 131–133, *see also* Artifacts
  domestic, 12, 14–15, 88, 143–145,
    193–194, 200–201, *see also* Heating
    devices
  farming, 95, 148, 150, 198–199
  stock-raising, 12, 14, 95, 147, 197

F

Facilities, on homesites, 12, 14–15, 19, 87–88, 143, 193,
    see also Customary use area
  and annual stay, 87, 143, 193
  and class transformation, 204–205
  storage, 87, 143, 193
Family, defined, 2, *see also* Household; Outfit; Resi-
    dence group
Farming, 11, 16, 19, 33, 34, 104, 107, 158, *see also*
    Fields
  division of labor, *see* Labor
  equipment and tools, *see* Equipment and
    tools
  and large-scale stock owners, 34, 107
  and money income, 198–199
  and range subdivision, 95, 150
  tasks, 95, 148, 198–199
Farmington, 152–153
Fat Salt, 52, 118–120, 147, 172
Faunal remains, 35, 40–41, 111, 160, *see also* Livestock;
    Meat
Fields, 11, 14, 21, 32, *see also* Customary use area
  number, 72, 136, 186
  and physiography, 72–74, 137, 187
  size, 72, 107, 136, 186
  slope-wash, defined, 74
  and water, 73–74, 137, 187
Flotation samples, *see* Botanical remains
Food, 24, 35, 88, 109, 110, 112, 159–160, *see also*
    Artifacts; Botanical remains; Faunal remains
Food stamps, 156, 158
Fort Defiance, 20, 21–23, 27–28, 30, 50, 54, 152–153
Fort Fauntleroy, 21, 22, *see also* Bear Spring
Fort Lyon, 21, *see also* Fort Fauntleroy
Fort Sumner, 7, 22–23, 50

Franciscan Fathers, 26, *see also* Saint Michaels; Weber,
    Anselm
Fred Harvey Company, 25
Fuzzy Face, 65–66

G

Gallup, 27, 109, 144, 145, 160, 194, 195, *see also* Coal
    mines
Game, wild, 16, 41, *see also* Corrals, antelope; Faunal
    remains
Ganado Mucho, 19, 23, 27
General Allotment Act, 7–8, *see also* Allotments
General Dynamics, 153
Gish, defined, 95, *see also* Equipment and tools
Goats, *see* Livestock; Stock raising
Goldtooth, Charley, 172–174
Graham, Gib, 105–106, 116, 119, 120, 122, *see also*
    Wildcat Trading Post
Gray-Eyed Woman, 53, 57, 60, 63, 64–66, 70, 127, 181
  descendants, 53, 66, 120, 129–130,
    173–174, 181
Grazing permits, *see* Permits
Grazing regulation, 9, 12, 99–103
Grazing tracts, 11–12, 14, 32, 202
  discontiguous, 69–70, 135, 186
  and non-Navajo ranchers, 186
  number, 69, 135, 186
  and physiography, 70, 72, 135, 186
  and roads, 186
  size, 69, 135, 186
  and stripmining, 186, 202–205
  and water, 72, 135–136, 186
Gulf Oil Company, 153, *see also* Coal mines

H

Haile, Berard, 100
Handicrafts, 10, 19, 24–26, 31, 33, 102, 104, 158, *see
    also* Blacksmithing; Silversmithing; Weaving
Harvesting, 134, *see also* Farming
He Walks Around clan, 28, 50
Headmen, 8, 19, 20, 27, 30, 45–46, 99–101, *see also*
    Ricos; Stock owners
  councils, 29, 99
Heating devices, 12, 84–85, 142–143, 193–194
Herders, hired, 14, 19, 33, 34, 54, 67, 103, 106, 119,
    146, 191, 195, *see also* Labor, stock-raising

History, oral, 4, 206
Hogan, *see* Dwellings
    herding, 84, 88, 142
Homesites, 11-12, 14, 32, 200-202, *see also* Homesteads;
        Sheep camps
    and class transformations, 204-205
    and money income, 189
    number, 74, 137, 187
    and physiography, 74-77, 137-139, 190
    and range subdivision, 74, 137
    and roads, 189-190
    and seasonal mobility, 74, 137-138, 188
    size, 74, 137, 188
    and water, 76, 137-138
Homestead Act, 7-8
Homesteads, 39, 62-63, 126-127, 180, *see also* Cus-
        tomary use area; Homesites
Homesteaders, *see* Settlers
Hoover Dam, *see* Boulder Dam
Horses, 104, 128, 131, 133, 195, 197, *see also* Livestock;
        Stock raising
House Concurrent Resolution 108, *see* Termination, of
        federal trusteeship
Household, 13, 44-45, 115, 206-207, 209, *see also* Cus-
        tomary use area
    defined, 2
    number, 44-45, 115, 166-168
    size, 44-45, 115, 166-168
Human Dependency Survey, 104-112, 207, 209
Hunters Point, 27, 45, 95, 121, 175, 183-184

I

Income, money, 13-14, 108, 110, 154-156, 159-162, *see
        also* Wage work; Welfare
Indian Land Consolidation Act, 202
Indian Reorganization Act, 100
Indian Self-Determination and Education Act, 154
Industrial capitalism, 1, 6-8, 12, 203-204, *see also* Indus-
        trialization
    and consumption patterns, 14-15, 155
    and demography, 12-13, 155
    and division of labor in family, 12-13,
        155
    and family sources of livelihood, 12-13,
        155
    and land tenure, 13-14, 155
    and overgrazing, 12, 155
    and range subdivision, 12, 155
    and spatial aspects of land use, 14-15,
        155-156
    and technology, 14-15, 155-156

Industrial reserve army, 9
Industrialization, 13-15, 151-156, *see also* Industrial
        capitalism
Influenza, Spanish, 54, 67
Interviews, *see* History, oral

J

Jim, Chee, 52, 118-120, 172, 175
Juan, 57
    descendants, 122, 131

K

Kids, *see* Livestock; Stock raising
King, Annie, 120, 174
    descendants, 120

L

Labor
    division of, in family, 10, 14, 26, 31, 79,
        104, 141, 191
    domestic, 12, 79, 191
    farming, 95, 148, 150, 198-199
    outmigration, 44-45, 102, 115, 121, 158,
        168
    stock-raising, 88, 146, 195
Labor-saving devices, 12, 14, 32, 87-88, 141, 147, *see
        also* Equipment and tools
Lambing, *see also* Stock raising
    camps, 63, 89
    drop-bunch, 89
Lambs, *see* Livestock; Stock raising
Land disputes, *see* Land tenure
Land grant
    railroad, 24, 29, 46, 105-106, 116, 122,
        168-169, *see also* Leases
    State of New Mexico, 46, 169
Land management district, 100-102
Land tenure, 13-14, 201-202
    communal, 11, 31, 45-46
    inherited, 11, 14, 32, 47, 116, 168-169,
        see also Matrilineality
    legal, 14, 105, 168, *see also* Allotments;
        Leases; Permits, livestock
    by original claim, 32, 116
    by purchase, 105-106, 116, 122, 168-169,
        172-176
    residual rights, 48-49, 118, 168, 171
Land use, defined, 2

Land-use community, 2, 45, *see also* Outfit
Lease townships
    carrying capacity, 41–42, 114, 164
    defined, 4
    first settlement, 27
    major drainages, described, 17
Leases
    grazing, 98, 105–106, 116, 169, *see also*
        Permits, livestock
    homesite, 169–170
    mineral, 98, 152–154, 168–171, *see also*
        Allotments
    of public land, 8–9, *see also* U.S. Graz-
        ing Service
    of railroad land, *see* Land grant
Lee, Robert, 198–199
Lefthanded Slim, 28, 53, 60
Little Warrior, 52
    descendants, 119–120, 172–173
Livestock, 16, 21, 31, 201–202, *see also* specific types;
        Stock raising
    distribution, by government, 23
    number, 33, 104–107, 157
    sale, 26, 99–102, 110–111, 160, 195, *see*
        also Prices
    subsistence minimum, defined, 33–34
    supplementary feeding, 147, 158, 195
    and wealth stratification, 34, 106, 157
Louis Reeder, 28
Louisiana Purchase, 19

M

Manuelito, 19–23, 46, *see also* Headmen
Manuelito, New Mexico, 16, 26, 34
Manufacturing, 152–154, *see also* Industrial capitalism
Matrilineality, 11, 14, 47–49, 116, 170–171
Meat, 10, 111, *see also* Faunal remains; Livestock
Merchant capitalism, 1, 6–8, 12, 203–204, *see also* Trad-
        ing posts; Wholesalers
    consumption patterns, 10, 35, 43, 103
    demography, 11, 44, 59, 103
    division of labor in family, 10, 44, 79,
        103
    family sources of livelihood, 10, 33, 43,
        103
    land tenure, 11, 45, 103
    overgrazing, 11, 41, 103
    range subdivision, 11, 42–43, 59, 103
    spatial aspects of land use, 11–12, 59,
        103
    technology, 12, 79–80, 88, 95, 103

Meriwether, David, 20
Mexican Springs, 57, 122
Mineral Leasing Act, 9, *see also* Leases
Missionaries, 29, *see also* Franciscan Fathers
Mobility, seasonal, 50–57, 118–122, 171–176, *see also*
        Customary use area
Morgan, Jacob C., 100–101
Mount Taylor, 16, 19

N

Narbona, 18, 20
Navajo–Hopi Long-Range Rehabilitation Act, 9, 151–152
Navajo Pre-Vocational Training Program, 153
Navajo Reservation
    additions to, 23, 29, 99
    treaty, 23
Navajo tribal business enterprises, 153
Navajo tribal council, 9, 28, 98–102
Navajo tribal government, 151–154

O

Oak Springs, 16, 20, 22, 57
Office of Navajo Economic Opportunity, 153
Oil and gas, 99, *see also* Leasing
Old Man Curly, 28, 53
Original claim, 27–28, 60, *see also* Land tenure
Ortega, Lotario, 120, 172–174, *see also* Divide Trading
        Post
Outfit, 11, 14, 48–49, 118, 168, 171
    defined, 2–3
    examples, 50–57, 118–122, 171–176
    and large stock owners, 49, 171
Ovens, 87, 143, 193, *see also* Facilities, on homesites
Overgrazing, 11, 13, 31, 41–42, 70, 98–103, 114,
        162–163, *see also* Grazing regulation; Permits

P

Participant observation, 3, 203
Pawn, 102, *see also* Trading posts
Pens, 12, 87, 143, 193, *see also* Facilities, on homesites
    on homesteads, 92, 196
    lamb, 12, 89, 143, 196
    on sheep camps, 92, 196
Permits, livestock, 98–102, 104–107, 157
Pittsburg and Midway Coal Mining Company, 153, 194,
        see also Coal mines
Plant foods, wild, 16, *see also* Botanical remains

Planting, 136–137, *see also* Farming

Pobres, 19, *see also* Stock owners, small-scale

Policy, federal Indian, 6–10, 12, 14, 29, 98–102, 151–154, *see also* U.S. Army; U.S. Bureau of Indian Affairs; U.S. Congress

Population, of lease townships, 11, 31, 44, 115–116, 166

Prices, 29–31, 102, 107, 109
   flour, 31, 107
   livestock, 26, 29, 31, 160
   wool, 10, 24, 25, 29, 30–31, 34, 107, 160

Production
   and atomistic decision-making, 1, 10
   diversification, by family, 13, 204–205
   family as basic unit, 1, 30, 115
   intensification, by family, 13, 204–205

Public domain, 26, 29

Pueblo Colorado Wash, 19, 20

Pueblo Indians
   hostilities with, 21
   trade with, *see* Trade

Pueblo Revolt, 16

R

Railroad, 8, 24, *see also* Land grant
   and employment, 45, 158

Ramadas, 87, 143, 148, 150, 193, *see also* Facilities, on homesites

Ranchers, *see* Settlers, non-Navajo

Rations, 23

Rattles, sheep, 95

Recession, economic, *see* Business cycle; Depression

Reconquest, Spanish, 16

Red Lake, 20, 28, 153

Relocation, 120–121, 168, 175–176, *see also* Stripmining

Residence, postmarital, 14, 47–48, 116–118, 170–171

Residence group, 13, 44–45, 115, 166, 206–207, 209
   defined, 2
   number, 44–45, 115, 166
   size, 44–45, 115, 166

Residents, absentee, 166–168

Revegetation, *see* Stripmining

Ricos, 19, *see also* Headmen; Stock owners, large-scale

Rio Puerco of the West, 16, 19, 27, 55, 173–174, 181

Rock Springs, 16, 21, 26, 27, 53, 103, 110, 129

S

Sadie, 120

Saint Michaels, 50, *see also* Cienega Amarilla; Franciscan Fathers

Saint Michaels Mission, 26, *see also* Coal Mines; Franciscan Fathers

Santa Fe Trail, 19

Savory grazing method, 202

Sawmill, 27

Schools, 29–30, 152, 155

Settlers, non-Navajo, 26, 28–29, 101, 176, 186, 190, *see also* Graham, Gib

Sex ratio, in lease townships, 44–45, 115, 166

Sharp, Tom, 57, 60, 69, 111, 122, 140, 173, 175–176

Shearing, *see* Stock raising

Sheep, *see* Livestock; Stock raising

Sheep camps, 38, 62–63, 126–127, 180, *see also* Customary use area; Homesites

Sheep Springs, 19, 20

Sheep units year long, defined, 42

Shiprock, 100, 152

Shorthair, 26

Silversmith, 27

Silversmithing, 35, 107, 158, *see also* Handicrafts

Sisters of the Blessed Sacrament, 26

Small, Mr., 34, 57, 62, 89

Smiley, 27, 28, 53–55, 60, 62, 95, 120–121, 182–183
   Billy, Mr. and Mrs., 120–121, 172–175
   descendants, 121

Soil Conservation Service, 99, 102

Speculators, land, 7–8, 10, 105, 116, 140, *see also* Graham, Gib

Springerville, 23

Springstead, A. L., 176

Stock owners, *see also* Livestock
   large-scale, 11, 27, 33, 34, 100, 106–107, 116, 122, 127, 140, 146
      and stock reduction, 98–100, 107, 118
   small-scale, 11, 107, 127, 140

Stock raising
   annual cycle, 89–90, 146–147, 195
   daily regime, 88–89, 146, 195
   division of labor, *see* Labor
   equipment and tools, *see* Equipment and tools
   and money income, 195–197
   sites used for, 88, 146–147, 195–196, *see also* specific types

Stock reduction program, *see* Grazing regulation

Stripmining, *see also* Coal mines
   and reclamation, 164, 201–202
   and relocation, 173–177, 200–202

Sumner, Edwin Vose, 20

Sweathouses, 19, 87, 143, 193

T

Tall, Mr., 175
Tall Mexican Clansman, 119, 172
Tall Red Streak Clansman, 118–120, 172
Tall Salt Clansman, 27, 50, 69
  descendants, 119–120, 159–160, 172–174,
    181
Taylor Grazing Act, 101
Termination, of federal trusteeship, 9–10, 151
They Are Raiding Along Behind Each Other, 54, 121,
    174–175, 181–185
Thompson, Margaret, 53, 65–67, 120, 127–130, 173, 181
Tinhouse, Mary and Fred, 67–68, 112, 121, 127,
    131–135, 147, 174–175, 181, 185
Tiny's Daughter, 57
  descendants, 57
Tohatchi, 19, 23
Tools, see Equipment and tools
Torrivio, 20, 21
Torrivio Ridge, 20
Towering House clan, members, 27, 69
Towering House Clansman, Mr., 34, 54, 57, 62, 89, 95,
    106, 111, 116, 122, 127, 131, 140, 147, 176
Towering House Woman, 56–57, 63, 122
  descendants, 57, 122
Trade
  with Pueblo Indians, 19, see also
    Artifacts
  slave, 16, 21, 22
Traders, see Trading posts
Trading posts, 11, 24–26, 30–32, 99, 101, 109, 151, 160,
    194
  and indebtedness of families, 1, 10–13,
    27, 29–32, 33, 102–103, 109–111,
    156, 157
Transportation, 14, 21, 22, 88, 108–109, 138, 143–144,
    152, 164–165, 184–185, 194–195, 197, 200
Treaty of 1868, 23
Tsayatoh Chapter, 4, 99, 105, 197
Tse Bonita Wash, see Lease townships
Turning Warrior, 121, 174–175, 181–185

U

Unemployment, 14, 154, 158–159, see also Wage work;
  Welfare
United Mine Workers of America, 159
U.S. Army, 7, 19–22
U.S. Bureau of Indian Affairs, 9, 98–102, 105, 116,
  152–154, see also Agency

U.S. Bureau of Land Management, 102, see also U.S.
  Grazing Service
U.S. Commissioner of Indian Affairs, see U.S. Bureau
  of Indian Affairs
U.S. Congress, 20, 24, 99, 151, see also Policy, federal
  Indian
U.S. Grazing Service, 101–102, 104–106, see also U.S.
  Bureau of Land Management
U.S. Indian Service, see U.S. Bureau of Indian Affairs
Ute Indians, 16, 21, 22
Utilities, public, 153, 194

W

Wage work, 13, 33, 34–35, 99–103, 104, 107–108,
    152–154, 158–159
War, Vietnam, 153
Wars
  Apache, 29
  Navajo, 18–22
Washington Pass, 20, 23
Water sources, 11, 41, 114, 124, 147, 164, 201, see also
    Customary use areas
  government development of, 99, 126,
    152, 194
Weaving, 33, 35, 107, 158, see also Handicrafts
Weber, Anselm, 29, see also Franciscan Fathers
Welfare, 13, 102, 152, 153, 158–159
Wheatfields, 21, 147
Wheeler-Howard bill, see Indian Reorganization Act
Whitegoat, Mr., 50, 68, 121
Whitegoat Curly, 50, 60, 62, 106, 111, 116, 118–120,
    127, 171–172
  widow of, 172–173, 175
Wholesalers, 30, 151
Wildcat Trading Post, 176, see also Graham, Gib
Wilson brothers, 183–185
Windbreaks, 87, 143, 150, 193, see also Facilities, on
    homesites
Window Rock, 100, 108, 152–154, 159, 160, 195
Woodpiles, 87, 143, 193, see also Facilities, on homesites
Wool, 24, 89, 110, 160, see also Livestock; Prices; Stock
    raising
World War I, 30, 34, 42–43, 80, 88, 120
World War II, 13, 98, 101–103, 104, 151

Z

Zarcillos Largos, 19–23, 46, see also Headmen
Zuni Mountains, 19
Zuni Pueblo, 22, see also Pueblo Indians